JUSTICE DELAYED

Also by Peter Irons

JUSTICE DELAYED

*The Record of the
Japanese American
Internment Cases*

Edited and with an Introduction by
Peter Irons

 Wesleyan University Press
Middletown, Connecticut

For Jack Herzig and Aiko Herzig-Yoshinaga
with affection and admiration

Introduction, headnotes, index copyright © 1989 by Peter Irons

All rights reserved

All inquiries and permissions requests should be addressed to the Publisher, Wesleyan University Press, 110 Mt. Vernon Street, Middletown, Connecticut 06457

LIBRARY OF CONGRESS CATALOGING-IN-PUBLICATION DATA

Justice delayed.

  Bibliography: p.
  Includes index.
  1. Japanese Americans—Legal status, laws, etc.
2. Japanese Americans—Civil rights. 3. Japanese
Americans—Evacuation and relocation, 1942–1945.
4. Writ of error coram nobis—United States.
I. Irons, Peter H., 1940–
KF7224.5.J87 1989   342.73′083   88-20880
ISBN 0-8195-5168-6   347.30283
ISBN 0-8195-6175-4 (pbk.)

Manufactured in the United States of America

FIRST EDITION, 1989
Wesleyan Paperback, 1989

Contents

Contents

Contents

Preface

Few episodes in American history have been as widely condemned as the wartime expulsion from the West Coast of the entire Japanese American population. More than 120,000 people, most of them native-born American citizens, were forced by military order into concentration camps—the government called them "relocation centers"—after the Japanese attack on Pearl Harbor. Inmates of these camps, hidden in deserts and swamps from California to Arkansas, spent an average of three years behind barbed-wire fences. Members of this ethnic minority were charged by political opportunists with disloyalty, tried by a hostile press, and found 'guilty by reason of race' in the drumhead tribunal of public opinion. Not one of the Japanese Americans sentenced to years of barren exile had been charged with any crime, given the right of legal counsel, or offered even the rudiments of due process under the Constitution.

Among this entire group, only three young men had the courage and conviction to challenge the military curfew and exclusion orders that preceded the mass internment of Japanese Americans. Minoru Yasui, Gordon Hirabayashi, and Fred Korematsu had very different backgrounds and divergent motivations for violating the military orders. After criminal conviction in 1942, each defendant took his case to the United States Supreme Court. The nation's highest court rebuffed each one and upheld the Army's power to order citizens into and then out of their homes, on the basis of ancestry alone.

Few decisions of the Supreme Court have been denounced as widely and for so long as those in the internment cases. The Court's eager deference to the military, and its adoption of the government's "racial disloyalty" argument, earned the enduring scorn of legal scholars. Japanese Americans rebuilt their shattered lives after the war and achieved through hard work and sacrifice a measure of influence, affluence, and respect. Despite their reputation as a "model minority," a well-meaning but unwelcome label, many Japanese Americans still bear the psychic scars of internment. Brought up to obey the law and respect the courts, they suffered an added pain from the Supreme Court decisions. Only in the internment cases, Japanese Americans knew, had the Court approved the punishment of citizens whose only crime was their ethnicity.

This book provides the record of the unprecedented legal campaign, four decades after the Court upheld the convictions, to clear the criminal records of the three defendants in the 1942 trials. Using an obscure federal law, lawyers for Min Yasui, Gordon Hirabayashi, and Fred Korematsu filed legal petitions in 1983 that asked federal judges to vacate their convictions and wipe them off the judicial record. These petitions raised serious charges of misconduct by the government lawyers and officials who handled the internment cases in the 1940s. Based on documents from the government's own files, the petitions alleged both the withholding of crucial evidence from the Supreme Court and the submission of false evidence to the justices.

The federal district judges assigned to these cases in 1983 held separate hearings on the petitions, and each judicial outcome reflected a different approach and attitude toward the unique and novel legal issues they raised. Each defendant ultimately secured vacation of the charges against him, an impressive victory of the legal campaign for vindication. This effort took more than five years to reach final decision, and one of the original defendants died before he could share the ultimate victory of his compatriots.

Justice Delayed is intended to offer a ground-level view of these historic cases. This record includes the full text of the original Supreme Court opinions in each case, the petition—identical in all three cases—filed in 1983 to vacate the criminal convictions, supporting legal briefs on both sides, excerpts from the oral arguments at the hearings, and the opinions of the district court and appellate judges who granted the petitions. Although much of the language is legal, the facts at issue are dramatic, the claims of both sides are irreconcilable, and the stakes in these cases are crucial and far-reaching.

I have included an introductory essay that recounts the legal effort to undo the internment cases and places the documents that follow in the context of this campaign. Although I have tried to provide a fair account, I make no pretense of objectivity or claims of completeness. This is a participant's view, not a historian's. Because I acted as a lawyer in these cases, there are certain privileged materials I could not include in my essay. My role as lawyer has ended, but I remain bound by these privileges. Needless to say, I did not have access to the government's files and deliberations, and could not satisfy my curiosity about what was said at high-level Justice Department and White House meetings on these cases. I suspect these conversations were as much political as legal in substance, but that should not surprise anyone. All cases that reflect the fundamental conflicts of state power and individual rights are political at their core, and lawyers and judges are equally aware of this reality, however much they deny its impact.

This book is both a sequel and supplement to my earlier account of the wartime internment cases, *Justice at War.* I ended that book, published in 1983, with a brief notice of the petitions filed by the test-case defendants and a thumbnail sketch of the issues they raised. This is a book of records, and that was a narrative history. Each can stand alone, and can be read without the other. But the reader who wants to explore the full context of these important and exciting cases is advised to read both, and to keep an eye on the newspapers. The internment story has not ended, and will not end until we have purged American society of the racism and intolerance that provoked the internment.

I have received much help in preparing this book, and can only acknowledge a fraction of my debt. The dedication to Jack Herzig and Aiko Herzig-Yoshinaga is more than deserved; not only did Jack and Aiko share their work with me in a selfless spirit, but they put me up (and put up with me) in Washington, and they continue their redress crusade with the essential mixture of realism and idealism that all such campaigns require for ultimate success. All the lawyers who volunteered their time and commitment to the coram nobis teams deserve credit for our success; Dale Minami, Don Tamaki, and Lori Bannai in particular have become my good friends and sources of inspiration. This was truly a collective effort, and could not have succeeded without the contribution of each volunteer. Min Yasui, Gordon Hirabayashi, and Fred Korematsu provided me with exemplars of courage, endurance, and true patriotism. Krista Kiger, my research assistant and now a seminary student, infused her work and my spirit with faith, hope, and love. Priscilla Long, who shares my life, approaches her own writing with such care and craft that mine has picked up a bit of her polish.

Finally, an appreciation to Horace Mann, whose plea to the graduates of Antioch College in 1859 struck a chord in me, an Antiochian a century later: "Be ashamed to die until you have won some victory for humanity."

P.I.

October 1988

JUSTICE DELAYED

Introduction: Righting a Great Wrong

by Peter Irons

"They did me a great wrong."

With these few words, spoken in a quiet but firm voice, Fred Korematsu launched an unprecedented legal effort in January 1982. Forty years earlier, along with two other men of Japanese ancestry, Gordon Hirabayashi and Minoru Yasui, Korematsu had defied the military curfew and evacuation orders that paved the roads to the barbed-wire compounds that encircled 120,000 Japanese Americans during World War II. Charged by the government with criminal offenses, all three young men were convicted in 1942 in federal courts. Without dissent, the United States Supreme Court in June 1943 affirmed the convictions of Hirabayashi and Yasui for curfew violations. The justices split over Korematsu's case in December 1944, with three dissenters from the majority opinion which upheld the evacuation orders that forced Japanese Americans into bleak, desolate internment camps.

Fred Korematsu worked as a shipyard welder in the San Francisco area when Japanese planes attacked Pearl Harbor on December 7, 1941. He had volunteered for military service before the war began, but the Navy and Coast Guard turned him away on medical grounds. Hoping to remain with his Caucasian fiancée and escape detection, Korematsu failed to obey the evacuation orders that Army troops tacked on telephone poles early in May 1942. These orders were based on Executive Order 9066, signed by President Franklin D. Roosevelt on February 19, 1942, which authorized military officials to exclude "any or all persons" from designated military zones. Three weeks after the evacuation deadline, police in the East Bay town of San Leandro responded to a tip and arrested Korematsu as he waited at a street corner for his fiancée. Although he first tried to conceal his identity from the police, someone in the station recog-

3

nized Korematsu and he quickly confessed his real name to the FBI agents summoned by the local police.

The young men who challenged the wartime military orders had acted alone, willing to risk imprisonment out of conviction that depriving one group of Americans of their liberty on the basis of ancestry alone could not be squared with the Constitution. Min Yasui had been a young lawyer in Portland, Oregon, when General John L. DeWitt imposed a curfew on all Japanese Americans. Hoping to force a legal test of military power over citizens, Yasui broke the curfew on its first night and spent nine months in solitary confinement after his arrest. Gordon Hirabayashi, a University of Washington senior, left school to work with the Quakers and turned himself in to the FBI when his evacuation notice came in May 1942. Charged with both curfew and evacuation violations, Hirabayashi spent five months in jail before his trial and conviction on both counts. Following their convictions, each man had been imprisoned in jail or in one of the internment camps.

Seated in his living room in San Leandro, close to the corner where the police grabbed him in 1942, Korematsu related the story of his arrest and trial to me in January 1982. I was then a member of the Legal Studies faculty at the University of Massachusetts and was doing research for a book on the wartime internment cases. Earlier I had interviewed Gordon Hirabayashi and Min Yasui for my book and had showed both men copies of documents from the Justice Department files on their cases. These documents, which I dug out of dusty cardboard boxes in October 1981, included internal complaints by government lawyers in 1943 and 1944 that their superiors were engaged in the "suppression of evidence" and had presented "lies" to the Supreme Court in the internment cases. The complaints, however, had been ignored.

I had explained to both Hirabayashi and Yasui that the newly discovered documents might make it possible to reopen their wartime cases and to clear their criminal records, despite the passage of forty years. Both men had responded with enthusiasm to this prospect and had authorized me to act on their behalf as attorney. Yasui was then the executive director of the Denver Commission on Community Relations, and Hirabayashi was a sociology professor at the University of Alberta in Canada. For years they had both hoped to find some way to reopen their cases but had been discouraged by law professors and lawyers who saw no opening in the judicial wall of "finality."

Although my initial meetings with Yasui and Hirabayashi were encouraging, I viewed my first encounter with Korematsu with trepidation. I had earlier written to him requesting an interview, but received no reply. I finally called him during a West Coast research trip and explained that I was writing a book about the internment cases and would like an interview. "I have some documents from the government file on your case that I think might interest you," I added. Cautious in tone, but obviously intrigued, Korematsu invited me to visit his home for an interview.

Korematsu and I were both formal and nervous when our first meeting began. Puffing on his pipe, Korematsu answered questions about his arrest and trial in a slow, deliberate voice, adding flashes of humor in describing his jail-house companions. He became animated and angry in recounting his first courtroom experience, when the judge set bail for his release pending trial, only to discover that the military police had orders to keep their prisoner in custody. Korematsu was escorted from the courtroom at gunpoint.

After Korematsu ended this account, I handed him about twenty pages of Justice Department documents. He read through the entire batch of papers in silence, pausing only to fiddle with his pipe. After what seemed to me an eternity, he looked up. "They did me a great wrong," he said of the officials who persuaded the Supreme Court to affirm his conviction. He then asked me an unexpected question: "Are you a lawyer?" When I answered that I was, Korematsu asked, "Would you be my lawyer?" I would be delighted to give him any help I could, I responded.

Korematsu and I discussed the prospect of reopening the three wartime internment cases. I explained as carefully and cautiously as possible the advantages and dangers of asking the federal courts to reopen cases that had been given a final decision by the Supreme Court almost four decades earlier. On the advantage side, the Justice Department records I had showed him made it possible to argue that prosecution of the cases had been infected with error and resulted in an injustice to the defendants.

The evidence at issue in the Justice Department records dealt with claims by General John L. DeWitt, the Army officer who directed the West Coast evacuation and internment programs, that Japanese Americans were disloyal as a racial group and had committed acts of espionage on behalf of Japan. DeWitt had made these claims in an official Army report that had been refuted by other federal agencies, including the Federal Communications Commission, the Office of Naval Intelligence, and the FBI. Disturbed by the "suppression of evidence" that attested to the overwhelming loyalty of Japanese Americans and by the presentation to the Supreme Court of DeWitt's "lies" about espionage by this group, two of the Justice Department lawyers assigned to the cases—Edward J.

Ennis and John L. Burling—had mounted a determined but futile effort to persuade Solicitor General Charles Fahy that he had an "ethical obligation" to give the Supreme Court the true facts in the cases. Over these protests, Fahy assured the Court in defending Korematsu's conviction that he stood behind every "line, word, and syllable" of DeWitt's disputed report.

Korematsu listened intently as I explained the factual and legal issues in the cases. Balanced against the documents that revealed misconduct by government lawyers were the relative lack of legal precedent in misconduct cases and the reluctance of federal judges to rule on cases that had been decided years ago by the Supreme Court. "In my opinion, you have a good chance of winning a reversal of your conviction," I told Korematsu, "but there is no guarantee of success, and it might take years before the cases are finally decided." Korematsu sat in silence, puffed his pipe for several minutes, and finally responded to my legal balance sheet. "I'll have to talk to my wife, but I want to go ahead." Kathryn Korematsu, who met Fred at a YMCA dance in Detroit after the war, was a tall, gracious native of South Carolina, and she quickly endorsed the effort to clear her husband's criminal record.

With the agreement of Fred Korematsu, the campaign to reopen and reverse the wartime internment cases began. All three men understood the significance and enormity of this task. Never before in American legal history had an effort been launched—let alone succeeded—to overturn convictions in cases that had been finally decided by the Supreme Court. Beyond the criminal records imposed on the three defendants, the Court's adoption of the government's "racial disloyalty" claims had imposed a collective stigma on Japanese Americans that many internment camp survivors still bore as a mark of shame. This effort would raise new and complex questions of law.

The legal procedure was so obscure and seldom used that few lawyers, let alone laypeople, had even heard of it. I described it in a letter to Fred Korematsu shortly after our first meeting: "It might help for me to explain in writing what these actions would involve. The legal procedure is called a petition for a writ of error coram nobis. What this means in English (lawyers like to use Latin to make people think what they do is mysterious) is that you would be asking the original trial court (in your case the federal court in San Francisco) to correct a fundamental error and injustice at your trial. The error would be the failure of the government to acknowledge that there was no evidence to support General DeWitt's claim that acts of sabotage and espionage by Japanese Americans required the curfew and evacuation, and no evidence to support his claim that Japanese Americans were disloyal. We now know, in fact, from government documents that General DeWitt had been told that there was no such evidence before he issued the curfew and evacuation orders, and that he disregarded what he had been told. Since the government had this evidence at the time of your trial, it was under an obligation to produce it. By failing to produce it, the court's judgment of guilty in your case was based on error and a fundamental injustice was committed. Since the government also failed to correct this error when the case was appealed to the Court of Appeals and then to the Supreme Court, the final decision in your case was also fundamentally unjust."

The coram nobis writ has been little used in American law, but it is one of the so-called "Ancient Writs" whose roots are deep in English common law. Designed to protect criminal defendants against arbitrary and unlawful action, coram nobis (the Latin words mean "error before us") is analogous to the more famous writ of habeas corpus, the "Great Writ" of English law that protects against unlawful detention. Habeas corpus is available to those who are being held in custody, while coram nobis is limited to those who have been released from custody after conviction and final judgment by the courts. Those who invoke coram nobis, limited by the Supreme Court to instances of "fundamental error" or "manifest injustice," face a high burden of proof; it cannot be used to reopen and reargue points of law the courts have decided, but only to raise errors of fact that were knowingly withheld by prosecutors from judges and defendants. With these legal hurdles to clear, only defendants who can prove the most outrageous and obvious governmental or prosecutorial misconduct have any real chance of winning in a coram nobis case.

Although I had uncovered the crucial Justice Department files in 1981, I was hardly the first lawyer to consider the reopening of the wartime internment cases. As early as 1945, Yale Law School professor Eugene V. Rostow blasted the Supreme Court decisions as a judicial "disaster" and urged that "the basic issues should be presented to the Supreme Court again, in an effort to obtain a reversal of these war-time cases." Rostow did not, however, suggest a procedural mechanism for returning the cases to the Supreme Court and overcoming the principle of finality, the judge-made doctrine that every case must have an end and that exhaustion of appeals is a mark of finality. More recently, Min Yasui and his friend Frank Chuman, a Los Angeles lawyer and former president of the Japanese American Citizens League (JACL), had consulted with law school

professors and discussed coram nobis as a possible remedy. The problem
was that none who explored the issue had evidence to satisfy the coram
nobis requirement that prosecutorial misconduct be demonstrated. Merely
suggesting the Supreme Court had erred in deciding legal and constitutional issues would not suffice.

The prospect of reopening the internment cases was greatly enhanced
by a development I had not known of when I began my research in August
1981. In 1980 Congress had created the Commission on Wartime Relocation and Internment of Civilians, a blue-ribbon panel charged with
reviewing the wartime "detention in internment camps of American citizens" and recommending "appropriate remedies" for congressional action. Chaired by Washington lawyer Joan Z. Bernstein, the CWR included
Representative Dan Lungren, a young California Republican, former
Senator Edward Brooke and Representative Robert Drinan of Massachusetts, and former Supreme Court Justice Arthur Goldberg among its nine
members.

Between July and December 1981, the CWR held twenty days of hearings across the country and listened to 750 witnesses, many of them former camp residents who had never before discussed their internment
experiences in public. The dikes of emotion broke as many survivors
expressed feelings of shame and anger in tearful words.

The commission held its final hearing at Harvard University on December 9, 1981, with witnesses from law schools that included Harvard,
New York University, Boston University, and the University of Washington. Invited to testify by CWR Research Director Charles D. Smith, I
prepared a fifteen-page statement summarizing my research to that time
and quoting from many of the Justice and War Department records I had
uncovered. Although my statement avoided direct charges of misconduct
by government lawyers, I noted "serious issues of ethical and professional responsibility" and suggested that the commission discuss measures "to insure that records and arguments presented by the government
to the Supreme Court will be made with full candor and disclosure" of the
relevant facts.

After presenting my statement, I was questioned by Judge William
Marutani of the Philadelphia Common Pleas Court, the only Japanese
American commissioner and a former internment camp resident. Suggesting that the "historical evidence" in my statement showed "a deliberate and knowing withholding of information" from the Supreme Court,
Marutani raised the issue of coram nobis as a possible remedy. "Under
the facts that you've indicated," he asked me, would coram nobis "per-

haps be available today? Therefore this entire matter [might] again be reviewed by the Supreme Court of the United States on the basis that material and relevant evidence was withheld from the court?" I noted in responding that coram nobis petitions by the original defendants "might not overrule the Supreme Court precedent" in the cases but might, if brought in the original trial court, "provide a judicial forum for reopening the evidentiary basis upon which their convictions were based" and "justify a reversal of a conviction."

The encouragement of Judge Marutani and other commission members stimulated me to organize a coram nobis effort. I then lived in Boston, although I moved to California in September 1982 to accept a position in the political science department of the University of California, San Diego. Preparing the coram nobis petitions would be a massive and complex undertaking requiring the participation of lawyers admitted to practice and experienced in West Coast courts. To begin the effort, I asked Min Yasui, a nonpracticing lawyer with wide contacts among the Japanese American community, to recommend lawyers who might volunteer their time and skills. Yasui sent me a list of ten lawyers he thought might be sympathetic, all of them Japanese American. I felt it was essential to recruit lawyers from San Francisco, Portland, and Seattle, the cities in which the defendants were tried in 1942. The only lawyer from these cities on Yasui's list was Dale Minami, who specialized in employment discrimination law as a partner in a small Bay Area firm. A 1971 graduate of Boalt Hall Law School at the University of California, Berkeley, Minami was the first president of the Asian Pacific Bar Association of California. Like most third-generation Japanese Americans, Minami learned of the wartime internment from his parents, who had been inmates of the isolated camp at Heart Mountain, Wyoming.

Dale Minami had already taken a position on the internment cases as an active member of Bay Area Attorneys for Redress (BAAR). This group of twenty lawyers and legal workers had submitted a fifty-seven-page statement, drafted as a legal brief, to the Commission on Wartime Relocation at its San Francisco hearing in July 1981. Branding the internment both immoral and unconstitutional, the BAAR statement charged that the Supreme Court opinions in the internment cases rested upon "racial stereotypes and myths devoid of scientific testimony, evidence or documentation." The Supreme Court "approved the concept of guilt by ethnic affiliation" in the opinions and thus ignored "the basic standard of individual guilt essential to our system of legal justice." The BAAR statement urged the CWR to declare that the Supreme Court decisions "were incorrect and should never be used as a precedent against any identifiable group."

Minami and other BAAR members had continued to meet informally after the 1981 CWR hearings, and hoped to contribute their legal skills to the "redress" movement that sought financial compensation from Congress for those who endured imprisonment in the internment camps. After Minami responded with enthusiasm to my request for legal help, I drafted a short memorandum that outlined the basis for a coram nobis attack on the internment cases and summarized the evidence of governmental misconduct I had uncovered. "My own assessment of the probable outcome of such petitions is that they would succeed," I wrote. "It is impossible, of course, to guarantee such outcomes. It is up to the three defendants in the final analysis to decide whether they want to proceed." I assured Minami that all three defendants had given their tentative approval of the proposal. "Having met all these men, I am impressed by their strength of character and conviction," I concluded. "I can't think of a more worthwhile project than to try to eradicate the legacy of racism that these cases left to our country. It would be, I think, a tribute to our legal system if the courts at last recognized that the internment was wrong."

When he received my initial memo, Minami circulated it to the BAAR group. He suggested that I visit the Bay Area to discuss the petition effort, and we set a meeting for early May. During the weeks that preceded this meeting, I prepared a first draft of a coram nobis petition, with a focus on the separate misconduct allegations and the documents that related to each of these. Meanwhile, Minami worked to expand the network of lawyers to Portland and Seattle. The only Japanese American lawyer he knew in Portland was Peggy Nagae, a 1977 graduate of the law school of Lewis and Clark College, who had clerked in Minami's firm as a law student. Then a member of a small Portland firm, she later became assistant dean of the University of Oregon Law School in Eugene. Gordon Hirabayashi and Dale Minami both suggested that Kathryn Bannai head the Seattle legal team. Kathryn had played an active role in the Seattle redress movement, and her sister, Lorraine, was also a lawyer in Minami's firm. As the petition effort took shape, these three lawyers— Dale Minami, Peggy Nagae, and Kathryn Bannai—assumed leadership of the legal teams in their respective cities.

More than a dozen volunteer lawyers and law students attended the two all-day sessions in Minami's home in Oakland. The serious business of our meetings was centered on legal strategy issues and topics for further research, not only to polish the coram nobis petitions but also to anticipate possible defenses by the government after the petitions were filed. These lengthy meetings were both exciting and exhausting, punctuated with breaks in which lawyers tossed Dale's foam-rubber basketball at a hoop on the wall and played video games on the television screen.

Two major questions dominated these first legal team meetings. I had prepared a draft petition that outlined the misconduct charges against the government, and we discussed and debated how to frame these charges, in which order to present them, and whether to include charges that struck some lawyers as minor or weak in legal precedent. As we hammered out agreement on these basic points, Bob Rusky and Karen Kai joined me as the primary petition drafters. Bob and Karen had been classmates at the University of San Francisco Law School and had married after graduation. Bob was the only legal team member who practiced in a large San Francisco firm, and his office donated essential clerical and copying services to our cases.

The other pressing strategy question took several months to settle. In what court or courts should we file the petitions? That we were preparing three separate cases, originally tried in 1942 in three different federal district courts, complicated this question. The federal law that authorized the coram nobis procedure did not specify the proper court, although all the cases we dug up in our research had been filed in the original trial court. This seemed logical, since the misconduct alleged in all these prior cases occurred at the trial level.

In the internment cases, the "suppression of evidence" that government lawyers had charged against their superiors took place before the Supreme Court. We also argued in our petitions that this evidence had been withheld from the trial courts and from the intermediate appellate court. Filing the petitions with the Supreme Court would have generated a burst of publicity, but we had no guarantee the justices would rule on the cases. If they were summarily dismissed, we might be out of court without any chance to appeal. If the petitions were sent back to lower courts, we would have lost several months. In the end, we chose the safest course and filed each petition in the original trial court. Because the cases involved similar legal issues and the government's misconduct had affected all three, our petitions were identical in content.

The most urgent task at the first meetings of the Korematsu legal team was to develop a structure for the overall coram nobis effort. Dale Minami was the natural choice to direct the group and serve as "lead counsel" in the courtroom. His experienced guidance, offered with self-deprecating humor, eased the legal team through conflicts over strategy and tactics. Aided by Lorraine Bannai, I assumed responsibility for factual research and further document searches. In looking for additional documents to bolster our petitions, Lori and I relied heavily on Aiko Herzig-Yoshinaga, the CWR's chief researcher, with whom I had begun to exchange findings early in my own research, and her husband, Jack Herzig, a retired lieutenant colonel in Army counterintelligence. After Aiko left the commission, she and Jack had turned their Washington apartment into an archive of internment files. Bob Rusky and Karen Kai, along with Dennis Hayashi, a lawyer at the Asian Law Caucus in Oakland, headed the legal research effort. More than a dozen lawyers and law students helped this group in plowing through cases in the search for legal precedent to buttress our misconduct charges.

Legal and factual research was only half the task of the coram nobis effort. Equally important, the lawyers agreed, was mounting as broad and intensive a public education campaign as possible. The primary goals of our campaign were to clear the criminal records of the three defendants and to obtain strong judicial findings on the misconduct charges. We also hoped for judicial findings that the internment program itself had been unlawful and unconstitutional. Even if achieved, these goals would lose their impact if the public failed to learn about the cases, the internment, and the continuing need to rectify this national mistake. The legal team devoted much time to plans for an outreach and education program to include media relations, liaison with the Japanese American community, contacts with church, labor, political, and civic groups, and funding.

Donald Tamaki volunteered to direct the education and outreach program. Don was a graduate of Boalt Hall Law School at the University of California, Berkeley, and then served as executive director of the Asian Law Caucus, which provided free legal services to the Asian community in areas such as housing, employment, and health care. Virtually from scratch, he mastered the skills of writing press releases, arranging press conferences, and juggling the demands of the media for interviews, photographs, and "exclusive" news. He also raised funds to cover the legal team's expenses and built a network of support from a wide spectrum of groups that endorsed our efforts. To funnel these funds and support to the coram nobis effort, Don constructed an umbrella group called the Committee to Reverse the Japanese American Wartime Cases, a cumbersome name but the best we could devise.

The legal team had initially planned to file the petitions in October 1982, but as work progressed over the summer it became obvious the date would have to be pushed back. Bay Area law students and undergraduates volunteered their services for legal and factual research, and a blizzard of memoranda swirled about the legal team meetings. One group of Berkeley undergraduates, students in a course on Asian American legal issues taught by Dale Minami and Don Tamaki, prepared a giant chart, some ten feet long, that matched all the important statements in the government documents, court briefs, and Supreme Court opinions, tracing their origins and connections. Despite the intense pace, a note of healthy irreverence marked the work; one lawyer addressed his memos to "Maximal Leader Minami" and signed them "Batty, Bilious Backroom Boy." The legal team began calling itself the "Western Defense Commandos," a play on the Army unit headed by General DeWitt.

After it became obvious that the October filing date was unrealistic, the legal team chose a tentative date of December 15. We had agreed to keep this date from the press, to avoid pressure on the defendants (whom the team now called "petitioners") and leaks that might alert the government to the charges the petitions would make. But it was impossible, given the widespread discussion of the coram nobis effort among Japanese Americans, to maintain a complete media blackout before the filings.

Two events in October created concern and consternation within the legal team. Late that month, someone provided the Japanese American press with a copy of an October 1 letter from Arthur J. Goldberg to Judge William Marutani. As a former Supreme Court justice and member of the Commission on Wartime Relocation, Goldberg had an aura of influence and a reputation as a judicial liberal. In his letter, Goldberg criticized the coram nobis effort as unnecessary and potentially damaging. Assuming that a petition attacking the Korematsu conviction alone would be filed in the Supreme Court, and without knowledge of the misconduct evidence that had been uncovered, Goldberg wrote that "it is my considered opinion that it is not necessary and indeed not procedurally possible to mount a legal attack to overrule Korematsu." Citing a 1954 case that outlawed racial discrimination by federal agencies and officials—a companion to the famous *Brown* school segregation case—Goldberg claimed that this opinion "overruled Korematsu on the equal protection issue."

"Based on my experience" as a Supreme Court justice and lawyer, Goldberg wrote to Marutani, a coram nobis effort directed at the Supreme Court "would be fruitless" and would undermine the "obvious and strong public interest in finality of a judgment." The coram nobis approach, he concluded, "runs the danger of legitimating this bad decision, in public perception, in the virtually certain event of denial by the Court of reopening the case."

Legal team members reacted to Goldberg's letter and the publicity it received with public restraint and private anger. We did not know for certain who had prompted the letter and released it to the press. We were also incensed by a *Washington Post* article in late October that quoted from Goldberg's letter, revealed our plan to file the petitions on December 15, and reported as fact that Supreme Court reversal of the internment cases "would work little or no change in the law," since later decisions "have dramatically expanded safeguards for racial minorities." The *Post* reporter, Fred Barbash, had called me and read the draft of his article to me, asking for corroboration and additional facts. I told him that many details in the story were wrong or speculative. When Barbash asked for copies of important documents the petitions would include, I offered them on the same condition asked of other reporters, that they not be published before the petitions were filed. Barbash refused, and the misinformation in his article reached the public (and government lawyers) before final decisions on filing the petitions were made by the legal team.

The press of work in completing the petitions, and doubts about December as a time to launch them, led to a final choice of January 19, 1983, as the filing date for the Korematsu petition in San Francisco. After consultation with the Portland and Seattle legal teams, we decided that their separate petitions would be filed two weeks later. Hectic meetings to polish the petitions, and several all-night sessions at the word processors in Bob Rusky's law office, preceded the filing date. Dom Tamaki spent hours on the telephone, urging newspaper and television people to attend the press conference scheduled after the court filing and patiently explaining the details of the cases and the coram nobis procedure to dozens of callers.

The three men who brought the test cases in 1942 had never met as a group until the day before we filed the Korematsu petition. Min Yasui and Gordon Hirabayashi had met a few times over the years, but Fred Korematsu had avoided any public appearances and was not active in the Japanese American community. After he agreed to challenge his conviction, Fred had his telephone number unlisted and asked Dom Tamaki to make sure "there won't be any television cameras on my lawn." Trailed by a CBS film crew, the three men finally met in the Oakland office of the Asian Law Caucus. Korematsu, who had recently undergone major surgery, looked gaunt and nervous, but he spoke with conviction and humor as he answered questions.

The morning of January 19, the legal team gathered at the office of the federal district court clerk in San Francisco to file the Korematsu petition. Cases were assigned to judges by computer, and the lawyers had some apprehension they might draw one of the more conservative judges from the fifteen who were available for assignment. We gave the petitions to an assistant clerk, who punched a docket number into a computer terminal, waited a minute, and then turned to the waiting lawyers with a wide smile on his face. "Congratulations," he announced. "You got Judge Patel." The lawyers exploded with whoops of joy and hand-slapping. Judge Marilyn Patel was probably the most sympathetic member of the district court bench. A graduate of Wheaton College and Fordham Law School in 1963, she left private practice in New York to join the Immigration and Naturalization Service in San Francisco in 1972. Patel, whose husband was an engineer of East Indian ancestry, became a judge on the Oakland Municipal Court in 1976. Four years later, President Jimmy Carter appointed her to the federal bench on the recommendation of Senator Alan Cranston. Patel had worked with and supported the National Organization for Women and other progressive groups, and the legal team members were naturally delighted that she would sit on the Korematsu case.

Jubilant with this stroke of good fortune, we rushed to the San Francisco Press Club near Union Square, where we joined the three petitioners in an appearance before a jammed crowd of more than a hundred newspaper, radio, and television reporters. After introductions by Don Tamaki, I explained the coram nobis procedure and summarized the misconduct charges in the petitions. "New evidence will put these cases in a new light," I concluded. Dale Minami stressed the importance of the coram nobis effort to the Japanese American community and the need to ask the judicial system to erase the wartime convictions. "We're not just asking for sympathy," he said, "but for the justice denied these men forty years ago."

The petitioners each spoke briefly, exhibiting both their differences in personality and their burning desire to clear their records. "I was born and schooled in Oakland," Korematsu said in his quiet voice. "I'm just like any other American." Gordon Hirabayashi, in his measured, professorial tone, explained why he defied the curfew and evacuation orders. "If I gave in to this, it would cause me to change my ideals, my beliefs, my whole philosophy of life," he said. "I knew I'd be accused of disloyalty, but I couldn't sit back and passively endorse the orders." Min Yasui, who often faced the press as an advocate of the redress movement, recalled "the nine months that I rotted in solitary confinement" after his wartime arrest and displayed a copy of the Constitution his father had given him as a school child in proclaiming his devotion to the American ideals the internment had ignored. Coverage of the filing and press conference by the national television networks and wire services pleased the legal team, which considered media coverage of the coram nobis effort an essential part of its educational campaign.

Petitions in the remaining two cases were filed at the end of January. The Yasui petition, filed in Portland by Peggy Nagae, was assigned to Judge Robert C. Belloni. Appointed to the federal bench by President Lyndon Johnson in 1967, Belloni served in the Army in World War II and had been active in Democratic politics before his appointment. The sixty-three-year-old judge did not have a substantial record on civil rights cases, and it was difficult to predict his reaction to the petition. None of the other Oregon federal judges, however, was noted as a civil rights liberal.

Fortunately, the judge assigned to the Hirabayashi case had an excellent reputation on civil rights issues. Judge Donald S. Voorhees, a native of Kansas and a graduate of Harvard Law School, practiced law in Seattle for more than twenty years before President Richard Nixon appointed him to the bench. Voorhees, born in 1916 and a Navy officer in World War II, had won praise from civil rights groups for his sweeping order in a Seattle school integration case. Lawyers admired his patience and courtroom courtesy, although he demanded that lawyers respect the court and witnesses and was known as a stickler for adherence to procedural rules.

Trial lawyers, in both private and government practice, keep files and exchange notes on the judges they practice before or may face in court. They can often predict whether a particular judge will be friendly or hostile, impartial or indifferent to their side. Lawyers know that absolute judicial impartiality is a myth and that judges have political biases just as most people do. Given this reality, we were delighted that judges Patel and Voorhees had drawn the Korematsu and Hirabayashi petitions, and we recognized that Judge Belloni was typical of his Oregon colleagues.

Filing the three petitions completed the first phase of the coram nobis effort and shifted the initiative to the government for its response and to the courts for decision. The legal teams had no idea how the government would respond. The options ranged from agreement with the petitions and the relief they sought to total opposition and a hard-line defense of the wartime internment. Given the advances in civil rights over the past four decades, the political clout of Japanese Americans on the West Coast, and the national mood of repentance for the internment, the latter option seemed unlikely. On the other hand, the Reagan administration and the Justice Department had cut back on civil rights enforcement, and our misconduct allegations implicated several former officials who were still alive and unrepentant. The most influential in this group was John J. McCloy, Assistant Secretary of War during the internment period and an unbending defender of the wartime program. McCloy had retained his influence in Washington and would likely object strenuously to any confession of error by the government.

The timing of the government's response was as uncertain as its substance. The petitions, although identical in form, had been filed in three separate courts, and federal judges had great discretion over their dockets. The coram nobis lawyers could not force any of the judges to act on the petitions or to set a date for the government's response. The Bay Area lawyers were delighted when Judge Patel, only two weeks after the Korematsu petition was filed, scheduled a status conference for March 14, 1983. This would allow her to set a timetable for proceedings in the case and get an idea of the positions of both sides.

While they prepared for their first court appearance on the petitions, the Bay Area lawyers consulted with the legal teams in Portland and Seattle about future strategy. Neither Judge Belloni nor Judge Voorhees had yet taken any action on the petitions, and we heard rumors that both judges had decided to wait until Judge Patel had ruled in the Korematsu case.

A long-awaited event that happened before the status conference gave the legal teams hope that the government would not oppose the petitions. In mid-February, the Commission on Wartime Relocation released a 467-page report of its internment investigation, entitled *Personal Justice Denied*. As the title suggested, the commission labeled the internment a "grave injustice" to Americans of Japanese ancestry. The commissioners agreed without dissent that the internment resulted from "race prejudice, war hysteria and a failure of political leadership." Although the report devoted only three pages to the Supreme Court opinions in the internment cases, it denounced the Korematsu decision in scathing terms. Discussing the Court's sanction of racial discrimination and its deference to military authority, the report found that "each part of the decision, questions of both factual review and legal principles, has been discredited or abandoned" by later decisions. "Today the decision in *Korematsu* lies overruled in the court of history," the report concluded. The commissioners did not issue their recommendations for redress with the report, announcing they would release them before the CWR disbanded on June 30, 1983.

The commission report became the centerpiece of the status conference on March 14, with copies of the blue-covered book on the tables of both sets of lawyers. Dale Minami and I appeared for Fred Korematsu, and we were matched with Victor Stone, a Justice Department lawyer from the Criminal Division in Washington. William McGivern of the local U.S. attorney's office joined Stone at the counsel table but played no role in the proceedings. Stone proved to be voluble and excitable at the podium, and his rapid speech and rambling locution often provoked judicial requests to slow down and clarify his points. A 1971 graduate of Harvard Law School, Stone had worked as a law student with the Prison Legal Assistance Project and the Civil Rights Research Committee, but he joined the criminal prosecution side after graduation.

Judge Patel got right to the point after she opened the courtroom proceedings. "Has the government filed anything yet in response to the petition?" she asked Stone, who replied that he had not. "How do you intend to respond?" she pressed on. Stone's answer made it clear that the government's strategy was to delay its response as long as possible. Brandishing his copy of the CWR report, Stone told Judge Patel that "we would prefer to be in a position where we had the conclusion of the commission's work placed before the Congress" before responding to the petition. It might be considered "a kind of interference if we started taking positions on these issues before they completed their work," Stone suggested. He assured Judge Patel the government intended to heed the commission's recommendations if possible, stating that "if they come down strongly for a particular result it may well be that the Executive will be interested, happy, eager" to join in the recommendations.

Stone urged Judge Patel to give him up to three months after the commission released its recommendations, hinting that they "may allow this court to avoid certain constitutional issues" raised in the petition and possibly end the case through a settlement. "I'm not entirely sure we'll have a controversy" after release of the recommendations, he stated. Dale Minami and I did not oppose Stone's request to delay his response for a "reasonable time" after the commission acted, and Judge Patel set a limit of no more than sixty days after the final commission report was issued.

The release of the long-awaited recommendations of the Commission on Wartime Relocation came on June 16, and set off a new round of disputes between Stone and the coram nobis lawyers. The most dramatic recommendation, and the one that captured the most media attention, was that Congress appropriate the funds to pay $20,000 to each of the roughly 60,000 survivors of the internment camps, a total redress payment of some $1.2 billion. All the commissioners except Congressman Dan Lungren endorsed the redress proposal, which prompted much comment on both sides. John J. McCloy, who had earlier defended the internment as "retribution" for the Pearl Harbor attack, denounced the redress proposal as "utterly unconscionable and unfair to all those who suffered from the attack on Pearl Harbor, none of whom were adequately compensated." McCloy defended the internment as "the most benign episode" of the war. "Nobody probably suffered as little as those ethnic Japanese who were moved," he told reporters.

The commission recommendation that directly affected the petitioners was one the legal teams did not welcome. The commissioners unanimously proposed "that the President pardon those who were convicted of violating the statutes imposing a curfew on American citizens on the basis of their ethnicity and requiring the ethnic Japanese to leave designated areas of the West Coast or to report to assembly centers." Their pardon proposal, the commissioners added, was "made without prejudice to cases currently before the courts," a cryptic statement the coram nobis lawyers could not decipher.

The pardon recommendation gave the Justice Department a way to avoid answering the petitions on their merits unless one of the judges forced an answer to the misconduct charges. The legal teams had advance word of the pardon proposal and had vainly protested that it would be useless and damaging. A few weeks before the recommendations were released, Angus Macbeth, special counsel to the CWR, called Dale Minami and asked whether the petitioners would accept a presidential pardon. Dale replied that he could not speak officially for all three men, but he was sure they would not accept a pardon. The coram nobis lawyers suspected that Arthur Goldberg, who had already deprecated their efforts, had pushed for the pardon proposal as a way of defusing the petitions.

The impact of the commission action became evident on June 17, the day after the recommendations were released. I had already scheduled a telephone call to Victor Stone on that day to discuss my visit to look through government records in his office the following week. When I called Stone, I asked for his reaction to the proposal and inquired whether it would affect the government's response to the Korematsu petition. After the CWR recommendations were issued, Judge Patel had ordered Stone to file the government's reply by August 29. Stone told me that he was pleased with the pardon proposal and that he thought the petitioners should also be pleased. "I would think they would welcome an official apology by the President," he said. Stone added that he would probably asked Judge Patel for an extension of the August 29 deadline, since "people in the department want me to prepare papers" on the pardon proposal and it would take considerable time to have them reviewed. Stone also told me he would not be working on the petition response while he dealt with the pardon issue.

Stone and I then sparred over the question of whether presidential pardons would "moot" the petitions, the legal term for ending a lawsuit by wiping out the dispute between the parties. Stone suggested that pardons "probably would" moot the petitions. I disagreed with this position. The only effect of a pardon, I reminded him, was to erase the civil disabilities (loss of voting rights and professional licenses) that followed criminal convictions; the conviction and finding of guilt remained on the record after a pardon. Stone did not dispute the legal issue, but replied that "I doubt that the judge would think that a pardon would be irrelevant" to the petitions.

Stone seemed quite anxious in this conversation that the petitioners agree to accept pardons, and he hinted that the "political officials" in the Justice Department would accept his recommendation that pardons be granted, although he stressed that he could not guarantee this outcome. What the petitioners wanted, I replied, was the judicial vacation of their convictions and action on the petitions, which raised serious charges of governmental misconduct. The call ended with my assurance that we would ask the petitioners for their response to the pardon proposal and get back to Stone.

I immediately called Dale Minami from Boston to report my talk with Stone and to request that Dale ask Fred Korematsu for his reaction. Within minutes, Stone called me back to report that he had just talked with the pardon attorney in the Justice Department, the official responsible for making pardon recommendations to the President. Stone was excited, and explained that the pardon attorney had told him that another form of presidential pardon existed, called a "pardon for innocence." Although rarely issued, this form of pardon was based on a finding by the President that the individual pardoned was innocent of the charges on which he or she had been convicted. Such findings, Stone told me, could be formally stated in the pardon document.

Stone seemed insistent that the petitioners could have no objection to pardons for innocence, and he asked me to respond to this possible action. Without agreeing that the three men would accept such pardons, I replied that any pardon would have to include a statement that the laws and military orders under which they were convicted were unlawful and unconstitutional. Stone did not object to this prospect, and hinted that we could propose any wording we wanted to that effect. I reminded him that I could give no commitments on the issue, and that the petitioners were determined to secure judicial hearings on their petitions. The only prospect that pardons for innocence might be accepted, I said, was dependent on the government's agreement to ask the district judges to vacate the convictions at the time the pardons were issued. Although Stone took a noncommittal stance on this proposal, he did not reject it, and this second conversation ended with my agreement to raise the issue with the petitioners and to advise Stone of their positions.

Although the coram nobis lawyers were initially angered that the CWR made the pardon recommendation over our objections and suspected that Stone would use it to further delay the government's response to the Korematsu petition, we soon decided that the proposal gave us additional flexibility in dealing with Stone. What he wanted to avoid at almost any cost, it seemed obvious, was a full-scale judicial hearing on the petitions' misconduct charges. I had made it clear that the petitioners would reject a general pardon, and Stone had virtually committed himself to "pardons for innocence" that would include wording drafted by the coram nobis lawyers. If that wording included everything the petitioners would want in a judicial opinion, Stone would wind up in a box.

After discussions with their respective clients, the lead attorneys on each legal team decided that any formal pardon offer from the government would be rejected in any form. Fred Korematsu was the most adamant of the three men. "We should be the ones pardoning the government," he told Dale Minami. Because Stone had not made a formal pardon offer, we agreed that this decision would not be communicated to the government unless an offer was made.

As the August 29 deadline approached, Stone hinted to me that the pardon proposal had run into opposition from "hard-liners" in the Justice Department, including some World War II veterans who opposed any concessions in the cases. The coram nobis lawyers were surprised, however, when Stone asked Judge Patel to extend the deadline by thirty days on the ground that I had indicated "that there is some possibility, however slim, that some form of Presidential action" in granting a pardon might be acceptable to Korematsu. We were even more surprised by Stone's claim to Judge Patel that an extension of time might "result in a voluntary withdrawal of the petition" by Korematsu. Before the President decided whether to grant the pardons the commission had requested, Stone argued, "it would be inappropriate to force the Government to take formal and public adversarial positions on the issues in this judicial proceeding at this time."

Dale Minami and I were resigned to the prospect that Judge Patel would give Stone the extra thirty days he requested, since such motions were rarely denied. But we took the opening that Stone's motion gave us to inform Judge Patel about the government's pardon plan, which we hoped she would recognize as a delaying tactic. I answered Stone with a statement to Judge Patel, opposing the extension request and noting that in every talk with Stone "I have made clear that Mr. Korematsu had indicated and reiterated his opposition to any form of presidential pardon."

As we expected, Judge Patel gave Stone the extra thirty days he requested. But her decision did not end the sparring over the pardon proposal. Stone sent a letter to Dale Minami accusing him of "inaccurately stating that an 'offer' of a pardon had been made" to Korematsu and chiding him for revealing to Judge Patel "our off-the-record talks" over the question. All discussions between the two sides on the issue ended on this acerbic note.

Although nothing came of the government's effort to induce the petitioners to accept presidential pardons, this episode is indicative of the high-level debate within the government over these sensitive cases. It seems clear that one faction wanted the easiest way out, one that would avoid alienating the Japanese American community, which had gained some measure of political clout on the West Coast. Another faction, including the "hard-liners" that Stone mentioned to me, was determined to defend the wartime internment to the bitter end. This group, perhaps influenced by John J. McCloy and Karl Bendetsen, the architect and engineer of the internment, responded to another political constituency, the vocal and virulent "Remember Pearl Harbor" lobby that opposed any form of redress to the internment camp survivors. The coram nobis lawyers never learned whether Stone's pardon proposals were serious, and

Fred Korematsu's emphatic rejection of any pardon had cut off that prospect of an out-of-court end to the petition effort.

The close of this episode made it certain that at least one of the three coram nobis petitions would receive a judicial hearing. What kind of hearing and the issues to be brought before Judge Patel depended on the government response that Victor Stone was drafting. The coram nobis lawyers could only guess about whether Stone would take a neutral stance on the petition or mount an all-out defense against the misconduct charges, which would require a full-scale evidentiary hearing. After the acrimonious dispute over the pardon proposals, it seemed unlikely that the government would take the option of supporting the petition.

The guessing ended when Stone filed the government's response on October 4, 1983. Covering less than two pages of text, the response tried to shift the initiative from the petitioner to the government by asking Judge Patel to vacate Korematsu's conviction on the government's motion. Confessing that the internment of Japanese Americans "was part of an unfortunate episode in our nation's history," the response stated that "the government has concluded—without any intention to disparage those persons who made the decisions in question—that it would not be appropriate to defend this forty year old misdemeanor conviction." Cast as an act of executive grace, much like the pardon Korematsu had scorned, the response argued that Judge Patel had no reason "to convene hearings or make findings about petitioner's allegations of governmental wrong-doing in the 1940s." Almost as an afterthought, the government concluded that "the petition should be dismissed." A tone of apology but not of contrition pervaded the brief document.

Judge Patel scheduled the hearing on the Korematsu petition for November 10, 1983, in the ceremonial courtroom of the federal courthouse in San Francisco. Well before the courtroom was opened, a crowd gathered in an atmosphere of emotion and anticipation. Many of those who attended were elderly Japanese Americans who had endured three years of imprisonment in barren internment camps in the desert and mountains. Cries of recognition broke the hallway chatter as former internees met campmates they had not seen for forty years. Television film crews flooded the scene with lights as Fred Korematsu, his wife Kathryn, and a dozen members of his volunteer legal team entered the building to face reporters. A chill winter wind had ruffled Fred Korematsu's sparse hair, and Kathryn smoothed it as he faced the cameras to explain why he had sought vindication more than four decades after his arrest and conviction.

Over three hundred spectators crowded the chamber when Judge Patel entered and took the bench. Serious and somewhat formal in expression, she was obviously conscious of the historic nature of the proceeding and the undercurrent of emotion in the courtroom. Fred and his lawyers, headed by Dale Minami, occupied one counsel table, while Victor Stone and William McGivern sat at the other. Dale chatted and joked with his colleagues before the session began, making last-minute changes in the statement he had drafted for the occasion. Stone appeared nervous as he shuffled through the stack of papers on his desk. He had just gotten off the telephone with his superiors in Washington, seeking final instructions on the government's position on the petition.

Judge Patel opened the session with a brisk review of the history of the case and the coram nobis petition, and she quickly announced that she did not consider the government's motion to vacate the conviction and dismiss the petition as a proper vehicle for judicial action. She had met with Minami and Stone before the session began to explain that she intended to deny the government's motion because the applicable rule of procedure did not allow the government to terminate prosecutions after the defendant had exhausted appeals and served his or her sentence. Judge Patel's decision on that issue, and her suggestion that the government might think twice about opposing the petition, had prompted Stone's hurried consultation with Washington officials.

Few spectators understood the legal issues as Judge Patel restated her decision and asked Stone and Minami if they wanted to address the government's motion for the record. Speaking rapidly, and with quick glances at his opponents, Stone began by stating that the government had asked Judge Patel to "grant the same substantive relief which Mr. Korematsu, as petitioner, has requested, namely that the conviction be vacated and the underlying information be dismissed." Stone referred in this last phrase to the original charge against Korematsu by the government. He went on to read a lengthy presidential proclamation, issued in 1976 by Gerald Ford, that characterized the wartime evacuation of Japanese Americans as a "set-back to fundamental American principles" and that expressed a national "resolve that this kind of action shall never again be repeated."

Stone very briefly defended the legal basis of the government's motion, conceding that his supporting cases "are quite ancient and do not carry federal authority which would normally be controlling over this Court."

Judge Patel then asked if the government still insisted that she dismiss the petition. Stone requested that she "grant us the indulgence of ten or twelve days" to decide whether opposition to the petition was "still a necessary part of our position," a request Judge Patel rejected. Dale knew he had won on this issue, and took only a minute at the podium to put his position on the record. Concluding that Stone's motion was "inappropriate," Judge Patel stated she would "treat it as essentially non-opposition to the petition and deal with the petition on the merits."

Dale Minami returned to the podium to argue, for the first time in an American court, that a criminal conviction upheld by the Supreme Court was so tainted that it should be vacated. In forceful, measured tones, Minami put his purpose in these words: "We are here today to seek a measure of the justice denied to Fred Korematsu and the Japanese American community forty years ago." He scorned the government's response as "excuses for not admitting error and for refusing to confront the real public interest in concluding this legal chapter."

Minami proceeded to the charges raised in the coram nobis petition. "The allegations we put forth are perhaps unique in legal history, charging that high government officials suppressed, altered and destroyed information and evidence in order to influence the outcome of a Supreme Court decision," he claimed. Minami then turned to the person whose decision to challenge his wartime conviction had initiated this unique proceeding. Fred Korematsu, he said, "lived forty years with the conviction while carrying the burden of losing the case which sanctioned the mass imprisonment of his people. For him to fight as a representative of all Japanese Americans virtually alone, when his community was either too young, too tired, too old, or too frightened to fight and risking imprisonment and a criminal record entitles him to some consideration. Surely after forty years of fighting, Fred Korematsu's interest is part of the public interest. For the Japanese American community, Fred's fight was their fight."

Minami had cast his statement not as a legal argument but to voice the hopes of an entire community: "For those Japanese Americans interned, for those ex-internees in the audience, for Fred Korematsu and for this court, this is the last opportunity to finally achieve the justice denied forty years ago." He ended with a request that Fred Korematsu be allowed to address the court, and Judge Patel agreed.

Korematsu spoke quietly to a hushed courtroom. "Your Honor," he began, "I still remember forty years ago when I was handcuffed and arrested as a criminal here in San Francisco." Speaking for all those who endured the "concentration camps" he had defied, Korematsu asked for the vindication he sought for himself and for those who suffered with him. "As long as my record stands in federal court, any American citizen can be held in prison or concentration camps without a trial or a hearing." He concluded with a simple request. "I would like to see the government admit that they were wrong and do something about it so this will never happen again to any American citizen of any race, creed or color."

Victor Stone seemed reluctant to follow Korematsu to the podium for his final arguments on the petition, and hurried through a brief statement. His only reference to the misconduct charges was to deny any "acts of suppression by the government that might have occurred when the cases were litigated" during wartime. Suggesting the petition had no legal ground, Stone ended by stating as a "symbolic matter" that acknowledgment of the internment as a national mistake "justifies vacating the conviction and dismissing the petition."

The focus of attention shifted to the bench as Stone returned to his counsel table. Judge Patel paused for a moment, then began reading the opinion she had composed before the hearing. She cited both the documents we had presented and the report of the Commission on Wartime Relocation as grounds for her decision. Labeling the government's petition response as "tantamount to a confession of error," she stated that a coram nobis petition was the appropriate vehicle "for the Court to correct fundamental errors in its record."

Judge Patel reminded her listeners of the limited scope of her authority as a district judge. She could not reverse the Supreme Court opinion of 1944 or correct any errors of law the justices may have made. Robbed by later cases of any value as legal precedent, she continued, the Court's opinion "stands as a constant caution that in times of war or declared military necessity our institutions must be vigilant in protecting constitutional guarantees." Judge Patel paused again, then stated firmly that "the petition for a writ of coram nobis is granted." She rose from the bench without further comment and left for her chambers.

The abrupt conclusion of the hearing left the courtroom in momentary silence. As the audience realized the impact of the judge's historic decision, silence turned to jubilation and tears. Several wept with long-suppressed tears, while others crowded around Fred Korematsu and his lawyers, pumping hands and clapping backs, adding words of gratitude. The crowd lingered in the courtroom as Korematsu, his family, and the legal team left to face the reporters and cameras, first in the courthouse lobby and then at the San Francisco Press Club. Asked why he waited forty years to seek vindication of his wartime defiance, Korematsu revealed both his reticence and resolve: "I had to do some deep thinking to reopen this case again, and I'm certainly glad I did."

The coram nobis lawyers did not have long to savor their initial victory. Hearings in the Yasui and Hirabayashi cases had not been scheduled at the time of the Korematsu hearing, but the judges assigned to those cases read the newspapers and were likely to act after waiting for the first decision. Judge Belloni in Portland was the first to move, setting a hearing on Min Yasui's petition for January 16, 1984.

Preparations for the Yasui hearing took place against the backdrop of two factors. One was the government's intention to appeal Judge Patel's decision, filed in the Ninth Circuit Court of Appeals on December 13, 1983. This Notice of Appeal did not commit the government to follow through but gave Victor Stone and his superiors time to wait for a decision on the Yasui petition before filing any appellate brief. Stone was aided by an agreement that his time to file a brief would be delayed until sixty days after Judge Patel issued her written opinion, which might take months from the hearing. If Judge Belloni dismissed or did not act on Yasui's petition, Stone's hand would be strengthened in this legal poker game.

Another factor the legal teams faced was the "class action redress suit" then pending in federal court in Washington, D.C. Spurred by William Hohri of Chicago, the National Council for Japanese American Redress had filed a suit in March 1983, after the coram nobis petitions were filed, on behalf of all internment camp survivors as a class. The suit listed twenty-one separate legal injuries the government had caused the internees and asked that each class member be awarded damages of $10,000 for each violation, a total potential award of some $24 billion. The injuries claimed by the camp survivors included "summary removal from their homes, imprisonment in racially segregated prison camps, and mass deprivations of their constitutional rights" by the government.

Although the coram nobis petitions and class action suit had no legal connection, both were facets of the overall "redress" movement and lawyers in the two efforts maintained contact. Several of the documents from the coram nobis petition were included in the class action suit as "direct evidence that the government knew of the falsity of its claim of military necessity" in defending the internment before the Supreme Court. The outcome of the Yasui hearing, the content of Judge Patel's opinion, and the legal impact of her opinion on the class action suit, were all factors likely to affect the government's final decision on appealing the Korematsu decision.

Once again, the legal teams could only guess about the government's position on the Yasui petition. Don Willner, a 1951 Harvard Law School graduate who headed a prestigious Portland firm, had joined Peggy Nagae in representing Min Yasui. Willner was an experienced trial lawyer who had often appeared before Judge Belloni. Yasui's lawyers were not surprised when Victor Stone, assigned to all three coram nobis cases, asked Judge Belloni to vacate Yasui's conviction and dismiss his petition, the same motion Judge Patel had denied. Days before the scheduled hearing, Stone filed with Judge Belloni a lengthy legal memo that supported the government's claim of power to dismiss criminal prosecutions after convictions had been entered. At the request of Yasui's lawyers, Karen Kai and I flew to Portland and worked around the clock for three days in Willner's office to draft and polish a reply to Stone's brief. This reply brief was filed only minutes before the hearing began.

Portland has a much smaller Japanese American community than San Francisco and Seattle, and the group that gathered to attend Yasui's hearing numbered only forty or fifty. But it more than filled the small courtroom, and about ten spectators stood along the back wall when Judge Belloni began the hearing. His response to this standing-room audience set the tone for the proceedings. "Anyone who is not seated will have to leave this courtroom," he brusquely ordered. Several people who could not squeeze onto the crowded benches left the chamber as Judge Belloni waited with an impatient look on his face.

The hearing opened on an inauspicious note for Yasui and his lawyers. Judge Belloni first asked Don Willner to "explain to me what this case is about." Willner gave a patient outline of the history of Yasui's case and the basis of his coram nobis petition, to which Judge Belloni responded with another question: "If you're talking about misconduct before the Supreme Court, why didn't you bring this case in that court?" Willner did his best to explain why the petition had been filed in the original trial court, but the judge seemed uninterested in the answer.

Peggy Nagae followed Willner to the podium and tried to educate Judge Belloni about the damage the internment had done to Japanese Americans and the need for a judicial response to this injustice. Min Yasui then addressed the court and put his oratorical skills to work. What he wanted most of all, Yasui told the judge, was to restore his faith in the Constitution and its guarantee of rights to those of all races and creeds. His conviction and the Supreme Court opinion that upheld it had damaged that faith, Yasui said, but had not destroyed it. Judicial action to clear his criminal record would restore his faith in the rule of law over military control.

Victor Stone took only a few minutes at the podium, and began with a claim that the two sides had no dispute over the relief Yasui was seeking. Although he still spoke in a rapid-fire fashion, Stone appeared more relaxed and comfortable than he had before Judge Patel. Before he left the podium, Stone suggested that Judge Belloni could best end the case by granting the government's motion to vacate Yasui's conviction and dismiss his petition. The hearing ended with Judge Belloni's assurance that he would take the government's motion under consideration and issue his ruling at a later date.

Judge Belloni took only ten days to decide the case. He granted the government's motion in a two-page order issued on January 26, 1984. He agreed with Stone that the two sides had asked for the "same relief" in vacating the conviction. "The only difference is that petitioner asks me to make findings of governmental acts of misconduct that deprived him of his Fifth Amendment rights." Listing the requested findings that no military necessity existed for the internment and that "the government knew about and withheld evidence refuting military necessity," Judge Belloni concluded that "I decline to make such findings forty years after the events took place." Yasui wanted to have "the court engage in fact finding which would have no legal consequences," he added. "Courts should not engage in that kind of activity."

The coram nobis lawyers were disappointed that Judge Belloni declined to consider the petition. Judge Patel had not yet issued her written opinion on the Korematsu petition, and Victor Stone—undoubtedly hoping to influence her opinion—sent her a copy of Judge Belloni's order for "the attention of the court." His move evidently annoyed Judge Patel, who promptly ruled that she found "such filing inappropriate and will not in any way consider the papers so filed."

Min Yasui appealed the dismissal of his petition to the Ninth Circuit Court of Appeals, arguing that Judge Belloni had erroneously granted the government's motion and pointing to Judge Patel's ruling on the issue as the proper approach. This appeal became entangled in technical questions about whether it had been filed on time; the appellate judges sent it back to Judge Belloni, who ruled that Yasui had met the time limits and returned the case to the Ninth Circuit judges. Before they decided his appeal, Yasui's time on earth expired, in November 1986, and his case died with him, a victim of the "mootness" doctrine and the government's stalling tactics. After his death, Yasui's family pressed a petition for review by the Supreme Court, more as a tribute to his indomitable spirit than a solid legal point. The Court's refusal in 1987 to consider the petition ended a gallant fight for one man's vindication.

The divergent outcomes of the hearings in San Francisco and Portland raised the stakes in the final coram nobis case, brought by Gordon Hirabayashi in Seattle. Judge Belloni's terse dismissal of Yasui's petition reminded the coram nobis lawyers that many—probably most—busy federal judges were unlikely to welcome the task of reopening "the partially healed wounds of an earlier period," as Judge Patel explained her reluctance to hold a full-scale hearing on the Korematsu petition. Victor Stone's success in Portland, the legal teams agreed, would lead him to put every remaining legal chip on the table in an effort to persuade Judge Voorhees to follow Judge Belloni's lead.

Judicial action began in the Hirabayashi case when Judge Voorhees scheduled a hearing for May 18, 1984, on the government's motion to dismiss the petition. A month before that date, on April 19, Judge Patel issued her written opinion on the Korematsu petition. This lengthy document closely followed the outline and wording of her oral opinion, adding case citations and historical detail to her conclusion that the government had no power to dismiss a prosecution after a defendant was released from custody. Judge Patel dealt with Korematsu's claims of governmental misconduct in blunt and accusing words. She held that "there is substantial support in the record that the government deliberately omitted relevant information and provided misleading information" to the Supreme Court in the 1940s. Conceding that "it cannot now be said what result would have obtained had the information been disclosed," she found this question irrelevant to the coram nobis proceeding, which turned on whether government lawyers had failed "to provide a full and accurate" factual record to the Supreme Court. Judge Patel added to her opinion a judicial scolding of the lawyers who failed in their duties: "The judicial process is seriously impaired when the government's law enforcement officers violate their ethical obligations to the court."

Victor Stone knew that Judge Voorhees would read his colleague's opinion with care and interest before the May hearing. He responded with a forty-one-page brief that lauded Judge Belloni's ruling as "correctly decided" and that said Judge Patel had "badly misconstrued" the law in denying the government's dismissal motion. Stone revealed his pique at Judge Patel in noting that she "refused to take note" of Judge Belloni's order and "did not even try to distinguish" that decision in her written opinion.

Stone devoted the bulk of his brief to three "jurisdictional" bars to judicial decision on Hirabayashi's petition. These arguments claimed that Judge Voorhees lacked jurisdiction and thus any power to decide the petition. Stone first argued that Hirabayashi suffered no continuing legal disabilities from his 1942 misdemeanor conviction, such as loss of civil rights or the remote prospect of harsher sentencing in a later criminal case. "Any lingering antagonism" to Hirabayashi, Stone wrote, reflected the "social consequences" of his wartime defiance and not "legal consequences which the law recognizes or redresses." The second jurisdictional bar that Stone raised rested on the government's agreement to vacate Hirabayashi's conviction and its assurance that no person could be prosecuted in the future for a similar offense. Consequently, Stone argued, "there is no continuing case or controversy" between the two sides that Judge Voorhees could decide. Any decision he might make would be an "advisory opinion" only, barred by the Constituion.

Stone argued finally that Hirabayashi had waited too long to bring his challenge, because the most important government documents disputing the wartime "military necessity" claim to the Supreme Court had been available since the late 1940s. In framing this point, known in legal jargon as a "laches" claim, Stone sidestepped the misconduct charges in the petition and argued that the Supreme Court had been exposed in 1943 to all the claims made by the petition in 1983. "In the Supreme Court," Stone said of attacks on the "military necessity" defense of the internment program, "Hirabayashi's attorneys made exactly the same arguments that they seek to resurrect now." All these jurisdictional bars, Stone concluded, required that the petition "must be denied without an evidentiary hearing." The prospect of such a hearing, in effect a trial on the misconduct charges with the government in the dock, clearly disturbed Stone and his superiors.

Judge Voorhees displayed his keen interest in the Hirabayashi case, and his concern for the crowd of spectators that gathered at the federal courthouse on May 18, by holding the hearing in the building's largest courtroom, borrowed for the occasion from the Court of Appeals. Like Judge Patel, he held up the proceedings until the audience found seats; he differed from her and Judge Belloni in his relaxed, almost folksy manner, pointing out empty seats to latecomers and chatting with his staff while he waited to begin. Kathryn Bannai was joined at the counsel table by several other lawyers, including Arthur Barnett, who advised Hirabayashi in

1942 and remained committed to the case at the age of seventy-five. The legal team also included Camden Hall, a 1965 University of Washington Law School graduate and member of a prestigious Seattle firm, and Rodney Kawakami, who graduated from the same school in 1976. Like Don Willner in Portland, Cam Hall had extensive trial experience; and he had often appeared before Judge Voorhees.

Both sides at the hearing understood the stakes. The coram nobis lawyers had asked Judge Voorhees to hold a full-scale evidentiary hearing at a later date, while the government heatedly opposed this request. Judge Voorhees opened the hearing by assuring the lawyers they could take all the time they needed for argument. Victor Stone, at his usual rapid pace, repeated the points in his brief at length and urged that the petition be dismissed. Stone had an additional card to play. The previous day, Judge Louis Oberdorfer in the District of Columbia had dismissed the class action suit of the internment camp survivors. He based this decision on statute of limitations grounds, which apply to civil but not criminal cases, holding that government records refuting the Army's "military necessity" claim had been available in the 1940s. Stone urged Judge Voorhees to follow this ruling, and to apply the "laches" defense to the petition as an analogy to the civil statute of limitations.

Judge Voorhees replied that he would read the class action opinion when he received a copy, but he noted the differences between civil and criminal cases. Judge Oberdorfer's opinion, in fact, offered the government very little in the coram nobis cases. He had carefully distinguished the civil damage suit from the Korematsu petition, quoting from Judge Patel's opinion on the "governmental misconduct" charges in the petition and noting that "evidence of the government's misconduct was not requisite to the filing of plaintiffs' claims" in the class action suit.

Cam Hall spoke briefly for Hirabayashi, reminding Judge Voorhees that the government had raised no substantive defense to the Korematsu and Yasui petitions, while the brief Stone filed before the Hirabayashi hearing discussed all the petition's misconduct charges. In his quiet, almost diffident tone, Hall pointed out that the case "has a fair amount of symbolic importance." Gordon Hirabayashi then spoke for himself, beginning in his lecture-hall fashion with an account of his teaching career in Third World countries. He had trouble, Hirabayashi said, answering questions of students who knew about the internment of Japanese Americans and wanted to know why the American government would imprison its own citizens on the basis of ancestry alone. His composure wavered as he recounted his 1942 trial in the same courthouse, when the government held his elderly parents in jail as witnesses at their son's trial. "They didn't have to keep them in jail," Hirabayashi said with an edge of bitterness, "and I'll never forgive the government for that."

Judge Voorhees ended the hearing with a ruling that denied the government's motion to dismiss the petition. Noting that Stone had addressed the misconduct charges at length, while denying their legal significance, the judge told the audience he believed Hirabayashi had a right to seek a hearing on his petition. "We can only admire his courage for standing up for his rights," he said of Hirabayashi. "What he really is seeking now is vindication of his honor, and I feel that he has that right."

A week after this initial hearing, Judge Voorhees issued an order that set a date for the evidentiary hearing for June 17, 1985, more than a year later. His order stated that Hirabayashi had "made a prima facie showing that evidence essential to his defense at his trial or upon his appeal may have been knowingly suppressed by the government," which thus had denied Hirabayashi his due process rights. The government would be free at the evidentiary hearing to answer the misconduct charges and to present evidence on the "laches" defense that Hirabayashi waited too long to bring his petition. Judge Voorhees did not, however, "intend to reexamine nor to rule upon the wisdom of the exclusion or curfew orders" Hirabayashi had been convicted of violating.

With more than a year to prepare for the evidentiary hearing in Seattle, the coram nobis lawyers began planning for a full-scale trial of their misconduct charges, with witnesses on both sides subject to examination and cross-examination. Although many central figures in the internment program had died, three men who had battled over the cases decided by the Supreme Court were alive and active, despite advanced age. Edward Ennis of the Justice Department and his wartime antagonists, Assistant Secretary of War John J. McCloy and Colonel Karl Bendetsen, had all testified before the Commission on Wartime Relocation in 1981 and remained firm in their wartime positions. The prospect of a trial with these witnesses on the stand, under oath, could hardly be equaled in drama and historical significance.

Well before the scheduled trial date, the government's reluctance to take a stand on the petition became evident in a series of foot-dragging steps. Judge Voorhees had set a date in December 1984 for Victor Stone to list the witnesses he intended to call and the documents he planned to introduce. Stone responded with a series of motions that again asked the judge to dismiss the petition or at least to postpone the evidentiary hearing until the Court of Appeals decided the Yasui case. Hirabayashi's lawyers opposed these motions and pressed Judge Voorhees to order the government to answer the petition.

Stone finally revealed the government's position in March 1985. His motion for a further postponement made it clear that "hard-liners" in the Justice Department and White House, where the final decisions over the case rested, had prevailed over any counsel of conciliation. The hearing should be postponed, Stone argued, because deciding Hirabayashi's petition would "require a difficult historical inquiry into the contents and distribution of World War II intelligence information, including the Magic Cables." The government had decided to adopt a last-ditch defense of the wartime military orders and to counter the misconduct charges with claims that General DeWitt and other officials had evidence of espionage by Japanese Americans on the West Coast. This tough, aggressive stance clearly signaled a political decision within the Reagan Administration to seek victory in the Hirabayashi case, if not before Judge Voorhees then at the appellate level.

Stone had kept the "Magic cables" up his sleeve for almost two years, and the coram nobis lawyers had waited to see whether he would pull them out. This defense rested on a handful of Japanese diplomatic cables that American cryptanalysts decoded in 1941. The cables were selected from some thirty-eight thousand between Tokyo and Japanese embassies and consulates around the world. The decoding effort, which continued through the war, proved such an intelligence coup that the decoders called it Magic.

The Magic defense was handed to Stone in 1983 by David D. Lowman, a retired official of the super-secret National Security Agency and a self-appointed critic of the Commission on Wartime Relocation. After his retirement, Lowman, who lived in Honolulu, had consulted for the NSA on the declassification and publication of the Magic cables, which were ultimately issued by the Defense Department in 1977 in an eight-volume set entitled *The MAGIC Background of Pearl Harbor.* On May 22, 1983, three months after the CWR issued its internment report, the *New York Times* ran a story under the headline "Japanese Cables Boasted of Spying." Lowman had fed some of the Magic cables to *Times* reporter Charles Mohr, who quoted Lowman as saying that officials who read the cables in 1941 "could easily conclude that thousands of resident Japanese were being organized into subversive organizations." Mohr noted that only "a few messages" in the eight-volume collection dealt with Japanese Americans, and his story did not quote from any cables that identified the source of any intelligence sent to Japan as an American of Japanese ancestry.

Lowman had initially blasted the CWR report as "badly flawed," and he followed with a barrage of articles and interviews. "I'm going to blow that commission out of the water," he promised a reporter for the right-wing Washington *Times* in July 1983. Lowman's charge of slipshod research clearly embarrassed the commission, and it issued an "addendum" to its report, which had stated that "not a single documented act of espionage" by an American of Japanese ancestry had occurred on the West Coast. The addendum reported that the commission "still stands" behind that claim after reviewing the Magic volumes.

Press accounts of Lowman's broadsides aroused concern on the coram nobis teams, then awaiting the government's answer to the Korematsu petition. I called Lowman in August 1983 and learned he had already talked several times with Victor Stone. "I sent him a great deal of information" about the cables, Lowman told me. He also admitted that the cables provided "no way of distinguishing the sources" of intelligence messages sent to Tokyo, which were prepared by Japanese military attachés in West Coast consulates.

The Magic issue remained dormant until Lowman testified before a House of Representatives subcommittee in June 1984, at hearings on bills to compensate internment camp survivors. Lowman submitted a forty-five-page statement that cited several Magic cables to show that "the frightening specter of massive espionage nets on the West Coast" gave President Roosevelt and other officials "genuine and legitimate cause for concern about the loyalty and actions" of Japanese Americans. Lowman displayed as an "espionage nugget" a cable to Tokyo that included details of airplane production in the Los Angeles area, suggesting that "second generations" in airplane plants had supplied the data.

Although Lowman received kid-glove treatment from panel members, his testimony was vigorously disputed by Jack Herzig, the retired counter-intelligence officer. Herzig and his wife, Aiko, in their close work with the coram nobis teams, had dug into unpublished Magic materials in the National Archives. Lowman had found only six cables that mentioned Japanese Americans as possible intelligence sources, Herzig noted. "There is not one bit of evidence in the Magic cables or in other finished intelligence that any Japanese-American has been recruited" for espionage, he concluded. Panel members listened to Herzig with evident skepticism and peppered him with hostile questions, a reflection of the subcommittee's conservative makeup.

The coram nobis lawyers learned in March 1985 that the government planned to rely on the Magic defense at the Seattle hearing, but they had prepared for this possibility, and the Herzigs continued to plow through boxes of cables in the National Archives. Although the legal team approached the hearings as a "documents case" that required few witnesses to corroborate the documentary record, they were delighted when Edward Ennis volunteered as their chief witness. Ennis, one of the Justice Department lawyers who protested in 1943, had appeared before the House subcommittee in September 1984 and had bluntly denied claims by John McCloy and Karl Bendetsen that Magic had played any role in the wartime evacuation decision. Ennis also repeated his 1943 charge that McCloy had withheld from him the Army's evacuation report, which he said "put the Department of Justice in a very awkward position in the Supreme Court."

Victor Stone made a final effort to persuade Judge Voorhees to put off the evidentiary hearing. Arguing that the hearing "overlaps into an area of current congressional concern," he suggested it was the job of Congress to "redress complaints of this sort." He also lumped Ennis with McCloy and Bendetsen as "elderly witnesses" who would have "only very dim and probably only marginally useful recollections of the key events" of the 1940s. Stone clearly did not relish the task of confronting Ennis in the courtroom. Judge Voorhees denied Stone's motion and ensured that the confrontation would take place.

More than forty years after he entered the federal courthouse in Seattle as a criminal defendant, Gordon Hirabayashi returned on June 17, 1985, to put his former prosecutors on trial. Close to a hundred spectators crowded the courtroom, with former internment camp inmates sharing the wooden benches with a small contingent of the local "Remember Pearl Harbor" group. Faced with a standing-room audience, Judge Voorhees opened the jury box to spectators and set a relaxed tone for the unprecedented hearing. Rod Kawakami and Cam Hall shared one counsel table with Hirabayashi and Arthur Barnett, who added a note of continuity with the 1942 trial; Victor Stone was joined at the other table by a stocky young associate, Richard Edwards. Piles of documents in boxes and folders crowded both tables. Whatever drama and detail the witnesses could add, this was primarily a "documents case," and both sides were primed with paper.

The hearing began on a sour note for Stone. Cam Hall asked Judge Voorhees to exclude from evidence several boxes of documents Stone had recently delivered to him, noting that Stone had not filed a list of exhibits before the hearing, as the rules required and the judge had ordered. Flustered and apologetic, Stone explained that he had been working furiously to prepare for trial and had lugged seventeen boxes of documents with him from Washington. When the judge asked if he had a list of exhibits, Stone suggested that the government had not been adequately informed of the scope of the hearing. This intimation of judicial laxity clearly annoyed Judge Voorhees. "I've heard from you all that I intend to hear on this," he replied firmly, displaying his impatience with pointless argument. More conciliatory in tone after this rebuke, Stone promised to file a handwritten list of exhibits that afternoon. Judge Voorhees looked down from the bench, smiled and said, "Too late."

After the session ended, Stone vented his frustration at an impromptu press conference with reporters who crowded around the counsel tables. "I don't know how much is left of the case," he complained to reporters who described him as "angry" at the judge's crucial ruling. Stone's remarks did not please Judge Voorhees. When Stone later tried to introduce an excluded document in questioning Edward Ennis, the judge sustained an objection by Cam Hall and cut off Stone's argument that he was simply trying to refresh Ennis's recollection. "I know you are angry about the court's ruling from the press accounts," Judge Voorhees said. "The ruling I made was not an unusual one. I will not allow 'refreshing recollection' to be a subterfuge."

After a day of scrapping over exhibits and witnesses, the hearing was adjourned for another day and resumed with opening arguments on both sides. "This case is an American case," Rod Kawakami began. "This is not just Gordon Hirabayashi's case, and this is more than just a Japanese American case. This is a case where an American citizen with a deep and abiding faith in American principles stood up and was one of the few voices to proclaim that as an American, evacuation and incarceration based solely on ancestry was contrary to the most fundamental concept of what being an American is all about." Methodical and deliberate in manner, Kawakami went on to detail the petition's misconduct allegations and to accuse the government of having been "so intent on defending the evacuation decision and to win at all costs" in the 1940s that it "fixed" the Hirabayashi case.

Explaining that "I had anticipated a slightly different opening statement," Victor Stone said he felt "obliged to respond" to Kawakami's accusations and asked the judge to "excuse me if I don't look that composed." Stone first denied that "this is a unique case, a Japanese American case," and described it as no different than "hundreds of kinds of criminal cases that are prosecuted every day" in the courts. He went on to denounce allegations that Japanese Americans had been deprived of their rights on racial grounds as "not only spurious but also almost incredible." Claiming that "we are not trying to bring up again allegations of Japanese American espionage," Stone nonetheless cited the Magic cables as evidence "Mr. Ennis may have been unaware of" during his wartime disputes with John J. McCloy.

Attention shifted from the lawyers when Edward Ennis, white-haired and dapper at seventy-seven, entered the courtroom and took the witness stand. Led by Cam Hall through an account of his lengthy government service, Ennis then confirmed the "suppression of evidence" charge he made to Solicitor General Charles Fahy in 1943, the central misconduct charge in Hirabayashi's petition. "And does that remain your view today?" Hall asked. Ennis answered with a firm "yes."

Ennis also corroborated his 1943 charge that John J. McCloy "deliberately withheld" from the Justice Department the report of General DeWitt that contradicted the government's Supreme Court brief in the Hirabayashi case on a crucial issue. The brief argued that Japanese Americans had been evacuated because the Army lacked time to conduct individual loyalty hearings, but the suppressed report argued that time was not a factor because there was *no* way to distinguish loyal Japanese Americans from the disloyal. Ennis testified that McCloy's deputy, Captain John Hall, "deceived me about the existence and nature of the report," and that the time-factor issue "was the whole center of our argument" to the Supreme Court. In questioning Ennis, Cam Hall pointedly noted the absence of McCloy and Karl Bendetsen, the Army colonel who engineered the internment and prepared the disputed report, from the government's list of witnesses. Hall left unstated his implication that Stone had been afraid of putting McCloy and Bendetsen on the stand to counter the misconduct charges Ennis had supported.

Stone's cross-examination of Ennis spanned two days. Much of this time was consumed with searches for documents by lawyers, judge, clerk, and witness, and by arguments over relevance and admissibility. Long stretches of tedium were broken by occasional flashes of humor, tension, or drama. At one point, as Ennis explained his wartime opposition to the evacuation of Japanese Americans from the West Coast, a Caucasian spectator shouted out, "There *was* a threat of invasion!" A firm vow by Judge Voorhees to eject any spectator who disrupted the hearing ended the interruption, but the incident showed the currents of conflicting emotions in the courtroom. A major point of Stone's questioning was his effort to show that Ennis had no access to Magic cables during the war, a point Judge Voorhees allowed Stone to make over Cam Hall's objection that the topic had no relevance to the petition's misconduct charges. Before he left the stand, Ennis frustrated Stone's repeated efforts to discredit his testimony as biased or poorly remembered.

Gordon Hirabayashi took the stand as the hearing moved to a second week of testimony. He added to an account of his wartime arrest and trial some of the reasons his criminal record left him "personally handicapped" after four decades. Hirabayashi read to Judge Voorhees two examples of "hate mail" he had received, accusing him and other Japanese Americans of responsibility for Pearl Harbor. His criminal conviction and the Supreme Court opinion that upheld it, he said, left a suspicion about loyalty that "hangs as a cloud over 120,000 Japanese Americans" who were shipped to internment camps. Some of this suspicion lingered in the courtroom. When Judge Voorhees asked a friendly question about Hirabayashi's early Boy Scout record, an unfriendly Caucasian spectator hissed, "Japs couldn't be Boy Scouts."

Victor Stone adopted an ingratiating manner in his cross-examination. "It is an honor and a privilege to have this conversation," he assured Hirabayashi. Stone's questions were aimed at reminding Judge Voorhees that Hirabayashi's original conviction stemmed from admitted violations of curfew and exclusion orders. When he posed a rhetorical question as to whether the government had ever charged Hirabayashi with disloyalty, the answer—"They put me in prison"—prompted a burst of courtroom laughter. Stone rephrased his question. Had the government ever accused Hirabayashi of espionage or sabotage? "If I were given that charge," he answered, "I would have had the chance to defend myself."

The government began its defense when Hirabayashi left the stand. William Hammond, a retired Army officer with wartime combat intelligence service, was the first of four military and FBI officials called by the government to testify about official fears that Japanese Americans posed a potential threat of espionage and sabotage on the West Coast. Brisk and businesslike, Hammond recalled under questioning by Richard Edwards his receipt of reports of radio transmissions and signal lights along the West Coast in the months after Pearl Harbor. The accuracy of such reports had been sharply questioned by the FBI and the Federal Communications Commission, and the Army's attribution of illicit signaling to Japanese Americans had prompted Edward Ennis to charge that "lies" had been submitted to the Supreme Court in the Army evacuation report.

Richard Edwards suggested in questioning Hammond that it was a "rational assumption" that Japanese Americans had been involved in signaling to offshore Japanese submarines, and Hammond's agreement that "the most likely friends of the enemy" were those of Japanese ancestry drew gasps of anger from the audience. Hammond conceded under cross-examination by Cam Hall that he had no personal knowledge or recollection of any connection between Japanese Americans and espionage. None of the government's remaining wartime witnesses—Richard Hamm of the Army and Richard Hood and Robert Mayer of the FBI—could recall any evidence of such a connection. Edwards and Stone seemed more intent, in questioning these witnesses, in showing that none could recall any racist remarks by General DeWitt.

The appearance of David Lowman as the government's star witness brought a buzz of courtroom anticipation. Cam Hall repeated for the record his continuing objection to the Magic cables as irrelevant, and was again overruled by Judge Voorhees, who said he would decide the issue after all the testimony. Victor Stone led Lowman through a recitation of his twenty-eight-year National Security Agency service and an explanation of how Magic had been broken and decoded before Pearl Harbor. Stone then pointed Lowman to a February 1942 military intelligence report that asserted that Japanese "espionage is now thoroughly organized and working underground" along the West Coast. "Is there information directly traceable to the Magic cables" in this report, Stone asked. "There were, in fact, espionage nets involving Japanese Americans," Lowman answered. Stone's purpose in connecting Magic to later intelligence reports was obviously to bolster his argument that General DeWitt and other officials had a rational basis for their internment orders.

Stone made much in his questioning of the cable Lowman had called an "espionage nugget" in his 1984 congressional testimony. This cable from Los Angeles to Tokyo included production figures for aircraft factories; although it indicated no source for the data, Lowman linked it with another cable suggesting "second generations" in the factories as espionage agents. When Cam Hall began his aggressive cross-examination, Lowman's nugget turned into fool's gold. "Weren't these same figures printed in the *Los Angeles Times* ten days before this cable was sent?" Hall asked, waving the article before Lowman, who promptly expanded his definition of intelligence sources to include the "open press."

Jack Herzig became the final witness at the hearing, called by Cam Hall to rebut Lowman's testimony. Herzig laid out his military counter-intelligence background and his research in the Magic cables, and conceded the existence of a Japanese intelligence network on the West Coast before the war. The arrest and deportation of Japanese military attachés in June 1941, he argued, had effectively broken this espionage ring. Herzig noted that only one Magic cable sent to Tokyo after this date had mentioned Japanese Americans, and that dealt with a request for census information. Victor Stone launched a bristling, hostile cross-examination, suggesting that Herzig was biased because his wife had worked for the Commission on Wartime Relocation and he supported the "redress" movement. Herzig refused to budge from his assertion that Magic represented nothing more than "raw data" and could not be considered "finished intelligence" on which American officials could rely for evidence of espionage by Japanese Americans.

The two-week hearing ended on a note of unintended hilarity. In a final effort to put some of his excluded documents in the record, Stone asked Judge Voorhees to accept as an "offer of proof" a sheaf of intelligence reports he claimed would prove the existence of a Japanese espionage ring in the United States after Pearl Harbor. The judge declined to read the whole batch but said, "I'll take a look at your best one." Stone riffled through his notes and handed one to the bench. After a quick glance, Judge Voorhees burst into laughter and told the audience, "I'll have to read it into the record: 'The intelligence net operating in England is made up of eight Welshmen, two Irishmen, eleven Scotsmen and two Spaniards.'" When the courtroom laughter subsided, the judge rejected Stone's offer of proof.

Confronted with a mound of documents, the testimony of a dozen witnesses, and his meticulous notes on the proceeding, Judge Voorhees told both sides when the hearing concluded that he would delay his decision on the petition until the lawyers submitted post-trial briefs with their summaries of evidence, testimony, and legal issues. The judge set deadlines for the briefs, with a final date of October 4, 1985. The lawyers packed their bulky files into cardboard boxes, the raw material for another round of briefs in a case that stretched back over four decades. Gordon Hirabayashi left the courthouse and faced the cameras and reporters for a last round of questions. In answer to one, he put his long crusade for vindication into a nutshell: "Ancestry is not a crime."

More than seven months passed before Judge Voorhees issued his written opinion on February 10, 1986. The judge made clear his admiration for Hirabayashi, presenting in detail his record as a Boy Scout and as a YMCA volunteer in college, and his refusal "as a matter of conscience" to obey the wartime curfew and evacuation orders. "The government presented no evidence that petitioner was anything other than a law-abiding, native-born American citizen," Judge Voorhees wrote of both the original trial and recent hearing.

The judge separated his analysis of the two convictions before him, looking first at Hirabayashi's violation of the evacuation order. From the mass of records submitted to him by both sides, Judge Voorhees singled out one for special scrutiny and grounded his opinion on this crucial document. Hirabayashi's petition charged that John J. McCloy of the War Department had withheld General DeWitt's original internment report, although Edward Ennis had officially requested access to the report in preparing the government's Supreme Court brief in the Hirabayashi case. The petition also charged that the original report had been altered at McCloy's order, and records of its existence concealed and destroyed.

Judge Voorhees put this disputed report under his judicial scalpel. General DeWitt had initially based his internment orders on racial grounds alone, with his bias and prejudice unconcealed. Japanese Americans belonged to an "enemy race" and were such a "dangerous element" on the West Coast that "military necessity required their immediate evacuation to the interior," he claimed. DeWitt also flatly contradicted the Justice Department, which argued to the Supreme Court that Japanese Americans had been evacuated because the Army lacked sufficient time to screen the group for loyalty. "It was not that there was insufficient time in which to make such a determination," DeWitt had confessed. His conviction that it would be "impossible" to separate the loyal and disloyal in this "tightly-knit racial group" had actually prompted his orders, DeWitt admitted to McCloy, who withheld this report from Ennis and the Supreme Court.

After he dissected this record in twenty pages of careful analysis, Judge Voorhees concluded that McCloy's action in withholding General DeWitt's report had "seriously prejudiced" the arguments that Hirabayashi's lawyers could have made against the government's "military necessity" claims. This action constituted "an error of the most fundamental character" and required the vacation of Hirabayashi's conviction on the evacuation charge, the judge concluded.

The only surprise in Judge Voorhees's opinion came at the end, where he painted the curfew imposed on Japanese Americans as a "relatively mild" burden "contrasted with the harshness of the exclusion order." Because the government, in his view, was not required to justify the curfew on "military necessity" grounds, misconduct in defending the exclusion order did not infect the curfew order. Judge Voorhees thus declined to vacate Hirabayashi's curfew conviction. Missing from the opinion was any mention of the disputed Magic cables on which the government hinged its case; the judge had allowed Victor Stone to make his record on this issue but had not budged from his initial skepticism about the relevance of Magic to the misconduct charges.

Shortly before Judge Voorhees issued his opinion, the Court of Appeals for the District of Columbia revived the class action redress suit that Judge Oberdorfer had dismissed. Judges J. Skelly Wright and Ruth Bader Ginsburg, two of the most liberal members of the circuit bench, reviewed a record similar to that before Judge Voorhees and concluded that "the Justice Department misled the Supreme Court when it argued that 'military necessity' justified a mass evacuation of Japanese-American citizens." Although they kept the case alive, the appellate judges knocked out all but one of the suit's damage claims under the doctrine of sovereign immunity, which requires the government's permission to file damage claims against it. The surviving claim rested on a federal statute that allows recovery for property losses.

William Hohri and his fellow plaintiffs asked the Supreme Court to reverse the sovereign immunity ruling and to reinstate the stricken claims. During argument on this appeal in April 1987, Solicitor General Charles Fried, a Harvard Law School professor on leave, expressed his opinion that the wartime Supreme Court rulings on the *Hirabayashi* and *Korematsu* cases were both morally and legally wrong. Fried argued, however, that the class action redress suit was barred by sovereign immunity and the statute of limitations; he additionally argued that it had been improperly heard in the District of Columbia appellate court and should have been decided by the Federal Circuit Court of Appeals, a recently created court with special functions. Ruling without an opinion in June 1987, the Supreme Court agreed with Fried and remanded the case to the new court. After a second round of arguments in March 1988, the suit was again dismissed, and the class-action plaintiffs asked the Supreme Court a second time to review the adverse ruling.

The remaining coram nobis case of Gordon Hirabayashi also reached an appellate court for review of Judge Voorhees's conflicting rulings. Neither side had gained all that it sought, and both sides filed appeals. Hirabayashi asked for reversal of his curfew conviction; the government for reinstatement of the exclusion order conviction.

After a lengthy briefing period, the appeals were argued in Seattle's federal courthouse on March 2, 1987. When Victor Stone walked into the clerk's office that morning and looked at the sheet listing the appellate panel, his face fell. The presiding judge, Alfred T. Goodwin, was a former World War II infantry captain and a Republican nominee of President Richard Nixon. The other two judges, however, both owed their judicial posts to President Jimmy Carter, who placed more women and blacks on the federal bench than any other president. Judge Mary M. Schroeder, partner in a prestigious Arizona law firm, had served in the Justice Department under President Lyndon Johnson. Judge Joseph J. Farris, a black native of Alabama, served as a state judge in Washington for ten years before his elevation to the federal bench in 1979.

Rod Kawakami smiled broadly when he looked at the panel list. His oral argument, low-key and matter-of-fact in tone, stressed that the curfew and evacuation orders had been fashioned by General DeWitt as part of a single plan that led to mass internment, and that both charges against Hirabayashi had been tainted by the same governmental misconduct. Kawakami fielded only a few questions and sat down after ten minutes at the podium.

Victor Stone scribbled a reminder to himself on a legal pad as he waited in the crowded courtroom: "Be low key." He began his argument by disparaging the case as a "history exercise" that had wasted two weeks of Judge Voorhees's time. If that was true, Judge Schroeder asked, why had the government bothered to appeal? The suggestion that he was wasting the appellate court's time rattled Stone, whose composure soon crumbled. His later interruption of a question from Judge Farris drew a rebuke: "You can't answer my question if you don't let me ask it." Stone's running dispute with Judge Farris over the government's wartime concealment of General DeWitt's racist beliefs prompted another rebuke: "This is the only time you get to talk, Mr. Stone, but I get to talk in the conference" on the case.

Stone once again raised the Magic cables in defending DeWitt, claiming they revealed an "underground network" of Japanese American spies. Stone also reminded the panel that President Ford had labeled the internment a "mistake" in 1976. Judge Schroeder asked why the government had not acted then to vacate the wartime convictions. Stone's answer brought gasps of disbelief from the audience: "We didn't think there was anyone out there who cared." His final words cast equal scorn on the Supreme Court and Judge Voorhees: "It would be unfortunate if this court held that one set of unprovable facts should be replaced by another set of unprovable facts." When Stone left the podium after forty-five minutes, he looked as if he never wanted to say another word about the internment cases. He never did, to any court.

More than seven months passed before the appellate panel issued in September 1987 a unanimous, thirty-nine-page opinion that Judge Schroeder wrote. She first observed that the Supreme Court's wartime opinions "have never occupied an honored place in our history." She cited numerous books and articles documenting that "the convictions were unjust," that they were based not on military necessity but on "racial stereotypes," and that General DeWitt's orders "caused needless suffering and shame for thousands of American citizens." Judge Schroeder reviewed the record presented before Judge Voorhees and agreed that "the information now in the public record constitutes objective and irrefutable proof of the racial bias that was the cornerstone of the internment orders."

Judge Schroeder also agreed that "the United States government doctored the documentary record" that was submitted to the Supreme Court. Had the "suppressed material been submitted to the Supreme Court," she wrote, "its decision probably would have been materially affected." Based on these findings of misconduct, Judge Schroeder disagreed with Judge Voorhees on Hirabayashi's curfew conviction. The two charges "were based upon simultaneous indictments, were tried together, briefed together, and decided together" by the Supreme Court. The government had "argued a single theory of military necessity" to support both convictions. This linkage of charges and arguments led the appellate judges to reverse Judge Voorhees on the curfew conviction and to remand the case to him with orders to "vacate both convictions."

Still unwilling to concede defeat, Justice Department hard-liners asked the Ninth Circuit panel to rehear the government's appeal before the entire bench of some thirty judges. Victor Stone had bowed out of the internment cases after almost five years, and Justice Department lawyer Jay Bybee filed the government's motion, which the appellate court curtly denied in a brief order on December 24, 1987. Three weeks later, on January 12, 1988, Judge Voorhees ended the journey for vindication that Gordon Hirabayashi had begun five years earlier. "Pursuant to the mandate of the United States Court of Appeals for the Ninth Circuit in this cause," Voorhees wrote, "petitioner's conviction on Count II of his indictment is hereby set aside." Supreme Court rules gave the government another sixty days, until February 22, 1988, to ask for review of this order. On that day, I called Jay Bybee and learned that Solicitor General Charles Fried had decided to end the internment litigation.

The words of Judge Voorhees provide a fitting close to this account of the coram nobis effort: "It is now conceded by almost everyone that the internment of Japanese Americans during World War II was simply a tragic mistake for which American society as a whole must accept responsibility. If, in the future, this country should find itself in a comparable national emergency, the sacrifices made by Gordon Hirabayashi, Fred Korematsu, and Minoru Yasui may, it is hoped, stay the hand of a government again tempted to imprison a defenseless minority without trial and for no offense."

From its beginning, the coram nobis effort was seen by all who took part as only one prong of a broad-scale redress campaign with three ultimate goals: legal vindication in the courts; monetary compensation from Congress; and a statement of national apology by the president. All three branches of government shared complicity in the wartime internment program, and all three needed to join in the final rectification of the "grave injustice" suffered by Japanese Americans. In 1988, forty-six years after President Franklin D. Roosevelt signed the internment order, these goals were achieved. In January 1988 the Justice Department abandoned its courtroom defense of the internment, although on October 31 the Supreme Court put an end to the *Hohri* suit for class-action redress by denying the last petition for certiorari in the case. In August 1988 Congress enacted a redress bill that provided $20,000 to each internment camp survivor, and on August 10 President Ronald Reagan added his signature to that bill and to the national apology it included.

The redress bill also provided for an educational fund to instruct future generations of Americans in the lessons of the internment. Gordon Hirabayashi put the lesson of this complex, painful, and tragic episode in American history into five simple words: "Ancestry is not a crime."

I

"Infringement on Individual Liberty"
1942-1944

Hirabayashi v. United States

Opinion of the U.S. Supreme Court*

<hr>

June 21, 1943

A University of Washington senior when World War II began, Gordon Hirabayashi left school to work for a Quaker relief group after the Army imposed curfew and evacuation orders on all persons of Japanese ancestry. When his turn for evacuation came, Hirabayashi refused to report and brought a legal challenge to the military orders. He was convicted on charges of violating both orders. At his one-day trial in Seattle, U.S. District Judge Lloyd Black referred to the Japanese as "unbelievably treacherous," and ordered the jury to convict Hirabayashi. In June 1943 the Supreme Court upheld this conviction on both charges. Although the Court's decision was unanimous, the concurring opinion of Justice Frank Murphy, which said the orders went to "the very brink of constitutional power," was originally prepared as a dissenting opinion. Murphy was talked out of his dissent by Justice Felix Frankfurter, who asserted that any break in unanimous support for the Army in wartime amounted to "playing into the hands of the enemy." Faced with this challenge to his patriotism, Murphy capitulated.

Response to questions certified by the Circuit Court of Appeals upon an appeal to that court from a conviction in the District Court upon two counts of an indictment charging violations of orders promulgated by the military commander of the Western Defense Command. This Court directed that the entire record be certified so that the case could be determined as if brought here by appeal. See 46 F. Supp. 657.

Messrs. Frank L. Walters and Harold Evans, with whom Messrs. Osmond K. Fraenkel, Arthur G. Barnett, Edwin M. Borchard, Brien McMahon, and William Draper Lewis were on the brief (Mr. Alfred J. Schweppe entered an appearance), for Hirabayashi.

Solicitor General Fahy, with whom Messrs. Edward J. Ennis, Arnold

*320 U.S. 81 (1943)

Raum, John L. Burling, and Leo Gitlin were on the brief, for the United States.

Briefs of amici curiae were filed by Messrs. Arthur Garfield Hays, Osmond K. Fraenkel, and A. L. Wirin on behalf of the American Civil Liberties Union; by Mr. A. L. Wirin on behalf of the Japanese American Citizens League; and by Mr. Jackson H. Ralston on behalf of the Northern California Branch of the American Civil Liberties Union,—in support of Hirabayashi; and by Messrs. Robert W. Kenny, Attorney General of California, I. H. Van Winkle, Attorney General of Oregon, Smith Troy, Attorney General of the State of Washington, and Fred E. Lewis, Chief Assistant and Acting Attorney General of the State of Washington, on behalf of those States,—urging affirmance.

Mr. Chief Justice Stone Delivered the Opinion of the Court

Appellant, an American citizen of Japanese ancestry, was convicted in the district court of violating the Act of Congress of March 21, 1942, 56 Stat. 173, which makes it a misdemeanor knowingly to disregard restrictions made applicable by a military commander to persons in a military area prescribed by him as such, all as authorized by an Executive Order of the President.

The questions for our decision are whether the particular restriction violated, namely that all persons of Japanese ancestry residing in such an area be within their place of residence daily between the hours of 8:00 p.m. and 6:00 a.m., was adopted by the military commander in the exercise of an unconstitutional delegation by Congress of its legislative power, and whether the restriction unconstitutionally discriminated between citizens of Japanese ancestry and those of other ancestries in violation of the Fifth Amendment.

The indictment is in two counts. The second charges that appellant, being a person of Japanese ancestry, had on a specified date, contrary to a restriction promulgated by the military commander of the Western Defense Command, Fourth Army, failed to remain in his place of residence in the designated military area between the hours of 8:00 o'clock p.m. and 6:00 a.m. The first count charges that appellant, on May 11 and 12, 1942, had, contrary to a Civilian Exclusion Order issued by the military commander, failed to report to the Civil Control Station within the designated area, it appearing that appellant's required presence there was a preliminary step to the exclusion from that area of persons of Japanese ancestry.

By demurrer and plea in abatement, which the court overruled (46 F. Supp. 657), appellant asserted that the indictment should be dismissed because he was an American citizen who had never been a subject of and had never borne allegiance to the Empire of Japan, and also because the Act of March 21, 1942, was an unconstitutional delegation of Congressional power. On the trial to a jury it appeared that appellant was born in Seattle in 1918, of Japanese parents who had come from Japan to the United States, and who had never afterward returned to Japan; that he was educated in the Washington public schools and at the time of his arrest was a senior in the University of Washington; that he had never been in Japan or had any association with Japanese residing there.

The evidence showed that appellant had failed to report to the Civil Control Station on May 11 or May 12, 1942, as directed, to register for evacuation from the military area. He admitted failure to do so, and stated it had at all times been his belief that he would be waiving his rights as an American citizen by so doing. The evidence also showed that for like reason he was away from his place of residence after 8:00 p.m. on May 9, 1942. The jury returned a verdict of guilty on both counts and appellant was sentenced to imprisonment for a term of three months on each, the sentence to run concurrently.

On appeal the Court of Appeals for the Ninth Circuit certified to us questions of law upon which it desired instructions for the decision of the case. See §239 of the Judicial Code as amended, 28 U. S. C. §346. Acting under the authority conferred upon us by that section we ordered that the entire record be certified to this Court so that we might proceed to a decision of the matter in controversy in the same manner as if it had been brought here by appeal. Since the sentences of three months each imposed by the district court on the two counts were ordered to run concurrently, it will be unnecessary to consider questions raised with respect to the first count if we find that the conviction on the second count, for violation of the curfew order, must be sustained. *Brooks* v. *United States*, 267 U.S. 432, 441; *Gorin* v. *United States*, 312 U.S. 19, 33.

The curfew order which appellant violated, and to which the sanction prescribed by the Act of Congress has been deemed to attach, purported to be issued pursuant to an Executive Order of the President. In passing upon the authority of the military commander to make and execute the order, it becomes necessary to consider in some detail the official action which preceded or accompanied the order and from which it derives its purported authority.

On December 8, 1941, one day after the bombing of Pearl Harbor by a Japanese air force, Congress declared war against Japan. 55 Stat. 795. On February 19, 1942, the President promulgated Executive Order No. 9066. 7 Federal Register 1407. The Order recited that "the successful prosecution of the war requires every possible protection against espionage and against sabotage to national-defense material, national-defense premises, and national-defense utilities as defined in Section 4, Act of April 20, 1918, 40 Stat. 533, as amended by the Act of November 30, 1940, 54 Stat. 1220, and the Act of August 21, 1941, 55 Stat. 655." By virtue of the authority vested in him as President and as Commander in Chief of the Army and Navy, the President purported to "authorize and direct the Secretary of War, and the Military Commanders whom he may from time to time designate, whenever he or any designated Commander deems such action necessary or desirable, to prescribe military areas in such places and of such extent as he or the appropriate Military Commander may determine, from which any or all persons may be excluded, and with respect to which, the right of any person to enter, remain in, or leave shall be subject to whatever restrictions the Secretary of War or the appropriate Military Commander may impose in his discretion."

On February 20, 1942, the Secretary of War designated Lt. General J. L. DeWitt as Military Commander of the Western Defense Command, comprising the Pacific Coast states and some others, to carry out there the duties prescribed by Executive Order No. 9066. On March 2, 1942, General DeWitt promulgated Public Proclamation No. 1. 7 Federal Register 2320. The proclamation recited that the entire Pacific Coast "by its geographical location is particularly subject to attack, to attempted invasion by the armed forces of nations with which the United States is now at war, and, in connection therewith, is subject to espionage and acts of sabotage, thereby requiring the adoption of military measures necessary to establish safeguards against such enemy operations." It stated that "the present situation requires as a matter of military necessity the establishment in the territory embraced by the Western Defense Command of Military Areas and Zones thereof"; it specified and designated as military areas certain areas within the Western Defense Command; and it declared that "such persons or classes of persons as the situation may require" would, by subsequent proclamation, be excluded from certain of these areas, but might be permitted to enter or remain in certain others, under regulations and restrictions to be later prescribed. Among the military areas so designated by Public Proclamation No. 1 was Military Area No. 1, which embraced, besides the southern part of Arizona, all the coastal region of the three Pacific Coast states, including the City of Seattle, Washington, where appellant resided. Military Area No. 2, designated by the same proclamation, included those parts of the coastal states and of Arizona not placed within Military Area No. 1.

Public Proclamation No. 2 of March 16, 1942, issued by General DeWitt, made like recitals and designated further military areas and zones. It contained like provisions concerning the exclusion, by subsequent proclamation, of certain persons or classes of persons from these areas, and the future promulgation of regulations and restrictions applicable to persons remaining within them. 7 Federal Register 2405.

An Executive Order of the President, No. 9102, of March 18, 1942, established the War Relocation Authority, in the Office for Emergency Management of the Executive Office of the President; it authorized the Director of War Relocation to formulate and effectuate a program for the removal, relocation, maintenance and supervision of persons designated under Executive Order No. 9066, already referred to; and it conferred on the Director authority to prescribe regulations necessary or desirable to promote the effective execution of the program. 7 Federal Register 2165.

Congress, by the Act of March 21, 1942, provided: "That whoever shall enter, remain in, leave, or commit any act in any military area or military zone prescribed, under the authority of an Executive Order of the President, by the Secretary of War, or by any military commander designated by the Secretary of War, contrary to the restrictions applicable to any such area or zone or contrary to the order of the Secretary of War or any such military commander, shall, if it appears that he knew or should have known of the existence and extent of the restrictions or order and that his act was in violation thereof, be guilty of a misdemeanor and upon conviction shall be liable" to fine or imprisonment, or both.

Three days later, on March 24, 1942, General DeWitt issued Public Proclamation No. 3. 7 Federal Register 2543. After referring to the previous designation of military areas by Public Proclamations Nos. 1 and 2, it recited that ". . . the present situation within these Military Areas and Zones requires as a matter of military necessity the establishment of certain regulations pertaining to all enemy aliens and all persons of Japanese ancestry within said Military Areas and Zones . . ." It accordingly declared and established that from and after March 27, 1942, "all alien Japanese, all alien Germans, all alien Italians, and all persons of Japanese ancestry residing or being within the geographical limits of Military Area

No. 1 . . . shall be within their place of residence between the hours of 8:00 p.m. and 6:00 a.m., which period is hereinafter referred to as the hours of curfew." It also imposed certain other restrictions on persons of Japanese ancestry, and provided that any person violating the regulations would be subject to the criminal penalties provided by the Act of Congress of March 21, 1942.

Beginning on March 24, 1942, the military commander issued a series of Civilian Exclusion Orders pursuant to the provisions of Public Proclamation No. 1. Each such order related to a specified area within the territory of his command. The order applicable to appellant was Civilian Exclusion Order No. 57 of May 10, 1942. 7 Federal Register 3725. It directed that from and after 12:00 noon, May 16, 1942, all persons of Japanese ancestry, both alien and non-alien, be excluded from a specified portion of Military Area No. 1 in Seattle, including appellant's place of residence, and it required a member of each family, and each individual living alone, affected by the order to report on May 11 or May 12 to a designated Civil Control Station in Seattle. Meanwhile the military commander had issued Public Proclamation No. 4 of March 27, 1942, which recited the necessity of providing for the orderly evacuation and resettlement of Japanese within the area, and prohibited all alien Japanese and all persons of Japanese ancestry from leaving the military area until future orders should permit. 7 Federal Register 2601.

Appellant does not deny that he knowingly failed to obey the curfew order as charged in the second count of the indictment, or that the order was authorized by the terms of Executive Order No. 9066, or that the challenged Act of Congress purports to punish with criminal penalties disobedience of such an order. His contentions are only that Congress unconstitutionally delegated its legislative power to the military commander by authorizing him to impose the challenged regulation, and that, even if the regulation were in other respects lawfully authorized, the Fifth Amendment prohibits the discrimination made between citizens of Japanese descent and those of other ancestry.

It will be evident from the legislative history that the Act of March 21, 1942, contemplated and authorized the curfew order which we have before us. The bill which became the Act of March 21, 1942, was introduced in the Senate on March 9th and in the House on March 10th at the request of the Secretary of War who, in letters to the Chairman of the Senate Committee on Military Affairs and to the Speaker of the House, stated explicitly that its purpose was to provide means for the enforcement of orders issued under Executive Order No. 9066. This appears in the committee reports on the bill, which set out in full the Executive Order and the Secretary's letter. 88 Cong. Rec. 2722, 2725; H. R. Rep. No. 1906, 77th Cong., 2d Sess.; S. Rep. No. 1171, 77th Cong., 2d Sess. And each of the committee reports expressly mentions curfew orders as one of the types of restrictions which it was deemed desirable to enforce by criminal sanctions.

When the bill was under consideration, General DeWitt had published his Proclamation No. 1 of March 2, 1942, establishing Military Areas Nos. 1 and 2, and that Proclamation was before Congress. S. Rep. No. 1171, 7th Cong., 2d Sess., p. 2; see also 88 Cong. Rec. 2724. A letter of the Secretary to the Chairman of the House Military Affairs Committee, of March 14, 1942, informed Congress that "General DeWitt is strongly of the opinion that the bill, when enacted, should be broad enough to enable the Secretary of War or the appropriate military commander to enforce curfews and other restrictions within military areas and zones"; and that General DeWitt had "indicated that he was prepared to enforce certain restrictions at once for the purpose of protecting certain vital national defense interests but did not desire to proceed until enforcement machinery had been set up." H. R. Rep. No. 1906, 77th Cong., 2d Sess., p. 3. See also letter of the Acting Secretary of War to the Chairman of the Senate Military Affairs Committee, March 13, 1942, 88 Cong. Rec. 2725.

The Chairman of the Senate Military Affairs Committee explained on the floor of the Senate that the purpose of the proposed legislation was to provide means of enforcement of curfew orders and other military orders made pursuant to Executive Order No. 9066. He read General DeWitt's Public Proclamation No. 1, and statements from newspaper reports that "evacuation of the first Japanese aliens and American-born Japanese" was about to begin. He also stated to the Senate that "reasons for suspected widespread fifth-column activity among Japanese" were to be found in the system of dual citizenship which Japan deemed applicable to American-born Japanese, and in the propaganda disseminated by Japanese consuls, Buddhist priests and other leaders, among American-born children of Japanese. Such was stated to be the explanation of the contemplated evacuation from the Pacific Coast area of persons of Japanese ancestry, citizens as well as aliens. 88 Cong. Rec. 2722–26; see also pp. 2729–30. Congress also had before it the Preliminary Report of a House Committee investigating national defense migration, of March 19, 1942, which approved the provisions of Executive Order No. 9066, and which recommended the evacuation, from military areas established under the Order, of all persons of Japanese ancestry, including citizens. H. R. Rep. No. 1911, 77th Cong., 2d Sess. The proposed legislation provided criminal sanctions for violation of orders, in terms broad enough to include the curfew order now before us, and the legislative history demonstrates that Congress was advised also that regulation of citizen and alien Japanese alike was contemplated.

The conclusion is inescapable that Congress, by the Act of March 21, 1942, ratified and confirmed Executive Order No. 9066. *Prize Cases*, 2 Black 635, 671; *Hamilton* v. *Dillin*, 21 Wall. 73, 96–97; *United States* v. *Heinszen & Co.*, 206 U.S. 370, 382–84; *Tiaco* v. *Forbes*, 228 U.S. 549, 556; *Isbrandtsen-Moller Co.* v. *United States*, 300 U.S. 139, 146–48; *Swayne & Hoyt, Ltd.* v. *United States*, 300 U.S. 297, 300–03; *Mason Co.* v. *Tax Comm'n*, 302 U.S. 186, 208. And so far as it lawfully could, Congress authorized and implemented such curfew orders as the commanding officer should promulgate pursuant to the Executive Order of the President. The question then is not one of the Congressional power to delegate to the President the promulgation of the Executive Order, but whether, acting in cooperation, Congress and the Executive have constitutional authority to impose the curfew restriction here complained of. We must consider also whether, acting together, Congress and the Executive could leave it to the designated military commander to appraise the relevant conditions and on the basis of that appraisal to say whether, under the circumstances, the time and place were appropriate for the promulgation of the curfew order and whether the order itself was an appropriate means of carrying the Executive Order for the "protection against espionage and against sabotage" to national defense materials, premises and utilities. For reasons presently to be stated, we conclude that it was within the constitutional power of Congress to prescribe this curfew order for the period under consideration and that its promulgation by the military commander involved no unlawful delegation of legislative power.

Executive Order No. 9066, promulgated in time of war for the declared purpose of prosecuting the war by protecting national defense resources from sabotage and espionage, and the Act of March 21, 1942, ratifying and confirming the Executive Order, were each an exercise of the power to wage war conferred on the Congress and on the President, as Commander in Chief of the armed forces, by Articles I and II of the Constitution. See *Ex parte Quirin*, 317 U.S. 1, 25–26. We have no occasion to consider whether the President, acting alone, could lawfully have made the curfew order in question, or have authorized others to make it. For the President's action has the support of the Act of Congress, and we are immediately concerned with the question whether it is within the constitutional power of the national government, through the joint action of Congress and the Executive, to impose this restriction as an emergency war measure. The exercise of that power here involves no question of martial law or trial by military tribunal. Cf. *Ex parte Milligan*, 4 Wall. 2; *Ex parte Quirin*, supra. Appellant has been tried and convicted in the civil courts and has been subjected to penalties prescribed by Congress for the acts committed.

The war power of the national government is "the power to wage war successfully." See Charles Evans Hughes, War Powers Under the Constitution, 42 A. B. A. Rep. 232, 238. It extends to every matter and activity so related to war as substantially to affect its conduct and progress. The power is not restricted to the winning of victories in the field and the repulse of enemy forces. It embraces every phase of the national defense, including the protection of war materials and the members of the armed forces from injury and from the dangers which attend the rise, prosecution and progress of war. *Prize Cases*, supra; *Miller* v. *United States*, 11 Wall. 268, 303–14; *Stewart* v. *Kahn*, 11 Wall. 493, 506–07; *Selective Draft Law Cases, 245 U.S. 366; McKinley* v. *United States*, 249 U.S. 397; *United States* v. *Macintosh*, 283 U.S. 605, 622–23. Since the Constitution commits to the Executive and to Congress the exercise of war power in all the vicissitudes and conditions of warfare, it has necessarily given them wide scope for the exercise of judgment and discretion in determining the nature and extent of the threatened injury or danger and in the selection of the means for resisting it. *Ex parte Quirin*, supra, 28–29; cf. *Prize Cases*, supra, 670; *Martin* v. *Mott*, 12 Wheat. 19, 29. Where, as they did here, the conditions call for the exercise of judgment and discretion and for the choice of means by those branches of the Government on which the Constitution has placed the responsibility of warmaking, it is not for any court to sit in review of the wisdom of their action or substitute its judgment for theirs.

The actions taken must be appraised in the light of the conditions with which the President and Congress were confronted in the early months of 1942, many of which, since disclosed, were then peculiarly within the knowledge of the military authorities. On December 7, 1941, the Japanese air forces had attacked the United States Naval Base at Pearl Harbor without warning, at the very hour when Japanese diplomatic representatives were conducting negotiations with our State Department ostensibly for the peaceful settlement of differences between the two countries. Simultaneously or nearly so, the Japanese attacked Malaysia, Hong

Kong, the Philippines, and Wake and Midway Islands. On the following day their army invaded Thailand. Shortly afterwards they sank two British battleships. On December 13th, Guam was taken. On December 24th and 25th they captured Wake Island and occupied Hong Kong. On January 2, 1942, Manila fell, and on February 10th Singapore, Britain's great naval base in the East, was taken. On February 27th the battle of the Java Sea resulted in a disastrous naval defeat to the United Nations. By the 9th of March Japanese forces had established control over the Netherlands East Indies; Rangoon and Burma were occupied; Bataan and Corregidor were under attack.

Although the results of the attack on Pearl Harbor were not fully disclosed until much later, it was known that the damage was extensive, and that the Japanese by their successes had gained a naval superiority over our forces in the Pacific which might enable them to seize Pearl Harbor, our largest naval base and the last stronghold of defense lying between Japan and the West Coast. That reasonably prudent men charged with the responsibility of our national defense had ample ground for concluding that they must face the danger of invasion, take measures against it, and in making the choice of measures consider our internal situation, cannot be doubted.

The challenged orders were defense measures for the avowed purpose of safeguarding the military area in question, at a time of threatened air raids and invasion by the Japanese forces, from the danger of sabotage and espionage. As the curfew was made applicable to citizens residing in the area only if they were of Japanese ancestry, our inquiry must be whether in the light of all the facts and circumstances there was any substantial basis for the conclusion, in which Congress and the military commander united, that the curfew as applied was a protective measure necessary to meet the threat of sabotage and espionage which would substantially affect the war effort and which might reasonably be expected to aid a threatened enemy invasion. The alternative which appellant insists must be accepted is for the military authorities to impose the curfew on all citizens within the military area, or on none. In a case of threatened danger requiring prompt action, it is a choice between inflicting obviously needless hardship on the many, or sitting passive and unresisting in the presence of the threat. We think that constitutional government, in time of war, is not so powerless and does not compel so hard a choice if those charged with the responsibility of our national defense have reasonable ground for believing that the threat is real.

When the orders were promulgated there was a vast concentration, within Military Areas Nos. 1 and 2, of installations and facilities for the production of military equipment, especially ships and airplanes. Important Army and Navy bases were located in California and Washington. Approximately one-fourth of the total value of the major aircraft contracts then let by Government procurement officers were to be performed in the State of California. California ranked second, and Washington fifth, of all the states of the Union with respect to the value of shipbuilding contracts to be performed.[1]

In the critical days of March 1942, the danger to our war production by sabotage and espionage in this area seems obvious. The German invasion of the Western European countries had given ample warning to the world of the menace of the "fifth column." Espionage by persons in sympathy with the Japanese Government had been found to have been particularly effective in the surprise attack on Pearl Harbor.[2] At a time of threatened Japanese attack upon this country, the nature of our inhabitants' attachments to the Japanese enemy was consequently a matter of grave concern. Of the 126,000 persons of Japanese descent in the United States, citizens and non-citizens, approximately 112,000 resided in California, Oregon and Washington at the time of the adoption of the military regulations. Of these approximately two-thirds are citizens because born in the United States. Not only did the great majority of such persons reside within the Pacific Coast states but they were concentrated in or near three of the large cities, Seattle, Portland and Los Angeles, all in Military Area No. 1.[3]

There is support for the view that social, economic and political conditions which have prevailed since the close of the last century, when the Japanese began to come to this country in substantial numbers, have intensified their solidarity and have in large measure prevented their assimilation as an integral part of the white population.[4] In addition, large

[1] State Distribution of War Supply and Facility Contracts—June 1940 through December 1941 (issued by Office of Production Management, Bureau of Research and Statistics, January 18, 1942); *Ibid.*—Cumulative through February 1943 (issued by War Production Board, Statistics Division, April 3, 1943).

[2] See "Attack upon Pearl Harbor by Japanese Armed Forces," Report of the Commission Appointed by the President, dated January 23, 1942, S. Doc. No. 159, 77th Cong., 2d Sess., pp. 12–13.

[3] Sixteenth Census of the United States, for 1940, Population, Second Series, Characteristics of the Population (Dept. of Commerce): California, pp. 10, 61; Oregon, pp. 10, 50; Washington, pp. 10, 52. See also H. R. Rep. No. 2124, 77th Cong., 2d Sess., pp. 91–100.

[4] Federal legislation has denied to the Japanese citizenship by naturalization (R. S. § 2169; 8 U. S. C. §703; see *Ozawa* v. *United States*, 260 U.S. 178), and the Immigration Act of 1924 excluded them from admission into the United States. 43 Stat. 161, 8 U. S. C. § 213. State legislation has denied to alien Japanese the privilege of owning land. 1 California General Laws (Deering,

numbers of children of Japanese parentage are sent to Japanese language schools outside the regular hours of public schools in the locality. Some of these schools are generally believed to be sources of Japanese nationalistic propaganda, cultivating allegiance to Japan.[5] Considerable numbers, estimated to be approximately 10,000, of American-born children of Japanese parentage have been sent to Japan for all or a part of their education.[6]

Congress and the Executive, including the military commander, could have attributed special significance, in its bearing on the loyalties of persons of Japanese descent, to the maintenance by Japan of its system of dual citizenship. Children born in the United States of Japanese alien parents, and especially those children born before December 1, 1924, are under many circumstances deemed, by Japanese law, to be citizens of Japan.[7] No official census of those whom Japan regards as having thus retained Japanese citizenship is available, but there is ground for the belief that the number is large.[8]

The large number of resident alien Japanese, approximately one-third of all Japanese inhabitants of the country, are of mature years and occupy positions of influence in Japanese communities. The association of the influential Japanese residents with Japanese Consulates has been deemed a ready means for the dissemination of propaganda and for the maintenance of the influence of the Japanese Government with the Japanese population in this country.[9]

As a result of these conditions affecting the life of the Japanese, both aliens and citizens, in the Pacific Coast area, there has been relatively

---

1931), Act 261; 5 Oregon Comp. Laws Ann. (1940) § 61–102; 11 Washington Rev. Stat. Ann. (Remington, 1933), §§ 10581–10582. It has also sought to prohibit intermarriage of persons of Japanese race with Caucasians. Montana Rev. Codes (1935), § 5702. Persons of Japanese descent have often been unable to secure professional or skilled employment except in association with others of that descent, and sufficient employment opportunities of this character have not been available. Mears, Resident Orientals on the American Pacific Coast (1927), pp. 188, 198–209, 402–03; H. R. Rep. No. 2124, 77th Cong., 2d Sess., pp. 101–38.

[5] Hearings before the Select Committee Investigating National Defense Migration, House of Representatives, 77th Cong., 2d Sess., pp. 11702, 11393–94, 11348.

[6] H. R. Rep. No. 1911, 77th Cong., 2d Sess., p. 16.

[7] Nationality Law of Japan, Article 1 and Article 20, § 3, and Regulations (Ordinance No. 26) of November 17, 1924,—all printed in Flournoy and Hudson, Nationality Laws (1929), pp. 382, 384–87. See also Foreign Relations of the United States, 1924, vol. 2, pp. 411–13.

[8] Statistics released in 1927 by the Consul General of Japan at San Francisco asserted that over 51,000 of the approximately 63,000 American-born persons of Japanese parentage then in the western part of the United States held Japanese citizenship. Mears, Resident Orientals on the American Pacific Coast, pp. 107–08, 429. A census conducted under the auspices of the Japanese government in 1930 asserted that approximately 47% of American-born persons of Japanese parentage in California held dual citizenship. Strong, The Second-Generation Japanese Problem (1934), p. 142.

[9] H. R. Rep. No. 1911, 77th Cong., 2d Sess., p. 17.

little social intercourse between them and the white population. The restrictions, both practical and legal, affecting the privileges and opportunities afforded to persons of Japanese extraction residing in the United States, have been sources of irritation and may well have tended to increase their isolation, and in many instances their attachments to Japan and its institutions.

Viewing these data in all their aspects, Congress and the Executive could reasonably have concluded that these conditions have encouraged the continued attachment of members of this group to Japan and Japanese institutions. These are only some of the many considerations which those charged with the responsibility for the national defense could take into account in determining the nature and extent of the danger of espionage and sabotage, in the event of invasion or air raid attack. The extent of that danger could be definitely known only after the event and after it was too late to meet it. Whatever views we may entertain regarding the loyalty to this country of the citizens of Japanese ancestry, we cannot reject as unfounded the judgment of the military authorities and of Congress that there were disloyal members of that population, whose number and strength could not be precisely and quickly ascertained. We cannot say that the war-making branches of the Government did not have ground for believing that in a critical hour such persons could not readily be isolated and separately dealt with, and constituted a menace to the national defense and safety, which demanded that prompt and adequate measures be taken to guard against it.

Appellant does not deny that, given the danger, a curfew was an appropriate measure against sabotage. It is an obvious protection against the perpetration of sabotage most readily committed during the hours of darkness. If it was an appropriate exercise of the war power its validity is not impaired because it has restricted the citizen's liberty. Like every military control of the population of a dangerous zone in war time, it necessarily involves some infringement of individual liberty, just as does the police establishment of fire lines during a fire, or the confinement of people to their houses during an air raid alarm—neither of which could be thought to be an infringement of constitutional right. Like them, the validity of the restraints of the curfew order depends on all the conditions which obtain at the time the curfew is imposed and which support the order imposing it.

But appellant insists that the exercise of the power is inappropriate and unconstitutional because it discriminates against citizens of Japanese ancestry, in violation of the Fifth Amendment. The Fifth Amendment contains no equal protection clause and it restrains only such discriminatory legislation by Congress as amounts to a denial of due process. *Detroit Bank* v. *United States*, 317 U.S. 329, 337–38, and cases cited. Congress may hit at a particular danger where it is seen, without providing for others which are not so evident or so urgent. *Keokee Coke Co.* v. *Taylor*, 234 U.S. 224, 227.

Distinctions between citizens solely because of their ancestry are by their very nature odious to a free people whose institutions are founded upon the doctrine of equality. For that reason, legislative classification or discrimination based on race alone has often been held to be a denial of equal protection. *Yick Wo* v. *Hopkins*, 118 U.S. 356; *Yu Cong Eng* v. *Trinidad*, 271 U.S. 500; *Hill* v. *Texas*, 316 U.S. 400. We may assume that these considerations would be controlling here were it not for the fact that the danger of espionage and sabotage, in time of war and of threatened invasion, calls upon the military authorities to scrutinize every relevant fact bearing on the loyalty of populations in the danger areas. Because racial discriminations are in most circumstances irrelevant and therefore prohibited, it by no means follows that, in dealing with the perils of war, Congress and the Executive are wholly precluded from taking into account those facts and circumstances which are relevant to measures for our national defense and for the successful prosecution of the war, and which may in fact place citizens of one ancestry in a different category from others. "We must never forget, that it is *a constitution* we are expounding," "a constitution intended to endure for ages to come, and, consequently, to be adapted to the various *crises* of human affairs." *McCulloch* v. *Maryland*, 4 Wheat. 316, 407, 415. The adoption by Government, in the crisis of war and of threatened invasion, of measures for the public safety, based upon the recognition of facts and circumstances which indicate that a group of one national extraction may menace that safety more than others, is not wholly beyond the limits of the Constitution and is not to be condemned merely because in other and in most circumstances racial distinctions are irrelevant. Cf. *Clarke* v. *Deckebach*, 274 U.S. 392, and cases cited.

Here the aim of Congress and the Executive was the protection against sabotage of war materials and utilities in areas thought to be in danger of Japanese invasion and air attack. We have stated in detail facts and circumstances with respect to the American citizens of Japanese ancestry residing on the Pacific Coast which support the judgment of the war-waging branches of the Government that some restrictive measure was urgent. We cannot say that these facts and circumstances, considered in the particular war setting, could afford no ground for differentiating citizens of Japanese ancestry from other groups in the United States. The fact alone that attack on our shores was threatened by Japan rather than another enemy power set these citizens apart from others who have no particular associations with Japan.

Our investigation here does not go beyond the inquiry whether, in the light of all the relevant circumstances preceding and attending their promulgation, the challenged orders and statute afforded a reasonable basis for the action taken in imposing the curfew. We cannot close our eyes to the fact, demonstrated by experience, that in time of war residents having ethnic affiliations with an invading enemy may be a greater source of danger than those of a different ancestry. Nor can we deny that Congress, and the military authorities acting with its authorization, have constitutional power to appraise the danger in the light of facts of public notoriety. We need not now attempt to define the ultimate boundaries of the war power. We decide only the issue as we have defined it—we decide only that the curfew order as applied, and at the time it was applied, was within the boundaries of the war power. In this case it is enough that circumstances within the knowledge of those charged with the responsibility for maintaining the national defense afforded a rational basis for the decision which they made. Whether we would have made it is irrelevant.

What we have said also disposes of the contention that the curfew order involved an unlawful delegation by Congress of its legislative power. The mandate of the Constitution that all legislative power granted "shall be vested in Congress" has never been thought, even in the administration of civil affairs, to preclude Congress from resorting to the aid of executive or administrative officers in determining by findings whether the facts are such as to call for the application of previously adopted legislative standards or definitions of Congressional policy.

The purpose of Executive Order No. 9066, and the standard which the President approved for the orders authorized to be promulgated by the military commander—as disclosed by the preamble of the Executive Order—was the protection of our war resources against espionage and sabotage. Public Proclamations Nos. 1 and 2 by General DeWitt, contain findings that the military areas created and the measures to be prescribed for them were required to establish safeguards against espionage and sabotage. Both the Executive Order and the Proclamations were before Congress when the Act of March 21, 1942, was under consideration. To the extent that the Executive Order authorized orders to be promulgated by the military commander to accomplish the declared purpose of the Order, and to the extent that the findings in the Proclamations establish that such was their purpose, both have been approved by Congress.

It is true that the Act does not in terms establish a particular standard to which orders of the military commander are to conform, or require findings to be made as a prerequisite to any order. But the Executive Order, the Proclamations and the statute are not to be read in isolation from each other. They were parts of a single program and must be judged as such. The Act of March 21, 1942, was an adoption by Congress of the Executive Order and of the Proclamations. The Proclamations themselves followed a standard authorized by the Executive Order—the necessity of protecting military resources in the designated areas against espionage and sabotage. And by the Act, Congress gave its approval to that standard. We have no need to consider now the validity of action if taken by the military commander without conforming to this standard approved by Congress, or the validity of orders made without the support of findings showing that they do so conform. Here the findings of danger from espionage and sabotage, and of the necessity of the curfew order to protect against them, have been duly made. General DeWitt's Public Proclamation No. 3, which established the curfew, merely prescribed regulations of the type and in the manner which Public Proclamations Nos. 1 and 2 had announced would be prescribed at a future date, and was thus founded on the findings of Proclamations Nos. 1 and 2.

The military commander's appraisal of facts in the light of the authorized standard, and the inferences which he drew from those facts, involved the exercise of his judgment. But as we have seen, those facts, and the inferences which could be rationally drawn from them, support the judgment of the military commander, that the danger of espionage and sabotage to our military resources was imminent, and that the curfew order was an appropriate measure to meet it.

Where, as in the present case, the standard set up for the guidance of the military commander, and the action taken and the reasons for it, are in fact recorded in the military orders, so that Congress, the courts and the public are assured that the orders, in the judgment of the commander, conform to the standards approved by the President and Congress, there is no failure in the performance of the legislative function. *Opp Cotton Mills* v. *Administrator*, 312 U.S. 126, 142–46, and cases cited. The essentials of that function are the determination by Congress of the legislative policy and its approval of a rule of conduct to carry that policy into execution. The very necessities which attend the conduct of military operations in time of war in this instance as in many others preclude

Congress from holding committee meetings to determine whether there is danger, before it enacts legislation to combat the danger.

The Constitution as a continuously operating charter of government does not demand the impossible or the impractical. The essentials of the legislative function are preserved when Congress authorizes a statutory command to become operative, upon ascertainment of a basic conclusion of fact by a designated representative of the Government. Cf. *The Aurora*, 7 Cranch 382; *United States* v. *Chemical Foundation*, 272 U.S. 1, 12. The present statute, which authorized curfew orders to be made pursuant to Executive Order No. 9066 for the protection of war resources from espionage and sabotage, satisfies those requirements. Under the Executive Order the basic facts, determined by the military commander in the light of knowledge then available, were whether that danger existed and whether a curfew order was an appropriate means of minimizing the danger. Since his findings to that effect were, as we have said, not without adequate support, the legislative function was performed and the sanction of the statute attached to violations of the curfew order. It is unnecessary to consider whether or to what extent such findings would support orders differing from the curfew order.

The conviction under the second count is without constitutional infirmity. Hence we have no occasion to review the conviction on the first count since, as already stated, the sentences on the two counts are to run concurrently and conviction on the second is sufficient to sustain the sentence. For this reason also it is unnecessary to consider the Government's argument that compliance with the order to report at the Civilian Control Station did not necessarily entail confinement in a relocation center.

Affirmed.

Mr. Justice Douglas, Concurring

While I concur in the result and agree substantially with the opinion of the Court, I wish to add a few words to indicate what for me is the narrow ground of decision.

After the disastrous bombing of Pearl Harbor the military had a grave problem on its hands. The threat of Japanese invasion of the west coast was not fanciful but real. The presence of many thousands of aliens and citizens of Japanese ancestry in or near to the key points along that coast line aroused special concern in those charged with the defense of the country. They believed that not only among aliens but also among citizens of Japanese ancestry there were those who would give aid and comfort to the Japanese invader and act as a fifth column before and during an invasion.[1] If the military were right in their belief that among citizens of Japanese ancestry there was an actual or incipient fifth column, we were indeed faced with the imminent threat of a dire emergency. We must credit the military with as much good faith in that belief as we would any other public official acting pursuant to his duties. We cannot possibly know all the facts which lay behind that decision. Some of them may have been as intangible and as imponderable as the factors which influence personal or business decisions in daily life. The point is that we cannot sit in judgment on the military requirements of that hour. Where the orders under the present Act have some relation to "protection against espionage and against sabotage," our task is at an end.

Much of the argument assumes that as a matter of policy it might have been wiser for the military to have dealt with these people on an individual basis and through the process of investigation and hearings separated those who were loyal from those who were not. But the wisdom or expediency of the decision which was made is not for us to review. Nor are we warranted where national survival is at stake in insisting that those orders should not have been applied to anyone without some evidence of his disloyalty. The orders as applied to the petitioner are not to be tested by the substantial evidence rule. Peacetime procedures do not necessarily fit wartime needs. It is said that if citizens of Japanese ancestry were generally disloyal, treatment on a group basis might be justified. But there is no difference in power when the number of those who are finally shown to be disloyal or suspect is reduced to a small per cent. The sorting process might indeed be as time-consuming whether those who were disloyal or suspect constituted nine or ninety-nine per cent. And the pinch of the order on the loyal citizens would be as great in any case. But where the peril is great and the time is short, temporary treatment on a group basis may be the only practicable expedient whatever the ultimate percentage of those who are detained for cause. Nor should the military be required to wait until espionage or sabotage becomes effective before it moves.

It is true that we might now say that there was ample time to handle the

[1] Judge Fee stated in *United States* v. *Yasui*, 48 F. Supp. 40, 44–45, the companion case to the present one, "The areas and zones outlined in the proclamations became a theatre of operations, subjected in localities to attack and all threatened during this period with a full scale invasion. The danger at the time this prosecution was instituted was imminent and immediate. The difficulty of controlling members of an alien race, many of whom, although citizens, were disloyal with opportunities of sabotage and espionage, with invasion imminent, presented a problem requiring for solution ability and devotion of the highest order."

problem on the individual rather than the group basis. But military decisions must be made without the benefit of hindsight. The orders must be judged as of the date when the decision to issue them was made. To say that the military in such cases should take the time to weed out the loyal from the others would be to assume that the nation could afford to have them take the time to do it. But as the opinion of the Court makes clear, speed and dispatch may be of the essence. Certainly we cannot say that those charged with the defense of the nation should have procrastinated until investigations and hearings were completed. At that time further delay might indeed have seemed to be wholly incompatible with military responsibilities.

Since we cannot override the military judgment which lay behind these orders, it seems to me necessary to concede that the army had the power to deal temporarily with these people on a group basis. Petitioner therefore was not justified in disobeying the orders.

But I think it important to emphasize that we are dealing here with a problem of loyalty not assimilation. Loyalty is a matter of mind and of heart not of race. That indeed is the history of America. Moreover, guilt is personal under our constitutional system. Detention for reasonable cause is one thing. Detention on account of ancestry is another.

In this case the petitioner tendered by a plea in abatement the question of his loyalty to the United States. I think that plea was properly stricken; military measures of defense might be paralyzed if it were necessary to try out that issue preliminarily. But a denial of that opportunity in this case does not necessarily mean that petitioner could not have had a hearing on that issue in some appropriate proceeding. Obedience to the military orders is one thing. Whether an individual member of a group must be afforded at some stage an opportunity to show that, being loyal, he should be reclassified is a wholly different question.

There are other instances in the law where one must obey an order before he can attack as erroneous the classification in which he has been placed. Thus it is commonly held that one who is a conscientious objector has no privilege to defy the Selective Service Act and to refuse or fail to be inducted. He must submit to the law. But that line of authority holds that after induction he may obtain through habeas corpus a hearing on the legality of his classification by the draft board.[2] Whether in the present

[2] See *United States* v. *Powell*, 38 F. Supp. 183; *Application of Greenberg*, 39 F. Supp. 13; *United States* v. *Baird*, 39 F. Supp. 392; *Micheli* v. *Paullin*, 45 F. Supp. 687; *United States* v. *Embrey*, 46 F. Supp. 916; *In re Rogers*, 47 F. Supp. 265; *Ex parte Stewart*, 47 F. Supp. 410; *United States* v. *Smith*, 48 F. Supp. 842; *Ex parte Robert*, 49 F. Supp. 131; *United States* v. *Grieme*, 128 F. 2d 811;

situation that remedy would be available is one of the large and important issues reserved by the present decision. It has been suggested that an administrative procedure has been established to relieve against unwarranted applications of these orders. Whether in that event the administrative remedy would be the only one available or would have to be first exhausted is also reserved. The scope of any relief which might be afforded—whether the liberties of an applicant could be restored only outside the areas in question—is likewise a distinct issue. But if it were plain that no machinery was available whereby the individual could demonstrate his loyalty as a citizen in order to be reclassified, questions of a more serious character would be presented. The United States, however, takes no such position. We need go no further here than to deny the individual the right to defy the law. It is sufficient to say that he cannot test in that way the validity of the orders as applied to him.

Mr. Justice Murphy, Concurring

It is not to be doubted that the action taken by the military commander in pursuance of the authority conferred upon him was taken in complete good faith and in the firm conviction that it was required by considerations of public safety and military security. Neither is it doubted that the Congress and the Executive working together may generally employ such measures as are necessary and appropriate to provide for the common defense and to wage war "with all the force necessary to make it effective." *United States* v. *Macintosh*, 283 U. S. 605, 622. This includes authority to exercise measures of control over persons and property which would not in all cases be permissible in normal times.[1]

It does not follow, however, that the broad guaranties of the Bill of Rights and other provisions of the Constitution protecting essential liberties are suspended by the mere existence of a state of war. It has been frequently stated and recognized by this Court that the war power, like the other great substantive powers of government, is subject to the limitations

---

Fletcher v. *United States*, 129 F. 2d 262; *Drumheller* v. *Berks County Local Board No. 1*, 130 F. 2d 610, 612. For cases arising under the Selective Draft Act of 1917, see *United States* v. *Kinkead*, 250 F 692; *Ex parte McDonald*, 253 F. 99; *Ex parte Cohen*, 254 F. 711; *Arbitman* v. *Woodside*, 258 F. 441; *Ex parte Thieret*, 268 F. 472, 476. And see 10 Geo. Wash. L. Rev. 827.

[1]*Schenck* v. *United States*, 249 U.S. 47; *Debs* v. *United States* 249 U.S. 211; *United States* v. *Bethlehem Steel Corp.*, 315 U.S. 289, 305; *Northern Pacific Ry. Co.* v. *North Dakota*, 250 U.S. 135; *Dakota Central Tel. Co.* v. *South Dakota*, 250 U.S. 163; *Highland* v. *Russell Car Co.*, 279 U.S. 253; *Selective Draft Law Cases*, 245 U.S. 366.

of the Constitution. See *Ex parte Milligan*, 4 Wall. 2; *Hamilton* v. *Kentucky Distilleries Co.*, 251 U.S. 146, 156; *Home Building & Loan Assn.* v. *Blaisdell*, 290 U.S. 398, 426. We give great deference to the judgment of the Congress and of the military authorities as to what is necessary in the effective prosecution of the war, but we can never forget that there are constitutional boundaries which it is our duty to uphold. It would not be supposed, for instance, that public elections could be suspended or that the prerogatives of the courts could be set aside, or that persons not charged with offenses against the law of war (see *Ex parte Quirin*, 317 U.S. 1) could be deprived of due process of law and the benefits of trial by jury, in the absence of a valid declaration of martial law. Cf. *Ex parte Milligan*, supra.

Distinctions based on color and ancestry are utterly inconsistent with our traditions and ideals. They are at variance with the principles for which we are now waging war. We cannot close our eyes to the fact that for centuries the Old World has been torn by racial and religious conflicts and has suffered the worst kind of anguish because of inequality of treatment for different groups. There was one law for one and a different law for another. Nothing is written more firmly into our law than the compact of the Plymouth voyagers to have just and equal laws. To say that any group cannot be assimilated is to admit that the great American experiment has failed, that our way of life has failed when confronted with the normal attachment of certain groups to the lands of their forefathers. As a nation we embrace many groups, some of them among the oldest settlements in our midst, which have isolated themselves for religious and cultural reasons.

Today is the first time, so far as I am aware, that we have sustained a substantial restriction of the personal liberty of citizens of the United States based upon the accident of race or ancestry. Under the curfew order here challenged no less than 70,000 American citizens have been placed under a special ban and deprived of their liberty because of their particular racial inheritance. In this sense it bears a melancholy resemblance to the treatment accorded to members of the Jewish race in Germany and in other parts of Europe. The result is the creation in this country of two classes of citizens for the purposes of a critical and perilous hour—to sanction discrimination between groups of United States citizens on the basis of ancestry. In my opinion this goes to the very brink of constitutional power.

Except under conditions of great emergency a regulation of this kind applicable solely to citizens of a particular racial extraction would not be regarded as in accord with the requirement of due process of law contained in the Fifth Amendment. We have consistently held that attempts to apply regulatory action to particular groups solely on the basis of racial distinction or classification is not in accordance with due process of law as prescribed by the Fifth and Fourteenth Amendments. Cf. *Yick Wo* v. *Hopkins*, 118 U.S. 356, 369; *Yu Cong Eng* v. *Trinidad*, 271 U.S. 500, 524–28. See also *Boyd* v. *Frankfort*, 117 Ky. 199, 77 S. W. 669; *Opinion of the Justices*, 207 Mass. 601, 94 N. E. 558. It is true that the Fifth Amendment, unlike the Fourteenth, contains no guaranty of equal protection of the laws. Cf. *Currin* v. *Wallace*, 306 U.S. 1, 14. It is also true that even the guaranty of equal protection of the laws allows a measure of reasonable classification. It by no means follows, however, that there may not be discrimination of such an injurious character in the application of laws as to amount to a denial of due process of law as that term is used in the Fifth Amendment.[2] I think that point is dangerously approached when we have one law for the majority of our citizens and another for those of a particular racial heritage.

In view, however, of the critical military situation which prevailed on the Pacific Coast area in the spring of 1942, and the urgent necessity of taking prompt and effective action to secure defense installations and military operations against the risk of sabotage and espionage, the military authorities should not be required to conform to standards of regulatory action appropriate to normal times. Because of the damage wrought by the Japanese at Pearl Harbor and the availability of new weapons and new techniques with greater capacity for speed and deception in offensive operations, the immediate possibility of an attempt at invasion somewhere along the Pacific Coast had to be reckoned with. However desirable such a procedure might have been, the military authorities could have reasonably concluded at the time that determinations as to the loyalty and dependability of individual members of the large and widely scattered group of persons of Japanese extraction on the West Coast could not be made without delay that might have had tragic consequences. Modern war does not always wait for the observance of procedural requirements that are considered essential and appropriate under normal conditions.

---

[2] For instance, if persons of an accused's race were systematically excluded from a jury in a federal court, any conviction undoubtedly would be considered a violation of the requirement of due process of law, even though the ground commonly stated for setting aside convictions so obtained in state courts is denial of equal protection of the laws. Cf. *Glasser* v. *United States*, 315 U.S. 60, with *Smith* v. *Texas*, 311 U.S. 128.

Accordingly I think that the military arm, confronted with the peril of imminent enemy attack and acting under the authority conferred by the Congress, made an allowable judgment at the time the curfew restriction was imposed. Whether such a restriction is valid today is another matter.

In voting for affirmance of the judgment I do not wish to be understood as intimating that the military authorities in time of war are subject to no restraints whatsoever, or that they are free to impose any restrictions they may choose on the rights and liberties of individual citizens or groups of citizens in those places which may be designated as "military areas." While this Court sits, it has the inescapable duty of seeing that the mandates of the Constitution are obeyed. That duty exists in time of war as well as in time of peace, and in its performance we must not forget that few indeed have been the invasions upon essential liberties which have not been accompanied by pleas of urgent necessity advanced in good faith by responsible men. Cf. Mr. Justice Brandeis concurring in *Whitney* v. *California*, 274 U.S. 357, 372.

Nor do I mean to intimate that citizens of a particular racial group whose freedom may be curtailed within an area threatened with attack should be generally prevented from leaving the area and going at large in other areas that are not in danger of attack and where special precautions are not needed. Their status as citizens, though subject to requirements of national security and military necessity, should at all times be accorded the fullest consideration and respect. When the danger is past, the restrictions imposed on them should be promptly removed and their freedom of action fully restored.

Mr. Justice Rutledge, Concurring

I concur in the Court's opinion, except for the suggestion, if that is intended (as to which I make no assertion), that the courts have no power to review any action a military officer may "in his discretion" find it necessary to take with respect to civilian citizens in military areas or zones, once it is found that an emergency has created the conditions requiring or justifying the creation of the area or zone and the institution of some degree of military control short of suspending habeas corpus. Given the generating conditions for exercise of military authority and recognizing the wide latitude for particular applications that ordinarily creates, I do not think it is necessary in this case to decide that there is no action a person in the position of General DeWitt here may take, and which he may regard as necessary to the region's or the country's safety, which will call judicial power into play. The officer of course must have wide discretion and room for its operation. But in this case that question need not be faced and I merely add my reservation without indication of opinion concerning it.

Yasui v. United States

Opinion of the U.S. Supreme Court *

June 21, 1943

A graduate of the University of Oregon Law School, Minoru Yasui held a reserve commission in the U.S. Army and worked for the Japanese consulate in Chicago when the war began. He resigned his job the day after the Pearl Harbor attack, immediately returning to Oregon to report for military service; but he was turned away because of his Japanese ancestry. Yasui challenged the military curfew order because he considered it unlawful discrimination on racial grounds, and he spent nine months in solitary confinement while he waited for trial. After his conviction in the U.S. District Court in Oregon, Judge James Alger Fee wrote an opinion holding the curfew order unconstitutional as applied to American citizens, but also holding that Yasui had renounced his citizenship by working for the Japanese government. The Supreme Court reversed Judge Fee on both issues, but it upheld the conviction by unanimous vote.

Response to questions certified by the Circuit Court of Appeals upon an appeal to that court from a conviction in the District Court for violation of a curfew order. This Court directed that the entire record be certified so that the case could be determined as if brought here by appeal.

Messrs. A. L. Wirin and E. F. Bernard (Mr. Ralph E. Moody was with the latter on the brief) for Yasui.

Solicitor General Fahy, with whom Messrs. Edward J. Ennis, Arnold Raum, John L. Burling, and Leo Gitlin were on the brief, for the United States.

Briefs of amici curiae were filed by Messrs. Arthur Garfield Hays, Osmond K. Fraenkel and A. L. Wirin on behalf of the American Civil Liberties Union; by Mr. A. L. Wirin on behalf of the Japanese American Citizens League; and by Mr. Jackson H. Ralston on behalf of the Northern California Branch of the American Civil Liberties Union,—in sup-

*320 U.S. 115 (1943)

port of Yasui; and by Messrs. Robert W. Kenny, Attorney General of California, I. H. Van Winkle, Attorney General of Oregon, and Smith Troy, Attorney General of the State of Washington, and Fred E. Lewis, Chief Assistant and Acting Attorney General of the State of Washington, on behalf of those States,—urging affirmance.

Mr. Chief Justice Stone Delivered the Opinion of the Court

This is a companion case to *Hirabayashi* v. *United States*, ante, p. 81.

This case comes here on certificate of the Court of Appeals for the Ninth Circuit, certifying to us questions of law upon which it desires instructions for the decision of the case. § 239 of the Judicial Code as amended, 28 U. S. C. § 346. Acting under that section we ordered the entire record to be certified to this Court so that we might proceed to a decision, as if the case had been brought here by appeal.

Appellant, an American-born person of Japanese ancestry, was convicted in the district court of an offense defined by the Act of March 21, 1942. 56 Stat. 173. The indictment charged him with violation, on March 28, 1942, of a curfew order made applicable to Portland, Oregon, by Public Proclamation No. 3, issued by Lt. General J. L. DeWitt on March 24, 1942. 7 Federal Register 2543. The validity of the curfew was considered in the *Hirabayashi* case, and this case presents the same issues as the conviction on Count 2 of the indictment in that case. From the evidence it appeared that appellant was born in Oregon in 1916 of alien parents; that when he was eight years old he spent a summer in Japan; that he attended the public schools in Oregon, and also, for about three years, a Japanese language school; that he later attended the University of Oregon, from which he received A. B. and LL. B. degrees; that he was a member of the bar of Oregon, and a second lieutenant in the Army of the United States, Infantry Reserve; that he had been employed by the Japanese Consulate in Chicago, but had resigned on December 8, 1941, and immediately offered his services to the military authorities; that he had discussed with an agent of the Federal Bureau of Investigation the advisability of testing the constitutionality of the curfew; and that when he violated the curfew order he requested that he be arrested so that he could test its constitutionality.

The district court ruled that the Act of March 21, 1942, was unconstitutional as applied to American citizens, but held that appellant, by reason of his course of conduct, must be deemed to have renounced his American citizenship. 48 F. Supp. 40. The Government does not undertake to support the conviction on that ground, since no such issue was tendered by the Government, although appellant testified at the trial that he had not renounced his citizenship. Since we hold, as in the *Hirabayashi* case, that the curfew order was valid as applied to citizens, it follows that appellant's citizenship was not relevant to the issue tendered by the Government and the conviction must be sustained for the reasons stated in the *Hirabayashi* case.

But as the sentence of one year's imprisonment—the maximum permitted by the statute—was imposed after the finding that appellant was not a citizen, and as the Government states that it has not and does not now controvert his citizenship, the case is an appropriate one for resentence in the light of these circumstances. See *Husty* v. *United States*, 282 U.S. 694, 703. The conviction will be sustained but the judgment will be vacated and the case remanded to the district court for resentence of appellant, and to afford that court opportunity to strike its findings as to appellant's loss of United States citizenship.

So ordered.

Korematsu v. United States

Opinion of the U.S. Supreme Court *

December 18, 1944

Fred Korematsu worked as a shipyard welder in the San Francisco area when the war began, and he lost his job because his union expelled all members of Japanese ancestry. Korematsu wanted to remain with his Caucasian fiancée, and when the Army posted exclusion orders in May 1942, he refused to report for evacuation. He altered his draft card and had minor plastic surgery to change his appearance, but he was ar- rested on a tip and his case brought to trial before U.S. District Judge Adolphus F. St. Sure in San Francisco. Korematsu was convicted of vio- lating the exclusion order. His case initially went before the Supreme Court with those of Hirabayashi and Yasui but was returned to the Court of Appeals on a technical issue. By the time it got back to the Supreme Court, Allied victory over Japan seemed assured and doubts about the continued internment of Japanese Americans had increased. Four mem- bers of the Court at first voted to reverse Korematsu's conviction, and two others expressed reservations, but the Court's final decision upheld the conviction by a vote of six to three.

Certiorari, 321 U.S. 760, to review the affirmance of a judgment of conviction.

Messrs. Wayne M. Collins and Charles A. Horsky argued the cause, and Mr. Collins was on the brief, for petitioner.

Solicitor General Fahy, with whom Assistant Attorney General Wech- sler and Messrs. Edward J. Ennis, Ralph F. Fuchs, and John L. Burling were on the brief, for the United States.

Messrs. Saburo Kido and A. L. Wirin filed a brief on behalf of the Japanese American Citizens League; and Messrs. Edwin Borchard, Charles A. Horsky, George Rublee, Arthur DeHon Hill, Winthrop Wadleigh, Osmond K. Fraenkel, Harold Evans, William Draper Lewis,

*323 U.S. 214 (1944)

76

and Thomas Raeburn White on behalf of the American Civil Liberties Union, as amici curiae, in support of petitioner.

Messrs. Robert W. Kenny, Attorney General of California, George Neuner, Attorney General of Oregon, Smith Troy, Attorney General of Washington, and Fred E. Lewis, Acting Attorney General of Washington, filed a brief on behalf of the States of California, Oregon and Washington, as amici curiae, in support of the United States.

Mr. Justice Black Delivered the Opinion of the Court

The petitioner, an American citizen of Japanese descent, was convicted in federal district court for remaining in San Leandro, California, a "Military Area," contrary to Civilian Exclusion Order No. 34 of the Commanding General of the Western Command, U.S. Army, which directed that after May 9, 1942, all persons of Japanese ancestry should be excluded from that area. No question was raised as to petitioner's loyalty to the United States. The Circuit Court of Appeals affirmed,[1] and the importance of the constitutional question involved caused us to grant certiorari.

It should be noted, to begin with, that all legal restrictions which curtail the civil rights of a single racial group are immediately suspect. That is not to say that all such restrictions are unconstitutional. It is to say that courts must subject them to the most rigid scrutiny. Pressing public necessity may sometimes justify the existence of such restrictions; racial antagonism never can.

In the instant case prosecution of the petitioner was begun by information charging violation of an Act of Congress, of March 21, 1942, 56 Stat. 173, which provides that

. . . whoever shall enter, remain in, leave, or commit any act in any military area or military zone prescribed, under the authority of an Executive Order of the President, by the Secretary of War, or by any military commander designated by the Secretary of War, contrary to the restrictions applicable to any such area or zone or contrary to the order of the Secretary of War or any such military commander, shall, if it appears that he knew or should have known of the existence and extent of the restrictions or order and that his act was in violation thereof, be guilty of a misdemeanor and upon conviction shall be liable to a fine of not to exceed $5,000 or to imprisonment for not more than one year, or both, for each offense.

[1] 140 F. 2d 289.

Exclusion Order No. 34, which the petitioner knowingly and admittedly violated, was one of a number of military orders and proclamations, all of which were substantially based upon Executive Order No. 9066, 7 Fed. Reg. 1407. That order, issued after we were at war with Japan, declared that "the successful prosecution of the war requires every possible protection against espionage and against sabotage to national-defense material, national-defense premises, and national-defense utilities. . . ."

One of the series of orders and proclamations, a curfew order, which like the exclusion order here was promulgated pursuant to Executive Order 9066, subjected all persons of Japanese ancestry in prescribed West Coast military areas to remain in their residences from 8 p.m. to 6 a.m. As is the case with the exclusion order here, that prior curfew order was designed as a "protection against espionage and against sabotage." In *Hirabayashi* v. *United States*, 320 U.S. 81, we sustained a conviction obtained for violation of the curfew order. The Hirabayashi conviction and this one thus rest on the same 1942 Congressional Act and the same basic executive and military orders, all of which orders were aimed at the twin dangers of espionage and sabotage.

The 1942 Act was attacked in the *Hirabayashi* case as an unconstitutional delegation of power; it was contended that the curfew order and other orders on which it rested were beyond the war powers of the Congress, the military authorities and of the President, as Commander in Chief of the Army; and finally that to apply the curfew order against none but citizens of Japanese ancestry amounted to a constitutionally prohibited discrimination solely on account of race. To these questions, we gave the serious consideration which their importance justified. We upheld the curfew order as an exercise of the power of the government to take steps necessary to prevent espionage and sabotage in an area threatened by Japanese attack.

In the light of the principles we announced in the *Hirabayashi* case, we are unable to conclude that it was beyond the war power of Congress and the Executive to exclude those of Japanese ancestry from the West Coast war area at the time they did. True, exclusion from the area in which one's home is located is a far greater deprivation than constant confinement to the home from 8 p.m. to 6 a.m. Nothing short of apprehension by the proper military authorities of the gravest imminent danger to the public safety can constitutionally justify either. But exclusion from a threatened area, no less than curfew, has a definite and close relationship to the prevention of espionage and sabotage. The military authorities, charged with the primary responsibility of defending our shores, concluded that curfew provided inadequate protection and ordered exclusion. They did so, as pointed out in our *Hirabayashi* opinion, in accordance with Congressional authority to the military to say who should, and who should not, remain in the threatened areas.

In this case the petitioner challenges the assumptions upon which we rested our conclusions in the *Hirabayashi* case. He also urges that by May 1942, when Order No. 34 was promulgated, all danger of Japanese invasion of the West Coast had disappeared. After careful consideration of these contentions we are compelled to reject them.

Here, as in the *Hirabayashi* case, supra, at p. 99,

. . . we cannot reject as unfounded the judgment of the military authorities and of Congress that there were disloyal members of that population, whose number and strength could not be precisely and quickly ascertained. We cannot say that the war-making branches of the Government did not have ground for believing that in a critical hour such persons could not readily be isolated and separately dealt with, and constituted a menace to the national defense and safety, which demanded that prompt and adequate measures be taken to guard against it.

Like curfew, exclusion of those of Japanese origin was deemed necessary because of the presence of an unascertained number of disloyal members of the group, most of whom we have no doubt were loyal to this country. It was because we could not reject the finding of the military authorities that it was impossible to bring about an immediate segregation of the disloyal from the loyal that we sustained the validity of the curfew order as applying to the whole group. In the instant case, temporary exclusion of the entire group was rested by the military on the same ground. The judgment that exclusion of the whole group was for the same reason a military imperative answers the contention that the exclusion was in the nature of group punishment based on antagonism to those of Japanese origin. That there were members of the group who retained loyalties to Japan has been confirmed by investigations made subsequent to the exclusion. Approximately five thousand American citizens of Japanese ancestry refused to swear unqualified allegiance to the United States and to renounce allegiance to the Japanese Emperor, and several thousand evacuees requested repatriation to Japan.[2]

We uphold the exclusion order as of the time it was made and when the petitioner violated it. Cf. *Chastleton Corporation* v. *Sinclair*, 264 U.S.

[2]Hearings before the Subcommittee on the National War Agencies Appropriation Bill for 1945, Part II, 608–726; Final Report, Japanese Evacuation from the West Coast, 1942, 309–327; Hearings before the Committee on Immigration and Naturalization, House of Representatives, 78th Cong. 2d Sess., on H. R. 2701 and other bills to expatriate certain nationals of the United States, pp. 37–42, 49–58.

543, 547; *Block* v. *Hirsh*, 256 U.S. 135, 154–5. In doing so, we are not unmindful of the hardships imposed by it upon a large group of American citizens. Cf. *Ex parte Kawato*, 317 U.S. 69, 73. But hardships are part of war, and war is an aggregation of hardships. All citizens alike, both in and out of uniform, feel the impact of war in greater or lesser measure. Citizenship has its responsibilities as well as its privileges, and in time of war the burden is always heavier. Compulsory exclusion of large groups of citizens from their homes, except under circumstances of direst emergency and peril, is inconsistent with our basic governmental institutions. But when under conditions of modern warfare our shores are threatened by hostile forces, the power to protect must be commensurate with the threatened danger.

It is argued that on May 30, 1942, the date the petitioner was charged with remaining in the prohibited area, there were conflicting orders outstanding, forbidding him both to leave the area and to remain there. Of course, a person cannot be convicted for doing the very thing which it is a crime to fail to do. But the outstanding orders here contained no such contradictory commands.

There was an order issued March 27, 1942, which prohibited petitioner and others of Japanese ancestry from leaving the area, but its effect was specifically limited in time "until and to the extent that a future proclamation or order should so permit or direct." 7 Fed. Reg. 2601. That "future order," the one for violation of which petitioner was convicted, was issued May 3, 1942, and it did "direct" exclusion from the area of all persons of Japanese ancestry, before 12 o'clock noon, May 9; furthermore it contained a warning that all such persons found in the prohibited area would be liable to punishment under the March 21, 1942 Act of Congress. Consequently, the only order in effect touching the petitioner's being in the area on May 30, 1942, the date specified in the information against him, was the May 3 order which prohibited his remaining there, and it was that same order, which he stipulated in his trial that he had violated, knowing of its existence. There is therefore no basis for the argument that on May 30, 1942, he was subject to punishment, under the March 27 and May 3 orders, whether he remained in or left the area.

It does appear, however, that on May 9, the effective date of the exclusion order, the military authorities had already determined that the evacuation should be effected by assembling together and placing under guard all those of Japanese ancestry, at central points, designated as "assembly centers," in order "to insure the orderly evacuation and resettlement of

Japanese voluntarily migrating from Military Area No. 1, to restrict and regulate such migration." Public Proclamation No. 4, 7 Fed. Reg. 2601. And on May 19, 1942, eleven days before the time petitioner was charged with unlawfully remaining in the area, Civilian Restrictive Order No. 1, 8 Fed. Reg. 982, provided for detention of those of Japanese ancestry in assembly or relocation centers. It is now argued that the validity of the exclusion order cannot be considered apart from the orders requiring him, after departure from the area, to report and to remain in an assembly or relocation center. The contention is that we must treat these separate orders as one and inseparable; that, for this reason, if detention in the assembly or relocation center would have illegally deprived the petitioner of his liberty, the exclusion order and his conviction under it cannot stand.

We are thus being asked to pass at this time upon the whole subsequent detention program in both assembly and relocation centers, although the only issues framed at the trial related to petitioner's remaining in the prohibited area in violation of the exclusion order. Had petitioner here left the prohibited area and gone to an assembly center we cannot say either as a matter of fact or law that his presence in that center would have resulted in his detention in a relocation center. Some who did report to the assembly center were not sent to relocation centers, but were released upon condition that they remain outside the prohibited zone until the military orders were modified or lifted. This illustrates that they pose different problems and may be governed by different principles. The lawfulness of one does not necessarily determine the lawfulness of the others. This is made clear when we analyze the requirements of the separate provisions of the separate orders. These separate requirements were that those of Japanese ancestry (1) depart from the area; (2) report to and temporarily remain in an assembly center; (3) go under military control to a relocation center there to remain for an indeterminate period until released conditionally or unconditionally by the military authorities. Each of these requirements, it will be noted, imposed distinct duties in connection with the separate steps in a complete evacuation program. Had Congress directly incorporated into one Act the language of these separate orders, and provided sanctions for their violations, disobedience of any one would have constituted a separate offense. Cf. *Blockburger* v. *United States*, 284 U.S. 299, 304. There is no reason why violations of these orders, insofar as they were promulgated pursuant to Congressional enactment, should not be treated as separate offenses.

The *Endo* case, post, p. 283, graphically illustrates the difference between the validity of an order to exclude and the validity of a detention order after exclusion has been effected.

Since the petitioner has not been convicted of failing to report or to remain in an assembly or relocation center, we cannot in this case determine the validity of those separate provisions of the order. It is sufficient here for us to pass upon the order which petitioner violated. To do more would be to go beyond the issues raised, and to decide momentous questions not contained within the framework of the pleadings or the evidence in this case. It will be time enough to decide the serious constitutional issues which petitioner seeks to raise when an assembly or relocation order is applied or is certain to be applied to him, and we have its terms before us.

Some of the members of the Court are of the view that evacuation and detention in an Assembly Center were inseparable. After May 3, 1942, the date of Exclusion Order No. 34, Korematsu was under compulsion to leave the area not as he would choose but via an Assembly Center. The Assembly Center was conceived as a part of the machinery for group evacuation. The power to exclude includes the power to do it by force if necessary. And any forcible measure must necessarily entail some degree of detention or restraint whatever method of removal is selected. But whichever view is taken, it results in holding that the order under which petitioner was convicted was valid.

It is said that we are dealing here with the case of imprisonment of a citizen in a concentration camp solely because of his ancestry, without evidence or inquiry concerning his loyalty and good disposition towards the United States. Our task would be simple, our duty clear, were this a case involving the imprisonment of a loyal citizen in a concentration camp because of racial prejudice. Regardless of the true nature of the assembly and relocation centers—and we deem it unjustifiable to call them concentration camps with all the ugly connotations that term implies—we are dealing specifically with nothing but an exclusion order. To cast this case into outlines of racial prejudice, without reference to the real military dangers which were presented, merely confuses the issue. Korematsu was not excluded from the Military Area because of hostility to him or his race. He *was* excluded because we are at war with the Japanese Empire, because the properly constituted military authorities feared an invasion of our West Coast and felt constrained to take proper security measures, because they decided that the military urgency of the situation demanded that all citizens of Japanese ancestry be segregated from the West Coast temporarily, and finally, because Congress, reposing its confidence in this time of war in our military leaders—as inevitably it must—determined that they should have the power to do just this. There was evidence of disloyalty on the part of some, the military authorities considered that the need for action was great, and time was short. We cannot—by availing ourselves of the calm perspective of hindsight—now say that at that time these actions were unjustified.

Affirmed.

Mr. Justice Frankfurter, Concurring

According to my reading of Civilian Exclusion Order No. 34, it was an offense for Korematsu to be found in Military Area No. 1, the territory wherein he was previously living, except within the bounds of the established Assembly Center of that area. Even though the various orders issued by General DeWitt be deemed a comprehensive code of instructions, their tenor is clear and not contradictory. They put upon Korematsu the obligation to leave Military Area No. 1, but only by the method prescribed in the instructions, i.e., by reporting to the Assembly Center. I am unable to see how the legal considerations that led to the decision in *Hirabayashi* v. *United States*, 320 U.S. 81, fail to sustain the military order which made the conduct now in controversy a crime. And so I join in the opinion of the Court, but should like to add a few words of my own.

The provisions of the Constitution which confer on the Congress and the President powers to enable this country to wage war are as much part of the Constitution as provisions looking to a nation at peace. And we have had recent occasion to quote approvingly the statement of former Chief Justice Hughes that the war power of the Government is "the power to wage war successfully." *Hirabayashi* v. *United States*, supra at 93; and see *Home Bldg. & L. Assn.* v. *Blaisdell*, 290 U.S. 398, 426. Therefore, the validity of action under the war power must be judged wholly in the context of war. That action is not to be stigmatized as lawless because like action in times of peace would be lawless. To talk about a military order that expresses an allowable judgment of war needs by those entrusted with the duty of conducting war as "an unconstitutional order" is to suffuse a part of the Constitution with an atmosphere of unconstitutionality. The respective spheres of action of military authorities and of judges are of course very different. But within their sphere, military authorities are no more outside the bounds of obedience to the Constitution than are judges within theirs. "The war power of the United States, like its other powers . . . is subject to applicable constitutional limitations," *Hamilton* v. *Kentucky Distilleries Co.*, 251 U.S. 146, 156. To recognize that military orders are "reasonably expedient military precautions" in time of war and yet to deny them constitutional legitimacy makes of the Constitution an instrument for dialectic subtleties not reasonably to be attributed to the hard-headed Framers, of whom a majority had had actual participation in war. If a military order such as that under review does not transcend the means appropriate for conducting war, such action by the military is as constitutional as would be any authorized action by the Interstate Commerce Commission within the limits of the constitutional power to regulate commerce. And being an exercise of the war power explicitly granted by the Constitution for safeguarding the national life by prosecuting war effectively, I find nothing in the Constitution which denies to Congress the power to enforce such a valid military order by making its violation an offense triable in the civil courts. Compare *Interstate Commerce Commission* v. *Brimson*, 154 U.S. 447; 155 U.S. 3, and *Monongahela Bridge Co.* v. *United States*, 216 U.S. 177. To find that the Constitution does not forbid the military measures now complained of does not carry with it approval of that which Congress and the Executive did. That is their business, not ours.

Mr. Justice Roberts, Dissenting

I dissent, because I think the indisputable facts exhibit a clear violation of Constitutional rights.

This is not a case of keeping people off the streets at night as was *Hirabayashi* v. *United States*, 320 U.S. 81, nor a case of temporary exclusion of a citizen from an area for his own safety or that of the community, nor a case of offering him an opportunity to go temporarily out of an area where his presence might cause danger to himself or to his fellows. On the contrary, it is the case of convicting a citizen as a punishment for not submitting to imprisonment in a concentration camp, based on his ancestry, and solely because of his ancestry, without evidence or inquiry concerning his loyalty and good disposition towards the United States. If this be a correct statement of the facts disclosed by this record, and facts of which we take judicial notice, I need hardly labor the conclusion that Constitutional rights have been violated.

The Government's argument, and the opinion of the court, in my judgment, erroneously divide that which is single and indivisible and thus make the case appear as if the petitioner violated a Military Order, sanctioned by Act of Congress, which excluded him from his home, by refusing voluntarily to leave and, so, knowingly and intentionally, defying the order and the Act of Congress.

The petitioner, a resident of San Leandro, Alameda County, California, is a native of the United States of Japanese ancestry who, according to the uncontradicted evidence, is a loyal citizen of the nation.

A chronological recitation of events will make it plain that the petitioner's supposed offense did not, in truth, consist in his refusal voluntarily to leave the area which included his home in obedience to the order excluding him therefrom. Critical attention must be given to the dates and sequence of events.

December 8, 1941, the United States declared war on Japan.

February 19, 1942, the President issued Executive Order No. 9066,[1] which, after stating the reason for issuing the order as "protection against espionage and against sabotage to national-defense premises, and national-defense utilities," provided that certain Military Commanders might, in their discretion, "prescribe military areas" and define their extent, "from which any or all persons may be excluded, and with respect to which the right of any person to enter, remain in, or leave shall be subject to whatever restrictions" the "Military Commander may impose in his discretion."

February 20, 1942, Lieutenant General DeWitt was designated Military Commander of the Western Defense Command embracing the westernmost states of the Union,—about one-fourth of the total area of the nation.

March 2, 1942, General DeWitt promulgated Public Proclamation No. 1,[2] which recites that the entire Pacific Coast is "particularly subject to attack, to attempted invasion . . . and, in connection therewith, is subject to espionage and acts of sabotage." It states that "as a matter of military necessity" certain military areas and zones are established known as Military Areas Nos. 1 and 2. It adds that "Such persons or classes of persons as the situation may require" will, by subsequent orders, "be excluded from all of Military Area No. 1" and from certain zones in Military Area No. 2. Subsequent proclamations were made which, together with Proclamation No. 1, included in such areas and zones all of California, Washington, Oregon, Idaho, Montana, Nevada and Utah, and the southern

[1] 7 Fed. Reg. 1407.   [2] 7 Fed. Reg. 2320.

portion of Arizona. The orders required that if any person of Japanese, German or Italian ancestry residing in Area No. 1 desired to change his habitual residence he must execute and deliver to the authorities a Change of Residence Notice.

San Leandro, the city of petitioner's residence, lies in Military Area No. 1.

On March 2, 1942, the petitioner, therefore, had notice that, by Executive Order, the President, to prevent espionage and sabotage, had authorized the Military to exclude him from certain areas and to prevent his entering or leaving certain areas without permission. He was on notice that his home city had been included, by Military Order, in Area No. 1, and he was on notice further that, at sometime in the future, the Military Commander would make an order for the exclusion of certain persons, not described or classified, from various zones including that in which he lived.

March 21, 1942, Congress enacted[3] that anyone who knowingly "shall enter, remain in, leave, or commit any act in any military area or military zone prescribed . . . by any military commander . . . contrary to the restrictions applicable to any such area or zone or contrary to the order of . . . any such military commander" shall be guilty of a misdemeanor. This is the Act under which the petitioner was charged.

March 24, 1942, General DeWitt instituted the curfew for certain areas within his command, by an order the validity of which was sustained in *Hirabayashi* v. *United States*, supra.

March 24, 1942, General DeWitt began to issue a series of exclusion orders relating to specified areas.

March 27, 1942, by Proclamation No. 4,[4] the General recited that "it is necessary, in order to provide for the welfare and to insure the orderly evacuation and resettlement of Japanese *voluntarily migrating* from Military Area No. 1, to restrict and regulate such migration"; and ordered that, as of March 29, 1942, "all alien Japanese and persons of Japanese ancestry who are within the limits of Military Area No. 1, be and they are hereby prohibited from leaving that area for any purpose until and to the extent that a future proclamation or order of this headquarters shall so permit or direct."[5]

[3] 56 Stat. 173.

[4] 7 Fed. Reg. 2601.

[5] The italics in the quotation are mine. The use of the word "voluntarily" exhibits a grim irony probably not lost on petitioner and others in like case. Either so, or its use was a disingenuous attempt to camouflage the compulsion which was to be applied.

No order had been made excluding the petitioner from the area in which he lived. By Proclamation No. 4 he was, after March 29, 1942, confined to the limits of Area No. 1. If the Executive Order No. 9066 and the Act of Congress meant what they said, to leave that area, in the face of Proclamation No. 4, would be to commit a misdemeanor.

May 3, 1942, General DeWitt issued Civilian Exclusion Order No. 34[6] providing that, after 12 o'clock May 8, 1942, all persons of Japanese ancestry, both alien and non-alien, were to be excluded from a described portion of Military Area No. 1, which included the County of Alameda, California. The order required a responsible member of each family and each individual living alone to report, at a time set, at a Civil Control Station for instructions to go to an Assembly Center, and added that any person failing to comply with the provisions of the order who was found in the described area after the date set would be liable to prosecution under the Act of March 21, 1942, supra. It is important to note that the order, by its express terms, had no application to persons within the bounds "of an established Assembly Center pursuant to instructions from this Headquarters . . ." The obvious purpose of the orders made, taken together, was to drive all citizens of Japanese ancestry into Assembly Centers within the zones of their residence, under pain of criminal prosecution.

The predicament in which the petitioner thus found himself was this: He was forbidden, by Military Order, to leave the zone in which he lived; he was forbidden, by Military Order, after a date fixed, to be found within that zone unless he were in an Assembly Center located in that zone. General DeWitt's report to the Secretary of War concerning the programme of evacuation and relocation of Japanese makes it entirely clear, if it were necessary to refer to that document,—and, in the light of the above recitation, I think it is not,—that an Assembly Center was a euphemism for a prison. No person within such a center was permitted to leave except by Military Order.

In the dilemma that he dare not remain in his home, or voluntarily leave the area, without incurring criminal penalties, and that the only way he could avoid punishment was to go to an Assembly Center and submit himself to military imprisonment, the petitioner did nothing.

June 12, 1942, an Information was filed in the District Court for Northern California charging a violation of the Act of March 21, 1942, in that petitioner had knowingly remained within the area covered by Exclu-

[6] 7 Fed. Reg. 3967.

sion Order No. 34. A demurrer to the information having been overruled, the petitioner was tried under a plea of not guilty and convicted. Sentence was suspended and he was placed on probation for five years. We know, however, in the light of the foregoing recitation, that he was at once taken into military custody and lodged in an Assembly Center. We further know that, on March 18, 1942, the President had promulgated Executive Order No. 9102[7] establishing the War Relocation Authority under which so-called Relocation Centers, a euphemism for concentration camps, were established pursuant to cooperation between the military authorities of the Western Defense Command and the Relocation Authority, and that the petitioner has been confined either in an Assembly Center, within the zone in which he had lived or has been removed to a Relocation Center where, as the facts disclosed in *Ex parte Endo* (post, p. 283) demonstrate, he was illegally held in custody.

The Government has argued this case as if the only order outstanding at the time the petitioner was arrested and informed against was Exclusion Order No. 34 ordering him to leave the area in which he resided, which was the basis of the information against him. That argument has evidently been effective. The opinion refers to the *Hirabayashi* case, supra, to show that this court has sustained the validity of a curfew order in an emergency. The argument then is that exclusion from a given area of danger, while somewhat more sweeping than a curfew regulation, is of the same nature,—a temporary expedient made necessary by a sudden emergency. This, I think, is a substitution of an hypothetical case for the case actually before the court. I might agree with the court's disposition of the hypothetical case.[8] The liberty of every American citizen freely to come and to go must frequently, in the face of sudden danger, be temporarily limited or suspended. The civil authorities must often resort to the expedient of excluding citizens temporarily from a locality. The drawing of fire lines in the case of a conflagration, the removal of persons from the area where a pestilence has broken out, are familiar examples. If the exclusion worked by Exclusion Order No. 34 were of that nature the *Hirabayashi* case would be authority for sustaining it. But the facts above recited, and those set forth in *Ex parte Endo*, supra, show that the exclusion was but a part of an over-all plan for forcible detention. This case

[7] 7 Fed. Reg. 2165.

[8] My agreement would depend on the definition and application of the terms "temporary" and "emergency." No pronouncement of the commanding officer can, in my view, preclude judicial inquiry and determination whether an emergency ever existed and whether, if so, it remained, at the date of the restraint out of which the litigation arose. Cf. *Chastleton Corp.* v. *Sinclair*, 264 U.S. 543.

cannot, therefore, be decided on any such narrow ground as the possible validity of a Temporary Exclusion Order under which the residents of an area are given an opportunity to leave and go elsewhere in their native land outside the boundaries of a military area. To make the case turn on any such assumption is to shut our eyes to reality.

As I have said above, the petitioner, prior to his arrest, was faced with two diametrically contradictory orders given sanction by the Act of Congress of March 21, 1942. The earlier of those orders made him a criminal if he left the zone in which he resided; the later made him a criminal if he did not leave.

I had supposed that if a citizen was constrained by two laws, or two orders having the force of law, and obedience to one would violate the other, to punish him for violation of either would deny him due process of law. And I had supposed that under these circumstances a conviction for violating one of the orders could not stand.

We cannot shut our eyes to the fact that had the petitioner attempted to violate Proclamation No. 4 and leave the military area in which he lived he would have been arrested and tried and convicted for violation of Proclamation No. 4. The two conflicting orders, one which commanded him to stay and the other which commanded him to go, were nothing but a cleverly devised trap to accomplish the real purpose of the military authority, which was to lock him up in a concentration camp. The only course by which the petitioner could avoid arrest and prosecution was to go to that camp according to instructions to be given him when he reported at a Civil Control Center. We know that is the fact. Why should we set up a figmentary and artificial situation instead of addressing ourselves to the actualities of the case?

These stark realities are met by the suggestion that it is lawful to compel an American citizen to submit to illegal imprisonment on the assumption that he might, after going to the Assembly Center, apply for his discharge by suing out a writ of habeas corpus, as was done in the *Endo* case, supra. The answer, of course, is that where he was subject to two conflicting laws he was not bound, in order to escape violation of one or the other, to surrender his liberty for any period. Nor will it do to say that the detention was a necessary part of the process of evacuation, and so we are here concerned only with the validity of the latter.

Again it is a new doctrine of constitutional law that one indicted for disobedience to an unconstitutional statute may not defend on the ground of the invalidity of the statute but must obey it though he knows it is no law and, after he has suffered the disgrace of conviction and lost his liberty by sentence, then, and not before, seek, from within prison walls, to test the validity of the law.

Moreover, it is beside the point to rest decision in part on the fact that the petitioner, for his own reasons, wished to remain in his home. If, as is the fact, he was constrained so to do, it is indeed a narrow application of constitutional rights to ignore the order which constrained him, in order to sustain his conviction for violation of another contradictory order.

I would reverse the judgment of conviction.

Mr. Justice Murphy, Dissenting

This exclusion of "all persons of Japanese ancestry, both alien and non-alien," from the Pacific Coast area on a plea of military necessity in the absence of martial law ought not to be approved. Such exclusion goes over "the very brink of constitutional power" and falls into the ugly abyss of racism.

In dealing with matters relating to the prosecution and progress of a war, we must accord great respect and consideration to the judgments of the military authorities who are on the scene and who have full knowledge of the military facts. The scope of their discretion must, as a matter of necessity and common sense, be wide. And their judgments ought not to be overruled lightly by those whose training and duties ill-equip them to deal intelligently with matters so vital to the physical security of the nation.

At the same time, however, it is essential that there be definite limits to military discretion, especially where martial law has not been declared. Individuals must not be left impoverished of their constitutional rights on a plea of military necessity that has neither substance nor support. Thus, like other claims conflicting with the asserted constitutional rights of the individual, the military claim must subject itself to the judicial process of having its reasonableness determined and its conflicts with other interests reconciled. "What are the allowable limits of military discretion, and whether or not they have been overstepped in a particular case, are judicial questions." *Sterling* v. *Constantin*, 287 U.S. 378, 401.

The judicial test of whether the Government, on a plea of military necessity, can validly deprive an individual of any of his constitutional rights is whether the deprivation is reasonably related to a public danger that is so "immediate, imminent, and impending" as not to admit of delay and not to permit the intervention of ordinary constitutional processes to alleviate the danger. *United States* v. *Russell*, 13 Wall. 623, 627–8; *Mitchell* v. *Harmony*, 13 How. 115, 134–5; *Raymond* v. *Thomas*, 91 U.S. 712, 716. Civilian Exclusion Order No. 34, banishing from a prescribed area of the Pacific Coast "all persons of Japanese ancestry, both alien and non-alien," clearly does not meet that test. Being an obvious racial discrimination, the order deprives all those within its scope of the equal protection of the laws as guaranteed by the Fifth Amendment. It further deprives these individuals of their constitutional rights to live and work where they will, to establish a home where they choose and to move about freely. In excommunicating them without benefit of hearings, this order also deprives them of all their constitutional rights to procedural due process. Yet no reasonable relation to an "immediate, imminent, and impending" public danger is evident to support this racial restriction which is one of the most sweeping and complete deprivations of constitutional rights in the history of this nation in the absence of martial law.

It must be conceded that the military and naval situation in the spring of 1942 was such as to generate a very real fear of invasion of the Pacific Coast, accompanied by fears of sabotage and espionage in that area. The military command was therefore justified in adopting all reasonable means necessary to combat these dangers. In adjudging the military action taken in light of the then apparent dangers, we must not erect too high or too meticulous standards; it is necessary only that the action have some reasonable relation to the removal of the dangers of invasion, sabotage and espionage. But the exclusion, either temporarily or permanently, of all persons with Japanese blood in their veins has no such reasonable relation. And that relation is lacking because the exclusion order necessarily must rely for its reasonableness upon the assumption that *all* persons of Japanese ancestry may have a dangerous tendency to commit sabotage and espionage and to aid our Japanese enemy in other ways. It is difficult to believe that reason, logic or experience could be marshalled in support of such an assumption.

That this forced exclusion was the result in good measure of this erroneous assumption of racial guilt rather than bona fide military necessity is evidenced by the Commanding General's Final Report on the evacuation from the Pacific Coast area.[1] In it he refers to all individuals of Japanese descent as "subversive," as belonging to "an enemy race" whose "racial strains are undiluted," and as constituting "over 112,000 potential ene-

[1] Final Report, Japanese Evacuation from the West Coast, 1942, by Lt. Gen. J. L. DeWitt. This report is dated June 5, 1943, but was not made public until January, 1944.

mies . . . at large today" along the Pacific Coast.[2] In support of this blan-
ket condemnation of all persons of Japanese descent, however, no reliable
evidence is cited to show that such individuals were generally disloyal,[3] or
had generally so conducted themselves in this area as to constitute a special menace to defense installations or war industries, or had otherwise by
their behavior furnished reasonable ground for their exclusion as a group.

Justification for the exclusion is sought, instead, mainly upon questionable racial and sociological grounds not ordinarily within the realm of
expert military judgment, supplemented by certain semi-military conclusions drawn from an unwarranted use of circumstantial evidence. Individuals of Japanese ancestry are condemned because they are said to be
"a large, unassimilated, tightly knit racial group, bound to an enemy
nation by strong ties of race, culture, custom and religion."[4] They are
claimed to be given to "emperor worshipping ceremonies"[5] and to "dual
citizenship."[6] Japanese language schools and allegedly pro-Japanese organizations are cited as evidence of possible group disloyalty,[7] together
with facts as to certain persons being educated and residing at length in

[2]Further evidence of the Commanding General's attitude toward individuals of Japanese ancestry
is revealed in his voluntary testimony on April 13, 1943, in San Francisco before the House Naval
Affairs Subcommittee to Investigate Congested Areas, Part 3, pp. 739–40 (78th Cong., 1st Sess.): "I
don't want any of them [persons of Japanese ancestry] here. They are a dangerous element. There is
no way to determine their loyalty. The west coast contains too many vital installations essential to the
defense of the country to allow any Japanese on this coast. . . . The danger of the Japanese was, and
is now—if they are permitted to come back—espionage and sabotage. It makes no difference
whether he is an American citizen, he is still a Japanese. American citizenship does not necessarily
determine loyalty. . . . But we must worry about the Japanese all the time until he is wiped off the
map. Sabotage and espionage will make problems as long as he is allowed in this area. . . ."

[3]The Final Report, p. 9, casts a cloud of suspicion over the entire group by saying that "while it
was *believed* that *some* were loyal, it was known that many were not." (Italics added.)

[4]Final Report, p. vii; see also pp. 9, 17. To the extent that assimilation is a problem, it is largely
the result of certain social customs and laws of the American general public. Studies demonstrate that
persons of Japanese descent are readily susceptible to integration in our society if given the opportunity. Strong, The Second-Generation Japanese Problem (1934); Smith, Americans in Process
(1937); Mears, Resident Orientals on the American Pacific Coast (1928); Millis, The Japanese Problem in the United States (1942). The failure to accomplish an ideal status of assimilation, therefore,
cannot be charged to the refusal of these persons to become Americanized or to their loyalty to Japan.
And the retention by some persons of certain customs and religious practices of their ancestors is no
criterion of their loyalty to the United States.

[5]Final Report, pp. 10–11. No sinister correlation between the emperor worshipping activities and
disloyalty to America was shown.

[6]Final Report, p. 22. The charge of "dual citizenship" springs from a misunderstanding of the
simple fact that Japan in the past used the doctrine of *jus sanguinis*, as she had a right to do under
international law, and claimed as her citizens all persons born of Japanese nationals wherever located.
Japan has greatly modified this doctrine, however, by allowing all Japanese born in the United States
to renounce any claim of dual citizenship and by releasing her claim as to all born in the United States
after 1925. See Freeman, "Genesis, Exodus, and Leviticus: Genealogy, Evacuation, and Law," 28
Cornell L. Q. 414, 447–8, and authorities there cited; McWilliams, Prejudice, 123–4 (1944).

[7]Final Report, pp. 12–13. We have had various foreign language schools in this country for
generations without considering their existence as ground for racial discrimination. No subversive

Japan.[8] It is intimated that many of these individuals deliberately resided "adjacent to strategic points," thus enabling them "to carry into execution a tremendous program of sabotage on a mass scale should any considerable number of them have been inclined to do so."[9] The need for protective custody is also asserted. The report refers without identity to "numerous incidents of violence" as well as to other admittedly unverified or cumulative incidents. From this, plus certain other events not shown to have been connected with the Japanese Americans, it is concluded that the "situation was fraught with danger to the Japanese population itself" and that the general public "was ready to take matters into its own hands."[10] Finally, it is intimated, though not directly charged or proved, that persons of Japanese ancestry were responsible for three minor isolated shellings and bombings of the Pacific Coast area,[11] as well as for unidentified radio transmissions and night signalling.

The main reasons relied upon by those responsible for the forced evacuation, therefore, do not prove a reasonable relation between the group characteristics of Japanese Americans and the dangers of invasion, sabotage and espionage. The reasons appear, instead, to be largely an accumulation of much of the misinformation, half-truths and insinuations that for years have been directed against Japanese Americans by people with racial and economic prejudices—the same people who have been among the foremost advocates of the evacuation.[12] A military judgment based

---

activities or teachings have been shown in connection with the Japanese schools. McWilliams, Prejudice, 121–3 (1944).

[8] Final Report, pp. 13–15. Such persons constitute a very small part of the entire group and most of them belong to the Kibei movement—the actions and membership of which are well known to our Government agents.

[9] Final Report, p. 10; see also pp. vii, 9, 15–17. This insinuation, based purely upon speculation and circumstantial evidence, completely overlooks the fact that the main geographic pattern of Japanese population was fixed many years ago with reference to economic, social and soil conditions. Limited occupational outlets and social pressures encouraged their concentration near their initial points of entry on the Pacific Coast. That these points may now be near certain strategic military and industrial areas is no proof of a diabolical purpose on the part of Japanese Americans. See McWilliams, Prejudice, 119–121 (1944); House Report No. 2124 (77th Cong., 2d Sess.), 59–93.

[10] Final Report, pp. 8–9. This dangerous doctrine of protective custody, as proved by recent European history, should have absolutely no standing as an excuse for the deprivation of the rights of minority groups. See House Report No. 1911 (77th Cong., 2d Sess.) 1–2. Cf. House Report No. 2124 (77th Cong., 2d Sess.) 145–7. In this instance, moreover, there are only two minor instances of violence on record involving persons of Japanese ancestry. McWilliams, What About Our Japanese-Americans? Public Affairs Pamphlets, No. 91, p. 8 (1944).

[11] Final Report, p. 18. One of these incidents (the reputed dropping of incendiary bombs on an Oregon forest) occurred on Sept. 9, 1942—a considerable time after the Japanese Americans had been evacuated from their homes and placed in Assembly Centers. See New York Times, Sept. 15, 1942, p. 1, col. 3.

[12] Special interest groups were extremely active in applying pressure for mass evacuation. See House Report No. 2124 (77th Cong., 2d Sess.) 154–6; McWilliams, Prejudice, 126–8 (1944).

upon such racial and sociological considerations is not entitled to the great weight ordinarily given the judgments based upon strictly military considerations. Especially is this so when every charge relative to race, religion, culture, geographical location, and legal and economic status has been substantially discredited by independent studies made by experts in these matters.[13]

The military necessity which is essential to the validity of the evacuation order thus resolves itself into a few intimations that certain individuals actively aided the enemy, from which it is inferred that the entire group of Japanese Americans could not be trusted to be or remain loyal to the United States. No one denies, of course, that there were some disloyal persons of Japanese descent on the Pacific Coast who did all in their power to aid their ancestral land. Similar disloyal activities have been engaged in by many persons of German, Italian and even more pioneer stock in our country. But to infer that examples of individual disloyalty prove group disloyalty and justify discriminatory action against the entire group is to deny that under our system of law individual guilt is the sole basis for deprivation of rights. Moreover, this inference, which is at the very heart of the evacuation orders, has been used in support of the abhorrent and despicable treatment of minority groups by the dictatorial tyrannies which this nation is now pledged to destroy. To give constitutional sanction to that inference in this case, however well-intentioned may have been the military command on the Pacific Coast, is to adopt one of the cruelest of the rationales used by our enemies to destroy the dignity of the individual and to encourage and open the door to discriminatory actions against other minority groups in the passions of tomorrow.

No adequate reason is given for the failure to treat these Japanese Americans on an individual basis by holding investigations and hearings to separate the loyal from the disloyal, as was done in the case of persons of German and Italian ancestry. See House Report No. 2124 (77th Cong., 2d Sess.) 247–52. It is asserted merely that the loyalties of this group

---

Mr. Austin E. Anson, managing secretary of the Salinas Vegetable Grower-Shipper Association, has admitted that "We're charged with wanting to get rid of the Japs for selfish reasons. . . . We do. It's a question of whether the white man lives on the Pacific Coast or the brown men. They came into this valley to work, and they stayed to take over. . . . They undersell the white man in the markets. . . . They work their women and children while the white farmer has to pay wages for his help. If all the Japs were removed tomorrow, we'd never miss them in two weeks, because the white farmers can take over and produce everything the Jap grows. And we don't want them back when the war ends, either." Quoted by Taylor in his article "The People Nobody Wants," 214 Sat. Eve. Post 24, 66 (May 9, 1942).

[13] See notes 4–12, supra.

"were unknown and time was of the essence."[14] Yet nearly four months elapsed after Pearl Harbor before the first exclusion order was issued; nearly eight months went by until the last order was issued; and the last of these "subversive" persons was not actually removed until almost eleven months had elapsed. Leisure and deliberation seem to have been more of the essence than speed. And the fact that conditions were not such as to warrant a declaration of martial law adds strength to the belief that the factors of time and military necessity were not as urgent as they have been represented to be.

Moreover, there was no adequate proof that the Federal Bureau of Investigation and the military and naval intelligence services did not have the espionage and sabotage situation well in hand during this long period. Nor is there any denial of the fact that not one person of Japanese ancestry was accused or convicted of espionage or sabotage after Pearl Harbor while they were still free,[15] a fact which is some evidence of the loyalty of the vast majority of these individuals and of the effectiveness of the established methods of combatting these evils. It seems incredible that under these circumstances it would have been impossible to hold loyalty hearings for the mere 112,000 persons involved—or at least for the 70,000 American citizens—especially when a large part of this number represented children and elderly men and women.[16] Any inconvenience that may have accompanied an attempt to conform to procedural due process cannot be said to justify violations of constitutional rights of individuals.

I dissent, therefore, from this legalization of racism. Racial discrimination in any form and in any degree has no justifiable part whatever in our democratic way of life. It is unattractive in any setting but it is utterly revolting among a free people who have embraced the principles set forth in the Constitution of the United States. All residents of this nation are kin in some way by blood or culture to a foreign land. Yet they are primarily and necessarily a part of the new and distinct civilization of the United

[14]Final Report, p. vii; see also p. 18.

[15]The Final Report, p. 34, makes the amazing statement that as of February 14, 1942, "The very fact that no sabotage has taken place to date is a disturbing and confirming indication that such action will be taken." Apparently, in the minds of the military leaders, there was no way that the Japanese Americans could escape the suspicion of sabotage.

[16]During a period of six months, the 112 alien tribunals or hearing boards set up by the British Government shortly after the outbreak of the present war summoned and examined approximately 74,000 German and Austrian aliens. These tribunals determined whether each individual enemy alien was a real enemy of the Allies or only a "friendly enemy." About 64,000 were freed from internment and from any special restrictions, and only 2,000 were interned. Kempner, "The Enemy Alien Problem in the Present War," 34 Amer. Journ. of Int. Law 443, 444–46; House Report No. 2124 (77th Cong., 2d Sess.), 280–1.

States. They must accordingly be treated at all times as the heirs of the American experiment and as entitled to all the rights and freedoms guaranteed by the Constitution.

Mr. Justice Jackson, Dissenting

Korematsu was born on our soil, of parents born in Japan. The Constitution makes him a citizen of the United States by nativity and a citizen of California by residence. No claim is made that he is not loyal to this country. There is no suggestion that apart from the matter involved here he is not law-abiding and well disposed. Korematsu, however, has been convicted of an act not commonly a crime. It consists merely of being present in the state whereof he is a citizen, near the place where he was born, and where all his life he has lived.

Even more unusual is the series of military orders which made this conduct a crime. They forbid such a one to remain, and they also forbid him to leave. They were so drawn that the only way Korematsu could avoid violation was to give himself up to the military authority. This meant submission to custody, examination, and transportation out of the territory, to be followed by immediate confinement in detention camps.

A citizen's presence in the locality, however, was made a crime only if his parents were of Japanese birth. Had Korematsu been one of four—the others being, say, a German alien enemy, an Italian alien enemy, and a citizen of American-born ancestors, convicted of treason but out on parole—only Korematsu's presence would have violated the order. The difference between their innocence and his crime would result, not from anything he did, said, or thought, different than they, but only in that he was born of different racial stock.

Now, if any fundamental assumption underlies our system, it is that guilt is personal and not inheritable. Even if all of one's antecedents had been convicted of treason, the Constitution forbids its penalties to be visited upon him, for it provides that "no attainder of treason shall work corruption of blood, or forfeiture except during the life of the person attainted." But here is an attempt to make an otherwise innocent act a crime merely because this prisoner is the son of parents as to whom he had no choice, and belongs to a race from which there is no way to resign. If Congress in peace-time legislation should enact such a criminal law, I should suppose this Court would refuse to enforce it.

But the "law" which this prisoner is convicted of disregarding is not found in an act of Congress, but in a military order. Neither the Act of Congress nor the Executive Order of the President, nor both together, would afford a basis for this conviction. It rests on the orders of General DeWitt. And it is said that if the military commander had reasonable military grounds for promulgating the orders, they are constitutional and become law, and the Court is required to enforce them. There are several reasons why I cannot subscribe to this doctrine.

It would be impracticable and dangerous idealism to expect or insist that each specific military command in an area of probable operations will conform to conventional tests of constitutionality. When an area is so beset that it must be put under military control at all, the paramount consideration is that its measures be successful, rather than legal. The armed services must protect a society, not merely its Constitution. The very essence of the military job is to marshal physical force, to remove every obstacle to its effectiveness, to give it every strategic advantage. Defense measures will not, and often should not, be held within the limits that bind civil authority in peace. No court can require such a commander in such circumstances to act as a reasonable man; he may be unreasonably cautious and exacting. Perhaps he should be. But a commander in temporarily focusing the life of a community on defense is carrying out a military program; he is not making law in the sense the courts know the term. He issues orders, and they may have a certain authority as military commands, although they may be very bad as constitutional law.

But if we cannot confine military expedients by the Constitution, neither would I distort the Constitution to approve all that the military may deem expedient. That is what the Court appears to be doing, whether consciously or not. I cannot say, from any evidence before me, that the orders of General DeWitt were not reasonably expedient military precautions, nor could I say that they were. But even if they were permissible military procedures, I deny that it follows that they are constitutional. If, as the Court holds, it does follow, then we may as well say that any military order will be constitutional and have done with it.

The limitation under which courts always will labor in examining the necessity for a military order are illustrated by this case. How does the Court know that these orders have a reasonable basis in necessity? No evidence whatever on that subject has been taken by this or any other court. There is sharp controversy as to the credibility of the DeWitt report. So the Court, having no real evidence before it, has no choice but to accept General DeWitt's own unsworn, self-serving statement, untested by any cross-examination, that what he did was reasonable. And thus it will always be when courts try to look into the reasonableness of a military order.

In the very nature of things, military decisions are not susceptible of intelligent judicial appraisal. They do not pretend to rest on evidence, but are made on information that often would not be admissible and on assumptions that could not be proved. Information in support of an order could not be disclosed to courts without danger that it would reach the enemy. Neither can courts act on communications made in confidence. Hence courts can never have any real alternative to accepting the mere declaration of the authority that issued the order that it was reasonably necessary from a military viewpoint.

Much is said of the danger to liberty from the Army program for deporting and detaining these citizens of Japanese extraction. But a judicial construction of the due process clause that will sustain this order is a far more subtle blow to liberty than the promulgation of the order itself. A military order, however unconstitutional, is not apt to last longer than the military emergency. Even during that period a succeeding commander may revoke it all. But once a judicial opinion rationalizes such an order to show that it conforms to the Constitution, or rather rationalizes the Constitution to show that the Constitution sanctions such an order, the Court for all time has validated the principle of racial discrimination in criminal procedure and of transplanting American citizens. The principle then lies about like a loaded weapon ready for the hand of any authority that can bring forward a plausible claim of an urgent need. Every repetition imbeds that principle more deeply in our law and thinking and expands it to new purposes. All who observe the work of courts are familiar with what Judge Cardozo described as "the tendency of a principle to expand itself to the limit of its logic." [1] A military commander may overstep the bounds of constitutionality, and it is an incident. But if we review and approve, that passing incident becomes the doctrine of the Constitution. There it has a generative power of its own, and all that it creates will be in its own image. Nothing better illustrates this danger than does the Court's opinion in this case.

It argues that we are bound to uphold the conviction of Korematsu because we upheld one in *Hirabayashi* v. *United States*, 320 U.S. 81, when we sustained these orders in so far as they applied a curfew require-

---

[1] Nature of the Judicial Process, p. 51.

ment to a citizen of Japanese ancestry. I think we should learn something from that experience.

In that case we were urged to consider only the curfew feature, that being all that technically was involved, because it was the only count necessary to sustain Hirabayashi's conviction and sentence. We yielded, and the Chief Justice guarded the opinion as carefully as language will do. He said: "Our investigation here does not go beyond the inquiry whether, in the light of all the relevant circumstances preceding and attending their promulgation, the challenged orders and statute *afforded a reasonable basis for the action taken in imposing the curfew*." 320 U.S. at 101. "We decide only the issue as we have defined it—we decide only that the *curfew order* as applied, and at the time it was applied, was within the boundaries of the war power." 320 U.S. at 102. And again: "It is unnecessary to consider whether or to what extent *such findings would support orders differing from the curfew order*." 320 U.S. at 105. (Italics supplied.) However, in spite of our limiting words we did validate a discrimination on the basis of ancestry for mild and temporary deprivation of liberty. Now the principle of racial discrimination is pushed from support of mild measures to very harsh ones, and from temporary deprivations to indeterminate ones. And the precedent which it is said requires us to do so is *Hirabayashi*. The Court is now saying that in *Hirabayashi* we did decide the very things we there said we were not deciding. Because we said that these citizens could be made to stay in their homes during the hours of dark, it is said we must require them to leave home entirely; and if that, we are told they may also be taken into custody for deportation; and if that, it is argued they may also be held for some undetermined time in detention camps. How far the principle of this case would be extended before plausible reasons would play out, I do not know.

I should hold that a civil court cannot be made to enforce an order which violates constitutional limitations even if it is a reasonable exercise of military authority. The courts can exercise only the judicial power, can apply only law, and must abide by the Constitution, or they cease to be civil courts and become instruments of military policy.

Of course the existence of a military power resting on force, so vagrant, so centralized, so necessarily heedless of the individual, is an inherent threat to liberty. But I would not lead people to rely on this Court for a review that seems to me wholly delusive. The military reasonableness of these orders can only be determined by military superiors. If the people ever let command of the war power fall into irresponsible and unscrupulous hands, the courts wield no power equal to its restraint. The chief restraint upon those who command the physical forces of the country, in the future as in the past, must be their responsibility to the political judgments of their contemporaries and to the moral judgments of history.

My duties as a justice as I see them do not require me to make a military judgment as to whether General DeWitt's evacuation and detention program was a reasonable military necessity. I do not suggest that the courts should have attempted to interfere with the Army in carrying out its task. But I do not think they may be asked to execute a military expedient that has no place in law under the Constitution. I would reverse the judgment and discharge the prisoner.

II

"A Grave Injustice"
1942 - 1982

Personal Justice Denied

Summary of Report of the Commission on Wartime
Relocation and Internment of Civilians, Washington, D.C.

December 1982

*Survivors of the internment camps kept their feelings of shame and anger
bottled up for years, but in the 1970s they finally ended the "silent years"
and began a campaign for redress and reparations. Early efforts to secure monetary compensation from Congress aroused opposition from
more cautious elements in the Japanese American community. Their tack,
to secure congressional approval of a study commission, succeeded in
1980 with establishment of the Commission on Wartime Relocation and
Internment of Civilians. This nine-member body included present and
former members of Congress, the Supreme Court, and the Cabinet. More
than 750 witnesses appeared before the commission, and its staff secured
and reviewed thousands of government documents. In a 467-page report
dated December 1982 but issued in February 1983, the commissioners
agreed unanimously that the internment had imposed a "grave injustice"
on Japanese Americans; all but one supported the recommendation that
Congress provide compensation of $20,000 for each survivor of the in-
ternment camps.*

Summary

The Commission on Wartime Relocation and Internment of Civilians
was established by act of Congress in 1980 and directed to

1. review the facts and circumstances surrounding Executive Order
Numbered 9066, issued February 19, 1942, and the impact of such
Executive Order on American citizens and permanent resident aliens;
2. review directives of United States military forces requiring the relocation and, in some cases, detention in internment camps of American

citizens, including Aleut civilians, and permanent resident aliens of the Aleutian and Pribilof Islands; and

3. recommend appropriate remedies.

In fulfilling this mandate, the Commission held 20 days of hearings in cities across the country, particularly on the West Coast, hearing testimony from more than 750 witnesses: evacuees, former government officials, public figures, interested citizens, and historians and other professionals who have studied the subjects of Commission inquiry. An extensive effort was made to locate and to review the records of government action and to analyze other sources of information including contemporary writings, personal accounts and historical analyses.

By presenting this report to Congress, the Commission fulfills the instruction to submit a written report of its findings. Like the body of the report, this summary is divided into two parts. The first describes actions taken pursuant to Executive Order 9066, particularly the treatment of American citizens of Japanese descent and resident aliens of Japanese nationality. The second covers the treatment of Aleuts from the Aleutian and Pribilof Islands.

Part I: Nisei and Issei*

On February 19, 1942, ten weeks after the Pearl Harbor attack, President Franklin D. Roosevelt signed Executive Order 9066, which gave to the Secretary of War and the military commanders to whom he delegated authority, the power to exclude any and all persons, citizens and aliens, from designated areas in order to provide security against sabotage, espionage and fifth column activity. Shortly thereafter, all American citizens of Japanese descent were prohibited from living, working or traveling on the West Coast of the United States. The same prohibition applied to the generation of Japanese immigrants who, pursuant to federal law and despite long residence in the United States, were not permitted to become American citizens. Initially, this exclusion was to be carried out by "voluntary" relocation. That policy inevitably failed, and these American citizens and their alien parents were removed by the Army, first to "assembly centers"—temporary quarters at racetracks and fairgrounds—

---

*The first generation of ethnic Japanese born in the United States are *Nisei*; the *Issei* are the immigrant generation from Japan; and those who returned to Japan as children for education are *Kibei*.

and then to "relocation centers"—bleak barrack camps mostly in desolate areas of the West. The camps were surrounded by barbed wire and guarded by military police. Departure was permitted only after a loyalty review on terms set, in consultation with the military, by the War Relocation Authority, the civilian agency that ran the camps. Many of those removed from the West Coast were eventually allowed to leave the camps to join the Army, go to college outside the West Coast or to whatever private employment was available. For a larger number, however, the war years were spent behind barbed wire; and for those who were released, the prohibition against returning to their homes and occupations on the West Coast was not lifted until December 1944.

This policy of exclusion, removal and detention was executed against 120,000 people without individual review, and exclusion was continued virtually without regard for their demonstrated loyalty to the United States. Congress was fully aware of and supported the policy of removal and detention; it sanctioned the exclusion by enacting a statute which made criminal the violation of orders issued pursuant to Executive Order 9066. The United States Supreme Court held the exclusion constitutionally permissible in the context of war, but struck down the incarceration of admittedly loyal American citizens on the ground that it was not based on statutory authority.

All this was done despite the fact that not a single documented act of espionage, sabotage or fifth column activity was committed by an American citizen of Japanese ancestry or by a resident Japanese alien on the West Coast.

No mass exclusion or detention, in any part of the country, was ordered against American citizens of German or Italian descent. Official actions against enemy aliens of other nationalities were much more individualized and selective than those imposed on the ethnic Japanese.

The exclusion, removal and detention inflicted tremendous human cost. There was the obvious cost of homes and businesses sold or abandoned under circumstances of great distress, as well as injury to careers and professional advancement. But, most important, there was the loss of liberty and the personal stigma of suspected disloyalty for thousands of people who knew themselves to be devoted to their country's cause and to its ideals but whose repeated protestations of loyalty were discounted—only to be demonstrated beyond any doubt by the record of Nisei soldiers, who returned from the battlefields of Europe as the most decorated and distinguished combat unit of World War II, and by the thousands of other Nisei who served against the enemy in the Pacific, mostly in military intelligence. The wounds of the exclusion and detention have healed in some respects, but the scars of that experience remain, painfully real in the minds of those who lived through the suffering and deprivation of the camps.

The personal injustice of excluding, removing and detaining loyal American citizens is manifest. Such events are extraordinary and unique in American history. For every citizen and for American public life, they pose haunting questions about our country and its past. It has been the Commission's task to examine the central decisions of this history—the decision to exclude, the decision to detain, the decision to release from detention and the decision to end exclusion. The Commission has analyzed both how and why those decisions were made, and what their consequences were. And in order to illuminate those events, the mainland experience was compared to the treatment of Japanese Americans in Hawaii and to the experience of other Americans of enemy alien descent, particularly German Americans.

The Decision to Exclude

The context of the decision. First, the exclusion and removal were attacks on the ethnic Japanese which followed a long and ugly history of West Coast anti-Japanese agitation and legislation. Antipathy and hostility toward the ethnic Japanese was a major factor of the public life of the West Coast states for more than forty years before Pearl Harbor. Under pressure from California, immigration from Japan had been severely restricted in 1908 and entirely prohibited in 1924. Japanese immigrants were barred from American citizenship, although their children born here were citizens by birth. California and the other western states prohibited Japanese immigrants from owning land. In part the hostility was economic, emerging in various white American groups who began to feel competition, particularly in agriculture, the principal occupation of the immigrants. The anti-Japanese agitation also fed on racial stereotypes and fears: the "yellow peril" of an unknown Asian culture achieving substantial influence on the Pacific Coast or of a Japanese population alleged to be growing far faster than the white population. This agitation and hostility persisted, even though the ethnic Japanese never exceeded three percent of the population of California, the state of greatest concentration.

The ethnic Japanese, small in number and with no political voice—the citizen generation was just reaching voting age in 1940—had become a convenient target for political demagogues, and over the years all the major parties indulged in anti-Japanese rhetoric and programs. Political bullying was supported by organized interest groups who adopted anti-Japanese agitation as a consistent part of their program: the Native Sons and Daughters of the Golden West, the Joint Immigration Committee, the American Legion, the California State Federation of Labor and the California State Grange.

This agitation attacked a number of ethnic Japanese cultural traits or patterns which were woven into a bogus theory that the ethnic Japanese could not or would not assimilate or become "American." Dual citizenship, Shinto, Japanese language schools, and the education of many ethnic Japanese children in Japan were all used as evidence. But as a matter of fact, Japan's laws on dual citizenship went no further than those of many European countries in claiming the allegiance of the children of its nationals born abroad. Only a small number of ethnic Japanese subscribed to Shinto, which in some forms included veneration of the Emperor. The language schools were not unlike those of other first-generation immigrants, and the return of some children to Japan for education was as much a reaction to hostile discrimination and an uncertain future as it was a commitment to the mores, much less the political doctrines, of Japan. Nevertheless, in 1942 these popular misconceptions infected the views of a great many West Coast people who viewed the ethnic Japanese as alien and unassimilated.

Second, Japanese armies in the Pacific won a rapid, startling string of victories against the United States and its allies in the first months of World War II. On the same day as the attack on Pearl Harbor, the Japanese struck the Malay Peninsula, Hong Kong, Wake and Midway Islands and attacked the Philippines. The next day the Japanese Army invaded Thailand. On December 13 Guam fell; on December 24 and 25 the Japanese captured Wake Island and occupied Hong Kong. Manila was evacuated on December 27, and the American army retreated to the Bataan Peninsula. After three months the troops isolated in the Philippines were forced to surrender unconditionally—the worst American defeat since the Civil War. In January and February 1942, the military position of the United States in the Pacific was perilous. There was fear of Japanese attacks on the West Coast.

Next, contrary to the facts, there was a widespread belief, supported by a statement by Frank Knox, Secretary of the Navy, that the Pearl Harbor attack had been aided by sabotage and fifth column activity by ethnic Japanese in Hawaii. Shortly after Pearl Harbor the government knew that this was not true, but took no effective measures to disabuse public belief that disloyalty had contributed to massive American losses on December 7, 1941. Thus the country was unfairly led to believe that both American citizens of Japanese descent and resident Japanese aliens threatened American security.

Fourth, as anti-Japanese organizations began to speak out and rumors from Hawaii spread, West Coast politicians quickly took up the familiar anti-Japanese cry. The Congressional delegations in Washington organized themselves and pressed the War and Justice Departments and the President for stern measures to control the ethnic Japanese—moving quickly from control of aliens to evacuation and removal of citizens. In California, Governor Olson, Attorney General Warren, Mayor Bowron of Los Angeles and many local authorities joined the clamor. These opinions were not informed by any knowledge of actual military risks, rather they were stoked by virulent agitation which encountered little opposition. Only a few churchmen and academicians were prepared to defend the ethnic Japanese. There was little or no political risk in claiming that it was "better to be safe than sorry" and, as many did, that the best way for ethnic Japanese to prove their loyalty was to volunteer to enter detention. The press amplified the unreflective emotional excitement of the hour. Through late January and early February 1942, the rising clamor from the West Coast was heard within the federal government and its demands became more draconian.

Making and justifying the decision. The exclusion of the ethnic Japanese from the West Coast was recommended to the Secretary of War, Henry L. Stimson, by Lieutenant General John L. DeWitt, Commanding General of the Western Defense Command with responsibility for West Coast security. President Roosevelt relied on Secretary Stimson's recommendations in issuing Executive Order 9066.

The justification given for the measure was military necessity. The claim of military necessity is most clearly set out in three places: General DeWitt's February 14, 1942, recommendation to Secretary Stimson for exclusion; General DeWitt's *Final Report: Japanese Evacuation from the West Coast, 1942*; and the government's brief in the Supreme Court defending the Executive Order in *Hirabayashi* v. *United States*. General DeWitt's February 1942 recommendation presented the following rationale for the exclusion:

In the war in which we are now engaged racial affinities are not severed by migration. The Japanese race is an enemy race and while many second and third generation Japanese born on United States soil, possessed of United States citizenship, have become "Americanized," the racial strains are undiluted. To conclude otherwise is to expect that children born of white parents on Japanese soil sever all racial affinity and become loyal Japanese subjects, ready to fight and, if necessary, to die for Japan in a war against the nation of their parents. That Japan is allied with Germany and Italy in this struggle is no ground for assuming that any Japanese, barred from assimilation by convention as he is, though born and raised in the United States, will not turn against this nation when the final test of loyalty comes. It, therefore, follows that along the vital Pacific Coast over 112,000 potential enemies, of Japanese extraction, are at large today. There are indications that these were organized and ready for concerted action at a favorable opportunity. The very fact that no sabotage has taken place to date is a disturbing and confirming indication that such action will be taken.

There are two unfounded justifications for exclusion expressed here: first, that ethnicity ultimately determines loyalty; second, that "indications" suggest that ethnic Japanese "are organized and ready for concerted action"—the best argument for this being the fact that it hadn't happened.

The first evaluation is not a military one but one for sociologists or historians. It runs counter to a basic premise on which the American nation of immigrants is built—that loyalty to the United States is a matter of individual choice and not determined by ties to an ancestral country. In the case of German Americans, the First World War demonstrated that race did not determine loyalty, and no negative assumption was made with regard to citizens of German or Italian descent during the Second World War. The second judgment was, by the General's own admission, unsupported by any evidence. General DeWitt's recommendation clearly does not provide a credible rationale, based on military expertise, for the necessity of exclusion.

In his 1943 *Final Report*, General DeWitt cited a number of factors in support of the exclusion decision: signaling from shore to enemy submarines; arms and contraband found by the FBI during raids on ethnic Japanese homes and businesses; dangers to the ethnic Japanese from vigilantes; concentration of ethnic Japanese around or near militarily sensitive areas; the number of Japanese ethnic organizations on the coast which might shelter pro-Japanese attitudes or activities such as Emperor-worshipping Shinto; and the presence of the Kibei, who had spent some time in Japan.

The first two items point to demonstrable military danger. But the reports of shore-to-ship signaling were investigated by the Federal Communications Commission, the agency with relevant expertise, and no identifiable cases of such signaling were substantiated. The FBI did confiscate arms and contraband from some ethnic Japanese, but most were items normally in the possession of any law-abiding civilian, and the FBI concluded that these searches had uncovered no dangerous persons that "we could not otherwise know about." Thus neither of these "facts" militarily justified exclusion.

There had been some acts of violence against ethnic Japanese on the West Coast and feeling against them ran high, but "protective custody" is not an acceptable rationale for exclusion. Protection against vigilantes is a civilian matter that would involve the military only in extreme cases. But there is no evidence that such extremity had been reached on the West Coast in early 1942. Moreover, "protective custody" could never justify exclusion and detention for months and years.

General DeWitt's remaining points are repeated in the *Hirabayashi* brief, which also emphasizes dual nationality, Japanese language schools and the high percentage of aliens (who, by law, had been barred from acquiring American citizenship) in the ethnic population. These facts represent broad social judgments of little or no military significance in themselves. None supports the claim of disloyalty to the United States and all were entirely legal. If the same standards were applied to other ethnic groups, as Morton Grodzins, an early analyst of the exclusion decision, applied it to ethnic Italians on the West Coast, an equally compelling and meaningless case for "disloyalty" could be made. In short, these social and cultural patterns were not evidence of any threat to West Coast military security.

In sum, the record does not permit the conclusion that military necessity warranted the exclusion of ethnic Japanese from the West Coast.

The conditions which permitted the decision. Having concluded that no military necessity supported the exclusion, the Commission has attempted to determine how the decision came to be made.

First, General DeWitt apparently believed what he told Secretary Stimson: ethnicity determined loyalty. Moreover, he believed that the ethnic Japanese were so alien to the thought processes of white Americans that it was impossible to distinguish the loyal from the disloyal. On this basis he believed them to be potential enemies among whom loyalty could not be determined.

Second, the FBI and members of Naval Intelligence who had relevant intelligence responsibility were ignored when they stated that nothing more than careful watching of suspicious individuals or individual reviews of loyalty were called for by existing circumstances. In addition, the opinions of the Army General Staff that no sustained Japanese attack on the West Coast was possible were ignored.

Third, General DeWitt relied heavily on civilian politicians rather than informed military judgments in reaching his conclusions as to what actions were necessary, and civilian politicians largely repeated the prejudiced, unfounded themes of anti-Japanese factions and interest groups on the West Coast.

Fourth, no effective measures were taken by President Roosevelt to calm the West Coast public and refute the rumors of sabotage and fifth column activity at Pearl Harbor.

Fifth, General DeWitt was temperamentally disposed to exaggerate the measures necessary to maintain security and placed security far ahead of any concern for the liberty of citizens.

Sixth, Secretary Stimson and John J. McCloy, Assistant Secretary of War, both of whose views on race differed from those of General DeWitt, failed to insist on a clear military justification for the measures General DeWitt wished to undertake.

Seventh, Attorney General Francis Biddle, while contending that exclusion was unnecessary, did not argue to the President that failure to make out a case of military necessity on the facts would render the exclusion constitutionally impermissible or that the Constitution prohibited exclusion on the basis of ethnicity given the facts on the West Coast.

Eighth, those representing the interests of civil rights and civil liberties in Congress, the press and other public forums were silent or indeed supported exclusion. Thus there was no effective opposition to the measures vociferously sought by numerous West Coast interest groups, politicians and journalists.

Finally, President Roosevelt, without raising the question to the level of Cabinet discussion or requiring any careful or thorough review of the situation, and despite the Attorney General's arguments and other information before him, agreed with Secretary Stimson that the exclusion should be carried out.

The Decision to Detain

With the signing of Executive Order 9066, the course of the President and the War Department was set: American citizens and alien residents of Japanese ancestry would be compelled to leave the West Coast on the basis of wartime military necessity. For the War Department and the Western Defense Command, the problem became primarily one of method and operation, not basic policy. General DeWitt first tried "voluntary" resettlement: the ethnic Japanese were to move outside the restricted military zones of the West Coast but otherwise were free to go wherever they chose. From a military standpoint this policy was bizarre, and it was utterly impractical. If the ethnic Japanese had been excluded because they were potential saboteurs and spies, any such danger was not extinguished by leaving them at large in the interior where there were, of course, innumerable dams, power lines, bridges and war industries to be disrupted or spied upon. Conceivably sabotage in the interior could be synchronized with a Japanese raid or invasion for a powerful fifth column effect. This raises serious doubts as to how grave the War Department believed the supposed threat to be. Indeed, the implications were not lost on the citizens and politicians of the interior western states, who objected in the belief that people who threatened wartime security in California were equally dangerous in Wyoming and Idaho.

The War Relocation Authority (WRA), the civilian agency created by the President to supervise the relocation and initially directed by Milton Eisenhower, proceeded on the premise that the vast majority of evacuees were law-abiding and loyal, and that, once off the West Coast, they should be returned quickly to conditions approximating normal life. This view was strenuously opposed by the people and politicians of the mountain states. In April 1942, Milton Eisenhower met with the governors and officials of the mountain states. They objected to California using the interior states as a "dumping ground" for a California "problem." They argued that people in their states were so bitter over the voluntary evacuation that unguarded evacuees would face physical danger. They wanted guarantees that the government would forbid evacuees to acquire land and that it would remove them at the end of the war. Again and again, detention camps for evacuees were urged. The consensus was that a plan for reception centers was acceptable so long as the evacuees remained under guard within the centers.

In the circumstances, Milton Eisenhower decided that the plan to move the evacuees into private employment would be abandoned, at least temporarily. The War Relocation Authority dropped resettlement and adopted confinement. Notwithstanding WRA's belief that evacuees should be returned to normal productive life, it had, in effect, become their jailer. The politicians of the interior states had achieved the program of detention.

The evacuees were to be held in camps behind barbed wire and released only with government approval. For this course of action no military justification was proffered. Instead, the WRA contended that these steps were necessary for the benefit of evacuees and that controls on their departure were designed to assure they would not be mistreated by other Americans on leaving the camps.

It follows from the conclusion that there was no justification in military necessity for the exclusion, that there was no basis for the detention.

The Effect of the Exclusion and Detention

The history of the relocation camps and the assembly centers that preceded them is one of suffering and deprivation visited on people against whom no charges were, or could have been, brought. The Commission hearing record is full of poignant, searing testimony that recounts the economic and personal losses and injury caused by the exclusion and the deprivations of detention. No summary can do this testimony justice.

Families could take to the assembly centers and the camps only what they could carry. Camp living conditions were Spartan. People were housed in tar-papered barrack rooms of no more than 20 by 24 feet. Each room housed a family, regardless of family size. Construction was often shoddy. Privacy was practically impossible and furnishings were minimal. Eating and bathing were in mass facilities. Under continuing pressure from those who blindly held to the belief that evacuees harbored disloyal intentions, the wages paid for work at the camps were kept to the minimal level of $12 a month for unskilled labor, rising to $19 a month for professional employees. Mass living prevented normal family communication and activities. Heads of families, no longer providing food and shelter, found their authority to lead and to discipline diminished.

The normal functions of community life continued but almost always under a handicap—doctors were in short supply; schools which taught typing had no typewriters and worked from hand-me-down school books; there were not enough jobs.

The camp experience carried a stigma that no other Americans suffered. The evacuees themselves expressed the indignity of their conditions with particular power:

On May 16, 1942, my mother, two sisters, niece, nephew, and I left . . . by train. Father joined us later. Brother left earlier by bus. We took whatever we could carry. So much we left behind, but the most valuable thing I lost was my freedom.

Henry went to the Control Station to register the family. He came home with twenty tags, all numbered 10710, tags to be attached to each piece of baggage, and one to hang from our coat lapels. From then on, we were known as Family #10710.

The government's efforts to "Americanize" the children in the camps were bitterly ironic:

An oft-repeated ritual in relocation camp schools . . . was the salute to the flag followed by the singing of "My country, 'tis of thee, sweet land of liberty"—a ceremony Caucasian teachers found embarrassingly awkward if not cruelly poignant in the austere prison-camp setting.

In some ways, I suppose, my life was not too different from a lot of kids in America between the years 1942 and 1945. I spent a good part of my time playing with my brothers and friends, learned to shoot marbles, watched sandlot baseball and envied the older kids who wore Boy Scout uniforms. We shared with the rest of America the same movies, screen heroes and listened to the same heart-rending songs of the forties. We imported much of America into the camps because, after all, we were Americans. Through imitation of my brothers, who attended grade school within the camp, I learned the salute to the flag by the time I was five years old. I was learning, as best one could learn in Manzanar, what it meant to live in America. But, I was also learning the sometimes bitter price one has to pay for it.

After the war, through the Japanese American Evacuation Claims Act, the government attempted to compensate for the losses of real and personal property; inevitably that effort did not secure full or fair compensation. There were many kinds of injury the Evacuation Claims Act made no attempt to compensate: the stigma placed on people who fell under the exclusion and relocation orders; the deprivation of liberty suffered during detention; the psychological impact of exclusion and relocation; the breakdown of family structure; the loss of earnings or profits; physical injury or illness during detention.

The Decision to End Detention

By October 1942, the government held over 100,000 evacuees in relocation camps. After the tide of war turned with the American victory at Midway in June 1942, the possibility of serious Japanese attack was no longer credible; detention and exclusion became increasingly difficult to defend. Nevertheless, other than an ineffective leave program run by the War Relocation Authority, the government had no plans to remedy the situation and no means of distinguishing the loyal from the disloyal. Total control of these civilians in the presumed interest of state security was rapidly becoming the accepted norm.

Determining the basis on which detention would be ended required the government to focus on the justification for controlling the ethnic Japanese. If the government took the position that race determined loyalty or that it was impossible to distinguish the loyal from the disloyal because "Japanese" patterns of thought and behavior were too alien to white Americans, there would be little incentive to end detention. If the government maintained the position that distinguishing the loyal from the disloyal was possible and that exclusion and detention were required only by the necessity of acting quickly under the threat of Japanese attack in early 1942, then a program to release those considered loyal should have been instituted in the spring of 1942 when people were confined in the assembly centers.

Neither position totally prevailed. General DeWitt and the Western Defense Command took the first position and opposed any review that would determine loyalty or threaten continued exclusion from the West Coast. Thus, there was no loyalty review during the assembly center period. Secretary Stimson and Assistant Secretary McCloy took the second view, but did not act on it until the end of 1942 and then only in a limited manner. At the end of 1942, over General DeWitt's opposition, Secretary Stimson, Assistant Secretary McCloy and General George C. Marshall, Chief of Staff, decided to establish a volunteer combat team of Nisei soldiers. The volunteers were to come from those who had passed a loyalty review. To avoid the obvious unfairness of allowing only those joining the military to establish their loyalty and leave the camps, the War Department joined WRA in expanding the loyalty review program to all adult evacuees.

This program was significant, but remained a compromise. It provided an opportunity to demonstrate loyalty to the United States on the battlefields; despite the human sacrifice involved, this was of immense practical importance in obtaining postwar acceptance for the ethnic Japanese. It opened the gates of the camps for some and began some reestablishment of normal life. But, with no apparent rationale or justification, it did not end exclusion of the loyal from the West Coast. The review program did not extend the presumption of loyalty to American citizens of Japanese descent, who were subject to an investigation and review not applied to other ethnic groups.

Equally important, although the loyalty review program was the first major government decision in which the interests of evacuees prevailed, the program was conducted so insensitively, with such lack of understanding of the evacuees' circumstances, that it became one of the most divisive and wrenching episodes of the camp detention.

After almost a year of what the evacuees considered utterly unjust treatment at the hands of the government, the loyalty review program began with filling out a questionnaire which posed two questions requiring declarations of complete loyalty to the United States. Thus, the questionnaire demanded a personal expression of position from each evacuee—a choice between faith in one's future in America and outrage at present injustice. Understandably most evacuees probably had deeply ambiguous feelings about a government whose rhetorical values of liberty and equality they wished to believe, but who found their present treatment in painful contradiction to those values. The loyalty questionnaire left little room to express that ambiguity. Indeed, it provided an effective point of protest and organization against the government, from which more and more evacuees felt alienated. The questionnaire finally addressed the central question of loyalty that underlay the exclusion policy, a question which had been the predominant political and personal issue for the ethnic Japanese over the past year; answering it required confronting the conflicting emotions aroused by their relation to the government. Evacuee testimony shows the intensity of conflicting emotions:

I answered both questions number 27 and 28 [the loyalty questions] in the negative, not because of disloyalty but due to the disgusting and shabby treatment given us. A few months after completing the questionnaire, U.S. Army officers appeared at our camp and gave us an interview to confirm our answers to the questions 27 and 28, and followed up with a question that in essence asked: "Are you going to give up or renounce your U.S. citizenship?" to which I promptly replied in the affirmative as a rebellious move. Sometime after the interview, a form letter from the Immigration and Naturalization Service arrived saying if I wanted to renounce my U.S. citizenship, sign the form letter and return. Well, I kept the Immigration and Naturalization Service waiting.

Well, I am one of those that said "no, no" on it, one of the "no, no" boys, and it is not that I was proud about it, it was just that our legal rights were violated and I wanted to fight back. However, I didn't want to take this sitting down. I was really angry. It just got me so damned mad. Whatever we do, there was no help from outside, and it seems to me that we are a race that doesn't count. So therefore, this was one of the reasons for the "no, no" answer.

Personal responses to the questionnaire inescapably became public acts open to community debate and scrutiny within the closed world of the camps. This made difficult choices excruciating:

After I volunteered for the [military] service, some people that I knew refused to speak to me. Some older people later questioned my father for letting me volunteer, but he told them that I was old enough to make up my own mind.

The resulting infighting, beatings, and verbal abuses left families torn apart, parents against children, brothers against sisters, relatives against relatives, and friends against friends. So bitter was all this that even to this day, there are many amongst us who do not speak about that period for fear that the same harsh feelings might arise up again to the surface.

The loyalty review program was a point of decision and division for those in the camps. The avowedly loyal were eligible for release; those who were unwilling to profess loyalty or whom the government distrusted were segregated from the main body of evacuees into the Tule Lake camp, which rapidly became a center of disaffection and protest against the government and its policies—the unhappy refuge of evacuees consumed by anger and despair.

The Decision to End Exclusion

The loyalty review should logically have led to the conclusion that no justification existed for excluding loyal American citizens from the West Coast. Secretary Stimson, Assistant Secretary McCloy and General Marshall reached this position in the spring of 1943. Nevertheless, the exclusion was not ended until December 1944. No plausible reason connected to any wartime security has been offered for this eighteen to twenty month delay in allowing the ethnic Japanese to return to their homes, jobs and businesses on the West Coast, despite the fact that the delay meant, as a practical matter, that confinement in the relocation camps continued for the great majority of evacuees for another year and a half.

Between May 1943 and May 1944, War Department officials did not make public their opinion that exclusion of loyal ethnic Japanese from the West Coast no longer had any military justification. If the President was unaware of this view, the plausible explanation is that Secretary Stimson and Assistant Secretary McCloy were unwilling, or believed themselves unable, to face down political opposition on the West Coast. General DeWitt repeatedly expressed opposition until he left the Western Defense Command in the fall of 1943, as did West Coast anti-Japanese factions and politicians.

In May 1944 Secretary Stimson put before President Roosevelt and the Cabinet his position that the exclusion no longer had a military justification. But the President was unwilling to act to end the exclusion until the first Cabinet meeting following the Presidential election of November 1944. The inescapable conclusion from this factual pattern is that the delay was motivated by political considerations.

By the participants' own accounts, there is no rational explanation for maintaining the exclusion of loyal ethnic Japanese from the West Coast for the eighteen months after May 1943—except political pressure and fear. Certainly there was no justification arising out of military necessity.

The Comparisons

To either side of the Commission's account of the exclusion, removal and detention, there is a version argued by various witnesses that makes a radically different analysis of the events. Some contend that, forty years later, we cannot recreate the atmosphere and events of 1942 and that the extreme measures taken then were solely to protect the nation's safety when there was no reasonable alternative. Others see in these events only the animus of racial hatred directed toward people whose skin was not white. Events in Hawaii in World War II and the historical treatment of Germans and German Americans shows that neither analysis is satisfactory.

Hawaii. When Japan attacked Pearl Harbor, nearly 158,000 persons of Japanese ancestry lived in Hawaii—more than 35 percent of the population. Surely, if there were dangers from espionage, sabotage and fifth column activity by American citizens and resident aliens of Japanese ancestry, danger would be greatest in Hawaii, and one would anticipate that the most swift and severe measures would be taken there. But nothing of the sort happened. Less than 2,000 ethnic Japanese in Hawaii were taken into custody during the war—barely one percent of the population of Japanese descent. Many factors contributed to this reaction.

Hawaii was more ethnically mixed and racially tolerant than the West Coast. Race relations in Hawaii before the war were not infected with the same virulent antagonism of 75 years of agitation. While anti-Asian feeling existed in the territory, it did not represent the longtime views of well-organized groups as it did on the West Coast and, without statehood, xenophobia had no effective voice in the Congress.

The larger population of ethnic Japanese in Hawaii was also a factor. It is one thing to vent frustration and historical prejudice on a scant two percent of the population; it is very different to disrupt a local economy and tear a social fabric by locking up more than one-third of a territory's people. And in Hawaii the half-measure of exclusion from military areas would have been meaningless.

In large social terms, the Army had much greater control of day-to-day events in Hawaii. Martial law was declared in December 1941, suspending the writ of habeas corpus, so that through the critical first months of the war, the military's recognized power to deal with any emergency was far greater than on the West Coast.

Individuals were also significant in the Hawaiian equation. The War Department gave great discretion to the commanding general of each defense area and this brought to bear very different attitudes toward persons of Japanese ancestry in Hawaii and on the West Coast. The commanding general in Hawaii, Delos Emmons, restrained plans to take radical measures, raising practical problems of labor shortages and transportation until the pressure to evacuate the Hawaiian Islands subsided. General Emmons does not appear to have been a man of dogmatic racial views; he appears to have argued quietly but consistently for treating the ethnic Japanese as loyal to the United States, absent evidence to the contrary.

This policy was clearly much more congruent with basic American law and values. It was also a much sounder policy in practice. The remarkably high rate of enlistment in the Army in Hawaii is in sharp contrast to the doubt and alienation that marred the recruitment of Army volunteers in the relocation camps. The wartime experience in Hawaii left behind neither the extensive economic losses and injury suffered on the mainland nor the psychological burden of the direct experience of unjust exclusion and detention.

The German Americans. The German American experience in the First World War was far less traumatic and damaging than that of the ethnic Japanese in the Second World War, but it underscores the power of war fears and war hysteria to produce irrational but emotionally powerful reactions to people whose ethnicity links them to the enemy.

There were obvious differences between the position of people of German descent in the United States in 1917 and the ethnic Japanese at the start of the Second World War. In 1917, more than 8,000,000 people in the United States had been born in Germany or had one or both parents born there. Although German Americans were not massively represented politically, their numbers gave them notable political strength and support from political spokesmen outside the ethnic group.

The history of the First World War bears a suggestive resemblance to the events of 1942: rumors in the press of sabotage and espionage, use of a stereotype of the German as an unassimilable and rapacious Hun, followed by an effort to suppress those institutions—the language, the press and the churches—that were most palpably foreign and perceived as the seedbed of Kaiserism. There were numerous examples of official and quasi-governmental harassment and fruitless investigation of German Americans and resident German aliens. This history is made even more disturbing by the absence of an extensive history of anti-German agitation before the war.

The promulgation of Executive Order 9066 was not justified by military necessity, and the decisions which followed from it—detention, ending detention and ending exclusion—were not driven by analysis of military conditions. The broad historical causes which shaped these decisions were race prejudice, war hysteria and a failure of political leadership. Widespread ignorance of Japanese Americans contributed to a policy conceived in haste and executed in an atmosphere of fear and anger at Japan. A grave injustice was done to American citizens and resident aliens of Japanese ancestry who, without individual review or any probative evidence against them, were excluded, removed and detained by the United States during World War II.

In memoirs and other statements after the war, many of those involved in the exclusion, removal and detention passed judgment on those events. While believing in the context of the time that evacuation was a legitimate exercise of the war powers, Henry L. Stimson recognized that "to loyal citizens this forced evacuation was a personal injustice." In his autobiography, Francis Biddle reiterated his beliefs at the time: "the program was ill-advised, unnecessary and unnecessarily cruel." Justice William O. Douglas, who joined the majority opinion in *Korematsu* which held the evacuation constitutionally permissible, found that the evacuation case "was ever on my conscience." Milton Eisenhower described the evacuation to the relocation camps as "an inhuman mistake." Chief Justice Earl Warren, who had urged evacuation as Attorney General of California, stated, "I have since deeply regretted the removal order and my own testimony advocating it, because it was not in keeping with our American concept of freedom and the rights of citizens." Justice Tom C. Clark, who had been liaison between the Justice Department and the Western Defense Command, concluded, "Looking back on it today [the evacuation] was, of course, a mistake."

THE COMMISSION ON WARTIME RELOCATION AND INTERNMENT
OF CIVILIANS

Joan Z. Bernstein, *Chair*

Daniel E. Lungren, *Vice-Chair*

Edward W. Brooke

Robert F. Drinan

Arthur S. Flemming

Arthur J. Goldberg

Ishmael V. Gromoff

William M. Marutani

Hugh B. Mitchell

Angus Macbeth, *Special Counsel*

III

"A Tragic Mistake"
1983 - 1987

Korematsu v. United States

Petition for Writ of Error Coram Nobis, U.S. District Court for the Northern District of California

January 19, 1983

Forty years after their criminal trials, the three men whose challenges to the internment of Japanese Americans had been rejected by the Supreme Court launched a joint campaign to secure the judicial reversal of their convictions. They based this effort on newly uncovered documents from government files, some of which disclosed that the Justice Department lawyers who handled the internment cases before the Supreme Court had charged their superiors with suppressing evidence and lying to the justices. The legal procedure for bringing a criminal case before the courts after appeals have been exhausted and sentences served is called a writ of error coram nobis. It can be granted only in cases of "fundamental error" at the trial or "manifest injustice" to the defendant. One kind of fundamental error is governmental misconduct in the form of withholding important evidence at trial or presenting false evidence. The three original defendants filed identical petitions for writs of coram nobis in their original trial courts: Fred Korematsu in San Francisco, Minoru Yasui in Portland, Oregon, and Gordon Hirabayashi in Seattle. Each petition included copies of documents (not reproduced here) that supported the charges of governmental misconduct.

Fred T. Korematsu ("Petitioner") alleges as follows:

Parties

A. *Petitioner*

Petitioner Fred Toyosaburo Korematsu is a citizen of the United States and a resident of San Leandro, California.

B. *Respondent*

Respondent is the United States of America.

Jurisdiction

Jurisdiction is conferred on this Court by 28 U.S.C. §1651. Included in the powers conferred on federal district courts by this section of the United States Code, known as the All-Writs Act, is the authority to issue writs of error coram nobis and thus to vacate the criminal convictions of defendants who have completed the sentences imposed on them after conviction.

Conviction by This Court of Petitioner

Petitioner was convicted in this Court on September 8, 1942 of one count of violation of Public Law 503, 56 Stat. 173. Petitioner was sentenced to a term of five years of probation and imposition of sentence was suspended. Following an order of the United States Supreme Court and subsequent decision by the United States Court of Appeals for the Ninth Circuit and the United States Supreme Court, Petitioner completed service of his probationary sentence.

Introduction

By this petition for writ of error coram nobis, Petitioner seeks to vacate his conviction in 1942 before this court for violation of Public Law 503. His conviction was upheld by the United States Supreme Court in 1944. Petitioner has recently discovered evidence that his prosecution was tainted, both at trial and during the appellate proceedings that followed, by numerous and related acts of governmental misconduct. Both separately and cumulatively, these acts of misconduct constituted fundamental error and resulted in manifest injustice to Petitioner, depriving him of rights guaranteed by the Fifth Amendment to the Constitution of the United States.

A. Relation of This Petition to Those Filed on Behalf of Gordon Hirabayashi and Minoru Yasui

This is an extraordinary petition in many ways. First, it seeks to vacate a conviction that led to a historic and widely cited and debated opinion of the Supreme Court. Second, the allegations of governmental misconduct made below raise the most fundamental questions of the ethical and legal obligations of government officials. Third, the alleged misconduct was committed not only before this court but also before the United States Supreme Court. Fourth, this petition is identical to separate petitions being filed on behalf of Gordon Hirabayashi and Minoru Yasui in the federal district courts in Seattle, Washington and Portland, Oregon, respectively. Hirabayashi and Yasui were also convicted in 1942 of violation of Public Law 503 and their convictions were upheld by the Supreme Court in 1943.

Although this petition is separate from those filed on behalf of Hirabayashi and Yasui, the remainder of this petition refers collectively to all three defendants as "Petitioners." This collective appellation and format requires explanation and justification. Three related factors make such a presentation not only reasonable but essential: (1) the virtual identity of the legal and constitutional issues raised in Petitioners' cases and decided by the Supreme Court; (2) the relevance of the evidence presented and discussed below to each of Petitioners' cases; and (3) the interrelated pattern of the acts of misconduct alleged below and their impact on each of Petitioners' cases. Petitioners will discuss in more detail below the operation of these factors in their cases; the point is made here to advise the court of the distinctive form of this petition.

B. Background of Petition and Relevance of Appendix

Petitioners' arrests and convictions arose from the decision to incarcerate Japanese Americans during World War II. This decision was initiated early in 1942 by military and civilian officials of the U.S. War Department and was subsequently ratified by President Roosevelt. The historical record makes clear that these officials acted largely in response to political and economic pressure fueled by wartime hysteria and prejudice against Japanese Americans. As a result of this pressure, some 110,000 Japanese Americans were forced into detention camps for an indefinite period, without the bringing of charges against them.

Adoption of the internment program was achieved over the strenuous opposition of officials of the U.S. Department of Justice, including the Attorney General and several of his subordinates. The grounds for this opposition included doubts about the necessity for mass evacuation and about the constitutionality of the detention without charges of American citizens. Although these Justice Department officials ultimately deferred to the War Department and the President, the relevance of their objections to the issues raised below requires discussion at some length of the events that preceded the evacuation decision. Petitioners respectfully refer the Court to the Appendix to this petition for presentation of these events.

C. Summary of Acts of Governmental Misconduct Alleged by Petitioners

In seeking the vacation of their respective convictions, Petitioners allege below the commission by government officials of numerous acts of misconduct during the entire course of their cases. A continuing and cumulative pattern of misconduct, designed to secure Petitioners' convictions and judicial approval of the evacuation and incarceration program, emerges from these related acts. While the pattern of misconduct alleged below is complex, when unraveled the acts involved can be grouped under four headings. A separate allegation that Petitioners' convictions violate current constitutional standards, which provide a ground for vacation, is made below under a fifth heading. The following summary of Petitioners' allegations is included at this point to assist the Court in dealing with this necessarily lengthy and complex petition.

Point One: Officials of the War Department altered and destroyed evidence and withheld knowledge of this evidence from the Department of Justice and the Supreme Court. In April 1943, General John L. DeWitt, who headed the Western Defense Command and issued the military orders at issue in Petitioners' cases, submitted an official report to the War Department on the evacuation and incarceration program. Justice Department officials had requested access to this Final Report for use in the government's Supreme Court briefs in *Hirabayashi* and *Yasui*. When War Department officials discovered that the report contained statements contradicting representations made by the Justice Department to the courts, they altered these statements. They subsequently concealed records of the report's receipt, destroyed records of its preparation, created records that falsely identified a revised version as the only report, and withheld the original version from the Justice Department. These acts were committed with knowledge that the contents of this report were material to the cases pending before the Supreme Court.

Point Two: Officials of the War Department and the Department of Justice suppressed evidence relative to the loyalty of Japanese Americans and to the alleged commission by them of acts of espionage. The government relied in Petitioners' cases on purported evidence of widespread disloyalty among the Japanese Americans and the alleged commission by them of acts of espionage. Presented to the courts as justification of the curfew and exclusion orders at issue, these claims were made in the Final Report of General DeWitt. Responsible officials knew that these claims were false. Reports of the Office of Naval Intelligence directly refuted DeWitt's disloyalty claims, while reports of DeWitt's own intelligence staff and of the Federal Bureau of Investigation and the Federal Communications Commission directly refuted DeWitt's espionage claims. Although the Final Report was before the Supreme Court in Petitioners' cases, these exculpatory reports were withheld from the Court despite the protest of government attorneys that such action constituted "suppression of evidence."

Point Three: Government officials failed to advise the Supreme Court of the falsity of the allegations in the Final Report of General DeWitt. When certain Justice Department attorneys learned of the exculpatory evidence discussed in Point Two, *infra*, they attempted to alert the Supreme Court to its existence and the falsity of the Final Report of General DeWitt. Their effort took the form of a crucial footnote in the government's *Korematsu* brief to the Court. This footnote explicitly repudiated DeWitt's espionage claims and advised the Court of the existence of countering evidence. Before submission of the brief, War Department officials intervened with the Solicitor General and urged removal of the footnote. As a result of this intervention, the Solicitor General halted printing of the brief and directed that the footnote be revised to the War Department's satisfaction. The *Korematsu* brief accordingly failed to advise the Court of the falsity of DeWitt's claims and thus misled the Court.

Point Four: The government's abuse of the doctrine of judicial notice and the manipulation of amicus briefs constituted a fraud upon the courts. Justice Department and War Department officials undertook separate but related efforts to present a false and misleading record to the courts in Petitioners' cases.

Even before trial of these cases, Justice Department officials decided to utilize the doctrine of judicial notice in presenting "evidence" that the "racial characteristics" of Japanese Americans predisposed them to disloyalty. Despite the rebuff of one trial judge, and knowledge by Justice Department attorneys that countering evidence existed, such tainted "evidence" was included in the Supreme Court briefs in Petitioners' cases. In addition, War Department officials made available to the attorneys general of the West Coast states the Final Report withheld from the Justice Department, and delegated a military officer to assist in preparing the amicus briefs submitted by these states to the Supreme Court. Justice Department attorneys later learned of these acts and concluded they were unlawful, but failed to report these acts to the Supreme Court.

Point Five: Petitioners are also entitled to relief on the ground that their convictions are based on governmental orders that violate current constitutional standards. The acts of misconduct alleged in the preceding Points provide ample ground for the vacation of Petitioners' convictions. With Petitioners' cases before this Court through the instant petition, the application of current constitutional standards provides an additional ground for vacation. The racial classification involved in the military orders at issue is subject to the "strict scrutiny" standard laid out in subsequent Supreme Court opinions. The government now has the task of *proving* that such a racial classification is essential to fulfill a compelling governmental interest and that no less restrictive alternative is available. Petitioners argue that application of this standard requires vacation of their convictions.

D. Relevant Statute and Orders at Issue in Petitioners' Cases

For the convenience of this Court, the pertinent provisions of the statute and orders at issue in Petitioners' cases are presented below, along with a summary of the structure and operations of the evacuation and incarceration program of which they formed the legal basis.[1]

President Roosevelt signed Executive Order 9066 on February 19, 1942. This order was a broad measure which declared in pertinent part:

Whereas, The successful prosecution of the war requires every possible protection against espionage to national-defense material, national-defense premises and national-defense utilities . . . . :

Now therefore, By virtue of the authority vested in me as President of the United States, and Commander in Chief of the Army and Navy, I hereby authorize and direct the Secretary of War, and the Military Commanders whom he may from time to time designate, whenever he or any designated Commander deems such action necessary or desirable, *to prescribe military areas . . . from which any or all persons may be excluded*, and with respect to which, the right of any person to enter, remain in, or leave shall be subject to whatever restriction the Secretary of War or the appropriate Military Commander may impose in his discretion.[2]

---

[1] The statute and orders applicable to each Petitioner are presented in the Supreme Court opinions in their respective case, to which this court is respectfully referred. See *Hirabayashi* v. *United States*, 320 U.S. 81 (1943); *Yasui* v. *United States*, 320 U.S. 115 (1943); and *Korematsu* v. *United States*, 323 U.S. 214 (1944).

[2] 7 Fed. Reg. 1407. Emphasis added.

On February 20, 1942, Secretary of War Henry L. Stimson exercised the authority granted him in Executive Order 9066 by designating Lt. General John L. DeWitt as Military Commander of the area included in the Western Defense Command, which included the eight westernmost states in the continental United States. General DeWitt first implemented this grant of authority by issuing Public Proclamation No. 1 on March 2, 1942.[3] This Proclamation established six designated "military areas" within the Western Defense Command. Military Area No. 1 included the western halves of California, Oregon and Washington, and the southern half of Arizona. Military Area No. 2 included the remaining portions of those states, while the other four states within the Western Defense Command were each designated as a military area. In a press release issued on the same date, General DeWitt placed Japanese Americans on notice that "[e]ventually orders will be issued requiring all Japanese including those who are American-born to vacate all of Military Area No. 1."[4]

On March 21, 1942, President Roosevelt signed Public Law 503. This law was enacted to enforce the military orders authorized by Executive Order 9066 and imposed criminal penalties for their violation. The statute provided in pertinent part:

[W]hoever shall enter, remain in, leave, or commit any act in any military zone . . . contrary to the restrictions applicable to any such area or zone . . . shall, if it appears he knew or should have known of the existence and extent of the restrictions or order and that this act was in violation thereof, be guilty of a misdemeanor and upon conviction shall be liable to a fine of not to exceed $5,000 or to imprisonment for not more than one year, or both, for each offense.[5]

On March 24, 1942, General DeWitt issued the first military order following enactment of Public Law 503. Public Proclamation No. 3 imposed a curfew on German and Italian aliens, and *all persons* of Japanese ancestry. This curfew required all designated persons to be in their residences between the hours of 8:00 p.m. and 6:00 a.m.[6]

General DeWitt then instituted the internment phase of the mass evacuation program. Public Proclamation No. 4, issued on March 27, 1942, prohibited *all* Japanese Americans from leaving Military Area No. 1 after March 29. This "freeze order" was accompanied by the first of a series of Civilian Exclusion Orders that required the Japanese Americans subject

[3] 7 Fed. Reg. 2320.
[4] Western Defense Command, Press Release No. 3, March 3, 1942, quoted in Jacobus tenBroek et al., *Prejudice, War and the Constitution*, p. 117.
[5] 56 Stat. 173.
[6] 7 Fed. Reg. 2543.

to each order to report to a Civilian Control Center for processing. After processing each person was transferred under guard to an Assembly Center. The first Civilian Exclusion Order required the evacuation of all Japanese Americans from Bainbridge Island, Washington. A total of 108 such orders, each of which affected approximately 1000 Japanese Americans, was issued over a period that ended on June 12, 1942.[7]

Prior to March 27, 1942, the War Department began construction of ten Relocation Centers located in unpopulated areas of California, Arizona, Colorado, Wyoming, Idaho and Arkansas. These Relocation Centers were administered by the War Relocation Authority, a civilian agency established by President Roosevelt on March 18, 1942 pursuant to Executive Order 9102. These centers were guarded by U.S. Army troops and each was designated a "military area" over which General DeWitt retained authority.[8]

Between March and October 31, 1942, the War Department interned a total of 109,347 persons of Japanese ancestry. By the end of this period all Japanese Americans who had resided within the boundaries of Military Areas No. 1 and 2 were confined within the Relocation Centers. Release of the last Japanese Americans held in custody occurred on March 20, 1946, almost four years after the internment program had begun.[9]

E. History of Petitioners' Cases

Minoru Yasui was the first of the three Petitioners arrested for violation of the military orders. Yasui violated the curfew imposed by Public Proclamation No. 3 and was arrested in Portland, Oregon, on March 28, 1942. Gordon Hirabayashi violated both the curfew and Civilian Exclusion Order No. 57 and was arrested in Seattle, Washington, on May 12, 1942. Fred Korematsu violated Civilian Exclusion Order No. 34 and was arrested in San Leandro, California, on May 30, 1942.

Charges based on these violations were brought against each Petitioner by indictment or information in the respective United States District

---

[7] To ensure that no Japanese Americans were overlooked by any of these exclusion orders, General DeWitt issued Public Proclamation No. 7 on June 8, 1942, which read in part: "Should there be any areas remaining in Military Area No. 1 from which Japanese have not been excluded, the exclusion of all Japanese from these areas is provided for in this proclamation." 7 Fed. Reg. 4498.

[8] 7 Fed. Reg. 2165.

[9] War Relocation Authority, *Semi-Annual Report, January 1 to June 30, 1946*, p. 13; quoted in tenBroek, et al., Note 13, supra, p. 13.

Courts in Portland, Seattle and San Francisco. All three Petitioners pled not guilty to the charges against them and each filed a demurrer to the indictment or information. Each demurrer was subsequently denied after hearing. Fred Korematsu was found guilty on September 8, 1942 and was sentenced to five years probation with imposition of sentence suspended. Gordon Hirabayashi was found guilty on October 20, 1942 on the two counts brought against him and sentenced to ninety days on each count, with sentences to run concurrently. Minoru Yasui was found guilty on November 16, 1942 and was sentenced to one year imprisonment and a fine of $5,000.

On September 11, November 16, and November 20, 1942, Korematsu, Hirabayashi and Yasui each appealed their respective convictions to the United States Court of Appeals for the Ninth Circuit. The Circuit Court heard oral arguments in Hirabayashi's and Yasui's cases on March 27, 1943. Invoking a rarely used procedure, the Circuit Court certified the cases to the United States Supreme Court without opinion. Korematsu's appeal was argued in the Circuit Court on April 18, 1943 and was also certified to the Supreme Court on the limited procedural question of whether a suspended sentence was appealable.

The Supreme Court heard oral arguments in all three cases on May 10 and 11, 1943. Ruling that an appeal was properly taken from the suspended probationary sentence, the Supreme Court remanded Korematsu's appeal to the Circuit Court on June 1, 1943. On June 21, 1943, the Supreme Court unanimously upheld the convictions of Hirabayashi and Yasui. In Yasui's case, however, the Court held that the District Judge had erred in ruling the curfew order unconstitutional as applied to citizens and in ruling that Yasui had forfeited his citizenship, and remanded the case to the District Court for resentencing.

On December 2, 1943, the Circuit Court sustained Korematsu's conviction with an opinion that cited the Supreme Court opinion in *Hirabayashi* as controlling. Korematsu's petition for certiorari was granted by the Supreme Court on March 27, 1944. The Court heard oral argument in the case on October 11 and 12, 1944. In a six-to-three decision issued on December 18, 1944, the Supreme Court upheld Korematsu's conviction. The Court ruled on the same day in a unanimous opinion in *Ex parte Endo* (on an appeal from denial of a habeas corpus petition brought by an interned Japanese American) that Congress had not authorized the continuing detention of a concededly loyal citizen.

F. Summary of the Impact of Governmental Misconduct on the Factual and Legal Issues Presented in Petitioners' Cases and Decided by the Supreme Court

The government's misconduct was complex in execution and long in duration. To understand the significance of such misconduct requires an explanation of the legal and factual premises upon which the courts, and the Supreme Court in particular, based their decisions in these cases.

The stated purpose of Executive Order 9066 was to provide "every possible protection against espionage and against sabotage" to national defense facilities.[10] On March 2, 1942, under the authority of Executive Order 9066, General DeWitt issued Public Proclamation No. 1, which did the following:

1. Recited that the entire Pacific coast was "subject to espionage and acts of sabotage, thereby requiring the adoption of military measures necessary to establish safeguards against such enemy operations;"

2. Established Military Area No. 1 which included approximately 90% of the Japanese Americans on the mainland; and

3. Announced the planned evacuation of the Japanese American population from this area.[11]

Each of the subsequent military orders affecting Japanese Americans relied upon the findings set forth in Public Proclamation No. 1 for their justification and authority.

In upholding the constitutionality of these orders, the Supreme Court relied heavily upon the ostensible purpose of these orders, as set forth in Executive Order 9066 and Public Law 503, and upon the military's purported "findings" of a threat of espionage and sabotage from the West Coast Japanese Americans.

From the outset, however, in order to justify the incarceration of Japanese Americans, the military and the War Department destroyed, suppressed and manipulated evidence so as to create an appearance of a military threat from allegedly disloyal elements within the Japanese American population. Ultimately, attorneys for the Justice Department became aware of such evidence, but capitulated to the War Department's and military's tactics, and suppressed and distorted the "evidence" they chose to place before the Supreme Court in Petitioners' cases. Unfortu-

[10]7 Fed. Reg. 1407.
[11]7 Fed. Reg. 2320.

nately, the Supreme Court accepted the government's factual picture of a purported military threat as a true and complete representation of the basis of the military orders and explicitly based its decisions upholding the constitutionality of these orders upon the military's ostensible apprehension of a danger of espionage and sabotage from the Japanese Americans.

Explaining its inquiry into the constitutionality of the military orders at issue in *Hirabayashi* and *Yasui*, the Supreme Court stated:

[O]ur inquiry must be whether in the light of all the facts and circumstances, there was any substantial basis for the conclusion, in which Congress and military commander united, that the curfew as applied was a protective measure necessary to meet the threat of sabotage and espionage which would substantially affect the war effort and which might reasonably be expected to aid a threatened enemy invasion.[12]

Observing that "racial discriminations are in most circumstances irrelevant and therefore prohibited," the Court explained the fundamental legal and moral context in which it made its inquiry:

Distinctions between citizens solely because of their ancestry are by their very nature odious to a free people whose institutions are founded upon the doctrine of equality. For that reason, legislative classification or discrimination based on race alone has often been held to be a denial of equal protection. *Yick Wo v. Hopkins*, 118 U.S. 356 . . . ; *Yu Cong Eng v. Trinidad*, 271 U.S. 500 . . . ; *Hill v. Texas*, 316 U.S. 400. . . . We may assume that these considerations would be controlling here were it not for the fact that the danger of espionage and sabotage, in time of war and of threatened invasion, calls upon the military authorities to scrutinize every relevant fact bearing on the loyalty of populations in the danger areas.[13]

In *Korematsu*, the Court similarly explained at the very outset of its opinion that:

[A]ll legal restrictions which curtail the civil rights of a single racial group are immediately suspect. That is not to say that all such restrictions are unconstitutional. It is to say that courts must subject them to the most rigid scrutiny. Pressing public necessity may sometimes justify the existence of such restrictions; racial antagonism never can.[14]

Under this standard, the military orders establishing the curfew and ordering the removal of the Japanese Americans from the West Coast required for their justification:

[12] *Hirabayashi* v. *United States*, supra, 320 U.S. at 95.
[13] *Id*. at 100.
[14] *Korematsu* v. *United States*, supra, 323 U.S. at 216.

Nothing short of apprehension by the proper military authorities of the gravest imminent danger to the public safety . . .[15]

Notwithstanding this language, the Court in both *Hirabayashi* and *Korematsu* accepted without question, but clearly not without misgivings, the "facts" presented to it by the government in support of the constitutionality of the military orders.[16] Upholding the factual basis of the orders at issue in *Hirabayashi*, the Court concluded:

[W]e cannot reject as unfounded the judgment of the military authorities and that of Congress that there were disloyal members of [the Japanese American] population, whose number and strength could not be precisely and quickly ascertained. We cannot say that the war-making branches of the government did not have ground for believing that in a critical hour such persons could not readily be isolated and separately dealt with, and constituted a menace to the national defense and safety, which demanded that prompt and adequate measures be taken to guard against it.[17]

Again, in the specific context of its response to the argument that Public Law 503 effected an unconstitutional delegation of powers, the Court in *Hirabayashi* declared:

[T]he findings of danger from espionage and sabotage, and of the necessity of the curfew order to protect against them, have been duly made. . . .

The military commander's appraisal of facts . . . , and the inferences which he drew from those facts, involved the exercise of his informed judgment. . . . [T]hose facts . . . support [his] judgment, that the danger of espionage and sabotage to our military resources was imminent. . . .[18]

Finally, in *Korematsu*, the Court reaffirmed its prior analysis and conclusion in *Hirabayashi* and added:

Like curfew, exclusion of those of Japanese origin was deemed necessary because of the presence of an unascertained number of disloyal members of the

---

[15]*Id.* at 218.

[16]Notwithstanding the Supreme Court's conclusion that racial classifications are "odious to a free people," are "immediately suspect" and should be subject to the "most rigid scrutiny," by failing to apply these principles in reviewing the constitutionality of the military orders promulgated by DeWitt, the Court abdicated its responsibilities to Petitioners and to the Constitution. In this respect, entirely independent of the manifest injustices put at issue by the instant petition, Petitioners respectfully submit that the Court's original decisions in *Korematsu*, *Hirabayashi* and *Yasui* were themselves fundamentally in error. Indeed, by their consistent reliance upon the principles of strict scrutiny first articulated in *Korematsu* and *Hirabayashi*, subsequent decisions of the Supreme Court have made clear that the Court erred in Petitioners' cases in failing to apply in fact the most rigid scrutiny of the invidious racial classifications established by the military orders. See, e.g., *Bolling* v. *Sharpe*, 347 U.S. 497, 499 (1954); *McLaughlin* v. *Florida*, 379 U.S. 184, 192 (1964); *Loving* v. *Virginia*, 388 U.S. 1, 11 (1967).

[17]*Hirabayashi* v. *United States*, supra, 320 U.S. at 99.

[18]*Id.* at 103–104.

group, most of whom were no doubt loyal to this country. It was because we could not reject the finding of the military authorities that it was impossible to bring about an immediate segregation of the disloyal from the loyal that we sustained the validity of the curfew order as applying to the whole group. In the instant case, temporary exclusion of the entire group was rested by the military on the same ground.[19]

As the Court's choice of language in these passages makes evident, the Court upheld the constitutionality of the military orders at issue in both *Hirabayashi* and *Korematsu* on "findings" of facts by General DeWitt. The "facts" upon which the Court relied, however, were not facts at all. Composed of half-truths and outright lies, the "facts" presented to the Court resulted from a deliberate and knowing attempt by the highest rank-ing military and civilian officials in the United States government to de-stroy, suppress and withhold highly credible evidence that no such threat from Japanese Americans as posited by DeWitt ever existed. In place of such evidence, these officials fabricated a factual record composed of other "evidence," some of which had been discredited as early as January 1942, and argued that the military orders leading to the incarceration of the Japanese American people were justified by such fabrications.

Had the true facts been presented to the Supreme Court, the Court could not have concluded even that "[w]e cannot reject as unfounded the judgment of the military authorities," or that "[w]e cannot say that the war-making branches of the government did not have ground for believ-ing" in the threat ostensibly posed by Japanese Americans. As Petitioners will show, that the military had no such ground was known, not only to DeWitt, but to the Navy, the FBI, the FCC, the War Department and the Department of Justice, and should have been divulged to the Court. As the destruction, suppression and fabrication of evidence was critically material to Petitioners' constitutional challenges, Petitioners' respective convictions must be vacated.

Statement of the Case

Point One: Officials of the War Department Altered and Destroyed Evidence and Withheld Knowledge of this Evidence from the Department of Justice and the Supreme Court

As noted above, General DeWitt's Final Report on the evacuation of Japanese Americans is of central significance to the allegations of govern-

---

[19] *Korematsu* v. *United States*, supra, 323 U.S. at 218–219.

mental misconduct made in this petition. This official report was prepared to justify the evacuation decision and contained the "disloyalty" and "espionage" claims on which DeWitt purported to base his recommendation for mass evacuation. Until now, it has been believed that there was only one "Final Report." Petitioners have discovered the existence of a prior version which had been printed and formally transmitted to the War Department.

This initial version contained statements known by the War Department to be material to the loyalty issue raised before the Supreme Court in *Hirabayashi* and *Yasui*. Moreover, War Department officials knew that statements in the initial version contradicted representations already made to the Courts by the Department of Justice and undermined the credibility of General DeWitt. In order to "clean up" the Report, War Department officials willfully altered these statements to conceal the contradictions. In addition, War Department officials destroyed records and altered and concealed other records to withhold from the Justice Department and the Supreme Court any evidence that an original version of the Report had existed and had been formally submitted to the War Department.

A. The Justice Department requested evidence from the War Department for use in the Government's briefs in Hirabayashi *and* Yasui. On April 5, 1943, after certification by the Court of Appeals, the Supreme Court ordered up the entire records in the *Hirabayashi* and *Yasui* cases. Argument was set for the week of May 10, 1943. Edward J. Ennis, Director of the Alien Enemy Control Unit of the Department of Justice, undertook supervision of the preparation of briefs in both cases.[1]

To prepare the briefs, Ennis formally requested the War Department "to supply any published material in the War Department's possession on the military situation on the West Coast at the time of the evacuation to be used in the *Hirabayashi* brief in the Supreme Court."[2] Ennis also reported to Solicitor General Fahy with respect to this request on April 19, 1943:

[1] Ennis intended to address the major issues of the curfew and evacuation in the *Hirabayashi* brief, since Hirabayashi had been convicted of violating both the curfew order and the evacuation order applicable to him. Given the fact that Yasui had been convicted only of curfew violation, and that the District Judge had held that Yasui had forfeited his United States citizenship, a holding with which the United States disagreed, Ennis proposed submitting a "short brief" in the *Yasui* case "discussing the special question of the defendant's citizenship" and referring the Supreme Court to the *Hirabayashi* brief for discussion of the curfew issue. Memorandum, Edward J. Ennis to Solicitor General Fahy, April 19, 1943, Folder 3, Box 37, Charles Fahy Papers, Franklin D. Roosevelt Library, Hyde Park, New York [cited hereafter as Fahy Papers]. See Exhibit A.

[2] Memorandum, Edward J. Ennis to Herbert Wechsler, September 30, 1944, Folder 3, Box 37, Fahy Papers. This memorandum was written in connection with the preparation of the Government's brief to the Supreme Court in the *Korematsu* case. See Exhibit B.

In this connection the War Department has today received a printed report from General DeWitt about the Japanese evacuation and is now determining whether it is to be released so that it may be used in connection with these cases. The War Department has been requested to furnish any published materials which may be helpful.[3]

Ennis made this request for the purpose of "assisting the Court . . . in the presentation of the factual material" relating to the curfew and evacuation issues raised in the *Hirabayashi* and *Yasui* cases. The relevance of material in the possession of the War Department, as the agency responsible for the mass evacuation program and for the military orders that precede and accompanied this program, is obvious.

B. War Department officials altered the Final Report to conceal contradictions with representations made to the courts by the Department of Justice. Ennis had requested a copy of the Final Report which had been formally transmitted to the War Department by General DeWitt on April 15, 1943. Ten copies of the Report had been printed and bound, and six of these copies had been sent to the War Department. Two of these copies went to Assistant Secretary of War John J. McCloy. In a transmittal letter to McCloy dated April 15, 1943, DeWitt noted that the Report had been shipped Air Express because it was needed for the preparation of the Government's Supreme Court briefs:

These are going forward via Air Express because I am advised that there is an urgent need of the material contained therein for use in the preparation of the Federal Government's briefs in the cases now pending before the Supreme Court of the United States challenging the constitutionality of the entire program.[4]

In reviewing the initial version of the Final Report, McCloy discovered a statement by General DeWitt that prompted him to direct that the Report be altered and withheld from the Justice Department. The objectionable statement appeared in Chapter II, entitled "Need for Military Control and for Evacuation." This chapter included both the "military necessity" and "disloyalty" claims made by DeWitt in support of the evacuation. The significant paragraph is quoted below in full:

Because of the ties of race, the intense feeling of filial piety and the strong bonds of common tradition, culture and customs, this population [Japanese Americans] presented a tightly-knit racial group. It included in excess of 115,000 persons deployed along the Pacific Coast. Whether by design or accident, virtually al-

[3] Note 1, supra.

[4] Letter, General DeWitt to McCloy, April 15, 1943, File 319.1, Section I, Records of the Western Defense Command and Fourth Army, Civil Affairs Division, Record Group 338, National Archives and Record Service [NARS], Washington, D.C. See Exhibit C.

ways their communities were adjacent to very vital shore installations, war plants, etc. While it was believed that some were loyal, it was known that many were not. *It was impossible to establish the identity of the loyal and the disloyal with any degree of safety. It was not that there was insufficient time in which to make such a determination; it was simply a matter of facing the realities that a positive determination could not be made, that an exact separation of the "sheep from the goats" was unfeasible.*[5]

The underscored portion of this paragraph is significant for several reasons. First, DeWitt's assertion that it was "impossible" to separate the loyal and the disloyal among the Japanese Americans contradicted De- Witt's own prior statement of the subject. On December 26, 1941, at a time of greater military uncertainty and potential danger of Japanese at- tack on the West Coast, DeWitt had opposed mass evacuation with the statement that "I think we can weed the disloyal out of the loyal and lock them up if necessary."[6] DeWitt offered no evidence in the Final Report to explain his change in opinion. What he did offer were simply supposi- tions that the "racial characteristics" of Japanese Americans predisposed them to disloyalty.

Second, officials of the War Department and Department of Justice— including McCloy and Attorney General Biddle—had known since early 1942 that reports from responsible intelligence agencies flatly contra- dicted DeWitt's claim that it was impossible to separate the loyal from the disloyal. Evidence of this knowledge and the reports on which it was based is detailed in the following section of this petition.

Third, the statement that considerations of time had not been a factor in the mass evacuation decision contradicted the position consistently taken by the Department of Justice before the courts. Counsel for Hirabayashi and Yasui argued at length in their briefs to the Supreme Court that the prior experience of the British government in conducting individual loy- alty hearings for enemy aliens demonstrated the feasibility of this less restrictive alternative to mass evacuation. DeWitt's elimination of the time factor from the evacuation equation was directly and critically rele- vant to this central question.

McCloy had not expected to receive the Final Report in printed and bound form before he had an opportunity to review it. He communicated

---

[5] *Final Report, Japanese Evacuation From the West Coast, 1942*, [initial version], p. 9, *ibid.* Emphasis added. See Exhibit D.
[6] Transcript of telephone conversation, General DeWitt and General Allen W. Gullion, Provost Marshal General, United States Army, December 26, 1941, File 311.3 (Telephone conversations, DeWitt, 1942–43), Record Group 338, Records of the Western Defense Command, National Ar- chives and Records Service, Washington, D.C.

his surprise to Colonel Karl Bendetsen in a telephone conversation on April 19, 1943:

The arrangement that I understood was that you were going to submit a galley that you could go over and we could work on that and make any suggestions. . . . [T]he letter of transmittal is already printed and signed—completed—done— pat. That is what disturbs me. The whole thing disturbs me. The whole thing disturbs me—frankly.[7]

At the end of this conversation McCloy ordered Colonel Bendetsen to report to Washington for consultation on the Final Report. Bendetsen subsequently reported to General DeWitt on May 3, 1943, that McCloy objected:

. . . to that portion of Chapter II which said in effect that it is absolutely impossible to determine the loyalty of Japanese no matter how much time was taken in the process. He said that he had no objection to saying that time was of the essence and that in view of the military situation and the fact *that there was no known means of making such a determination with any degree of safety* the evacuation was necessary.[8]

McCloy then instructed Captain John M. Hall of his staff to revise the paragraph from the Final Report quoted above. Hall revised the last two sentences of this paragraph to read as follows:

To complicate the situation, no ready means existed for determining the loyal and the disloyal with any degree of safety. It was necessary to face the realities— a positive determination could not be made.[9]

Hall's revision produced more than a semantic change. It resulted in the complete alteration of DeWitt's original statement and its meaning. DeWitt obviously claimed that it was "impossible" to segregate the Japanese Americans on the basis of loyalty because he assumed that their "racial characteristics" predisposed them to disloyalty. Hall's unsupported statement that "no ready means existed" by which loyalty could be determined shifted the argument to the question of practicality and concealed the racist underpinning of DeWitt's equally unsupported claim. More important, Hall's revision concealed from the Justice Department

[7]Transcript of telephone conversation, Colonel Bendetsen and McCloy, April 19, 1943, note 4, supra. See Exhibit E.

[8]Memorandum, Colonel Bendetsen to General DeWitt, May 3, 1943, Note 4, supra. Emphasis in original. See Exhibit F.

[9]Memorandum, "Suggested changes by Capt. Hall in 'Final Report: Japanese Evacuation From the West Coast—1942'", [no recipient or date noted], *ibid*. See Exhibit G. This alteration appeared in the published version of the Final Report, Japanese Evacuation From the West Coast, 1942, Washington, D.C.: Government Printing Office, 1943. [Hereinafter cited as DeWitt, Final Report.]

DeWitt's express admission that the time required to pursue the less restrictive alternative of segregation by loyalty had not been a factor in the mass evacuation decision.

The impact of this alteration of the Final Report on Petitioners' cases is undeniable. Barred by McCloy from access to the original version of the Report, the Justice Department erroneously asserted to the Supreme Court in *Hirabayashi* and *Yasui* that lack of sufficient time for a loyalty determination had necessitated the adoption of the program of mass evacuation. The *Hirabayashi* brief, incorporated by reference on this point in the *Yasui* brief, included this assertion: "Many months, or perhaps years, would be required for such [loyalty] investigations and hearings."[10] In view of DeWitt's original statement on this question, the consequence of this assertion was to mislead the Court on this crucial issue.

The Supreme Court's reliance on this misleading and erroneous assertion is evident. The Court upheld the curfew order at issue in both *Hirabayashi* and *Yasui* on the ground that DeWitt had determined that the Japanese American population included "disloyal members . . . whose number and strength could not be precisely and quickly ascertained" and that "such persons could not readily be isolated and separately dealt with" by any means other than the curfew.[11] Later, in *Korematsu*, the Court upheld the exclusion order at issue (and the mass evacuation program as well) with quotation of this same excerpt from *Hirabayashi*.[12]

The altered version of the Final Report was presented to the Supreme Court in *Korematsu* after its public release in 1944. Justice Murphy's dissent in *Korematsu* provides a clear indication that the outcome of Petitioners' cases might have differed had the Court not been misled on this issue. "No adequate reason is given for the failure to treat these Japanese Americans on an individual basis by holding investigations and hearings to separate the loyal from the disloyal," Justice Murphy wrote in reference to the Final Report. Rather, "it is asserted that the loyalties of this group 'were unknown and time was of the essence'."[13] This interior quotation from the Final Report reflected, of course, the alteration of the original version directed by McCloy. Had the Court been aware of DeWitt's initial statement, other members of the Court might well have shared Justice Murphy's doubts.

[10]*Hirabayashi* v. *United States*, 320 U.S. 81 (1943), Brief for the United States, pp. 62–65.
[11]*Hirabayashi* v. *United States*, supra, 320 U.S. 81, 99.
[12]*Korematsu* v. *United States*, 323 U.S. 214, 218 (1943).
[13]*Id*. at 241 (Murphy, J., dissenting).

War Department officials destroyed records of the original version of the Final Report and concealed records of its existence from the Department of Justice. After the alteration of the Final Report to eliminate General DeWitt's damaging statements, War Department officials destroyed records of the receipt of the initial version sent to the War Department and records used in its preparation. On May 9, 1943, Colonel Bendetsen transmitted to General James Barnett, Assistant Chief of Staff of the Western Defense Command, the following order from DeWitt:

Take action to call in all copies previously sent to WD [War Department] less enclosures and to have WD destroy all records of receipt of report as when final revision is forwarded letter of transmittal will be redated.[14]

Two days later, on May 11, DeWitt sent a telegram to the Army Chief of Staff requesting return of the six printed copies of the Final Report that had been sent to the War Department on April 15. DeWitt also requested that "your record [of] receipt of same be cancelled for reason rewritten report in process."[15]

War Department records were subsequently altered to conceal the receipt of the initial version of the Final Report. On June 7, 1943, Captain Hall returned to Colonel Bendetsen the original and copy of General DeWitt's letter of transmittal dated April 15. "War Department records have been adjusted accordingly," Hall reported to Bendetsen.[16]

The final step in the destruction of records took place on June 29, 1943. On that day, the following document was submitted to Bendetsen's office by Warrant Officer Theodore E. Smith:

I certify that this date I witnessed the destruction by burning of the galley proofs, galley pages, drafts and memorandums of the original report of the Japanese Evacuation.[17]

While these records were being destroyed, the altered version of the Final Report was printed and, on June 5, 1943, submitted to the War Department by General DeWitt.[18] This date has a particular significance to the *Hirabayashi* and *Yasui* cases. Although arguments in these cases

---

[14] Telegram, Colonel Bendetsen to General Barnett, May 9, 1943, File 319.1, Note 4, *supra*. See Exhibit H.

[15] Telegram, General DeWitt to Chief of Staff, United States Army, May 11, 1943, *ibid*. See Exhibit I.

[16] Letter, Captain Hall to Colonel Bendetsen, June 7, 1943, *ibid*. See Exhibit J.

[17] Memorandum, Warrant Officer Junior Grade Theodore E. Smith, June 29, 1943, *ibid*. See Exhibit K.

[18] DeWitt, *Final Report*, p. vii.

before the Supreme Court had taken place several weeks earlier, the Court's opinions were not issued until June 21, 1943. The Justice Department's request to the War Department for material relevant to these cases had been made in April and was still outstanding. Notwithstanding this request, and their knowledge that the Final Report had been officially requested, War Department officials did not release the Report until January 1944.

Justice Department officials gained access to the altered version of the Final Report only after its release to the press. The purge of War Department records gave them no hint that any other version of the Report had ever existed. Not until the recent discovery by Petitioners of a copy of the original version in the files of the Western Defense Command, and of the records relating to its alteration, did this shocking episode come to light. The deliberate alteration and destruction of evidence material to issues raised in Petitioners' cases and decided adversely to them by the Supreme Court speaks for itself.

Point Two: Officials of the War Department and the Department of Justice Suppressed Evidence Relative to the Loyalty of Japanese Americans and to the Alleged Commission by Them of Acts of Espionage

The alteration of the original version of the Final Report, and the destruction of records of its preparation, were directly related to the suppression of authoritative intelligence reports showing that the "evidence" upon which General DeWitt relied to support his assertions of a threat from Japanese Americans was false. These reports conclusively refuted both the disloyalty and espionage allegations made in the Final Report in support of mass evacuation.

Officials of the War Department and the Department of Justice were aware since early 1942 of reports that dealt with the disloyalty and espionage issues. These reports had been submitted by the Office of Naval Intelligence (ONI), the Military Intelligence Division of DeWitt's command (MID), the Federal Bureau of Investigation (FBI), and the Federal Communications Commission (FCC). Collectively, these reports refuted every allegation made in the Final Report. However, *none* of this exculpatory evidence was presented to the courts which considered Petitioners' cases. Instead, over the objections of the attorneys responsible for the briefs in these cases, the Justice Department knowingly presented to the courts the false factual picture created by DeWitt and the War Department in support of the incarceration program.

A. The disloyalty and espionage allegations made in the Final Report. Allegations that Japanese Americans constituted a disloyal element among the West Coast population, and that members of this group had committed acts of espionage, provided the twin foundations of DeWitt's justification of mass evacuation in the Final Report. DeWitt's actions could in fact be justified only on an asserted link between these separate allegations. Acts of espionage were in the province of military and civilian intelligence and law enforcement agencies. The mass evacuation and incarceration of all Japanese Americans depended on an assertion of widespread disloyalty among this group and upon the related assertion that they were predisposed to sympathy to Japan and would commit acts of espionage to further Japanese war aims.

General DeWitt made such an explicit linkage between disloyalty and espionage in his Final Report. He expressed it in the following terms:

In his estimate of the situation, the Commanding General found a tightly-knit, unassimilated racial group, substantial numbers of whom were engaged in pro-Japanese activities. . . . He had no alternative but to conclude that the Japanese [Americans] constituted a potentially dangerous element from the viewpoint of military necessity—that military necessity required their immediate evacuation to the interior. . . . There were hundreds of reports nightly of signal lights visible from the coast, and of intercepts of unidentified radio transmissions. . . . The problem required immediate solution.

It called for the application of measures not then in being.[1]

Long before he submitted the Final Report to the War Department, DeWitt had expressed his belief that Japanese Americans were disloyal as a group in statements that literally reeked of racism. On January 4, 1942, more than a month before he recommended mass evacuation, DeWitt made the following statement to an official of the Department of Justice:

I have little confidence that the enemy aliens are law-abiding or loyal in any sense of the word. Some of them, yes; many, no. Particularly the Japanese. *I have no confidence in their loyalty whatsoever.* I am speaking now of the native-born Japanese. . . .[2]

---

[1] *Final Report: Japanese Evacuation From the West Coast, 1942*, Washington, D.C.: Government Printing Office, 1943 [hereafter cited as DeWitt, *Final Report*], pp. 8–9.

[2] Transcript, Conference in Office of General DeWitt, January 4, 1942, File 014.31, Box 7, Record Group 338 [Records of the Western Defense Command and Fourth Army], National Archives and Records Service, Washington, D.C. Emphasis added. See Exhibit L.

The Final Report included a revealing expression of DeWitt's belief that the "racial characteristics" of Japanese Americans predisposed them to disloyalty. DeWitt included in the Report the text of the "Final Recommendation" he submitted to the Secretary of War on February 14, 1942. The following statement appeared in this document:

In the war in which we are now engaged racial affinities are not severed by migration. *The Japanese race is an enemy race* and while many second and third generation Japanese born on United States soil, possessed of United States citizenship, have become 'Americanized', *the racial strains are undiluted.* . . . It, therefore, follows that along the vital Pacific coast over 112,000 potential enemies, of Japanese extraction, are at large today.[3]

DeWitt's final public statement about the loyalty of Japanese Americans came shortly before his transfer from the Western Defense Command in June 1943. Testifying before a congressional committee on April 13, 1943, he stated that "it makes no difference whether he is an American citizen or not."[4]

These statements do more than document the consistency of DeWitt's hostility toward Japanese Americans as a racial group. His expression of "no confidence" in the loyalty of Japanese Americans led to the fabrication of "evidence" that members of this group had committed acts of espionage. The espionage allegations in the Final Report thus provide a classic example of the self-fulfilling prophecy in operation.

The Final Report shows the consequence of DeWitt's linkage of disloyalty and espionage. DeWitt included in his "Final Recommendation" for mass evacuation the following prediction that Japanese Americans would engage in acts of espionage:

Hostile naval and air raids *will be assisted by enemy agents signaling from the coastline* and the vicinity thereof; and by supplying and otherwise assisting enemy vessels and by sabotage.[5]

Having predicted in the "Final Recommendation" that Japanese Americans would commit espionage, DeWitt was forced by the logic of his prophecy to include "evidence" of espionage in the Final Report. DeWitt

---

[3] DeWitt, *Final Report*, p. 3. Emphasis added.

[4] Quoted in San Francisco *Chronicle*, April 14, 1943. The printed text of General DeWitt's testimony does not contain the first statement quoted above. That testimony, as printed, read in relevant part: "I don't want any of them [persons of Japanese ancestry] here. They are a dangerous element. There is no way to determine their loyalty. . . . The danger of the Japanese was, and is now—if they are permitted to come back—espionage and sabotage. It makes no difference whether he is an American citizen, he is still a Japanese. . . ." Hearings, House Naval Affairs Subcommittee to Investigate Congested Areas, 78th Cong., 1st Sess., Part 3, pp. 739–740.

[5] DeWitt, *Final Report*, p. 33. Emphasis added.

made two separate allegations of espionage activities in his Report. One dealt with radio communications from the mainland to Japanese submarines off the coast; the other with the transmission of visual signals to offshore Japanese vessels.

DeWitt first stated that his recommendation of mass evacuation was:

. . . in part based upon the interception of unauthorized radio communications which had been identified as emanating from certain areas along the coast. Of further concern to him was the fact that for a period of several weeks following December 7th [1941], substantially every ship leaving a West Coast port was attacked by an enemy submarine. *This seemed conclusively to point to the existence of hostile shore-to-shore (submarine) communication.*[6]

The second espionage allegation in the Final Report came in a section that charged the Department of Justice with having "impeded" the search for "arms, cameras and other contraband" in the possession of Japanese Americans by insisting that premises occupied by citizens could be searched only with the warrant required by the Fourth Amendment. DeWitt accompanied this criticism with the following statement:

There were hundreds of reports nightly of signal lights visible from the coast. . . . Signaling was often observed at premises which could not be entered without a warrant because of mixed [i.e., alien and citizen] occupancy.[7]

It should be noted that these related allegations of disloyalty and espionage were the only "evidence" offered by General DeWitt to support the mass evacuation and incarceration of Japanese Americans. These allegations in the Final Report were presented to the Supreme Court in Petitioners' cases as the basis of the "military necessity" argument in support of the military orders at issue. It also deserves notice that DeWitt did not directly charge that any of the alleged acts of espionage had been committed by Japanese Americans. Presumably because no person—of Japanese ancestry or otherwise—was charged with espionage on the West Coast, DeWitt resorted to implication rather than accusation.

B. Officials of the War Department and the Department of Justice suppressed the report of the Office of Naval Intelligence on the loyalty of Japanese Americans.

1. Preparation and contents of the ONI Report. The responsibility of the Office of Naval Intelligence (ONI) for the investigation of the Japanese American population on the West Coast originated in June 1939. At that time, in response to increasing tension between the United States and

---

[6]*Id*. at 4. Emphasis added.
[7]*Id*. at 8.

Japan, President Roosevelt ordered a reorganization of the government's intelligence activities on the West Coast.[8] The "Delimitation Agreement" of June 4, 1940 further coordinated the operations of civilian and military intelligence agencies and specifically assigned primary responsibility for investigation of the Japanese American population on the West Coast to the ONI.[9]

Among the most significant of the intelligence reports suppressed by government officials in Petitioners' cases was the ONI report on its investigation of the Japanese Americans submitted to the Chief of Naval Operations on January 26, 1942. Entitled "Report on Japanese Question," this document discussed in detail the question of the loyalty of Japanese Americans on the West coast. It had been prepared by Lieutenant Commander Kenneth D. Ringle, the official most knowledgeable about Japanese Americans among the personnel of all federal intelligence agencies both before and during the war.[10]

Pursuant to his duties on the intelligence staff of the Eleventh Naval District, with headquarters in Los Angeles, Commander Ringle assumed primary responsibility for the investigation of the loyalty of Japanese Americans. He maintained close contact with Japanese Americans and with officials in other intelligence agencies. His periodic reports, in particular that of January 26, 1942, thus constituted the most expert and definitive intelligence on the loyalty question.

In his report of January 26, 1942, Commander Ringle concluded that the vast majority of Japanese Americans were loyal to the United States and presented little danger to military security. He admitted that a small number among the entire Japanese American population represented a potential military danger, noting that:

. . . there are among the Japanese, both alien and United States citizens, certain individuals, either deliberately placed by the Japanese government or actuated by a fanatical loyalty to that country, who would act as saboteurs or agents. *This*

[8] United States Navy, Office of Naval Intelligence, "United States Naval Administration in World War II," n.d., pp. 66–69. See Exhibit M.

[9] *Ibid.*

[10] Memorandum, "Japanese Question, Report on," Lieutenant Commander K. D. Ringle to Chief of Naval Operations, January 26, 1942, File BIO/ND 11BF37/A8–5, Records of the United States Navy. See Exhibit N. Note the following statement of Ringle's background and experience: "(a) Three years of study of the Japanese language and the Japanese people as a naval language student attached to the United States Embassy in Tokyo from 1928 to 1931. (b) One year's duty as Assistant District Intelligence Officer, Fourteenth Naval District (Hawaii) from July 1936 to July 1937. (c) Duty as Assistant District in charge of Naval intelligence matters in Los Angeles and vicinity from July 1940 to the present time." Pp. 3–4.

number is estimated to be less than three percent of the total, or about 3500 in the *entire* United States.[11]

Commander Ringle added to this estimate the significant statement that the identities of the potentially disloyal were easily discoverable:

. . . of the persons mentioned . . . above, *the most dangerous are either already in custodial detention* or are members of such organizations as the Black Dragon Society, the Kaigun Kyokai (Navy League), or the Haimusha Kai (Military Service Men's League), or affiliated groups. *The membership of these groups is already fairly well known* to the Naval Intelligence service or the Federal Bureau of Investigation. . . .[12]

On the basis of these informed estimates and his personal knowledge of the Japanese Americans, Commander Ringle came to the following conclusion:

That, in short, the entire 'Japanese Problem' has been magnified out of its true proportion, largely because of the physical characteristics of the people; that it is no more serious than the problems of the German, Italian, and Communistic portions of the United States population, and, finally that it should be handled on the basis of the *individual*, regardless of citizenship, and *not* on a racial basis.[13]

Most importantly, in accordance with the existing "Delimitation Agreement" between the federal intelligence agencies, Commander Ringle's report was available to both the Federal Bureau of Investigation and to General DeWitt through the staff of the Military Intelligence Division (MID) of the Western Defense Command.

2. The Government's knowledge of the ONI Report. It is significant that the ONI Report came to the personal attention of both Attorney General Biddle and Assistant Secretary of War McCloy *before* General DeWitt issued the curfew and exclusion orders applicable to Petitioners. Biddle transmitted the report to McCloy on March 9, 1942, with a letter that read: "You will be interested in the enclosed confidential report of the Office of Naval Intelligence with respect to the Japanese situation on the West Coast." [14] McCloy responded on March 21, 1942, with a letter that included the following:

I spent some time on the West Coast, returning yesterday, and while out there *I talked at some length with Commander Ringle* and other officials of the Office of

[11] *Id.* at 2.
[12] *Ibid.*
[13] *Id.* at 3.
[14] Biddle to McCloy, March 9, 1942, File ASW014.311 [Eastern Defense Command, Exclusion Order Reports], Entry 47, Box 6, Record Group 107, Records of the Assistant Secretary of War, National Archives and Records Service, Washington, D.C. See Exhibit O.

Naval Intelligence, 12th Naval District. *I was greatly impressed with Commander Ringle's knowledge* of the Japanese problem along the coast.[15]

Additionally, the substance and conclusions of the ONI Report came to the attention of officials of the Department of Justice during preparation of the Government's brief to the Supreme Court in the *Hirabayashi* case. Subsequent to his preparation of the report of January 26, 1942, Commander Ringle prepared, at the request of officials of the War Relocation Authority (WRA), an expanded 57-page report entitled "The Japanese Question in the United States."[16] This report discussed in detail such questions as dual citizenship, the Shinto religion, the education in Japan of the American-born "Kibei" group, and the basic loyalty of Japanese Americans. On each of these questions, Commander Ringle for the War Relocation Agency controverted every piece of "evidence" submitted to the Supreme Court on the loyalty issue by the Department of Justice in Petitioners' cases.

The ONI Report of January 26, 1942, along with excerpts from the report submitted to the WRA on June 15, 1942, was subsequently published in summary form in the October, 1942 issue of *Harper's Magazine*. This article was anonymously published under the title "The Japanese in America, The Problem and Solution," under the pseudonym "An Intelligence Officer."[17] In April, 1943, this article came to the attention of Edward J. Ennis of the Department of Justice, who was then responsible for preparation of the Government's brief to the Supreme Court in the *Hirabayashi* case. Ennis subsequently identified Commander Ringle as the author of the magazine article and obtained copies of the reports on which it was based.[18]

3. The Government's suppression of the ONI Report. On April 30, 1943, Ennis informed Solicitor General Fahy of his knowledge of the ONI Report and its contents. Given the importance of the memorandum from Ennis to Fahy, it is quoted below at length:

. . . I have repeatedly been told that the Army, before the war, agreed in writing to permit the Navy to conduct its Japanese intelligence work for it. I think it follows, therefore, that to a very considerable extent the Army . . . is bound by the opinion of the Naval officers in Japanese matters. Thus, had we known that

[15] McCloy to Biddle, March 21, 1942, See Exhibit P.
[16] Memorandum, "The Japanese Question in the United States," Lt. Commander K. D. Ringle, June 15, 1942, "Commander Ringle File." Box 573, Record Group 210, Records of the War Relocation Authority, National Archives and Records Service, Washington, D.C.
[17] *Harper's Magazine*, Vol. 185, No. 1109 (October 1942), p. 489.
[18] Memorandum, Ennis to Solicitor General, April 30, 1943, File 146-42-20, #8, Records of the Department of Justice. See Exhibit Q.

the Navy thought that 90 percent of the evacuation was unnecessary, we could strongly have urged upon General DeWitt that he could not base a military judgment to the contrary upon Intelligence reports, as he now claims to do.

Lt. Com. Ringle's full memorandum is somewhat more complete than the version published in Harpers and I think you will be interested in reading it. . . . [I]t is my opinion that *this is the most reasonable and objective discussion* of the security problem presented by the presence of the Japanese minority. In view of the inherent reasonableness of this memorandum and in view of the fact that *we now know that it represents the view of the Intelligence agency having the most direct responsibility for investigating the Japanese* from the security viewpoint, I feel that we should be extremely careful in taking any position on the facts more hostile to the Japanese than the position of Lt. Com. Ringle. . . . Furthermore, in view of the fact that the Department of Justice is now representing the Army in the Supreme Court of the United States and is arguing that a partial, selective evacuation was impracticable, we must consider most carefully what our obligation to the Court is in view of the fact that *the responsible Intelligence agency regarded a selective evacuation as not only sufficient but preferable.* It is my opinion that certainly one of the most difficult questions in the whole case is raised by the fact that the Army did not evacuate people after any hearing or on any individual determination of dangerousness, but evacuated the entire racial group. . . . Thus, in one of the crucial points of the case the Government is forced to argue that individual, selective evacuation would have been impracticable and insufficient when *we have positive knowledge that the only Intelligence agency responsible for advising General DeWitt gave him advice directly to the contrary.*

In view of this fact, I think we should consider very carefully whether we do not have a duty to advise the Court of the existence of the Ringle memorandum and of the fact that this represents the view of the Office of Naval Intelligence. It occurs to me that *any other course of conduct might approximate the suppression of evidence.*[19]

Despite this clear warning of the Government's duty to the Supreme Court, the Solicitor General ignored Ennis' memorandum. Although the Attorney General, the Assistant Secretary of War, and the Solicitor General each had personal knowledge of the existence and contents of the ONI Report, and knew that it controverted statements made to the Court on the loyalty issue, the Government's briefs to the Supreme Court in *Hirabayashi* and *Yasui* contained no mention whatsoever of the ONI Report.

4. The impact of suppression of the ONI Report on Petitioners' cases. Suppression of the ONI report had a direct and adverse impact on the outcome of Petitioners' cases. The report made clear that allegedly disloyal members of the Japanese American population could easily have

[19] *Ibid.*

been identified and segregated. As a less restrictive alternative to the mass evacuation and incarceration of the entire group, this would have been an admittedly preferable course. However, in contradiction of the ONI Report, the Government claimed in its *Hirabayashi* brief that such an alternative was impossible:

If those Japanese who might aid the enemy were either known or readily identifiable, the task of segregating them would probably have been comparatively simple. However, *the identities of the potentially disloyal were not readily discoverable.*[20]

The Government thus concluded that mass evacuation was necessary: "Since they [the disloyal] were not easily identifiable, the only certain way of removing them was to remove the group as a whole."[21]

The Government made a similar claim in its *Korematsu* brief:

There was a basis for concluding that some persons of Japanese ancestry, although American citizens, had formed an attachment to, and sympathy and enthusiasm for, Japan. It was also evident that *it would be impossible quickly and accurately to distinguish these persons from other citizens of Japanese ancestry.*[22]

The Government's claims on this issue clearly affected the opinions of the Supreme Court. The Court expressed its agreement with these claims in the following statement in its *Hirabayashi* opinion:

Whatever views we may entertain regarding the loyalty to this country of the citizens of Japanese ancestry, we cannot reject as unfounded the judgment . . . that *there were disloyal members of that population, whose number and strength could not be precisely and quickly ascertained.* We cannot say that the war-making branches of the Government did not have ground for believing that . . . *such persons could not readily be isolated and separately dealt with. . . .*[23]

The Supreme Court also cited this passage in the *Korematsu* opinion in upholding the exclusion order at issue.[24]

The importance of the ONI Report to Petitioners' cases cannot be over-stressed. Based on first-hand knowledge and access to all relevant information on the loyalty of Japanese Americans, it explicitly recommended against mass evacuation or other restrictive measures directed against

[20] *Hirabayashi* v. *United States*, 320 U.S. 81 (1943), Brief for the United States, p. 61.

[21] *Ibid.* These arguments were presented by reference to the Supreme Court in the *Yasui* brief. 320 U.S. 115 (1943), Brief for the United States, p. 8.

[22] *Korematsu* v. *United States*, 323 U.S. 214 (1944), Brief for the United States, p. 12. Footnote omitted.

[23] *Hirabayashi* v. *United States*, supra, 320 U.S. 81, 99.

[24] *Korematsu* v. *United States*, supra, 323 U.S. 214, 218.

Japanese Americans as a group. The ONI Report also directly refuted the unsupported disloyalty allegations made by General DeWitt in his Final Report. The suppression of this crucial document both from the courts and from Petitioners clearly constituted an egregious act of governmental misconduct.

C. *Officials of the War Department suppressed reports of the Military Intelligence Division that refuted the espionage allegations in the Final Report.* Among the most important records that show the falsity of the espionage allegations made by General DeWitt in his Final Report are those of DeWitt's own Military Intelligence Division (MID, or G-2). The suppression of these G-2 reports is of particular significance to Petitioners' cases, since they were submitted to DeWitt personally by members of his staff *before* the recommendation for mass evacuation and since they directly refuted DeWitt's statements in the Final Report.

Beginning on January 3, 1942, MID officials submitted directly to DeWitt a weekly "G-2 Periodic Report" that included assessments of enemy capabilities and intelligence sources. These reports were based on radio monitoring, aerial and naval reconnaissance, and reports from G-2 installations along the West Coast from San Diego to Alaska.[25] The first five of these weekly reports, dated January 3 through January 31, 1942, identically stated:

The enemy's probable knowledge of our situation has not been gained by observation or reconnaissance but by information learned during peace *and the activities of fifth-columnists.*[26]

Beginning on February 7, 1942, and continuing through May 16, 1942—at which time all of the military orders applicable to Petitioners had been issued—these G-2 reports contained a significant revision and uniformly stated:

The enemy's probable knowledge of our situation has not been gained by observation or reconnaissance but by information learned during peace by the activities of accredited, diplomatic, military and naval attachés and their agents.[27]

As noted above, DeWitt cited in his Final Report as a justification for mass evacuation "hundreds of reports nightly of signal lights visible from

[25] The reports for this period are located in Records of the Western Defense Command, G-2 Section, Weekly Intelligence Reports, 1942-1946, Record Group 338, Boxes 28-29, National Records Center, Suitland, Maryland. Those reports submitted through February 28, 1942, were signed by Colonel D. A. Stroh; those submitted through March 21, 1942, by Colonel J. H. Harrington; and those submitted through May 16, 1942 by Colonel John Weckerling.

[26] G-2 Periodic Report, No. 3, January 31, 1942. *Id.* Emphasis added. See Exhibit R.

[27] G-2 Periodic Report, No. 20, May 16, 1942, *Id.* Emphasis added. See Exhibit S.

the coast" and "the nightly observation of visual signal lamps from constantly changing locations. . . ."[28] The obvious implication of these statements was that Japanese Americans had been signaling to Japanese submarines off the coast. However, an Air Force intelligence report submitted to DeWitt on February 26, 1942 stated:

Numerous flares, signal lights, and unidentified naval surface craft have been reported, but not included in this report because of:

(1) The unreliability of source, or
(2) Improbability of information, or
(3) Negative investigation reports have included more reasonable or more probable natural causes for reported phenomena.[29]

Although DeWitt's own intelligence staff could find no evidence of espionage by Japanese Americans, DeWitt included such allegations in his Final Report and suppressed the G-2 reports that refuted his allegations. Suppression of the reports that eliminated prior references to "fifth-column" activities had a direct impact on Petitioners' cases. The Government's briefs to the Supreme Court stressed the "fifth-column" threat allegedly posed by Japanese Americans, and the Court specifically noted in *Hirabayashi* "the menace of the 'fifth column'" in the context of the Court's expression of "grave concern" about the loyalty of Japanese Americans.[30] Suppression of the exculpatory evidence contained in the G-2 reports thus constituted an act of governmental misconduct.

D. Officials of the War Department and the Department of Justice suppressed reports of the Federal Bureau of Investigation and the Federal Communications Commission that refuted the espionage allegations in the Final Report.

1. Initial reports of the FBI and FCC on espionage. Well before the outbreak of war between the United States and Japan, the Federal Bureau of Investigation (FBI) and the Federal Communications Commission (FCC) were actively engaged in the investigation of espionage activities on the West Coast and elsewhere in the country. After the Japanese attack on Pearl Harbor and the declaration of war on Japan, officials of both agencies worked closely with General DeWitt and his intelligence staff in this field. Reports of the FBI and FCC were available to Dewitt *before* his recommendation of the mass evacuation and incarceration of Japanese Americans that refuted the espionage allegations made in the Final Report. In addition, Justice Department officials failed to bring these reports

---

[28] DeWitt, *Final Report*, p. 8.
[29] 4th Air Force Periodic Intelligence Report, February 26, 1942, note 25, supra.
[30] *Hirabayashi* v. *United States*, supra, 320 U.S. at 96.

to the attention of the courts or Petitioners despite their exculpatory nature and their obvious relevance to Petitioners' cases.

The FBI played a direct role in the investigation of espionage. Pursuant to a secret directive issued by President Roosevelt in 1939, the FBI was assigned to investigate cases of "actual or strongly presumptive espionage or sabotage" within the United States. Accordingly, prior to and during the war the FBI conducted investigations of alleged acts of espionage or sabotage by Japanese Americans both on its own initiative and at the request of military intelligence agencies and state and local police.[31]

In March 1941, the FBI participated in the "surreptitious entry" of the Japanese consulate in Los Angeles, an undertaking of the Office of Naval Intelligence under the leadership of Lt. Commander Ringle.[32] Based on the lists of Japanese agents and sympathizers obtained in this raid and records seized during the subsequent arrest of Japanese agent Tachibana, the Japanese espionage network on the West Coast was dismantled in June 1941.[33] The names of those discovered to be Japanese sympathizers or spies were added to the Justice Department's "ABC" list of dangerous aliens. Some 1,370 Japanese aliens on the "ABC" list were arrested within five days of the Pearl Harbor attack.

FBI Director J. Edgar Hoover ordered a follow-up investigation of possible Japanese American espionage after the consular break-in. On November 8, 1941, Nat J. L. Pieper, Special Agent in Charge of the San Francisco FBI office, reported to Hoover that:

. . . practical results of espionage investigations of Japanese have been meager . . . [T]he reason for lack of practical results is that although surveillances, spot checks, and a thorough and logical investigation of individuals reported to be engaged in espionage activities has been conducted, no evidence has been obtained indicating that any have been guilty of violating any federal statutes for which prosecution would lie.[34]

In the period that followed the outbreak of war, the FBI continued to investigate all reports of espionage and sabotage. A number of these reports were transmitted to the FBI by Army personnel under the command of General DeWitt. Included were reports that Japanese Americans had committed acts of sabotage against the electric power lines and had lit "arrows of fire" designed to point Japanese airplanes toward military

---

[31] Note 8, supra.

[32] See Appendix, infra, note 7.

[33] *Ibid.*

[34] Memorandum, Special Agent in Charge N.J.L. Pieper to J. Edgar Hoover, November 8, 1941, File 100-71-1, Records of the Federal Bureau of Investigation. See "Memorandum on Pearl Harbor Attack and Bureau's Activities Before and After." *Id.*

targets. Hoover discussed these reports in a December 17, 1941, memorandum to senior members of his staff. Reporting on a telephone conversation with Pieper, Hoover noted that:

. . . there was no sense in the Army losing their heads as they did in the Bonneville Dam Affair, where the power lines were sabotaged by cattle scratching their backs on the wires, or the "arrows of fire" near Seattle, which was only a farmer burning brush as he had done for years.[35]

At no time in the period that preceded completion of the mass evacuation and incarceration of Japanese Americans did FBI reports substantiate any of the claims later made by General DeWitt in his Final Report of acts of espionage or sabotage.

The Federal Communications Commission was responsible for all radio monitoring in the United States before and during the war. Shortly after Pearl Harbor General DeWitt requested that the FCC supplement existing stationary monitoring facilities with mobile directionfinding intercept units to detect shore-to-ship radio transmissions. Subsequently, on January 9, 1942, DeWitt and his staff met with George E. Sterling, Chief of the FCC's Radio Intelligence Division. Sterling informed DeWitt at this meeting that the FCC's round-the-clock surveillance of the entire radio communications spectrum would detect any illicit radio transmitters.[36]

Following a discussion at this meeting of the FCC's capabilities and expertise, DeWitt established the Radio Intelligence Center (RIC) under the direction of the FCC. RIC operated as the central clearance agency on matters relating to radio intelligence and communications. Both the Army and Navy maintained direct telephone communications with RIC and had liaison personnel at the Center.[37]

Sterling came away from the meeting with DeWitt on January 9, 1942 with an impression that DeWitt and his staff were incompetent in the radio intelligence field. He expressed this attitude in a candid and scathing memorandum dated January 9:

The General launched into quite a discourse on the Japanese and other foreign language programs, *radio transmitters operated by enemy agents in California*

[35] Memorandum, J. Edgar Hoover to Mr. Tolson, Mr. Tamm, and Mr. Ladd, December 17, 1941, File 100-97-1-67, Records of the Federal Bureau of Investigation. See Exhibit T.

[36] Memorandum, "Conference With General DeWitt at San Francisco, Friday January 9th [1942]," Files of the Radio Intelligence Division, Record Group 173, Records of the Federal Communications Commission, National Archives and Records Service, Washington, D.C. See Exhibit U.

[37] Memorandum, Fly to Biddle, April 4, 1944, Box 37, Folder 3, Fahy Papers, FDRL. See Exhibit V.

sending messages to ships at sea, and a general discussion of the enemy aliens and all Japanese in the area followed.

Since Gen'l DeWitt seemed concerned and, in fact, *seemed to believe that the woods were full of Japs with transmitters*, I proceeded to tell him and his staff the organization [of the FCC radio monitoring program]. I know it virtually astounded the General's staff officers. . . .

Frankly, I have never seen an organization that was so hopeless to cope with radio intelligence requirements. . . . The personnel is unskilled and untrained. Most are privates who can read only ten words a minute. They know nothing about signal identification, wave propagation and other technical subjects, so essential to radio intelligence procedure. They take bearings with loop equipment on Japanese stations in Tokio. . . and report to their commanding officers that they have fixes on Jap agents operating transmitters on the West Coast. These officers, knowing no better, pass it on to the General and he takes their word for it. *It's pathetic to say the least.* . . .

Furthermore, Army reports Navy stations as being Japs and vice versa. . . . Whenever a station cannot be identified they call F.C.C. Consequently, it is easy to understand the hundreds of calls that have been made to the F.C.C. office in S.F. They look to the F.C.C. as an authority on all matters pertaining to radio communications other than their own.[38]

Despite Sterling's assurance that the FCC had detected no illicit radio transmissions, and the constant communication of his staff with RIC personnel, DeWitt continued to accuse Japanese Americans of radio espionage. DeWitt's charges were accepted as fact at the highest levels of command. On January 25, 1942, only 15 days after DeWitt's meeting with Sterling, Secretary of War Stimson urged Attorney General Biddle to accept DeWitt's first written evacuation proposal on the basis of these unfounded charges:

In recent conferences with General DeWitt, he has expressed great apprehension because of the presence on the West Coast of many thousand alien enemies. As late as yesterday, 24 January, he stated over the telephone that shore-to-ship and ship-to-shore radio communications, undoubtedly coordinated by intelligent enemy control were continually operating. . . . The alarming and dangerous situation just described, in my opinion, calls for immediate and stringent action.[39]

Although the FBI and FCC found no evidence of Japanese American involvement in espionage or sabotage, DeWitt deliberately included in his Final Report the discredited allegations of shore-to-ship signaling and

---

[38] Note 36, supra. Emphasis added.

[39] Stimson to Biddle, January 25, 1942, Record Group 107, Records, the Assistant Secretary of War, National Archives and Records Service, Washington, D.C. Quoted in R. Daniels, *The Decision to Relocate the Japanese Americans* (J. B. Lippincott Co. 1975) pp. 23–24.

radio transmissions. These allegations formed the core of the "military necessity" argument for the mass evacuation and incarceration of Japanese Americans. DeWitt included no mention in the Final Report of the FBI and FCC investigations and findings of which he had knowledge.

2. FBI and FCC refutations of DeWitt's espionage allegations. As noted above, War Department officials withheld release of the Final Report until January 1944. The falsity of DeWitt's espionage allegations was thus concealed from the Justice Department during considerations of the *Hirabayashi* and *Yasui* cases by the Supreme Court. Justice Department officials learned of the Report's release on January 20, 1944, through an article in the Washington Post headlined "Japs Attack All Ships Leaving Coast." Attorney General Biddle shortly thereafter requested reports from the FBI and FCC on the veracity of DeWitt's charges. This action was prompted by Edward J. Ennis and John L. Burling of the Alien Enemy Control Unit, who were then responsible for preparation of the Government's brief to the Supreme Court in the *Korematsu* case.

FBI Director Hoover submitted a detailed report to the Attorney General on February 7, 1944, entitled "Reported Bombing and Shelling of the West Coast." In his cover memorandum to this report, Hoover summarized the FBI's findings:

Certain statements were made in the report indicating that immediately after the attack on Pearl Harbor there was a possible connection between the sinking of United States ships by Japanese submarines and alleged Japanese espionage activity on the West Coast. It was also indicated that there had been shore-to-ship signaling, either by radio or lights, at this time.

As indicated in the attached memorandum, there is no information in the possession of this Bureau as the result of investigations conducted relative to submarine attacks and espionage activity on the West Coast which would indicate that attacks made on ships or shores in the area immediately after Pearl Harbor have been associated with any espionage activity ashore or that there has been any illicit shore-to-ship signaling, either by radio or lights.[40]

In an additional comment on DeWitt's allegations of shore-to-ship signaling, Hoover stated:

Every complaint in this regard has been investigated, but in no case has any information been obtained which would substantiate the allegations that there has been illicit signaling from shore-to-ship since the beginning of the war.[41]

[40] Memorandum, J. Edgar Hoover to the Attorney General, February 7, 1944, Folder—Japanese Relocation Cases III, Box 37, Fahy Papers, Franklin D. Roosevelt Library, Hyde Park, N.Y. [hereafter cited as Fahy Papers, FDRL]. The date indicated is that of receipt of the memorandum by the Office of the Attorney General. See Exhibit W.

[41] *Ibid.*

Preceding the Attorney General's request for an FCC report on DeWitt's charges, John L. Burling met on February 23, 1944, with George E. Sterling, Chief of the Radio Intelligence Division of the FCC. Burling's report to Ennis of this meeting stated the following:

Mr. Sterling read to me reports transmitted by his representatives of their discussions with General DeWitt's radio intelligence officers, in which it was explained to the Army men that their fixing operations were being poorly conducted. . . . His men also reported to the Army in every case in which the Army referred a complaint to them, and thus *the Army had notice that every complaint was unfounded.*[42]

On February 26, 1944, Attorney General Biddle requested a report from FCC Commissioner James L. Fly. In response to a request from Fly for material to assist in the FCC report, Sterling submitted a detailed memorandum dated March 25, 1944 on the activities of the Radio Intelligence Center established at DeWitt's order and its coordination with DeWitt's intelligence staff. This memorandum covered the period from December 1, 1941 to July 1, 1942 and concluded:

During this entire period of operation, no illegal radio stations were found within the confines of the Evacuated Area of the Western Defense Command.[43]

Most significantly, in a report to Biddle dated April 4, 1944, Commissioner Fly brought Sterling's January 9, 1942 memorandum to the attention of the Attorney General. This report similarly concluded:

There were no radio signals reported to the Commission which could not be identified, or which were unlawful. Like the Department of Justice, the Commission knows of no evidence of any illicit radio signaling in this area during the period in question.[44]

Although Biddle had received the reports from Hoover and Fly *six months* before it submitted its brief to the Supreme Court in *Korematsu*, the government's briefs make no mention whatsoever of the findings of the FBI and the FCC; nor was the existence of these reports ever disclosed to Korematsu's attorneys. As will be discussed below, the veracity of the Final Report was allowed to go unchallenged before the Supreme Court although the Justice Department had in its possession authoritative evidence that the allegations against the Japanese Americans set forth in DeWitt's Report were patently false. Indeed, the FBI and FCC reports

[42] Burling to Ennis, February 23, 1944, Section 23, File 146-13-7-2-0, Records of the Department of Justice. Emphasis added. See Exhibit X.

[43] Memorandum to the Chief Engineer, March 25, 1944, note 36, supra. See Exhibit Y.

[44] Fly to Biddle, April 4, 1944, Folder 3, Box 37, Fahy Papers, FDRL. See Exhibit V.

were suppressed even though Ennis had written to Biddle as early as February 26, 1944, the same day that Biddle had requested the FCC report, apprising him that:

[The Final Report] stands as practically the only record of causes for the evacuation and unless corrected will continue to do so. Its practical importance is indicated by the fact that already it is being cited in the briefs in the *Korematsu* case in the Supreme Court on the constitutionality of the evacuation.[45]

Thus, the suppression of the FBI and FCC findings that began with the *Hirabayashi* and *Yasui* cases was again perpetrated on the Court in *Korematsu*.

The suppression of the ONI Report, the G-2 reports, and the findings and reports of the FBI and FCC constituted egregious governmental misconduct which prejudiced Petitioners and subverted the entire course of the judicial process in their cases.

Point Three: Government Officials Failed to Advise the Supreme Court of the Falsity of the Allegations in the Final Report of General DeWitt

As shown above, officials of the War Department and Department of Justice had personal knowledge that the allegations of disloyalty and espionage in the Final Report of General DeWitt were false. Reports submitted to these officials by responsible intelligence agencies provided a conclusive refutation of these allegations, and discredited the "military necessity" claim offered by DeWitt in support of the mass evacuation and incarceration of Japanese Americans. These reports contained exculpatory evidence of direct relevance to the central issues in Petitioners' cases, and their suppression constituted prejudicial misconduct by governmental officials.

Government attorneys responsible for the Supreme Court brief in the *Korematsu* case subsequently attempted to advise the Court of the falsity of the Final Report. At the insistence of the War Department, Justice Department officials disregarded this effort and prevented the Court from learning of the exculpatory intelligence reports. This failure to advise the Court of these crucial reports constituted a still further act of governmental misconduct.

A. Government attorneys attempted to advise the Supreme Court of the

---

[45] Memorandum, Edward Ennis to Attorney General Biddle, February 26, 1944, Box 37, Folder 3, Fahy Papers, FDRL, Hyde Park, New York. See Exhibit Z.

falsity of the Final Report. As noted above, the War Department withheld the Final Report from the Justice Department until January 19, 1944, when it was released to the press.[1] Justice Department officials then conducted an independent investigation of the Report's espionage allegations. After receiving reports from the Federal Bureau of Investigation and the Federal Communications Commission which directly refuted these allegations, government attorneys responsible for the Supreme Court brief in the pending *Korematsu* case attempted to advise the Court of their existence. Thus, John L. Burling, Assistant Director of the Alien Enemy Control Unit of the Justice Department, inserted the following footnote in the Department's brief to the Supreme Court in *Korematsu*:

The Final Report of General DeWitt (which is dated June 5, 1943, but which was not made public until January, 1944) is relied on in this brief for statistics and other details concerning the actual evacuation and the events that took place subsequent thereto. The recital of the circumstances justifying the evacuation as a matter of military necessity, however, is in several respects, particularly with reference to the use of illegal radio transmitters and to shore-to-ship signaling by persons of Japanese ancestry, *in conflict with information in possession of the Department of Justice*. In view of the contrariety of the reports on this matter we do not ask the Court to take judicial notice of the recitals of those facts contained in the Report.[2]

The insertion of this significant footnote was designed to advise the Supreme Court that the Justice Department possessed evidence which refuted the espionage allegations in the Final Report. Burling explained the importance of this footnote in a memorandum to Assistant Attorney General Herbert Wechsler, who directed the War Division of the Department:

You will recall that General DeWitt's report makes flat statements concerning radio transmitters and ship-to-shore signalling which are categorically denied by the FBI and the Federal Communications Commission. *There is no doubt that these statements are intentional falsehoods . . .*[3]

The proposed footnote was set in print and circulated with the brief to War Department and Justice Department officials for final approval. Burling anticipated that the War Department would object to this repudiation of the asserted justification for General DeWitt's military orders. He appealed to Wechsler for support:

[1] See Point One, supra.
[2] Memorandum, John L. Burling to Assistant Attorney General Herbert Wechsler, September 11, 1984, File 146-42-7, Records of the Department of Justice. Emphasis added. See Exhibit AA.
[3] *Ibid*. Emphasis added.

I assume that the War Department will object to the footnote and I think that we should resist any further tampering with it with all our force.[4]

The *Korematsu* brief was due in printed form at the Supreme Court on October 5, 1944. During the last week of September, a printed copy was sent to Assistant Secretary of War John J. McCloy for his comments.

B. At the insistence of the War Department, Justice Department officials altered the Burling footnote and thus failed to advise the Supreme Court of the falsity of the Final Report. Shortly after they received the *Korematsu* brief, War Department officials undertook a shocking campaign designed to remove the footnote drafted by Burling. In a report to his superior, Edward J. Ennis, dated October 2, 1944, Burling described the War Department's campaign of intervention and manipulation:

Although the War Department was furnished with a first draft of the brief last April and although it had a copy of the page proof for about a week, the War Department did not react to the brief until the morning of September 30 when Captain [Adrian S.] Fisher [of the staff of Assistant Secretary of War McCloy] called you and suggested a change. It became necessary for you to suggest the possibility to Captain Fisher that the brief had gone for final printing and, presumably, as a result of this, Mr. McCloy called the Solicitor General and particularly referred to the footnote. *Presumably at Mr. McCloy's request, the Solicitor General had the printing stopped at about noon.*[5]

When he learned that Solicitor General Fahy had stopped the printing of the government's brief at the insistence of McCloy, Ennis immediately prepared a memorandum to Assistant Attorney General Wechsler "strongly recommending that the footnote be kept in its existing form." Among the "various exhibits illustrating the falsity of the DeWitt report" that Ennis attached to this memorandum were the FBI and FCC reports previously submitted to the Attorney General. Wechsler in turn forwarded Ennis's memorandum and the appended documents to Solicitor General Fahy.[6]

Ennis urged in this memorandum that the disputed footnote was necessary to advise the Supreme Court that the Justice Department knew DeWitt's espionage allegations to be untrue. He stated that alteration or removal of the footnote would amount to a breach of the Department's ethical responsibilities and an abuse of the judicial notice doctrine:

[4] *Ibid.*

[5] Memorandum, John L. Burling to Edward Ennis, October 2, 1944, *ibid.* Emphasis added. See Exhibit BB.

[6] Memorandum, Edward Ennis to Herbert Wechsler, September 30, 1944, Folder 3, Box 37, Fahy Papers. See Exhibit B.

This Department has an ethical obligation to the Court to refrain from citing it [the Final Report] as a source of which the Court may properly take judicial notice if the Department knows that important statements in the source are untrue and if it knows as to other statements that there is such contrariety of information that judicial notice is improper.[7]

Ennis added that the Justice Department had an additional obligation to the Japanese Americans falsely accused by DeWitt of espionage activities:

The general tenor of the report is not only that there was a reason to be apprehensive, but also to the effect that overt acts of treason were being committed. *Since this is not so it is highly unfair to this racial minority that these lies, put out in an official publication, go uncorrected.* This is the only opportunity which this Department has to correct them.[8]

Despite this clear warning of the duty owed to the Supreme Court by the Department of Justice, neither Wechsler nor Fahy answered the memorandum submitted by Ennis. According to Burling, Fahy met with Captain Fisher at the request of Assistant Secretary McCloy on Saturday evening, September 30, 1944. Burling later reported to Ennis that at this meeting:

Captain Fisher took the position that *he would not defend the accuracy of the report* but that the Government would deal with sufficient honesty with the [Supreme Court] if it would merely refrain from reciting the report without affirmatively flagging our criticism thereof.[9]

At the conclusion of the September 30 meeting, Solicitor General Fahy directed Wechsler to reach a compromise on the disputed footnote by Monday, October 2. Accordingly, Wechsler drafted the following two alternatives as a substitute for the original footnote:

1. "We have specifically recited in this brief the facts relating to the justification for the evacuation, of which we ask the court to take judicial notice; and we rely upon the Final Report only to the extent that it relates to such facts."
2. "We do not ask the court to notice judicially such particular details recited in the report as justification for the evacuation as the use of illegal radio transmitters and shore-to-ship signaling by persons of Japanese ancestry, which conflict with information derived from other sources."[10]

Wechsler read the alternative drafts to Captain Fisher by telephone on the morning of October 2. In this conversation, Wechsler explained that

---

[7] *Ibid.*   [8] *Ibid.*
[9] Note 5, supra.
[10] Memorandum, Captain Fisher to McCloy, October 2, 1944, File 014.311, Western Defense Command Exclusion Orders (Korematsu), Box 9, Record Group 107, National Archives. See Exhibit CC.

the first alternative was designed to "drop out any reference to matters in controversy" and that it had been phrased in "the gentlest conceivable way." [11] After this conversation, Fisher called Burling at the Justice Department and told him that "although the War Department did not agree to either alternative, nevertheless the first would be preferable." [12]

The War Department's victory in persuading the Justice Department to alter the Burling footnote kept the Supreme Court from learning of vitally important exculpatory evidence which undermined the factual justification for DeWitt's military orders. The consequence of the government's failure to expose the falsity of the Final Report is apparent in the Supreme Court's opinion in *Korematsu*, for, in upholding the constitutionality of the exclusion order at issue, the Court found that it "has a definite and close relationship to the prevention of espionage and sabotage." [13]

The inherent incredibility of the Final Report was evident to Justice Jackson, who expressed skepticism in his dissenting opinion in *Korematsu*:

How does the Court know that these orders have a reasonable basis in necessity? No evidence whatever has been taken by this or any other court. There is a sharp controversy as to the credibility of the DeWitt report. So the Court, having no real evidence before it, has no choice but to accept General DeWitt's own unsworn, self-serving statement, untested by any cross-examination, that what he did was reasonable. [14]

Evidence on the credibility of DeWitt's allegations existed at the time of Petitioners' trials and subsequent appeals. The failure of the government to advise the Court of this evidence constituted misconduct that both violated ethical standards of conduct and subverted the judicial process.

Point Four: The Government's Abuse of the Doctrine of Judicial Notice and the Manipulation of Amicus Briefs Constituted a Fraud upon the Courts

Petitioners' cases proceeded from trial through decision by the Supreme Court on a record intentionally fashioned to assure their convictions. The acts of alteration, destruction and suppression of evidence alleged in the instant petition separately constituted misconduct that deprived Peti-

[11] Transcript of telephone conversation, Fisher and Wechsler, October 2, 1944, *ibid.* See Exhibit DD.
[12] Note 10, supra.
[13] *Korematsu* v. *United States*, supra, 323 U.S. 214, 218.
[14] *Id.* at 245.

tioners of their constitutional rights. The cumulative effect of these acts of misconduct was calculated to induce the courts to rely on false and misleading statements.

In addition, the government's abuse of the doctrine of judicial notice and its manipulation of amicus briefs were intentionally designed to place an equally false and misleading record before the courts. The acts of misconduct alleged above deprived Petitioners and the courts a full and accurate factual record; those alleged below show that the records actually submitted to the courts by the government were tainted and presumptively affected the outcome of Petitioners' cases. The acts alleged below thus constituted a fraud upon the courts.

A. *The government abused the doctrine of judicial notice during the course of Petitioners' cases.* During the entire course of Petitioners' cases, the government's attempt to demonstrate the alleged "disloyalty" of Japanese Americans involved abuse of the doctrine of judicial notice. The effort to show that the "racial characteristics" of Japanese Americans predisposed them to disloyalty, and to the commission of espionage and sabotage, began, in fact, before any of the Petitioners were tried.

Minoru Yasui was the first of Petitioners to be tried. On May 29, 1942, the month before Yasui's trial took place, the U.S. Attorney for Oregon requested the advice of Maurice Walk, Assistant Solicitor of the War Relocation Authority:

Insofar as the rules of evidence permit, I wish to introduce evidence to support the proclamation of the Western Defense Command . . . affecting the Japanese *by reason of their racial characteristics* and belief which stamp and distinguish them from other nationalities.[1]

Walk responded on June 6, 1942, advising the U.S. Attorney to include in the trial record "facts justifying the exclusion of American citizens of Japanese descent from the declared military zones." He stated that, given the unavailability of evidence necessary to prove the disloyalty of Japanese Americans, reliance on judicial notice was necessary to establish the military's belief in collective disloyalty as evidentiary fact:

In my judgment, we have got to recognize that the facts relied on to vindicate the legality of this differential treatment are *not susceptible of proof by the ordinary types of evidence.* We shall probably, therefore, be compelled to rely greatly on the doctrine of judicial notice.[2]

---

[1]Letter, Carl C. Donaugh to Maurice Walk, May 29, 1942, Box 337, Record Group 210 [Records of the War Relocation Authority], National Archives and Records Service, Washington, D.C. Emphasis added.

[2]Letter, Maurice Walk to Carl C. Donaugh, June 6, 1942. *Id.* See Exhibit EE.

The source and purpose of this advice on trial strategy is significant. As Assistant Solicitor of the WRA, Walk had no direct responsibility for the prosecution of Petitioners. However, the WRA administered the "relocation centers" in which Japanese Americans were incarcerated, and WRA officials anticipated legal challenges to their power to detain those being held in the centers. Walk's advice in the *Yasui* case was designed to utilize that trial as a "dry run" of a strategy based on the doctrine of judicial notice, for later application to expected challenges to incarceration. Walk made clear that the success of this strategy in the *Yasui* case would establish the "military necessity" foundation for subsequent exclusion and detention cases:

It is of great importance to us, in planning the strategy of a case which will necessarily involve the validity of the detention of Japanese Americans as well as their exclusion from military areas, to know *just how far we are likely to go with the doctrine of judicial notice*. For this reason . . . I hope that you will find it possible to urge the foregoing consideration upon the court in the approaching trial of Minoru Yasui.[3]

In a lengthy memorandum to the U.S. Attorney in Oregon, Walk listed eleven "propositions" relating to the alleged existence and danger of a "fifth column" of Japanese Americans. These propositions reflected nothing more than supposition and racial stereotypes about Japanese Americans. The following excerpts from Walk's memorandum exemplify this bias:

There is a Japanese fifth column in this country of undisclosed and undetermined dimensions. *It is composed of American citizens of Japanese descent, and will be used as an instrument of espionage and sabotage.* A fifth column exists by virtue of successfully pretending loyalty to the country of citizenship and successfully concealing all evidence of its activities from the constituted authorities.

A great majority of American citizens of Japanese descent are loyal to this country; but it is impossible during this period of emergency to make a particular investigation of the loyalty of each person in the Japanese community. *Such an investigation would be hampered in any case by the difficulties which the Caucasian experiences with Oriental psychology.*[4]

Walk further advised that, under the doctrine of judicial notice, evidence should be introduced that dealt with those Japanese Americans educated in Japan, those who adhered to the Shinto religion and those who had "dual nationality" as a result of Japan's citizenship laws. Each of these statements of "fact" assumed the consequent disloyalty of Japa-

---

[3] *Ibid.* Emphasis added.
[4] *Ibid.* Emphasis added.

nese Americans. Walk concluded by urging that the U.S. Attorney employ the judicial notice doctrine in the *Yasui* trial to place these "propositions" on the record.[5]

In response to this advice, the U.S. Attorney attempted to introduce "evidence" of racial characteristics of Japanese Americans in the *Yasui* trial. The government first sought to present this evidence through the testimony of an unidentified "expert witness." The U.S. Attorney informed the court of:

. . . the availability of a man who is familiar, by reason of long residence and contact, with the Orient, and in particular the Japanese people . . . who is available to testify as to . . . *the Japanese as a race of people* and their ideals and culture *and their type of loyalty* . . . under which circumstances such as the present condition of war between Japan and the United States.[6]

Walk's strategy received an initial setback in the *Yasui* trial. Counsel for Yasui responded to the U.S. Attorney's attempt to place the "expert witness" on the stand with a statement that he would "object to any testimony or dissertation by some man as to his conclusions as to what some of the Japanese [Americans] might do under certain circumstances."[7] The trial judge informed the U.S. Attorney that "I have no interest in this matter at all," and the proffered witness was withdrawn.[8]

Although government attorneys retreated from this approach in the subsequent *Hirabayashi* and *Korematsu* trials, the judicial notice strategy was refined for use in the appellate proceedings in Petitioners' cases. This strategy was outlined in a memorandum prepared by Nanette Dembitz of the Alien Enemy Control Unit of the Department of Justice. Entitled "Method of Presenting Facts Relevant to the Constitutionality of Japanese Evacuation Program," this memorandum urged the following approach:

It appears that facts as to the following matters should be presented to the Court: The number of persons of Japanese ancestry, both alien and non-alien, in the

---

[5] *Ibid.* For example, the reference to the "indeterminable" number of adherents of Shinto concluded: "It is impossible to predict how such persons would act if any army of the Emperor of Japan were landed upon our shores." The final three "propositions" were predicated on the assumption that public hostility toward Japanese Americans would justify their detention. The Government's brief to the Supreme Court in *Hirabayashi* pressed this "preventive detention" argument, notwithstanding that it had no factual or constitutional support. Brief for the United States, pp. 31–32.

[6] The transcript of the *Yasui* trial is found in *Yasui* v. *United States*, 320 U.S. 115 (1943), Brief for the United States and Record. Record, pp. 206–207. Emphasis added. The Government also offered the testimony of an official of the Lumber and Sawmill Workers Union at the *Yasui* trial in order to show that hostility toward Japanese Americans "threatened to affect the very war production effort," and that "their own safety demands that there be a certain type. . . of restriction" such as the curfew at issue. The District Judge sustained an objection to this testimony. Record, pp. 201–207.

[7] *Id.* at 207.

[8] *Id.* at 208.

United States; . . . *the lack of assimilation of such persons in the population as a whole*; the existence of methods by which the loyalty of such persons to Japan might have been encouraged, such as the activities of Japanese Consuls, the return of such persons to Japan for education, the dual citizenship of American citizens, and activities of Shinto priests; the engagement of such persons in espionage and sabotage. . . .[9]

After a canvass of existing precedent on this question, Dembitz offered the following advice:

As to the facts in point with respect to the Japanese program, it appears that all of them could be established to the Court's satisfaction without the introduction of evidence and that even the citation of documentary authority would not be necessary with respect to many of them; however, it is obvious that as much documentary authority as is available should be used. *It would also appear that the facts could be sufficiently established, without the use of evidence, so that the Court would refuse an offer of evidence to contradict these facts.*[10]

Justice Department attorneys adopted the approach suggested by Dembitz in preparation of the briefs submitted to the Supreme Court in Petitioners' cases. The "racial characteristics" argument was presented most extensively in the government's *Hirabayashi* brief, with the "evidence" presented in that brief incorporated by reference in the *Yasui* and *Korematsu* briefs as well.[11]

The government sought judicial notice of "evidence" that allegedly proved the disloyalty of Japanese Americans and their consequent predisposition to commit acts of espionage and sabotage. However, government officials had knowledge of contrary evidence on each of these issues. The report of the Office of Naval Intelligence, submitted by Lieutenant Commander Ringle in January 1942, refuted the "disloyalty" claims made by General DeWitt and subsequently repeated in the government's briefs to the Supreme Court. Officials of the War and Justice Departments knew of the ONI report as early as March 1942. In March 1944, the Federal Bureau of Investigation and the Federal Communications Commission reported to the Justice Department that DeWitt's espionage allegations were false. Nonetheless, the government continued to press the doctrine of judicial notice on the courts so as to introduce

[9]Memorandum, Nanette Dembitz to John L. Burling, August 11, 1942, File 31.090, Box 332, Record Group 210, National Archives. See Exhibit FF (only pp. 1–6 and 17–18 attached). Emphasis added.

[10]*Id.* at 17. Emphasis added. It should be noted that this memorandum followed by a month the refusal by Judge Fee at the trial of Minoru Yasui to hear direct evidence on the disloyalty issue, on the ground of irrelevance.

[11]See these briefs generally.

"facts" which were either false or contradicted by evidence in the government's possession.

The Supreme Court's reliance on the "disloyalty" evidence presented under the judicial notice doctrine is evident in its opinions in Petitioners' cases, as illustrated in the following excerpt from *Hirabayashi*:

Whatever views we may entertain regarding the loyalty to this country of the citizens of Japanese ancestry, we cannot reject as unfounded the judgment of the military authorities and of Congress that *there were disloyal members of that population*, whose number and strength could not be precisely and quickly ascertained.[12]

An examination of the records presented in these cases clearly reveals the government's abuse of judicial notice. Nanette Dembitz, who recommended that the government rely on this doctrine and who signed the government's brief in *Hirabayashi*, subsequently recanted her position and she authoritatively discussed the abuse of the judicial notice doctrine in *Hirabayashi* and subsequent decisions. In an article published June 1945 in the Columbia Law Review, entitled "Racial Discrimination and the Military Judgment: The Supreme Court's *Korematsu* and *Endo* Decisions," Dembitz examined virtually every piece of "evidence" submitted to the Supreme Court in each of Petitioners' cases. She asserted that the doctrine of judicial notice is not applicable if "there is a bona fide dispute about the existence of the fact" at issue. She cited countering evidence of many of the "facts" presented to the Supreme Court and criticized the use of the doctrine to admit racial stereotype and public prejudices as evidentiary fact.[13]

Dembitz concluded that the "facts" placed on record by the government were not facts susceptible to judicial notice:

A "reasonable" man *could not and would not* have come to a positive conclusion, on the basis of the available documentary data, that most of the supposed influences toward disloyalty did in fact exist; *a belief in their existence could not be said to rest on "reasonable or substantial grounds"* insofar as the phrase

[12] *Hirabayashi* v. *United States*, 320 U.S. 81, 99 (1943).

[13] 45 Col. L. Rev. 175, 185, n. 9. Ms. Dembitz quoted the statement in *Hirabayashi* that governmental authorities "have constitutional power to appraise the danger [posed by Japanese Americans] in the light of facts of public notoriety." She then noted that "the opinion itself shows that the danger was appraised not in the light of the 'facts' reasonably established by consideration of an adequate amount of data but of widely held suspicions, such as may be possessed by every group of society with respect to every other group. A typical instance is the statement, frequently and positively made, that the persons of Japanese ancestry have close filial ties and are thus easily dominated by their parents, as contrasted with the findings by reputable sociologists that the second-generation generally strive to disassociate themselves from the ways of their parents even more than in the usual immigrant families."

connotes that a fact is established by a preponderance of evidence after weighing of an adequate amount of data on both sides.[14]

In view of the government's knowledge of contrary evidence on the central "disloyalty" issue, the long-range strategy initiated before Petitioners' trials and pursued during the entire course of their cases constituted an abuse of the doctrine of judicial notice and resulted in a fraud upon the courts.

B. The War Department manipulated the amicus briefs of the West Coast states and unlawfully submitted "evidence" withheld from the Department of Justice. As noted above, in April 1943, the Justice Department had requested the Final Report of General DeWitt to assist in preparation of the Supreme Court brief in the *Hirabayashi* case. Because of their concern about certain statements in the Final Report on the "military necessity" issue, however, War Department officials withheld the Final Report from the Justice Department until January 1944.

Despite this act by War Department officials, they *did* release the initial version of the Final Report for presentation to the Supreme Court in the *Hirabayashi* case. General DeWitt personally delegated a member of his legal staff, Captain Herbert E. Wenig, to assist the Attorney General of California in preparing the amicus brief submitted on behalf of the three West Coast states.[15] Captain Wenig was then a member of the Judge Advocate's staff of the Western Defense Command. Wenig prepared an amicus brief which included lengthy excerpts, without attribution, from the initial version of the Final Report. Most of these excerpts presented a "racial characteristics" argument designed to persuade the Court that Japanese Americans were inherently disloyal. The following excerpt from the amicus brief illustrates the central point of this argument:

The Japanese of the Pacific Coast area on the whole have remained a group apart and *inscrutable to their neighbors.* They represent an unassimilated, homoge-

[14] *Id*. at 185–186. Emphasis added.

[15] Letter, Attorney General Robert Kenny to Colonel Joel Watson, May 1, 1943, Hirabayashi File, Record Group 153 [Records of the Judge Advocate General's Office], Washington National Records Center, Suitland, Maryland. Attorney General Kenny wrote as follows: ". . . I greatly appreciate the assistance being rendered this office by Lieutenant [sic] Herbert E. Wenig, whom General DeWitt has designated to provide liaison with this office." It is additionally significant that the War Department also collaborated with the West Coast states in the preparation in 1944 of an amicus brief to the Supreme Court in the *Korematsu* case. The Judge Advocate General noted this collaboration in a letter to the Deputy Chief of Staff of the Western Defense Command: "This letter will confirm understanding just had with you and approved by General Emmons [who succeeded General DeWitt in September, 1943] that the Judge Advocate section collaborate fully, but informally, with the Attorneys General of the states mentioned in the preparation of a joint brief to be filed by them

neous element which in varying degrees is closely related through ties of race, language, religion, custom and ideology to the Japanese Empire.[16]

The amicus brief concluded that these "racial characteristics" created a reasonable suspicion that Japanese Americans would engage in espionage and sabotage:

The facts just reviewed indicate that because of the racial, cultural, religious and ideological ties and sympathies with Japan and the various causes which have kept the Japanese apart, there would be a sufficient number that could be used as a fifth column in assisting in sabotage or espionage or giving aid in the event of an attempted attack.[17]

In a highly misleading manner, the amicus brief also presented to the Supreme Court the espionage allegations made in the Final Report. After reciting three alleged incidents of Japanese attack on the West Coast in 1942, the brief drew the following conclusion:

There was an increasing indication that the enemy had knowledge of our patrols and naval dispositions, for ships leaving west coast ports were being intercepted and attacked regularly by enemy submarines.[18]

The amicus brief assured the Supreme Court that the "facts" presented to the Court were deserving of judicial notice:

. . . the Court may take notice of many of the facts to be stated because *they are generally notorious* and are . . . matters of public concern upon which the Court may inform itself by reference to documentary evidence of any other reliable source.[19]

---

as amici curiae in the above mentioned case." Judge Advocate General to Deputy Chief of Staff, March 31, 1944, Korematsu File. *Ibid.*

[16] Brief of the States of California, Oregon and Washington as Amici Curiae, p. 11. Emphasis added. Compare the following statement in the *Final Report*: "Here was a relatively homogeneous, unassimilated element bearing a close relationship through ties of race, religion, language, custom, and indoctrination to the enemy." DeWitt, *Final Report*, p. 15. The extent of reliance in the brief of the West Coast States on the *Final Report* is substantial. Statements on pp. 10, 11, 14–20, 22–23, and 25–26 of the West Coast brief are taken directly from the latter source.

[17] *Id.* at 26.

[18] *Id.* at 10. The statement quoted above misleadingly compressed into one charge two allegations made against Japanese Americans in the *Final Report*, which read as follows: "In summary, the Commanding General was confronted with *the Pearl Harbor experience*, which involved a positive enemy knowledge of our patrols, naval dispositions, etc., on the morning of December 7th; [and] with the fact that ships leaving West Coast ports were being intercepted regularly by enemy submarines. . . ." DeWitt, *Final Report*, p. 18. Emphasis added. Notwithstanding the obvious suspicion of General DeWitt that Japanese Americans had aided in both the Japanese attack on Pearl Harbor and subsequent submarine attacks on shipping, he did not directly link the two episodes. In stating as a fact that such a linkage existed, the states' amicus brief misled the Supreme Court. See discussion of War Department involvement in the preparation of this brief under Point Three, *infra.*

[19] *Id.* at 8.

These "generally notorious" facts were, in truth, no more than the unsupported allegations of an interested party. By making the Final Report available to the West Coast states, and delegating Captain Wenig to assist in preparing the amicus brief, General DeWitt sought to perpetrate a fraud upon the courts. By concealing the Final Report from the Department of Justice, while assuring its introduction through friendly amici, DeWitt manipulated the judicial process and in fact committed a fraud upon the Court. Significantly, when the Justice Department belatedly learned of DeWitt's actions after Supreme Court decision of *Hirabayashi*, it properly condemned his unlawful behavior:

It is also to be noted that parts of the [Final Report] which, in April 1942 [sic] could not be shown to the Department of Justice in connection with the *Hirabayashi* case in the Supreme Court, were printed in the brief amici curiae of the States of California, Oregon and Washington. In fact the Western Defense Command *evaded the statutory requirement* that this Department represent the Government in this litigation *by preparing the erroneous and intemperate brief* which the States filed.[20]

In upholding the constitutionality of the military orders under which petitioners were prosecuted and convicted, the Supreme Court relied upon the very "facts" purportedly demonstrating the disloyalty of the Japanese Americans that the states' amicus brief, with the aid of General DeWitt, presented to the Court. That the government possessed other evidence refuting the charges asserted in the amicus brief, renders DeWitt's manipulation of the judicial process that much more egregious. The false factual picture presented to the Court by means of the government's abuse of judicial notice and manipulation of the states' amicus brief led the Court in *Hirabayashi* to conclude that the military orders at issue:

. . . were defense measures for the avowed purpose of safeguarding the military area in question, at a time of threatened air raids and invasion by the Japanese forces, from the danger of espionage and sabotage.[21]

Such a deliberate manipulation of the judicial process constituted a fraud upon the Court.

---

[20]Memorandum, Edward J. Ennis to Herbert Wechsler, September 30, 1944, Folder 3, Box 37, Fahy Papers. Emphasis added. See Exhibit B.
[21]*Hirabayashi* v. *United States*, supra, 320 U.S. at 94–95.

Point Five: Petitioners Are Also Entitled to Relief on the Ground That Their Convictions Are Based on Governmental Orders That Violate Current Constitutional Standards

Petitioners further allege that their convictions are based on governmental orders that violate current substantive constitutional standards. Nearly forty years ago, the Supreme Court sustained the constitutionality of the government's decision to impose a curfew on and then to evacuate all Japanese Americans living on the West Coast. In doing so, however, the Court did not in fact apply the same type of "strict scrutiny" of suspect classifications that would be applied today. The Court deferred to the government's unproven assertions that a grave danger of espionage and sabotage existed, that Japanese Americans should be regarded as potential saboteurs, and that an appropriate method of combatting this perceived danger was first to impose a curfew on all persons of Japanese ancestry and then to evacuate and detain this entire racial group.

In racial discriminations cases decided after *Korematsu*, the Court demanded far more from the government to justify the use of a racial classification that burdened or stigmatized a racial minority. The government now has the exceedingly difficult task of *proving* that it is essential to use such a classification to fulfill a compelling governmental interest and that no less restrictive alternative is available. The Court has consistently held, in cases decided after *Korematsu*, that the government has failed to meet this highly demanding burden of proof. Moreover, the Court has stated that the government's burden is particularly great when the Court is reviewing a criminal conviction based on a racial classification.

Judged by today's standards, the government plainly did not offer sufficient proof to justify the racial classification challenged in Petitioners' cases. Thus, Petitioners' convictions violate their right to equal protection, as applied through the Due Process Clause of the Fifth Amendment. A petition in the nature of a writ of error coram nobis is the appropriate means of remedying this fundamental constitutional defect in Petitioners' convictions.

Prayer for Relief

Petitioners respectfully submit that it would be impossible to find any other instance in American history of such a long standing, pervasive and unlawful governmental scheme designed to mislead and defraud the courts and the nation. By the misconduct set forth in detail above, the United States deprived petitioners of their rights to fair judicial proceedings guaranteed by the Fifth Amendment to the United States Constitution. Although successful to date, this fundamental and egregious denial of civil liberties cannot be permitted to stand uncorrected.

Wherefore, petitioner Fred Toyosaburo Korematsu respectfully prays:

1. That judgment of conviction be vacated;
2. That the military orders under which he was convicted be declared unconstitutional;
3. That his indictment be dismissed;
4. For costs of suit and reasonable attorneys' fees;
5. For such other relief as may be just and proper.

Dated: January 19, 1983

Respectfully submitted,

By: Peter Irons
By: Dale Minami
    Minami, Tomine & Lew

Appendix

Petitioners have presented above those facts that relate to the issuance of Executive Order 9066 and enactment of Public Law 503, and the promulgation of the military orders applicable to Japanese Americans on the West Coast. Petitioners consider it necessary as well to recount in this Appendix those significant events that preceded and led to the adoption of these measures. Such a recounting will enable the Court to place in proper context the origins of the internment program and the allegations of governmental misconduct made throughout this Petition. In particular, the steps taken before the Pearl Harbor attack to combat espionage and sabotage, the political pressures that culminated in the internment program, and the concomitant debate among government officials over the necessity for and constitutionality of this program, are of central importance to this Petition.

A. *Steps Taken by the Government Before the Pearl Harbor Attack to Combat Espionage and Sabotage*

It is relevant to claims advanced by the government during Petitioners' cases to recount the steps taken before the Japanese attack on Pearl Harbor to protect the West Coast area against potential espionage and sabotage. Predicated on apprehensions of an eventual state of war between Japan and the United States, planning in this regard began in June, 1939 with a secret directive issued by President Roosevelt. The President ordered that "the investigation of all espionage, counter-espionage and sabotage matters be controlled and handled" jointly by the Federal Bureau of Investigation (FBI), the Military Intelligence Division of the Army (MID), and the Office of Naval Intelligence of the Navy (ONI).[1]

A year later, on June 4, 1940, the President's order that such intelligence operations be "coordinated" by these three agencies was modified by a "Delimitation Agreement" that assigned to the FBI control over cases of "actual or strongly presumptive espionage or sabotage, including the names of individuals definitely known to be connected with subversive activities." Significantly, this agreement delegated to ONI primary responsibility for the collection and dissemination of intelligence relating to the Japanese American population, presumably because of the proximity of segments of this population to naval installations along the West Coast.[2]

Within the United States Department of Justice, responsibility for pre-war planning for the treatment of potential "alien enemies" was delegated to the Special Defense Unit. Personnel of this Unit compiled extensive lists of "subversive" and "dangerous" aliens of German, Italian and Japanese citizenship. In collated form, these lists were informally known as the "ABC" list, so called from the listing of three categories of aliens in descending order of potential danger.[3] By mid-1941, some six

---

[1] United States Navy, Office of Intelligence, "United States Naval Administration in World War II," n.d., pp. 66–69. See Exhibit M.

[2] *Ibid.*

[3] Those listed in category "A" were the "known dangerous" aliens, which included among the Japanese American population "fishermen, produce distributors, Shinto and Buddhist priests, influential businessmen, and members of the Japanese Consulate." Those in category "B" were considered "potentially dangerous" but had not been thoroughly investigated, while those in category "C" had not been connected to Japanese intelligence activities but "were watched because of their pro-Japanese inclinations and propagandist activities." This last group included Japanese language instructors, martial arts instructors, travel agents, and newspaper editors. Office of Naval Intelligence, "Japanese Organizations and Societies Engaged in Propaganda, Espionage and Cultural Work," ONI File A8-5/EF37, ONI Records, National Archives and Records Service, Washington, D.C.

months before the Pearl Harbor attack, the "ABC" list included the names of more than 2,000 aliens of Japanese descent.[4] This group included virtually the entire leadership of the West Coast population of Japanese Americans, the vast majority of them aliens by virtue of restrictive Federal legislation.[5]

The FBI and military intelligence agencies submitted to the Special Defense Unit the names of Japanese Americans considered potentially dangerous for inclusion on the "ABC" list. Some of these names were taken from public sources such as the publications of Japanese American organizations and newspapers such as the Rafu Shimpo in Los Angeles.[6] A more significant source of names was the list of Japanese sympathizers and espionage agents seized in March, 1941 during an illegal break-in and burglary of the Japanese consulate in Los Angeles. This break-in was planned and executed by Lieutenant Commander Kenneth D. Ringle of ONI, with the aid of the FBI. This intelligence operation effectively dismantled a Japanese espionage network on the West Coast and led in June, 1941, to the arrest of Itaru Tachibana, a Japanese naval officer posing as an English language student. Along with the records photographed by Government agents during the consular break-in, and those seized when Tachibana was arrested, were lists of agents who had gathered intelligence on behalf of the Japanese government in the form of maps, lists of Army and Navy installations, data on defense factories, and the locations of power lines and dams.[7]

B. Steps Taken After the Pearl Harbor Attack to Deal With Japanese Americans Considered Dangerous

The significance to Petitioners' cases of the consular break-in and the arrest of Tachibana lies in subsequent conclusions by the FBI about their impact on Japanese intelligence operations. As noted above in Point Two, FBI officials concluded that the break-in and arrests had ended any substantial threat of espionage and sabotage on the West Coast by Japanese

[4] *Ibid.* See also Custodial Detention Files, File 100-2-60-3, Sections 180–190, Records of the Federal Bureau of Investigation. The "ABC" list was formally known as the Custodial Detention Index.

[5] The Immigration Act of 1924 excluded Japanese from admission into the United States. 43 Stat. 161. Federal law, also enacted in 1924, denied to the Japanese citizenship by naturalization. 8 U.S.C. §703 (1924).

[6] Note 3, supra.

[7] This account is based on Kenneth D. Ringle, Jr., "What Did You Do Before the War, Dad?", *The Washington Post Magazine*, December 6, 1981, p. 54. Petitioners believe that FBI records of the consular break-in are located in File 65-13888, Records of the FBI. These records have been requested by Kenneth D. Ringle, Jr., but have not been released by the FBI.

Americans.[8] The available records of the FBI and military intelligence agencies disclose no evidence of espionage or sabotage in the period that followed Pearl Harbor. In fact, these records affirmatively disclaim the commission of such acts on the West Coast.[9]

It is relevant as well to note that the Department of Justice moved, immediately after the Pearl Harbor attack, to arrest all those aliens of Japanese descent included in the "ABC" list. During the night of December 7–8, 1941, FBI and military agents, assisted by local police, arrested 736 alien Japanese on the West Coast. Within four days, the number of Japanese arrested reached 1,370. By the end of the "ABC" roundup in February, 1942, a total of 2,192 alien Japanese on the mainland had been arrested and interned for some period of time.[10]

Following these arrests, the Attorney General directed that the Department of Justice establish a network of Alien Enemy Hearing Boards across the country. Most of the 92 hearing boards included one or more lawyers as members. Aliens who had been arrested and interned were afforded informal hearings at which, Biddle noted, "any 'fair' evidence could be admitted" that bore on the loyalty of the alien. Close to two-thirds of those initially detained were subsequently released outright or on parole by the hearing boards on a finding that they posed no danger to the United States.[11] However, most of the Japanese Americans released after such a finding were then placed in Relocation Centers on the order of General DeWitt. Those Japanese Americans released from internment by the Department of Justice were placed in custody by the War Department on the basis of orders issued without hearings and predicated on an assumption that the "racial characteristics" of Japanese Americans as a group predisposed them to disloyalty and the commission of espionage and sabotage.

C. Political Pressures for the Evacuation of Japanese Americans

The public record discloses no evidence of any substantial public hostility toward Japanese Americans in the weeks that followed the Pearl Harbor attack.[12] Similarly, the official record discloses no suggestions

---

[8] Memorandum, J. Edgar Hoover to Mr. Tolson, Mr. Tamm, and Mr. Ladd, December 17, 1941, File 100-97-1-67, Records of the FBI. See Exhibit T.

[9] These records are discussed under Point Two, supra.

[10] Department of Justice, Press Releases, December 8 and 13, 1941, February 16, 1942; quoted in Jacobus tenBroek, et al., *Prejudice, War and the Constitution*, p. 101.

[11] Francis Biddle, *In Brief Authority*, pp. 208–209.

[12] "Agitation for a mass evacuation of the Japanese did not reach significant dimensions until more

within the Government for restrictive measures against Japanese Americans as a group for close to two months after Pearl Harbor. In fact, General DeWitt initially expressed opposition to a proposal that the Army institute the internment of all Japanese Americans in California. He expressed this opposition in a telephone conversation on December 26, 1941 with Major General Allen W. Gullion, Provost Marshal General of the Army. Gullion passed on to General DeWitt a recommendation for internment made by the Washington, D.C. representative of the Los Angeles Chamber of Commerce. General DeWitt responded to this recommendation as follows:

I thought that thing out to my satisfaction . . . if we go ahead and arrest the 93,000 Japanese [in California], native born and foreign born, we are going to have an awful job on our hands and are very liable to alienate the loyal Japanese from disloyal. . . . I'm very doubtful that it would be common sense procedure to try and intern or to intern 117,000 Japanese in this theater. . . . I don't think it's a sensible thing to do. . . . An American citizen, after all, is an American citizen. And while they all may not be loyal, I think we can weed the disloyal out of the loyal and lock them up if necessary.[13]

During the month that followed this expression by General DeWitt of opposition to the evacuation or internment of Japanese Americans, public pressures for such moves remained relatively limited.[14] However, the situation changed dramatically following the release to the press on January 25, 1942, of the so-called "Roberts Report" on the Pearl Harbor attack. This report was issued by a commission appointed by President Roosevelt and chaired by Associate Justice Owen J. Roberts of the United States Supreme Court. In addition to finding that the Army and Navy commanders in Hawaii had been negligent in preparing for a possible Japanese attack, the report included the following statement:

There were, prior to December 7, 1941, Japanese spies on the island of Oahu. Some were Japanese consular agents and others were persons having no open relations with the Japanese foreign service. These spies collected, and through

than a month after the outbreak of war." Stetson Conn, et al., *United States Army in World War II: The Western Hemisphere: Guarding the United States and Its Outposts*, p. 120. This volume, issued by the Office of the Chief of Military History, Department of the Army, in 1964, is part of the official history of the armed services during World War II. The Court is directed to Chapter V, "Japanese Evacuation From the West Coast," for an authoritative discussion of the origins of the mass evacuation program.

[13] Telephone conversation, General DeWitt with General Gullion, December 26, 1941, File 311.3, Records of the Western Defense Command, Civil Affairs Division; quoted in *id.*, p. 118.

[14] Note 12, supra. See also tenBroek, et al., Note 10, supra, pp. 73–80. This study is the product of the University of California Japanese American Evacuation and Resettlement Study, an academic project begun in February, 1942 and supported by funding from the University of California, the

various channels, transmitted, information to the Japanese Empire respecting the military and naval establishments and dispositions on the island.[15]

Although unsupported by any cited evidence, the implied assertion that Japanese Americans had performed espionage activities on behalf of Japan was widely put in explicit terms by the West Coast press.[16] Public concern about the "danger" posed by Japanese Americans quickly turned into a campaign of pressure on both military and civilian officials for the mass evacuation of Japanese Americans from the West Coast.[17] DeWitt's exposure to this pressure is evident from his report of a January 27 meeting with Governor Culbert Olson of California. In a telephone conversation of January 29 with Major Karl R. Bendetsen of the Provost Marshal General's office, DeWitt made the following statement:

There's a tremendous volume of public opinion now developing against the Japanese of all classes, that is aliens and non-aliens, to get them off the land, and in Southern California . . . they are bringing pressure on the government to move all the Japanese out. As a matter of fact, it's not being instigated or developed by people who are not thinking but by the best people of California. Since the publication of the Roberts Report they felt that they were living in the midst of a lot of enemies. They don't trust the Japanese, none of them.[18]

In addition to pressure for mass evacuation from state officials such as Governor Olson, military officials were subjected to pressure from members of the West Coast Congressional delegation. On January 30, 1942, Major Bendetsen represented Provost Marshal Gullion at a meeting in Washington with members of this delegation, at which he was presented with a six-point proposal for action against Japanese Americans in the form of a recommendation to President Roosevelt. This proposal included two significant elements:

1. A designation by the War Department of critical areas throughout the country and territorial possessions.

2. Immediate evacuation of all such critical areas of all enemy aliens and their families, including children under 21 whether aliens or not.[19]

Rockefeller Foundation, and the Columbia Foundation. Although not an official government project, this comprehensive study received the cooperation of the Research Branch of the Civil Affairs Division, Western Defense Command. *Id.*, p. xiii.

[15] *Congressional Record*, Vol. 88, Part 8, p. A261.

[16] "The publication of the report of the Roberts Commission . . . on 25 January had a large and immediate effect both on public opinion and on government action." tenBroek, et al., Note 10, supra, p. 121.

[17] *Id.*, pp. 81–96.

[18] Telephone conversation, General DeWitt with Major Bendetsen, January 28, 1942; quoted in Conn, et al., Note 12, supra.

[19] Memorandum, Major Bendetsen to General Gullion, January 31, 1942, File PMG 384.4,

In a telephone conversation with Major Bendetsen on January 31, General DeWitt indicated his agreement with the recommendation of the West Coast Congressional delegation. DeWitt expressed his support for the mass evacuation of Japanese Americans as a protection against possible acts of sabotage: "The only positive answer to that question is evacuation of all enemy aliens on the West Coast, and their resettlement or internment and the positive control [of such a program] military or otherwise." General DeWitt made clear his endorsement of the mass evacuation of all American citizens of Japanese ancestry: "All Japanese, irrespective of citizenship."[20]

One fact of great significance emerges from this record: Between the month from the end of December, 1941 to the end of January, 1942, General DeWitt changed his position on mass evacuation from that of opposition as not "a sensible thing to do" to support of the evacuation of all persons of Japanese ancestry, "irrespective of citizenship." It will be shown below that during this period, and afterward as well, no evidence reached General DeWitt or any other responsible government official that indicated that Japanese Americans posed any danger of espionage or sabotage on the West Coast. In fact, intelligence reports prepared by the FBI and other federal agencies directly refuted all such allegations. The conclusion is inescapable that General DeWitt's endorsement of mass evacuation resulted both from his often-expressed racial hostility toward Japanese Americans and from pressure from state and congressional politicians.

D. The Debate Within the Federal Government Over Proposals for the Mass Evacuation of Japanese Americans

Officials of both the War Department and the Department of Justice initially opposed the proposals for mass evacuation. The grounds for such opposition included doubts about the military necessity for evacuation and the constitutionality of an evacuation program that included American citizens. This opposition was expressed at a meeting in the office of

---

Records of the Western Defense Command. According to Conn, et al., "The Congressional recommendations were a verbatim copy of a draft submitted by a representative of the Los Angeles Chamber of Commerce." Note 12, supra, p. 123, n. 27. Major Bendetsen interpreted this recommendation, in reporting to General Gullion on January 31, 1942, as "calling for the immediate evacuation of all Japanese from the Pacific coastal strip including Japanese citizens [sic] of the age of 21 and under . . ." *Id.*, p. 123.

[20]Telephone conversation, General DeWitt with Major Bendetsen, January 31, 1942, Records of the Provost Marshal General, National Archives and Records Service, Washington, D.C.

Attorney General Biddle on February 1, 1942, attended by Assistant Secretary of War McCloy.[21]

At this meeting, Biddle submitted to McCloy the draft of a press release to be signed and issued jointly by the Attorney General and Secretary of War Stimson. The initial sections of this press release announced agreement by the two Departments on steps to bar enemy aliens from limited areas that surrounded vital military installations on the West Coast, none of which involved restrictions on citizens. The proposed release concluded with this sentence: "The Department of War and the Department of Justice are in agreement that the present military situation does not at this time require the removal of American citizens of the Japanese race."[22]

At McCloy's request, the Attorney General agreed to withhold issuance of the proposed release until General DeWitt could respond to it. Provost Marshal Gullion called DeWitt later that day and read to him the text of the press release. General DeWitt was emphatic in his response to the sentence quoted above: "I wouldn't agree to that."[23] As a consequence of this objection by General DeWitt, this sentence was removed from the press release.

Following the meeting on February 1 between the Attorney General and McCloy, Secretary of War Stimson became personally involved in the debate over mass evacuation. On February 3, Stimson met with General Gullion to discuss recommendations from General DeWitt for the designation of "military areas" from which Japanese aliens would be excluded by order of the Attorney General. Stimson recorded this conversation in his official diary as follows:

General DeWitt . . . is very anxious about the situation and has been clamoring for the evacuation of the Japanese of the area surrounding the intensely important area at San Diego, Los Angeles, San Francisco and Puget Sound, where are located some of the most important airplane factories and naval shipyards. He thinks he has evidence that regular communications are going out from Japanese spies in those regions to submarines off the coast assisting in the attacks by the latter which have been made upon practically every ship that has gone out. If we based our evacuations upon the ground of removing enemy aliens, it will not get rid of the Nisei [native-born Japanese American citizens] who are . . . the more dangerous ones. If on the other hand we evacuate everybody including citizens,

---

[21] Also in attendance at this meeting were Provost Marshal General Gullion, Major Bendetsen, FBI Director Hoover, Assistant to the Attorney General James H. Rowe, Jr., and Edward J. Ennis, Director of the Alien Enemy Control Unit of the Department of Justice.

[22] Telephone conversation, General DeWitt with General Gullion, February 1, 1942. Note 20, supra.

[23] Ibid.

we must base it as far as I can see upon solely the protection of specified plants. *We cannot discriminate among our citizens on the ground of racial origin.* We talked the matter over for quite a while and then postponed it in order to hear further from General DeWitt who has not yet outlined all of the places that he wishes protected.[24]

Two elements of this statement by Stimson require comment. First, General DeWitt had been personally informed, almost a month before this meeting, that reports of communications from the coast to Japanese submarines had been investigated by the Federal Communications Commission and found to be baseless. Second, Stimson at this point recognized that the proposed evacuation of American citizens of Japanese ancestry had no constitutional basis.

Notwithstanding the doubt expressed by Stimson, Assistant Secretary of War McCloy undertook to suggest to General DeWitt a way around the constitutional barriers to the evacuation of citizens from the major West Coast cities. In a telephone conversation with General DeWitt on February 3, after the meeting between Stimson and General Gullion, McCloy made the following suggestion:

Now, my suggestion is that (after we have talked it over with General Gullion and Major Bendetsen) we might call those [cities] military reservations in substance, and exclude everyone—whites, yellows, blacks, greens—from that area and then license back into the area those whom we felt there was no danger to be expected from. . . . You see, then we cover ourselves with the legal situation is taken care of [sic] in a way because *in spite of the constitution* you can eliminate from any military reservation anyone—any American citizen, as we could exclude everyone and then by a system of permits and licenses permitting those to come back into that area who were necessary to enable that area to function as a living community. *Everyone but the Japs—.*[25]

During this conversation with General DeWitt, McCloy requested that he submit to the War Department a formal recommendation on the evacuation issue, and dispatched Major Bendetsen (who was shortly promoted to Lieutenant Colonel) to the West Coast to assist in drafting his recommendation. On February 10, 1942, Colonel Bendetsen submitted to General DeWitt a memorandum headed "Evacuation of Japanese from the Pacific Coast." This memorandum stated that there was "no disagreement in any quarter regarding the necessity for placing all Japanese in the same category" regardless of citizenship. This statement was in fact erro-

[24] Entry of February 3, 1942, Henry L. Stimson Diaries, Yale University Library, New Haven, Connecticut. Emphasis added.

[25] Telephone conversation, General DeWitt with Mr. McCloy, February 3, 1942. Emphasis added. Note 2, supra.

neous and misleading as an expression of the views of Secretary Stimson, who had recently stated to General Gullion his doubts about the constitutionality of any mass evacuation of citizens. Colonel Bendetsen then noted that it was "highly improbable that the Secretary will accept the recommendation of the entire evacuation [of Japanese Americans] from the coastal strip." This statement referred to the proposal by General DeWitt that Japanese Americans be evacuated from the entire area that extended some two hundred miles eastward from the coastline. Colonel Bendetsen concluded with the following statement:

... any recommendation should be predicated on the military necessity involved and this in turn can be developed only after a consideration of all the factors such as loss of vegetable production which may be consequent [from farms operated by Japanese Americans], and other economic dislocations which may ensue. These later factors can be weighed only from the standpoint of the military disadvantages which may be involved. If from the military standpoint, the military disadvantage involved in the loss of vegetable production which may result from a complete evacuation from the Pacific Coast is sufficiently great to outweigh the military advantage, then and only then should the recommendation for evacuation be confined to selected areas.[26]

The significance of this memorandum emerges in its contrast with the "Final Recommendation" submitted on February 14, 1942, by General DeWitt to Secretary Stimson. In balancing "military necessity" against the possible "loss of vegetable production" from the farms operated by Japanese Americans, Colonel Bendetsen demonstrated that the subsequent evacuation recommendation was less a purely military decision than a matter of the "economic dislocation" that evacuation might produce.

E. The "Final Recommendation" and the Evacuation Decision

During the period that preceded receipt by the War Department of the "Final Recommendation" of General DeWitt, debate within the Government over the evacuation issue centered on the "licensing" proposal advanced by Assistant Secretary of War McCloy. Secretary of War Stimson and Attorney General Biddle maintained their constitutional doubts about the evacuation of Japanese American citizens during this period. Stimson met with McCloy on February 10, 1942, to review the interim proposal by General DeWitt that some 88 limited areas along the Coast (containing military installations, defense factories, and public utilities) be evacuated

[26]Memorandum, Colonel Bendetsen to General DeWitt, February 10, 1942, Records of the Western Defense Command.

of all enemy aliens and Japanese American citizens. Following this meeting, Stimson recorded the following in his official journal:

The second generation Japanese [native-born citizens] can only be evacuated as part of a total evacuation, giving access to the areas only by permits, or by frankly trying to put them out on the ground that their racial characteristics are such that we cannot understand or trust even the citizen Japanese. The latter is the fact but I am afraid *it will make a tremendous hole in our constitutional system.*[27]

On February 12, 1942, Attorney General Biddle addressed a letter to Stimson stating that the Department of Justice lacked the personnel and facilities to undertake a mass evacuation program. Biddle added the following to his letter:

I have no doubt that the Army can legally, at any time, evacuate all persons in a specified territory if such action is deemed essential from a military point of view for the protection and defense of the area. No legal problem arises where Japanese citizens are evacuated; but American citizens of Japanese origin could not, in my opinion, be singled out of an area and evacuated with the other Japanese. However, the result might be accomplished by evacuating all persons in the area and then licensing back those whom the military authorities thought were not objectionable from a military point of view.[28]

It should be noted that the "licensing" proposal, as a means for the evacuation of Japanese Americans from limited "military areas" received no further consideration after February 11, 1942. On that date Stimson discussed the evacuation issue with President Roosevelt, on the basis of a memorandum summarizing the "questions to be determined re Japanese exclusion" by the President. This memorandum presented the following questions for decision by the President:

1. Is the President willing to authorize us to move Japanese citizens [American citizens of Japanese descent] as well as aliens from restricted areas?

2. Should we undertake withdrawal from the entire strip DeWitt originally recommended, which involves a number over 110,000 people, if we included both aliens and Japanese citizens?

3. Should we undertake the intermediate step involving, say, 70,000 which includes large communities such as Los Angeles, San Diego, and Seattle?

[27] Entry of February 10, 1942. Emphasis added. Note 27, supra.

[28] Letter, Attorney General Biddle to Secretary of War Stimson, February 2, 1942, Record Group 407, National Archives and Records Service, Washington, D.C.

4. Should we take any lesser step such as the establishment of re-stricted areas around airplane plants and critical installations, even though General DeWitt states that in several, at least, of the large communities this would be wasteful, involve difficult administrative problems, and might be a source of more continuous irritation and trouble than 100 percent withdrawal from the area?[29]

Stimson discussed these questions with the President over the tele-phone on February 11, 1942. No record has been located of any notation of this discussion by the President, but Stimson recorded in his official journal of that day that he "fortunately found that [President Roosevelt] was very vigorous about it and [he] told me to go along on the line that I had myself thought the best."[30]

Stimson did not record which of the alternative courses he thought best. However, later that day McCloy stated in a telephone conversation with Colonel Bendetsen that "we have carte blanche to do whatever we want to do as far as the President's concerned" and that the President had specifically authorized the evacuation of citizens, subject only to the qualification, "Be as reasonable as you can."[31]

Following this conversation, Colonel Bendetsen returned from San Francisco to Washington to meet with War Department officials on the evacuation issue. He brought with him the "Final Recommendation" of General DeWitt in the form of a memorandum to the Secretary of War headed "Evacuation of Japanese and other Subversive Persons from the Pacific Coast." Included in this memorandum were allegations about the commission of acts of espionage and sabotage by Japanese Americans and slurs on this group as members of an "enemy race." The knowing falsity of these allegations is discussed below.[32] The significance of these statements in the "Final Recommendation" to this Appendix lies in their presentation to Stimson as justification for the mass evacuation of Japa-nese Americans from the West Coast. General DeWitt put his formal recommendation in the following words:

That the Secretary of War procure from the President direction and authority to designate military areas in the combat zone of the Western Theater of Operations

[29] Memorandum, for Record (unsigned), February 11, 1942, File 014.311, Records of the As-sistant Secretary of War, *ibid.*

[30] Entry of February 11, 1942, Note 27, supra.

[31] Telephone conversation, Assistant Secretary McCloy with Colonel Bendetsen, February 11, 1942, File 311.3 (Tel Convs, Bendetsen, Feb-Mar 42), Records of the Western Defense Command.

[32] See discussion under Points Two and Three, supra.

(*if necessary to include the entire combat zone*), from which, in his discretion, he may exclude *all Japanese*, all alien enemies, and all other persons suspected for any reason by the administering military authorities of being actual or potential saboteurs, espionage agents, or fifth columnists.[33]

F. Adoption of the "Final Recommendation" and the Issuance of Executive Order 9066

The "Final Recommendation" of General DeWitt, backed by verbal authorization from the President to proceed with the drafting of an evacuation program, became the basis for a crucial series of meetings on February 17 and 18, 1942. Secretary Stimson first met on February 17 with Assistant Secretary McCloy, Colonel Bendetsen, Provost Marshal Gullion, and General Mark Clark, the latter representing General George C. Marshall, Chief of Staff of the Army. Stimson described the meeting in his official journal as follows:

Finally we worked the matter into a situation where we could take immediate steps beyond the ones which I had already authorized General DeWitt on the coast to do. A proposed order for the President was outlined and General Gullion undertook to have it drafted tonight. War Department orders will fill in the application of this Presidential order. These were notified and Gullion is also to draft them. It will involve the tremendous task of moving between fifty and one hundred thousand people from their homes and ultimately locating them in new places away from the coast.[34]

On the same day, February 17, Attorney General Biddle sent a letter to President Roosevelt, objecting to mass evacuation as unnecessary. Biddle put his objections in the following words:

For several weeks there have been increasing demands for evacuation of all Japanese, aliens and citizens alike, from the West Coast states. A great many of the West Coast people distrust the Japanese, various special interests would welcome their removal from good farm land and the elimination of their competition, some of the local California radio and press have demanded evacuation, the West Coast Congressional Delegation are asking the same thing and finally, Walter Lipman [sic] and Westbrook Pegler [nationally syndicated newspaper columnists] recently have taken up the evacuation cry on the ground that attack on the West Coast and widespread sabotage is imminent. My last advice from the War Department is that *there is no evidence of imminent attack* and from the F.B.I. that *there is no evidence of planned sabotage*.[35]

[33] DeWitt, *Final Report*, p. 36. Emphasis added.
[34] Entry of February 17, 1942, Note 27, supra.
[35] Memorandum, Attorney General Biddle to President Roosevelt, February 17, 1942, Folder—

Notwithstanding this objection to evacuation, Biddle met on the evening of February 17 with McCloy and General Gullion to draft a proposed Executive Order for submission to the President. Accompanying Biddle at this meeting were James H. Rowe, Jr., Assistant to the Attorney General, and Edward J. Ennis, director of the Alien Enemy Control Unit of the Department of Justice. In his memoirs, Biddle described this meeting as follows:

General Gullion had an executive order ready for the President to sign. Rowe and Ennis argued strongly against it. But the decision had been made by the President. It was, he said, a matter of military judgment. I did not think I should oppose it any further. The Department of Justice, as I had made it clear to him from the beginning, was opposed to and would have nothing to do with the evacuation.[36]

The following day, February 18, 1942, Biddle met with Stimson and members of their staffs to go over the proposed Executive Order. In final form, the order was approved and taken to the White House by Rowe for submission to the President. Executive Order 9066 was signed by President Roosevelt on February 19, and its pertinent provisions are cited above in the Statement of Facts.

G. Conclusion

There can be no doubt that the decision to evacuate and intern the Japanese American population on the West Coast was a direct consequence of two facts: first, General DeWitt's capitulation to the pressures exerted by state and federal officials; and second, his belief that the "racial characteristics" of Japanese Americans predisposed them to disloyalty. Until the end of January 1942, DeWitt expressed opposition to mass evacuation and agreement that the Army could "weed the disloyal out of the loyal" among the Japanese Americans. The arrest and internment of those on the "ABC" list convinced the Department of Justice that no significant threat of espionage or sabotage remained on the West Coast.

However, following the publication of the sensational, but undocumented allegations of spying by Japanese Americans in Hawaii that were made in the "Roberts Report," and the pressures exerted on General

---

C.F. Hawaii, Confidential File, President's Secretary's Files, Franklin D. Roosevelt Library, Hyde Park, New York. Emphasis added.

[36] Note 11, supra, p. 219.

DeWitt by Governor Olson and members of the West Coast Congressional delegation, General DeWitt submitted to the War Department a "Final Recommendation" for the evacuation of all persons of Japanese ancestry on the West Coast. This recommendation cited no evidence that Japanese Americans posed a danger of espionage or sabotage.

Responsible officials of both the War Department and the Department of Justice harbored serious doubts about the constitutionality of mass evacuation and restrictive measures directed at Japanese Americans as a group. Notwithstanding these doubts, they finally bowed to the claims of General DeWitt that "military necessity" required mass evacuation. These officials consequently approved the "Final Recommendation" of General DeWitt and drafted for submission to the President the Executive Order that empowered General DeWitt to issue the military orders at issue in Petitioners' cases and to implement the mass evacuation and internment of the Japanese American population of the West Coast.

ATTORNEYS OF RECORD FOR PETITIONER FRED T. KOREMATSU

Dennis W. Hayashi   Karen N. Kai
Donald K. Tamaki   Russell Matsumoto
Michael J. Wong   Dale Minami
Robert L. Rusky   Lorraine K. Bannai
Peter Irons

Korematsu v. United States

Memorandum of Points and Authorities in Support of
Petition for Writ of Error Coram Nobis, U.S. District
Court for the Northern District of California

January 19, 1983

*The coram nobis petitions were based on charges of governmental mis-
conduct in the trials and appeals of the internment cases in the 1940s.
These charges were initially made by the government's own lawyers and
were supported by documents from the government's own files at agencies
such as the Justice Department, FBI, Office of Naval Intelligence, and
Federal Communications Commission. To prevail in the courts, the petitioners needed both the factual record of governmental misconduct and
legal precedent for their claims that acts of misconduct had violated their
rights to fair trials and due process of law. The legal memorandum
drafted by the coram nobis lawyers cited forty-three cases as precedent
for vacating the wartime convictions. The "pattern of misconduct" by
government lawyers and officials, the memorandum argued, constituted a
"fraud upon the courts" that required judicial action to clear the criminal records of the three petitioners.*

Petitioner, Fred Toyosaburo Korematsu, submits the following memorandum in support of his petition for writ of error coram nobis.

Preliminary Statement

In separate but identical Petitions, Gordon Hirabayashi, Minoru Yasui,
and Fred Toyosaburo Korematsu challenge their respective convictions
under Public Law 503 which imposed criminal penalties on Japanese
Americans for violation of military curfew and exclusion orders during
World War II. Although each Petitioner brings his challenge in the respective United States District Court in which he was convicted, the intercon-
nected pattern of misconduct which tainted each of their trials and appeals

can only be understood by considering all three cases together. Because the government's course of misconduct permeated all Petitioners' cases, references to "Petitioners" is intended to include each Petitioner.

Petitioners have recently discovered evidence of governmental misconduct in the prosecution of their respective cases which effectively denied them fair trials and appeals in violation of the United States Constitution. Specifically, the Petitioners contend (1) that the government destroyed and suppressed evidence which controverted its own legal assertion of wartime military necessity; (2) that the government submitted false and inaccurate information to the courts with knowledge of its falsity; and, (3) that the destruction and suppression of evidence and the submission of false evidence were compounded by the government's failure to disclose exculpatory evidence. Petitioners further allege that these acts, in conjunction with an improper request by the government for judicial notice of facts known to be false and manipulation of amicus curiae briefs constituted a fraud upon the courts. Considering the acts of misconduct separately and in their cumulative effect, it is clear that Petitioners' constitutional rights to due process were fundamentally and systematically violated.

I. Relief by Writ of Error Coram Nobis is Available to Correct Fundamental Errors Which Deprived Petitioners of Due Process Rights Under the United States Constitution

Under 28 U.S.C. §1651, a petition in the nature of the common law writ of error coram nobis is available to challenge federal criminal convictions obtained by errors of such fundamental character as to render the underlying proceeding irregular and invalid. *United States* v. *Morgan*, 346 U.S. 502 (1954). The *Morgan* case established the district court's power, under 28 U.S.C. §1651, to grant relief by the writ even after a petitioner has fully served his sentence. *Id* at 513. Similarly, in *United States* v. *Danks*, 357 F. Supp. 190, 196 (D. Hawaii 1973), the court stated, "Coram nobis must be kept available as a post conviction remedy to prevent 'manifest injustice' even where the removal of the prior conviction will have little present effect on the petitioner."

The courts have exercised their power under this writ not only where errors during trial are of constitutional dimension but also where the errors are so fundamental that serious injustice would arise if coram nobis relief were not allowed. *United States* v. *Wickham*, 474 F. Supp. 113, 116 (C.D. Cal. 1979).

The allegations of misconduct in the instant petition lie squarely within the ambit of coram nobis. The various acts of suppression and destruction of evidence, the presentation of false evidence, and the generalized course of fraud on the court directly affected Petitioners' rights to fair proceedings. In similar situations, the courts have held that "prosecutorial misconduct may so pollute a criminal prosecution so as to require a new trial, especially when the taint in the proceedings seriously prejudices the accused." *United States* v. *Taylor*, 648 F.2d 565, 571 (9th Cir.), cert. denied, 454 U.S. 866 (1981). The court in *Taylor* held that a new trial is appropriate "when the prosecution has knowingly used perjured testimony or withheld materially favorable evidence from the defense."

Although procedurally distinct, a petition for writ of error coram nobis and a habeas corpus petition under 28 U.S.C. §2255 are substantively equivalent. See *Morgan*, 346 U.S. 510–11; *Taylor*, 648 F.2d at 573. Thus, prescinding from 28 U.S.C. §2255, a criminal defendant may challenge a criminal conviction not only for lack of jurisdiction or constitutional error, but also to remedy claimed errors of either law or fact "presenting exceptional circumstances constituting a fundamental defect which inherently results in a complete miscarriage of justice." *United States* v. *Addonizio*, 442 U.S. 178, 185 (1979). The legal significance of this petition extends beyond the fate of three individuals. The government's misconduct in Petitioners' cases not only resulted in the denial of their rights to fair proceedings but also legitimized the mass imprisonment of 110,000 Japanese Americans during World War II without trials. The constitutional violations alleged are no less significant some forty years later. As expressed by the United States Supreme Court in *Chessman* v. *Teets*, 354 U.S. 156 (1957), constitutional error cannot be minimized by the passing of time:

Evidently it also needs to be repeated that the overriding responsibility of this Court is to the Constitution of the United States, no matter how late it may be that a violation of the Constitution is found to exist. . . . We must be deaf to all suggestions that a valid appeal to the Constitution . . . comes too late, because courts, including this Court, were not earlier able to enforce what the Constitution demands. The proponent before the Court is not the petitioner but the Constitution of the United States.

Id. at 165.

II. The Government's Failure to Adhere to Established Standards of Prosecutorial Conduct Violated Petitioners' Due Process Rights

The petition submitted in this case discloses a pattern of conduct by government prosecutors and agents calculated to assure Petitioners' convictions and to gain court approval of wartime actions. In manipulating Petitioners' cases in this way, the prosecution abrogated its duty to the courts, the constitution and the defense. As first declared in *Berger* v. *United States*, 295 U.S. 78 (1935), agents of any prosecutorial entity, including attorneys, police, and other investigators, must be held to a definite standard of conduct in order to ensure the right to a fair and impartial trial guaranteed by the due process clause of the Fifth and Fourteenth Amendments. The breach of this standard by government prosecutors and their agents in the instant cases constitutes a basis to reverse Petitioners' convictions.

In *Berger*, the prosecutor, in closing argument to the jury, improperly charged the defendant with suppression of evidence. In language which has become the classic statement of the prosecution's duty, the court reversed the conviction, stating,

The United States Attorney is the representative not of an ordinary party to a controversy, but of a sovereignty whose obligation to govern impartially is as compelling as its obligation to govern at all; and whose interest, therefore, in a criminal prosecution is not that it shall win a case, but that justice shall be done. As such, he is in a peculiar and very definite sense a servant of the law, the twofold aim of which is that guilt shall not escape or innocence suffer. He may prosecute with earnestness and vigor—indeed, he should do so. But, while he may strike hard blows, he is not at liberty to strike foul ones. It is as much his duty to refrain from improper methods calculated to produce a wrongful conviction as it is to use every legitimate means to bring about a just one.

Id. at 88.

Similarly, prosecutors, as representatives of the state, have been admonished that " '[a] criminal trial is not a game in which the State's function is to outwit and entrap its quarry. The State's pursuit is justice, not a victim.' " *Imbler* v. *Craven*, 298 F. Supp. 795, 809 (C.D. Cal. 1969), aff'd sub nom., *Imbler* v. *State of California*, 424 F.2d 631 (9th Cir.), cert. denied, 400 U.S. 865 (1970), quoting *Giles* v. *Maryland*, 386 U.S. 66, 100 (1967)(Fortas, J., concurring).

The courts have consistently asserted that the responsibility of the government prosecutor to represent the interests of the State includes his duty to assure that convictions are obtained only within the constraints of the Constitution. As recently as 1979, in *Gannett Co.* v. *DePasquale*, 443 U.S. 368, 384 (1979), the Supreme Court reaffirmed the prosecutorial standard of conduct set forth in *Berger*: "The responsibility of the prosecutor as a representative of the public surely encompasses a duty to protect the societal interest in an open trial. But this responsibility also requires him to be sensitive to the due process rights of a defendant to a fair trial." Should this safeguard of the "ethical responsibilities of the prosecutor" fail, "review remains available under due process standards." *United States* v. *Ash*, 413 U.S. 300, 320 (1973).

The government fell far short of meeting these standards of prosecutorial conduct in Petitioners' cases. While the government finally won court approval of the military orders, it did so by keeping material evidence from the court, by submitting false evidence and, more importantly, by sacrificing Petitioners' constitutional rights to fair trial.

III. The Prosecution's Use of False Evidence and the Suppression of Materially Favorable Evidence in the Hirabayashi, Yasui, and Korematsu Cases Constituted a Denial of Due Process Requiring Vacating of Petitioners' Convictions

In order to present the strongest possible cases to the courts, the government suppressed key reports from military and government agencies. These reports authoritatively refuted the government's justification of the curfew and exclusion orders. In presenting evidence known to be inaccurate and false, the government placed a "tailored" factual record before the court as a basis for its "military necessity" claim. Had courts been provided with accurate and credible facts, the military orders would not have been upheld against Petitioners' constitutional attacks.

Beginning with *Mooney* v. *Holohan*, 294 U.S. 103 (1935) (per curiam), the courts have consistently held that either prosecutorial suppression of material evidence favorable to a defendant, or knowing presentation of false evidence, constitutes a denial of due process requiring a reversal of convictions so obtained.[1] Each ground stands as an independent basis for reversal. In *Mooney*, the petitioner claimed that the prosecution had

---

[1] See *Pyle* v. *Kansas*, 317 U.S. 213 (1942); *Alcorta* v. *Texas*, 355 U.S. 28 (1957) (per curiam); *Hysler* v. *Florida*, 315 U.S. 411 (1942); *Woollomes* v. *Heinze*, 198 F.2d 577 (9th Cir. 1952), cert. denied, 344 U.S. 929 (1953).

knowingly elicited false testimony and suppressed evidence useful to the defense in order to obtain the defendant's conviction. In ruling for the appellant, the court emphasized the importance of protecting against such conduct:

[The due process] requirement, in safeguarding the liberty of the citizen against deprivation through the action of the State, embodies the fundamental conceptions of justice which lie at the base of our civil and political institutions. It is a requirement that cannot be deemed to be satisfied by mere notice and hearing if a State has contrived a conviction through the pretence of a trial which in truth is but used as a means of depriving a defendant of liberty through a *deliberate deception of court* and jury by the presentation of testimony known to be perjured. Such a contrivance by a State to procure the conviction and imprisonment of a defendant is as inconsistent with the rudimentary demands of justice as is the obtaining of a like result by intimidation.

Id. at 112 (Citation omitted. Emphasis added.)

Subsequent cases have both affirmed and expanded *Mooney's* basic pronouncement of due process protection against instances of suppression of submission of false evidence. Thus, in *Napue* v. *Illinois* 360 U.S. 264 (1959) the Supreme Court ruled that post conviction relief was available to vacate a conviction where the prosecutor knowingly failed to correct false testimony which was relevant to a witness' credibility. In so holding, the court found evidence of credibility to be material enough to warrant relief. See also *Loraine* v. *United States*, 396 F.2d 335, 339 (9th Cir. 1968), cert. denied, 393 U.S. 933 (1968).

In the landmark case of *Brady* v. *Maryland*, 373 U.S. 83 (1963), the court held that the prosecution's suppression of evidence favorable to the accused and material to guilt or punishment could violate due process regardless of the good or bad faith of the prosecution:[2]

We now hold that the suppression by the prosecution of evidence favorable to an accused upon request violates due process where the evidence is material either to guilt or to punishment, irrespective of the good faith or bad faith of the prosecution.

The principle of *Mooney v. Holohan* is not punishment of society for misdeeds of a prosecutor but avoidance of an unfair trial to the accused. Society wins not only when the guilty are convicted but when criminal trials are fair; our system of justice suffers when any accused is treated unfairly. An inscription on the walls of the Department of Justice states the proposition candidly for the federal do-

---

[2]See also *Smith* v. *Phillips*, _____ U.S. _____, 71 L.Ed. 2d 78, 87 (1982) (". . . the touchstone of due process analysis in cases of alleged prosecutorial misconduct is the fairness of the trial, not the culpability of the prosecutor".; *United States* v. *Hibler*, 463 F.2d 455 (9th Cir. 1972).

main: "The United States wins its point whenever justice is done its citizens in the courts."[3]

Enlarging the due process principle of *Brady* further in cases involving suppression or false evidence, the courts have clearly stated that such actions violate constitutional rights even when committed by government representatives other than the individual trial/appellate attorney. In the leading case of *Barbee* v. *Warden, Maryland Penitentiary*, 331 F.2d 842 (4th Cir. 1964), the court ruled that the defendant was entitled to have his conviction set aside because the prosecutor failed to disclose potentially exculpatory evidence which was withheld by the police. The court held that even though the police, rather than the prosecutor, withheld the information, the resulting denial of due process was the same:

. . . the effect of the nondisclosure [is not] neutralized because the prosecuting attorney was not shown to have had knowledge of the exculpatory evidence. Failure of the police to reveal such material evidence in their possession is equally harmful to a defendant whether the information is purposely, or negligently, withheld. And it makes no difference if the withholding is by officials other than the prosecutor. The police are also part of the prosecution, and the taint on the trial is no less if they, rather than the State's Attorney, were guilty of the nondisclosure. If the police allow the State's Attorney to produce evidence pointing to guilt without informing him of other evidence in their possession which contradicts this inference, state officers are practicing deception not only on the State's Attorney but on the court and the defendant. "The cruelest lies are often told in silence." If the police silence as to the existence of the reports resulted from negligence rather than guile, the deception is no less damaging.

Id at 846.

The court emphasized that the state's duty to assure the fairness of the proceedings and to achieve justice extends beyond the prosecuting attorneys to the enforcement agency of the state itself:

The duty to disclose is that of the state which ordinarily acts through the prosecuting attorney; but if he too is the victim of police suppression of the material information, the state's failure is not on that account excused. We cannot condone the crime by questionable inferences which might be refuted by undisclosed and unproduced documents then in the hands of the police. To borrow a phrase

---

[3] Although the defense in *Mooney* made a specific request for evidence in the possession of the prosecution, such a request is not a prerequisite to holding the government to its duty to disclose. In *United States* v. *Hibler*, supra, the court stated, "That defense counsel did not specifically request the information, that a 'diligent' defense attorney might have discovered the information on his own with sufficient research, or that the prosecution did not suppress the evidence in bad faith, are not conclusive; due process can be denied by failure to disclose alone."

from Chief Judge Briggs, this procedure passes "beyond the line of tolerable imperfection and falls into the field of fundamental unfairness."[4]

Id. (footnotes omitted).

In 1976, apparently seeing the need to establish uniform standards for application of *Mooney* and its progeny, the Supreme Court rendered its decision in *United States* v. *Agurs*, 427 U.S. 97 (1976). *Agurs* remains today as the yardstick by which challenges to convictions based on false or suppressed evidence must be measured. The court in *Agurs* identified three situations involving suppression of evidence and defined for each category the circumstances in which a conviction may be vacated:

1. Misconduct cases typified by *Mooney*, 294 U.S. 103, where the prosecution introduces perjured testimony or false evidence which it knows or should know is false, a conviction will be reversed if the false evidence is considered material to a conviction. The evidence is material if there is "any reasonable likelihood" that the false evidence or testimony could have affected the judgment. *Agurs*, 427 U.S. at 103.

In Petitioners' trials and appeals, the Justice Department and other governmental agencies knew that charges of Japanese American espionage and sabotage were refuted by other authoritative evidence to the contrary. Relying upon the government's factual misrepresentations, the Supreme Court upheld the constitutionality of Petitioners' convictions. As argued in more detail in subsection II(B) of this Memorandum, Petitioners' convictions should be reversed on this ground alone.

2. The second classification of cases are those illustrated by *Brady*, 373 U.S. 83, where a request is made by the defense for specific evidence, and the prosecution fails to comply. *Agurs*, 427 U.S. at 104. As this category is not applicable to the instant petition, it will not be considered in detail.

3. The final group of cases are those illustrated by *Agurs* itself, wherein exculpatory evidence suppressed is known to the defense and no request for the evidence is made. 427 U.S. at 106. The prosecution's duty to produce such evidence arises from the "obviously exculpatory character" of the evidence, which "is so clearly supportive of a claim of innocence" that the prosecution is put on notice of its duty to produce it. *Id.* at 106. A violation of due process arises if, within the context of the entire

---

[4] For reaffirmation of this basic principle, that any government misconduct is the responsibility of the prosecution, see *Giglio* v. *United States*, 405 U.S. 150, 154 (1972); *Ray* v. *United States*, 588 F.2d 601, 603 (8th Cir. 1978).

record, "the omitted evidence creates a reasonable doubt that did not otherwise exist." *Id.* at 112.

As argued in subsection II(A) immediately following, the government suppressed various documents and reports obviously exculpatory in character. Critical language in General DeWitt's original Final Report, as well as facts presented in other government investigative documents exposed the lack of any factual basis for the military orders. This evidence would have supported Petitioners' constitutional challenges and the failure to disclose these documents subverted Petitioners' due process rights.

A. The Government Suppressed Material Evidence Contradicting the "Military Necessity" Justification Underlying the Curfew and Exclusion Orders

The test established by the Supreme Court in the third category of *United States v. Agurs*, 427 U.S. 97, requires the prosecution to disclose exculpatory evidence. While the government's suppression of such evidence in Petitioners' cases is more fully described in Points One, Two and Three of the petition, the following discussion points out the materiality of the suppressed evidence under the *Agurs* standard.

The government's factual allegations regarding sabotage and espionage were the sole focus of the Court's constitutional inquiry in Petitioners' cases. The Supreme Court in *Hirabayashi* v. *United States*, 320 U.S. 81 (1943) and *Yasui* v. *United States*, 320 U.S. 115 (1943) made it clear that the government's claim of military necessity and therefore constitutionality of the military orders, succeeded or failed on whether its claims regarding the disloyalty and disloyal acts of Japanese Americans were justified. The Court framed the essential question in *Hirabayashi* v. *United States*: "Whether in the light of all the facts and circumstances there was any substantial basis for the conclusion . . . that the curfew as applied was a protective measure necessary to meet the threat of sabotage and espionage . . ." *Hirabayashi*, 320 U.S. at 95.

In *Korematsu* v. *United States*, 323 U.S. 212, 218 (1944), the Court stated that an even greater factual showing would be required to support the government's claim: "[n]othing short of apprehension of the gravest imminent danger to the public safety can constitutionally justify either [the curfew or exclusion order]."

That the government's allegations of Japanese American espionage and sabotage were material to the Supreme Court's holdings is obvious from the Court opinions themselves. In *Hirabayashi*, the Court stated:

[We] cannot reject as unfounded the judgment of the military authorities and that of Congress that there were disloyal members of [the Japanese American] population, whose number and strength could not be precisely and quickly ascertained. We cannot say that the war-making branches of the government did not have ground for believing that in a critical hour such persons could not readily be isolated and separately dealt with, and constituted a menace to the national defense and safety, which demanded that prompt and adequate measures be taken to guard against it.

320 U.S. at 99. The Court added,

[T]he findings of danger from espionage and sabotage, and of the necessity of the curfew order to protect against them, have been duly made. . . .

The military commander's appraisal of facts . . . , and the inferences which he drew from those facts, involved the exercise of his informed judgment . . . [T]hose facts . . . support (his) judgment . . . , that the danger of espionage and sabotage to our military resources was imminent. . . .

Id. at 103–104.

In *Korematsu*, the Court reaffirmed the position taken in *Hirabayashi*, adding that

Like curfew, exclusion of those of Japanese origin was deemed necessary because of the presence of an unascertained number of disloyal members of the group, most of whom we have no doubt were loyal to this country. It was because we could not reject the finding of the military authorities that it was impossible to bring about an immediate segregation of the disloyal from the loyal that we sustained the validity of the curfew order as applying to the whole group. In the instant case, temporary exclusion of the entire group was rested by the military on the same ground.

323 U.S. at 218, 219.

The Court's decisions on the constitutionality of the military orders, therefore, rested on the premise that wartime necessity existed supporting the promulgation of official measures. Evidence contradicting such necessity would clearly have been material to the Court's finding and its consequent judgments. Each of the documents suppressed refuted different aspects of the government's case and, viewed as a whole, the suppressed evidence would have fatally undermined the government's position that any security threat by the Japanese American populace existed. A short examination of documents and their individual significance underscores this point.

1. Suppression of General DeWitt's Final Report. As outlined in Point

One of the petition, it was assumed until recently that only one draft of the Final Report, dated June 5, 1943, was composed. An initial draft, however, has been discovered which was originally withheld not only from the defense but also from other governmental agencies, including the Department of Justice. The initial draft contained statements contrary to positions taken by the United States in its argument to the Supreme Court. These statements were either excised or altered for the express purpose of avoiding an "unfavorable reaction" by the Supreme Court. Needless to say, the Supreme Court never received this initial draft and all copies of the initial draft were recalled. Eventually, the galley proof, galley pages, drafts and memoranda of the original report were destroyed by burning.

Among the statements in the initial draft which were altered or excised and suppressed were the following:

1. "It was impossible to establish the identity of the loyal and disloyal with any degree of safety."
2. "It was *not* that there was *insufficient time* in which to make such determination; it was simply a matter of facing the realities that a positive determination would not be made, that an exact separation of the 'sheep from the goats' was unfeasible." (Emphasis added.)

Officials of the War Department excised and altered these statements in the DeWitt Report because they stood in direct opposition to the government's position that the reason for mass evacuation was insufficiency of time to hold individual hearings. In addition, the statements contradicted prior statements made by DeWitt thus impairing his credibility. The statements were excised and redrafted to state that "no ready means existed for determining the loyal and disloyal . . ."

Ignorant of DeWitt's statements that insufficiency of time was *not* the reason for the military actions, the Department of Justice continued to argue to the courts that the justification for the orders was, in fact, insufficiency of time. The government had stated in its brief to the United States Supreme Court in *Hirabayashi*: ". . . it would be impossible quickly and accurately to distinguish those persons [who had formed an attachment to, and sympathy and enthusiasm for, Japan] from other citizens of Japanese ancestry." Brief for United States in *Hirabayashi v. United States*, p. 12.

2. *Suppression of the Report of the Office of Naval Intelligence (ONI) on Japanese American loyalty*. As set forth in more detail in Point Two of the Petition, the ONI was assigned by Presidential Order to investigate the West Coast Japanese American population. The ONI's official report con-

cluded that the majority of Japanese Americans were loyal to the United States. Further, the ONI asserted that not only could the disloyal be identified but that a mechanism for distinguishing between the loyal and disloyal could have been established. Indeed, other authorities, such as the FBI, recognized that the Japanese Americans presented no grave threat to this country's security.

The ONI Report was sent to Attorney General Francis Biddle in 1942 and was known to the prosecution throughout the trials and appeals of Petitioners' cases. Yet this report was never presented to either the courts or Petitioners. Given the assertions in the second DeWitt Final Report that the loyalty of Japanese Americans could not readily be distinguished with any certainty, the ONI report was material to any factual rebuttal by Petitioners.

3. Suppression of the Reports of the Army Military Intelligence Division (G-2), the Federal Communications Commission (FCC), and the Federal Bureau of Investigation (FBI). Central to the United States' argument justifying the curfew and exclusion was the alleged potential for espionage and sabotage by Japanese Americans. In his Final Report, DeWitt argued that the military orders were justified because Japanese Americans were predisposed to acts of espionage and sabotage. In support of his allegations, he cited the interception of unauthorized radio communications and reports of unauthorized signal lights, implying that Japanese Americans were responsible for such acts.

Both the War Department and the Department of Justice possessed evidence which flatly refuted these allegations *before* the *Hirabayashi* case was decided. This evidence was suppressed from the trial courts and the United States Supreme Court (as outlined in Point Two of the Petition). Official records of the Army Military Intelligence Division, FBI and FCC specifically rejected DeWitt's claim that Japanese Americans committed, or were prepared to commit, acts of espionage or sabotage. The chairman of the FCC, in fact, reported to the Attorney General that every shore-to-ship signal had been investigated and no substantiation of illicit signaling was ever discovered. General DeWitt was informed of this as early as January 9, 1942, yet maintained in his Final Report that illicit radio communication had occurred with the implication of participation by Japanese Americans.

Reviewing the above-described documents suppressed by the government, their materiality to Petitioners' cases under the standard in *United States* v. *Agurs*, 427 U.S. 97 becomes evident. Each document contained facts which contradicted government assertions of "military necessity" and thus each was "obviously exculpatory in character," *Id.* at 107.[5] Additionally, these records of the Army Military Intelligence Division, FBI and FCC, would have further undercut the credibility of General DeWitt as a source of accurate factual information concerning the threat posed by the Japanese Americans. Without contrary evidence, however, the courts in general and Supreme Court in particular were left with a biased, prefabricated record. The frustration over the inadequacies of the record was expressed by Justice Jackson in his dissent in *Korematsu,*

> How does the Court know that these orders have a reasonable basis in necessity? No evidence whatever on that subject has been taken by this or any other court. There is sharp controversy as to the credibility of the DeWitt report. So the Court, having no real evidence before it, has no choice but to accept General DeWitt's own unsworn, self-serving statement, untested by any cross-examination, that what he did was reasonable.

323 U.S. at 245.

B. The Submission of False Evidence Which the Prosecutor Knew or Should Have Known to Be False, and the Failure to Correct or Disclose Such Falsity Violated Petitioners' Due Process Rights to Fair Proceedings.

The submission of false evidence by the Department of Justice falls within the first category of suppression cases defined by *Agurs*, 427 U.S. at 106. As discussed in the previous section of this memorandum, the prosecution suppressed evidence which would have proven its proferred evidence to be false. In addition, the prosecution presented the courts with "evidence" of espionage and sabotage associated with Japanese Americans stemming from disloyalty. This "evidence" was contradicted by information in the possession of the government. The Court, unaware of the falsity of these allegations, relied on these "facts" to uphold the constitutionality of the curfew and exclusion orders.

Rather than repeat the previous discussion and the detailed account in Points One, Two and Three of the petition, the following summarizes the false evidence submitted: (1) The government asserted that the military orders were necessary because there was insufficient time to separate the loyal from the disloyal. This contention was undermined by statements in

[5] Even if this court considers the suppressed information merely the opinions of military officials, it has been held that due process is violated when the prosecution fails to inform the defense that contrary opinions exist. *Ashley* v. *Texas*, 319 F.2d 80, 85 (5th Cir. 1963), cert. denied, 375 U.S. 931 (1963).

DeWitt's original Report which were excised and altered to conceal evidence from the court. (2) The DeWitt Report's "findings" of unauthorized signal lights and illicit radio communications, suggesting possibilities of sabotage and espionage by Japanese Americans, were directly refuted by responsible governmental agencies. Further, DeWitt's allegations of espionage and sabotage among Japanese Americans were flatly contradicted by the Army Military Intelligence Division, the FBI and the FCC. Both the Solicitor General of the United States and the Attorney General of the United States knew that DeWitt's allegations were refuted by other agencies, yet failed to disclose its falsity to the United States Supreme Court. (3) DeWitt's assertion that it was impossible to ascertain the loyalty of Japanese Americans was controverted by the report of the Office of Naval Intelligence which was responsible for investigating the loyalty of West Coast Japanese Americans.

It is established law that a conviction of a defendant based on false evidence is "inconsistent with the rudimentary demands of justice . . ." *Mooney* v. *Holohan*, 294 U.S. at 112. Following *Mooney*, courts have consistently held that the prosecutor's knowing use of false evidence is unconstitutional. *Pyle* v. *Kansas*, 317 U.S. 213; *Hysler* v. *Florida*, 315 U.S. 411; *Giglio* v. *United States*, 405 U.S. 150. It is not only improper for the prosecution to affirmatively misrepresent facts, but it is just as improper for the prosecution to create an inference of guilt by omitting material facts. As stated in *Imbler* v. *Craven*, 298 F. Supp. 795, 809 (C.D. Cal. 1969) aff'd, sub nom., *Imbler* v. *State of California*, 424 F.2d 631 (9th Cir.), cert. denied, 400 U.S. 865 (1970), quoting *Giles* v. *Maryland*, 386 U.S. 66, 100 (1967) (Fortas, J., concurring):

. . . omissions and half-truths are equally damaging and prohibited, and their use is no less culpable. Creating an *inference* that a fact exists when in fact to the knowledge of the prosecution it does not, constitutes the knowing use of false testimony.

"Evidence may be false either because it is perjured, or, though not in itself factually inaccurate, because it creates a false impression of facts which are known not to be true." (Citations omitted. Emphasis added.)

As noted in *Agurs*, 427 U.S. at 103, a conviction obtained through the use of false evidence must be set aside "if there is any reasonable likelihood that the false evidence could have affected the judgment of the jury" or, in this case, the court before whom the constitutional question was presented.

In Petitioners' cases, the central issue before the Court was whether the military had an adequate factual justification for the curfew and exclusion of Japanese Americans. The false evidence described herein was offered on this central issue, painting a false and misleading picture of imminent threat to the security of the West Coast. Whether by affirmative misrepresentation, suggestive inference or by failure to disclose contrary evidence, the government knowingly and purposefully made a false impression on the courts. Given the government's manipulation of this evidence and the Supreme Court's finding of military necessity on the factual record before them, there is clearly more than a "reasonable likelihood" that the false evidence affected the court's judgment.

IV. The Prosecution's Bad Faith in Intentionally Destroying Evidence Material to the Petitioners' Defenses Prejudiced Petitioners' Rights to Fair Proceedings in Violation of the Due Process Clause of the United States Constitution

As discussed in Point One of the Petition and Section III of this Memorandum, several branches of government collaborated to destroy the original DeWitt Final Report. This destruction not only constituted suppression of evidence, but also raises an independent ground of misconduct upon which this court may base vacation of Petitioners' convictions.

When the prosecution and affiliated government agencies are responsible for the loss or destruction of evidence, the courts will find a due process violation if bad faith lies behind the government's actions. This standard should be distinguished from the standard applicable to suppression cases discussed above; in suppression cases, a due process violation will be found on the basis of the materiality of the evidence, "irrespective of the good faith or bad faith of the prosecution." *Brady* v. *Maryland*, 373 U.S. 83.

In 1974, the Ninth Circuit established an explicit test for vacation of convictions based on destruction of evidence. In *United States* v. *Heiden*, 508 F.2d 898 (9th Cir. 1974), the court was confronted with destruction of marijuana prior to the appellant's trial. The court declared that

When there is loss or destruction of such evidence, we will reverse a defendant's conviction if he can show (1) bad faith or connivance on the part of the government or (2) that he was prejudiced by the loss of evidence.

Id. at p. 902.

Prior to *Heiden*, the courts had established that the loss or destruction of evidence by the prosecution could violate defendant's constitutional rights if the prosecutor acted in bad faith. See *United States* v. *Augenblick*,

393 U.S. 348 (1969); *United States* v. *Bryant*, 439 F.2d 642 (D.C. Cir. 1971); *United States* v. *Henry*, 487 F.2d 912 (9th Cir. 1973).

It is significant to note that after *Heiden*, the courts have suggested that prejudice will be presumed if there is intentional destruction of evidence by the prosecution. As stated in *United States* v. *Arra*, 630 F.2d 836, 849–850 (1st Cir. 1980), where the government erased a tape of their surveillance of the appellants,

It may be, though we do not now so decide, that intentional wrongful misconduct on the part of the government would warrant an assumption that the evidence destroyed would have been favorable to the defense.

In the instant cases, the various government and military authorities purposefully and methodically collected all copies of the original DeWitt Final Report and had them destroyed. The conclusion is inescapable that the intent behind the destruction was to keep any evidence contrary to the government's legal position away from the Court. This intent is underscored by governmental agents' efforts to destroy not only the original Final Report but to alter and cover up any records of that original Report's existence. Such a blatant exhibition of bad faith falls squarely within the type of misconduct prohibited by *Heiden*, 508 F.2d 898.

The destruction of the Final Report was prejudicial to the Petitioners' defense. The government's claim of military necessity rested on the assumption that there was insufficient time to determine the loyalty of Japanese Americans on an individual basis. Yet, General DeWitt's own statements that insufficiency of time was not the reason for the orders, were destroyed with the original Final Report. Petitioners were thereby prejudiced in their ability to challenge the factual justification for the military orders put forth by the government. The bad faith exhibited by the War Department in destroying the original Final Report was so egregious and calculated that the court should presume that the evidence destroyed favored the Petitioners. *Arra*, 630 F.2d 836.

V. The Pattern and Practice of Generalized Misconduct by the Government Constituted a Fraud on the Court Resulting in Further Deprivation of Petitioners' Due Process Rights

Fraud on the court ". . . is that species of fraud which does, or attempts to, defile the court itself or is a fraud perpetrated by officers of the court so that the judicial machinery cannot perform in the usual manner its important task of adjudicating cases that are presented for adjudication." *Bulloch* v. *United States*, 95 F.R.D. 123, 143 (D. Utah 1982)(citations omitted).

Petitioners contend that the government executed a systematic plan to impede the administration of justice in their cases. Considered in its totality, these acts amounted to a fraud on the court, warranting relief from Petitioners' convictions.

Officials of the War Department, Justice Department, the Military, and the Executive branch acted in concert to effectuate a plan which: (1) deprived the court of relevant and material evidence necessary for a full adjudication of the underlying criminal actions, and (2) introduced into the proceedings information which was known to be false, misleading and prejudicial. This plan was intended to validate the government orders which ultimately resulted in the exclusion and imprisonment of an entire sector of the citizenry.

A. Development of a Standard for Fraud on the Court

The federal courts are empowered by rules of equity to grant relief from judgments which are "manifestly unconscionable." *Hazel-Atlas Glass Co.* v. *Hartford-Empire Co.*, 322 U.S. 238, 244–45 (1944)(citation omitted). In *Hazel-Atlas*, the Supreme Court granted relief some fifteen years after entry of a patent infringement judgment; the defendant had moved for vacation of the judgment on discovering a fraud upon the court. The fraud occurred when the Circuit Court of Appeals granted a patent based upon the submission of a document purporting to be an independent industry opinion. In fact, the article given to the court had been written by one of the attorneys for the appellant.

In setting aside the judgment, the court found that appellant had misled the court through a deliberately planned and carefully executed scheme to defraud the court. The court exercised its extraordinary power to set aside judgments because of the great public interest in maintaining the integrity of the judicial process. *Id.* at 246.

These equitable powers were recently exercised in *Bulloch* v. *United States*, 95 F.R.D. 123. In *Bulloch*, the court invalidated a twenty-six-year-old judgment for the government in an action filed by sheep owners for injuries caused by nuclear testing. In that case, the court found that the government's misconduct in making false and deceptive misrepresentations, intentionally withholding evidence, and generally manipulating the processes of the court amounted to fraud on the court. The court found the fraud to be even more egregious because the government "enjoyed a virtual monopoly of knowledge in comparison to that independently available to the plaintiff sheep owners, their attorneys and, indeed, the Court . . ." *Id*. at 144.

The criminal courts have also been invested with such equitable powers to prevent intrinsic fraud. *United States* v. *Frank*, 520 F.2d 1287, 1292 (2d Cir. 1975), cert. denied, 423 U.S. 1087 (1976). This power results from the reservation by the court of an inherent authority to regulate and supervise the administration of criminal justice. *United States* v. *Cortina*, 630 F.2d 1207, 1214 (7th Cir. 1980). Finding that false statements within an affidavit constitute fraud on the judicial system, *Cortina* held that the court's supervisory powers over government officials are at their "strongest and most defensible" when ordering sanctions against governmental fraud. *Id*.

These supervisory powers are referred to in *United States* v. *Banks*, 383 F. Supp. 389, 392 (D.S.D. 1974), appeal dismissed sub nom., *United States* v. *Means*, 513 F.2d 1329 (8th Cir. 1975). In *Banks*, the misconduct involved the use of perjured testimony, conspiracy, suppression of documents, illegal and unconstitutional use of military personnel, and the violation of ethical, professional, and moral standards.

B. Materiality

The materiality of a scheme that misleads and deceives the court must be viewed in the totality of the government's conduct. While no single component of the plan may have clouded the administration of justice, the theory of fraud on the court requires that the entire practice be examined for the overall effect on the judgment of the court. The court in *Hazel-Atlas* discussed the required showing of the materiality of the fraud:

Whether or not (the fraud) was the primary basis for that ruling, the article did impress the court, as shown by the Court's opinion. *Doubtless it is wholly impossible accurately to appraise the influence that the article exerted on the judges. But we do not think that circumstances call for such an attempted appraisal.* Hartford's officials and lawyers thought the article material. They conceived it in an effort to persuade a hostile Patent officer to grant their patent application, and went to considerable trouble and expense to get it published. Having lost their infringement suit based on the patent in the District Court wherein they did not specifically emphasize the article, they urged the article upon the Circuit Court and prevailed. They are in no position now to dispute its effectiveness.

322 U.S. at 246–47 (emphasis added).

From an examination of the opinions of the Supreme Court in Petitioners' cases, it is clear that the misinformation proffered by the government did enter into the judicial decision. Such a strict determination is not required, however, under *Hazel-Atlas*. It is sufficient that the offending party deem the evidence important to its case. Thus, the offending party should be precluded from denying the effectiveness of the misinformation submitted to the court.

C. Government Misconduct in Hirabayashi, Korematsu and Yasui as Fraud on the Court

Petitioners contend that governmental abuses rose to the level of an intentional and contrived program to mislead the Court. This process of deceit has been presented in detail in the instant Petition. Collectively and cumulatively, the government's acts deprived both Petitioners and the courts of information vital to the determination of constitutionality of the military orders.

Compounding this misconduct, the government further manipulated the court's processes by introducing before the court information on racial characteristics of Japanese Americans which was prejudicial, racially-biased, irrelevant and of dubious credibility. The government offered this evidence of racial characteristics, and of the propensity of Japanese Americans toward disloyalty, through the doctrine of judicial notice. According to Rule 201(b) of the Federal Rules of Evidence, "a judicially noticed fact must be one not subject to reasonable dispute in that it is either (1) generally known within the territorial jurisdiction of the court, or (2) capable of accurate and ready determination by resort to sources whose accuracy cannot be reasonably questioned."

The doctrine, which provides a process of streamlining the presentation of adjudicative facts, is reserved for those points which are unquestionably true. If there is bona fide dispute about the truth of the fact and the court believes that the truth is not or cannot be established to a convincing degree, the court should refuse judicial notice and remand for further evidence. Dembitz, *Racial Discrimination and the Military Judgments: The Supreme Court's Korematsu and Endo Decisions*, Colum. Rev. 177, 185 n.39 (1945).

The government used the doctrine of judicial notice to prove facts which it could not establish by other means. Given the government's knowledge of contradictory evidence, the use of judicial notice illustrates clearly the extent to which the government manipulated both the facts and the court's processes to win Petitioners' cases at all costs.

Another example of governmental misconduct was the War Department's manipulation of amicus curiae. While the War Department withheld DeWitt's Final Report from the Department of Justice, it furnished the report to the California State Attorney General for use in preparing the amicus brief of the West Coast states in *Hirabayashi*. In addition, to assure that the allegations in the Final Report would be introduced by amici, the military actively assisted the states in the preparation of their brief.

The course and scope of governmental misconduct in Petitioners' cases make application of the court's supervisory powers seem most appropriate. The court has exercised such equitable powers both in civil actions such as *Bulloch*, 95 F.R.D. 123, and in criminal cases such as *Banks*, 383 F. Supp. at 392, and *Cortina*, 630 F.2d 1216. The application of the court's broad supervisory powers seems particularly appropriate in Petitioners' cases for the government's misconduct had a much wider impact than on Petitioners' cases alone.

Ultimately, the government's misconduct resulted in the validation of a program which excluded and evacuated 110,000 Americans of Japanese ancestry. The government's actions violated the integrity of the judicial process itself and, as in *Hazel-Atlas*, this offense against the court provides adequate grounds for setting aside Petitioners' convictions.

VI. The Cumulative Effect of All the Acts of Governmental Misconduct Operated to Deny Petitioners Due Process Rights to a Fair Trial and Appeal

Petitioners additionally urge that the course of conduct undertaken by the government, viewed in its totality, represents an aggregate violation of due process rights. The cumulative effect of the acts of misconduct described in the petition demand extraordinary relief from the court.

The courts have found a denial for due process based on cumulative errors at trial. *United States* v. *Semensohn*, 421 F.2d 1206, 1210 (2d Cir. 1970). Where no one individual error would require reversal of a conviction, the court may ascribe due process violations to the total effect of errors which cast serious doubt on the fairness of a trial. *United States* v. *Guglielmini*, 384 F.2d 602, 607 (2d Cir. 1967). The court must examine such cumulative effect in close legal cases, where such an effect could have made the difference between conviction and acquittal. *United States v. Bledsole*, 531 F.2d 888, 892 (8th Cir. 1976).

In *United States ex rel. Marzeno* v. *Gengler*, 574 F.2d 730, 736–37 (3d Cir. 1978), the court commented on the cumulative effect of multiple non-disclosures of evidence: "Certainly, the effect of each non-disclosure must not only be considered alone, for the cumulative effect of non-disclosures might require reversal even though, standing alone, each bit of omitted evidence may not be sufficiently 'material' to justify a new trial." *United States ex rel. Marzeno* v. *Gengler*, 574 F.2d 730, 736–37 (3rd Cir. 1978).

Petitioners submit that the acts of government misconduct separately and cumulatively violated their due process rights. This pattern of misconduct has been discussed extensively in the Petition and in this Memorandum and will not be repeated here. When considered as a whole, the government's repeated abuse of the judicial process resulted in the denial to Petitioners of a fair proceedings.

Conclusion

The pattern of governmental misconduct described insured Petitioners' convictions at trial as well as the affirmance of those convictions on appeal. In securing Petitioners' convictions, the government also won court approval for the mass exclusion of one ethnic minority. The convictions stand today, not because Petitioners committed any wrong to society but because they were persons of Japanese ancestry. Petitioners urge this court to carefully weigh the complete record of governmental abuses, in each of its components and as a whole, and do justice where it was denied forty years ago.

Dated: January 19, 1983

Peter Irons
Dale Minami

Korematsu v. United States

Government's Response and Motion, U.S. District Court for the Northern District of California

October 4, 1983

Fred Korematsu's coram nobis petition, filed in the U.S. district court in San Francisco on January 19, 1983, was assigned to Judge Marilyn Hall Patel. The U.S. Department of Justice, represented in court by Victor Stone of the Criminal Division, sought to put off the government's response to the petition until the report and recommendations of the Commission on Wartime Relocation had been released. That report flatly rejected the "military necessity" claim the government had relied on before the Supreme Court in the 1940s and thus undercut any current government defense of the wartime convictions. After high-level discussions in the Justice Department and the White House, the government answered the Korematsu petition with a brief response that characterized the internment as an "unfortunate episode" in American history and agreed with the vacation of Korematsu's conviction. However, the government admitted no wrongdoing in the cases and asked Judge Patel to dismiss the petition without a hearing.

In 1942, petitioner was one of a very few standard bearers who chose to challenge the propriety of World War II military orders which resulted in the mass evacuation of over one-hundred thousand persons of Japanese ancestry from the west coast.

Although the judiciary questioned the wisdom of those military orders, *Korematsu* v. *United States*, 323 U.S. 214, 225 (Frankfurter, J., concurring), it affirmed petitioner's misdemeanor conviction because it upheld the very broad discretionary authority of the Legislative and Executive Branches of government acting together in wartime. *Korematsu* v. *United States*, 323 U.S. 214, 217–218 (1944).

Both of those branches of government have long since concluded that the mass evacuation was part of an unfortunate episode in our nation's history. In the 1976 presidential proclamation formally rescinding Executive Order 9066, President Ford praised the sacrifice and contributions of Japanese-Americans and called upon the American people to affirm with him the lesson "learned from the tragedy of that long-ago experience forever to treasure liberty and justice for each individual American, and resolve that this kind of action shall never again be repeated." Proclamation No. 4417, 41 Fed. Reg. No. 35 p. 7741 (Feb. 20, 1976).

The Legislative Branch has acted likewise. Even before the creation in 1980 of the Commission on Wartime Relocation and Internment of Civilians, Congress enacted 18 U.S.C. 4001(a) in 1971 which provides that "no citizen shall be . . . detained by the United States except pursuant to an Act of Congress." The only Act of Congress which had allowed such action, Public Law 77-503, then codified at 18 U.S.C. 1383 (which petitioner was convicted of violating in 1942), has been explicitly repealed. P.L. 94-412, Title V, §501(e), 90 Stat. 1258 (1976).

In this specific context, the government has concluded—without any intention to disparage those persons who made the decisions in question—that it would not be appropriate to defend this forty year old misdemeanor conviction. Because we believe that it is time to put behind us the controversy which led to the mass evacuation in 1942 and instead to reaffirm the inherent right of each person to be treated as an individual, it is singularly appropriate to vacate this conviction for non-violent civil disobedience. It is also the intention of the government to extend the same relief to other similarly situated individuals who request it.

There is, therefore, no continuing reason in this setting for this court to convene hearings or make findings about petitioner's allegations of governmental wrongdoing in the 1940's. Moreover, as the Commission found after spending three years and more than one-million dollars, no completely satisfactory answer can be reached about these emotion laden issues from this vantage point in history. See Addendum and Additional Views to Commission's Report.

Having recited above the current valid national interests to be served by vacating this misdemeanor conviction and dismissing the indictment at this time, the government hereby moves to vacate petitioner's conviction and dismiss the underlying indictment. See *Rinaldi* v. *United States*, 434 U.S. 22 (1978); and *United States* v. *Hamm*, 659 F. 2d 624, 631 (5th Cir. 1981)(en banc).

Thereupon, petitioner having received all the relief which this Court can render, the petition should be dismissed.

Dated: October 4, 1983

Respectfully submitted,

Stephen S. Trott, Assistant Attorney General, Criminal Division
Joseph P. Russoniello, United States Attorney

By: William T. McGivern, Jr., Chief Assistant United States Attorney
Victor Stone, Counsel for Special and Appellate Matters, General
   Litigation and Legal Advice Section, U.S. Department of Justice

Attorneys for Respondent

Korematsu v. United States

Transcript of Arguments on Coram Nobis Petition, U.S.
District Court for the Northern District of California

November 10, 1983

Judge Patel scheduled the hearing on Fred Korematsu's coram nobis petition for November 10, 1983. More than three hundred people, many of them elderly survivors of the internment camps, crowded the courtroom that day. Dale Minami, who headed Korematsu's legal team, argued for granting the petition. Victor Stone, who represented the government, asked that Judge Patel put off any ruling until the government had reviewed its position on the petition. Judge Patel rejected Stone's request, as well as Stone's argument that the government could vacate Korematsu's conviction without judicial action on his petition. The two lawyers then argued on the merits of the petition, and Korematsu made a brief but powerful statement to the court. Judge Patel ruled from the bench after the arguments, vacating Korematsu's conviction and granting his petition. Many of the spectators shed tears of joy and relief as the hearing ended.

Participants:

Judge Patel

Dale Minami for Fred Korematsu

Fred Korematsu

Victor Stone for United States

The Clerk: Criminal Action 27635-W MHP, United States versus Fred Toyosaburo Korematsu on Motion to Vacate Conviction and to Dismiss the Indictment.

The Court: The posture of this litigation is as follows: That in January of this year a petition for writ of coram nobis was filed by Petitioner Korematsu in this Court, this Court being the Court in which he was convicted in September of 1942, that conviction having been affirmed by the Supreme Court in 1944.

The conviction was for an offense under an Act of Congress of March 21, 1942 by reason of violation of an exclusion order denominating No. 34, which was issued pursuant to an executive order, that Executive Order No. 9066.

The petition was based upon several grounds having to do with misrepresentations made in the nature of supporting military necessity for the underlying executive order and exclusion orders implementing that executive order, and the Act of Congress as well as the arguments of military necessities supporting both the conviction and the affirmance of that conviction, as well as alleged failure to provide certain information to the Supreme Court in representing the nature of the military necessity in existence at that time.

With respect to the reasons for which that petition should be granted, I will hear from you now, Mr. Minami.

Mr. Minami: Your Honor, members of the Court staff, opposing counsel, co-counsel and members of the audience: We are here today to seek a measure of the justice denied to Fred Korematsu and the Japanese-American community 40 years ago.

At the outset, we dispute vigorously the characterization of the public interest which might support the granting of the petition as advanced by the government.

The government's definition of public interest is contained in the motion to vacate the conviction. If reviewed closely, the reasons advanced by the government are neither real nor substantial.

In effect, their position is to avoid a consideration of significant factual and constitutional issues.

The reasons may be summarized as follows as stated in the motion. "It is time to put behind us the controversy which led to the mass evacuation in 1942."

A second reason advanced is that "no completely satisfactory answer can be reached about these emotion-laden issues."

Simply put, these are not reasons, but excuses for not admitting error and for refusing to confront the real public interest in concluding this legal chapter.

It is uncontested that the Court has a duty to independently review the public interest in granting this petition.

In that context, we would like to set forth the public considerations that we believe are controlling in this case.

First, it must be recognized that we are dealing with an extraordinary case. The case was originally decided by the United States Supreme Court over 40 years ago. The allegations we put forth are perhaps unique in legal history, challenging that high government officials suppressed, altered and destroyed information and evidence in order to influence the outcome of a Supreme Court decision.

The case itself is enormously significant; as Fred Korematsu says, "My name must be known by every law student and lawyer in the country."

The case has been cited extensively and been the subject of law review articles over the years.

This is not just a 40-year-old misdemeanor, as the government characterizes it. This is a monumental precedent which affected deeply and irrevocably the lives of a hundred thousand Japanese-Americans, and countless numbers of friends and neighbors by mass banishment of a single racial minority group.

The total in lost property, lost opportunities, broken families and human suffering was staggering. This case also established some of the most criticized and controversial precedents in legal history.

First, the mass exclusion of an identifiable minority based on race without notice, without hearing, without an attorney was justified.

Secondly, military judgments in times of crises are virtually unreviewable by the courts, even though the courts are functioning and no martial law has been declared.

Korematsu v. *United States* has never been overruled and has never been reversed. Today we know that this Supreme Court decision rests on a non-existent factual foundation.

Evidence we have presented in this case underscores that assertion.

Some brief examples. Agencies responsible for the investigation and monitoring of Japanese-Americans felt that they presented no danger great enough to warrant mass exclusion.

Their opinions and reports were suppressed from the Supreme Court. Department of Justice officials felt an ethical duty to reveal evidence contrary to that offered to and accepted by the United States Supreme Court.

This evidence was likewise suppressed. Responsible government agencies, such as the Federal Communications Commission and the FBI flatly refuted claims presented to the Supreme Court as facts that Japanese-Americans were implicated in illegal signaling through radio and light transmissions to enemy vessels.

This evidence of refutation was also suppressed. The factual argument is described more fully in the petition supported by exhibits attached in the petition and the reply.

The conclusions of the Commission on Wartime Relocation and Internment of Civilians which was alluded to earlier are especially relevant here. As the Court undoubtedly recalls and as reflected in the transcripts of our court appearances on March 14th and May 9th, 1983, the government conceded great credibility to the Commission and its findings.

In fact, the schedule set for responding revolved around the issuance of the Commission report and recommendations.

The government indicated to this Court that the position of the U.S. government would rest strongly on the Commission findings and recommendations, and on March 14th when the Court referred to *Personal Justice Denied*, the report of the Commission, the attorney for the government stated, "I think there is a substantial amount of material in here," referring to *Personal Justice Denied*, "that directly bears on the issues in this case."

And at the same hearing, the government attorney agreed that it would be appropriate to take judicial notice of the government report.

I only recite these facts because it is clear from the record that the factual findings, the conclusions of *Personal Justice Denied*, had a great influence on the government's failure to respond in the motion to vacate.

So when the government offers little substantial reason for granting the petition, the record clearly indicates that the conclusions of *Personal Justice Denied* were the influential, if not controlling, reasons for their actions.

The Commission's findings, then, should be included in the grounds for granting the petition.

The conclusions made bear directly on the public interest and the conclusions made include the following: that no military necessity warranted the exclusion of Japanese from the West Coast; that Executive Order 9066 was not justified by military necessity; that General DeWitt's rationale that ethnicity determines loyalty does not provide a credible justification for the necessity of exclusion; that no evidence of imminent attack, no evidence of planned sabotage, no documented act of espionage, sabotage or fifth column activity was ever committed by an American of Japanese ancestry.

A final conclusion helps complete this picture. The broad historical causes which shaped these decisions, which included curfew, exclusion, imprisonment, were race prejudice, war hysteria and failure of political leadership.

These and other conclusions directly contradict the findings by the United States Supreme Court in 1944 in Fred Korematsu's case.

If the facts, as presented through the Commission, were known to the Supreme Court, we believe there would be a reasonable likelihood of a different result.

The government, however, is arguing that these findings, memorialized forever in a decision from the highest court of this land, now should be forgotten. It is arguing, in essence, that we should put the controversy behind us, that we should, in a sense, let old wounds heal.

But whose wounds need healing? The Japanese-Americans who have lived with the stigma of this decision for 40 years and who never received a judicial declaration of wrongfulness or wrongdoing or adequate compensation for their suffering, or is it the wounds of guilt, of high government officials who were responsible for this great civil rights disaster?

The government's approach turns the idea of public interest on its head. The government, in effect, is advocating letting the guilty go free and keeping the innocent imprisoned in the shame and suffering they endured for 40 years.

It is advocating keeping the public imprisoned in the ignorant notion that this was an "unfortunate" incident as the government describes.

Even the government's motion to vacate indicates an unwillingness to face the facts and the constitutional issues.

The motion states that the Commission found no completely satisfactory answer that can be reached about these emotion-laden issues, citing the addendum and Congressman Lungren's additional views.

To the contrary, the satisfactory answer was found and unanimously so by the Commission, that no military necessity existed to justify the exclusion; that the exclusion and detention was a result of hysteria, prejudice and failure of leadership.

The addendum confirmed that finding, and Congressman Lundgren, a member of the Commission, although his additional views raised concerns, stated specifically that he concurred with the findings of the Commission.

The attitude of the government to our serious allegations of misconduct and unconstitutionality of the military orders under which Fred Korematsu was convicted, is precisely why a judicial declaration of the grounds for granting the petition is necessary, because this was not an unfortunate incident. This was not a mistake. This was a deliberate and calculated plan to exclude and imprison a single minority group.

Yet the government has not completely admitted and recognized this wrong. For Fred Korematsu, the public interest grounds are clear. He lived 40 years with the conviction while carrying the burden of losing the case which sanctioned the mass imprisonment of his people.

For him to fight as a representative of all Japanese-Americans virtually alone, when his community was either too young, too tired, too old or too frightened to fight and risking imprisonment and a criminal record entitles him to some consideration.

Surely after 40 years of fighting, Fred Korematsu's interest is part of the public interest. For the Japanese-American community, Fred's fight was their fight.

Most knew in their hearts that the Korematsu exclusion and imprisonment was wrong, but they were too consumed with the business of survival to do anything about it.

They, too, have an interest in Fred's case, in Fred's vindication and to validate their own beliefs that they were not criminals in 1942.

Included in this community were a number of Japanese-Americans convicted of curfew and exclusion violations.

The government has offered to move for vacation of their conviction, but there is no guarantee that another judge in another venue or jurisdiction would find the public interest reasons suitable for granting the motion.

Findings in this Court would undoubtedly support the proper determination of public interest in another jurisdiction.

For this country, the entire incident is a lesson. A lesson that the government, including the executive, legislative and judicial branches allowed a grave injustice to occur.

We are not so naive to believe we have a perfect system, because no one has, but we are not so stupid to believe that we can deny our mistakes and our wrongs and still progress as a country.

As an institution, as a people, as a country, we will truly be condemned to relive history unless we learn its lessons.

In this sense, the public interest is not served by the government's refusal to confess error. Despite the evidence we have produced and despite the unequivocal findings of the Commission, unless the government confesses error or unless a judicial declaration includes a recognition of those errors, we *will* repeat these mistakes.

Clearly, the executive branch and the legislative branch have spoken and have acknowledged the grave constitutional error of exclusion and imprisonment of Japanese-Americans.

As mentioned earlier, President Ford, on February 19th of 1976, rescinded Executive Order 9066 calling the uprooting of loyal Americans a setback to fundamental American principles.

Even the major participants in the exclusion and detention decisions eventually repudiated their actions.

Earl Warren, who later became a great Chief Justice of the United States Supreme Court; Justice William O. Douglas, who voted to uphold the government's position in Hirabayashi and Korematsu, recanted in his later years and also Tom Clark, as a U.S. Attorney then, who later became a United States Supreme Court Justice, also repudiated his role.

Only the judicial system has not yet had the opportunity to recognize this wrong.

This is significant because the judicial system is so often the last refuge for powerless minorities such as Japanese-Americans who had neither the numbers nor the money to influence electoral politics.

The principle of judicial review is critical to our constitutional system. It is especially important when individual freedoms guaranteed by the Constitution are at stake.

The court, not Congress and not the executive, is the arbiter of the law and the ultimate protector of our freedoms.

Alexander Hamilton recognized that the necessary powers of the court is to "declare all acts contrary to the manifest tenor of the Constitution void. Without this, all the reservations of rights or privileges would amount to nothing."

Thus, there is no complete vindication without a judicial declaration of the constitutional wrongs inflicted on Japanese-Americans.

It is singularly appropriate for this Court to decide what public interest is served in granting this petition. That no military necessity existed to justify the military and executive orders; that critical evidence bearing on issues before the Supreme Court in 1944 was deliberately suppressed and had this evidence been produced before the Supreme Court, there existed a reasonable likelihood of a different result; that based upon these facts which demonstrated that no military necessity existed, Executive Order 9066 and military orders under which Fred Korematsu was convicted were unconstitutional.

The public interest, then, demands more than a sterile recitation that we should let bygones be bygones and requires that the real substantial reasons be exposed so that this tragedy will never be repeated.

The danger in accepting the government's reasons for granting the petition is the danger described by Justice Jackson `in a dissent in the

Korematsu case. In referring to a situation where the court validates a principle of law such as was upheld in *Korematsu* v. *United States*, Justice Jackson stated "The law lies around like a loaded weapon ready for the hand of any authority that can bring forward a plausible claim of urgent need."

For those Japanese-Americans interned, for those ex-internees in the audience, for Fred Korematsu and for this Court, this is the last opportunity to finally achieve the justice denied 40 years ago.

Thank you, very much.

The Court: Thank you.

Is there anything further, Mr. Minami?

Mr. Minami: If we may beg the Court's indulgence, Mr. Korematsu would like to make a statement to the Court.

The Court: I will allow him to do so at this time. Mr. Korematsu?

Mr. Korematsu: Your Honor, I still remember 40 years ago when I was handcuffed and arrested as a criminal here in San Francisco.

I was going to say here in this building, but it wasn't. It was on Mission Street, that building over there.

And I also remember Mr. Ernest Besig of the American Civil Liberties Union standing beside me at the hearing. He posted the bail of $5,000— Mr. Besig posted the bail of $5,000. And I was supposed to be free to go as a civilian, but as we were ready to go out the door the M.P.'s were there with guns and they said, "I'm sorry, you can't leave."

And they have orders from their commander. And so right away they raised the bail to $10,000 and so Mr. Besig said, "Well, we will just let you go with the M.P.'s and see what happens."

So that's how it was going back and forth. As an American citizen being put through this shame and embarrassment and also all Japanese-American citizens who were escorted to concentration camps, suffered the same embarrassment, we can never forget this incident as long as we live.

The horse stalls that we stayed in were made for horses, not human beings.

According to the Supreme Court decision regarding my case, being an American citizen was not enough. They say you have to look like one, otherwise they say you can't tell a difference between a loyal and a disloyal American.

I thought that this decision was wrong and I still feel that way. As long as my record stands in federal court, any American citizen can be held in prison or concentration camps without a trial or a hearing.

That is if they look like the enemy of our country. Therefore, I would like to see the government admit that they were wrong and do something about it so this will never happen again to any American citizen of any race, creed or color.

Thank you.

The Court: Thank you, Mr. Korematsu.

Does the Government have a response at this time?

Mr. Stone: Good morning, Your Honor. As the Court is well aware, the government has requested that the Court make the same substantive ruling and grant the same substantive relief which Mr. Korematsu, as petitioner, has requested, namely that the conviction be vacated and the underlying information be dismissed.

We do that in the context of a long history by the executive and legislative branches, which has recognized that this was a very unusual situation in the history of this nation that resulted in legislation on at least six, seven occasions to remedy different facets of this problem.

Initially in 1948 there was the Japanese-American Evacuation Claims Act as a result of one of the efforts of one of the amicus currently in this case, the Japanese-American Citizens League and . . . there was a further statute passed in 1971 which made it clear that no action such as Executive Order 9066, which was issued before there was legislative action, could ever again issue to imprison American citizens.

That statute was signed by President Nixon. It was followed by additional efforts, and again there was testimony before Congress, and Congress was well aware that it was intending, consciously, to limit the effect of this very case, *Korematsu* v. *United States*, as well as the Hirabayashi case and the precedent which the Supreme Court previously established.

And to that end in 1975, there was various legislation to repeal the statute under which Mr. Korematsu was convicted, and it was, in fact, repealed in 1976 and signed into law by President Ford.

At that time that that was underway, Japanese-American groups came into direct contact with the White House and asked what the continuing status of the executive order itself was, to which President Ford responded in an official proclamation, No. 4417, and I would like, at this point, to read it and make it part of the record.

It is entitled "An American Promise by the President of the United States of America, a Proclamation." It reads:

In this bicentennial year, we are commemorating the anniversary dates of many of the great events in American history. An honest reckoning, however, must include a recognition of our national mistakes as well as our national achievements.

Learning from our mistakes is not pleasant, but as a great philosopher once admonished, we must do so if we want to avoid repeating them.

February 19th is the anniversary of a sad day in American history. It was on that date in 1942, in the midst of the response to the hostilities that began on December 7, 1941, that Executive Order No. 9066 was issued, subsequently enforced by the criminal penalties of a statute enacted March 21, 1942, resulting in the uprooting of loyal Americans.

Over 100,000 persons of Japanese ancestry were removed from their homes, detained in special camps, and eventually relocated.

The tremendous effort by the War Relocation Authority and concerned Americans for the welfare of these Japanese-Americans may add perspective to that story, but it does not erase the setback to fundamental American principles.

Fortunately, the Japanese-American community in Hawaii was spared the indignities suffered by those on our mainland.

We now know what we should have known then—not only was that evacuation wrong, but Japanese-Americans were and are loyal Americans. On the battlefield and at home, Japanese-Americans —names like Hamada, Misumori, Marimoto, Noguchi, Yamasaki, Kido, Munemore and Miyamura—have been and continue to be written in our history for the sacrifices and the contributions they have made to the well-being and security of this, our common Nation.

The executive order that was issued on February 19, 1942, was for the sole purpose of prosecuting the war with the Axis Powers, and ceased to be effective with the end of those hostilities.

Because there was no formal statement of its termination, however, there is concern among many Japanese-Americans that there may yet be some life in that obsolete document. I think it appropriate, in this our Bicentennial Year, to remove all doubt on that matter, and to make clear our commitment in the future.

Now, therefore, I, Gerald R. Ford, President of the United States of America, do hereby proclaim that all the authority conferred by Executive Order No. 9066 terminated upon the issuance of Proclamation No. 2714, which formally proclaimed the cessation of the hostilities of World War II on December 31, 1946.

I call upon the American people to affirm with me this American Promise— that we have learned from the tragedy of that long-ago experience forever to treasure liberty and justice for each individual American, and resolve that this kind of action shall never again be repeated.

In witness whereof, I have hereunto set my hand this 19th day of February in the Year of Our Lord 1976, and of the Independence of the United States of America the 200th.

Gerald R. Ford.

And that is the substance of it. Subsequent to that, President Ford signed the legislation repealing the statute, as I previously mentioned, which Mr. Korematsu was convicted under.

Subsequent to that, largely both prior and subsequent, Congress passed statutes which provided special retirement provisions of the Social Security Act and the Federal Civil Service Act to grant special credit to people who had been interned.

Of course, more recently, several of the states, including California, have extended special compensation to former civil service employees.

And then in 1980, President Carter signed a bill which we have described at some length in our pleadings and which resulted in the formation of a Commission and the appropriation and expenditure of over a million dollars, so that Commission could again attempt to lay bare the record of what President Ford and President Nixon, and the Congress in 1948 as well, recognized was apparently done wrong during World War II, both as a lesson and as a mechanism which would forever guarantee the rights of these and all American citizens.

One of the recommendations which that Commission, which was established recently, came up with was a recommendation for the executive pardon of all those people convicted of violations which were still outstanding.

It was the decision of the executive branch to try and go further than that to affirmatively ask that the outstanding convictions and any underlying information or indictments be dismissed not only to this petitioner and others who have petitioned, but as to all of those people who suffered that legal result and wish to have it so done.

The government's response, Your Honor, is that the difficulties, many of the difficulties we have encountered emanate from the very same document which we have, of course, told the Court that it could recognize exists, namely the Commission's report.

To the extent that we are in a court of law and dealing with legal matters, that Commission's report has concluded and we find ourselves, I think, unanimous in agreeing with it, that it says "Today the decision in *Korematsu* lies overruled in the court of history." First, the Supreme Court, a little more than a year later in *Duncan* v. *Kahanamoku*, reviewed the imposition of martial law in Hawaii and struck it down, making adamantly clear that the principles and practices of American government are permeated by the belief that loyal citizens in loyal territory are to be governed by civil rather than military authority, and that when the military assumes civil functions, in such circumstances it will receive no deference from the courts in reviewing its actions, and later that each part of the decision, questions of both factual review and legal principles have been discredited or abandoned.

We don't think it lies around like a loaded gun and to that end, the legislative and executive branches have repealed any authority that any underlying statutes might once have had.

But this did not reach the conclusion, in fact, suggested exactly to the contrary, that there were particular acts of suppression by the government that might have occurred when the cases were litigated, particularly pages 8 and 237, it suggests contrary findings.

Now, to the extent it reaches those conclusions, those conclusions are not neatly applicable here. The standards for admissibility of evidence before the Commission and the standards of proof required and applied by that body are not the same as would be required and applied in a body of law, and although they might relate to the threshold question of whether the petitioner's petition could be entertained, they don't relate to the underlying question which, if it isn't a legal matter, is certainly a symbolic matter with which we completely agree with Mr. Korematsu and Mr. Minami, and that is that irrespective of specific proofs or facts, there is justification in light of the history of this republic and the efforts that it has made since that mistake, as the President of the United States described it was made, which justifies vacating the conviction and dismissing the petition.

Thank you, Your Honor.

Korematsu v. United States

Opinion of the Court, U.S. District Court for the Northern District of California*

April 19, 1984

Judge Patel issued her written opinion in the Korematsu case on April 19, 1984, five months after the hearing on the coram nobis petition. This opinion became a historic document in one important respect: never before had any judge vacated a criminal conviction that had been upheld by the Supreme Court on final appeal. Judge Patel's opinion reflects her awareness of the historic and current significance of both the case and the issues raised in the petition. Much of the opinion deals with questions of legal procedure and the status of the government's motion to dismiss the petition. Calling the government's response "tantamount to a confession of error," Judge Patel supported the petition's misconduct charges in strong language. She found "substantial support in the record that the government deliberately omitted relevant information and provided misleading information" to the Supreme Court. "The judicial process is seriously impaired," she concluded, "when the government's law enforcement officers violate their ethical obligations to the court."

William T. McGivern, Asst. U.S. Atty., San Francisco, Cal., Victor Stone, Counsel for Special & Appellate Matters, General Litigation & Legal Advice Section, U.S. Dept. of Justice, Washington, D.C., for defendant.

Dale Minami, Minami & Lew, San Francisco, Cal., Peter Irons, Leucadia, Cal., Robert L. Rusky, Hanson, Bridgett, Marcus, Vlahos & Stromberg, Ed Chen, Coblentz, Cahen, McCabe & Breyer, Eric Yamamoto, San Francisco, Cal., for plaintiff.

*584 F.Supp. 1406 (N.D.Cal. 1984)

OPINION

Patel, District Judge.

Fred Korematsu is a native born citizen of the United States. He is of Japanese ancestry. On September 8, 1942, he was convicted in this court of being in a place from which all persons of Japanese ancestry were excluded pursuant to Civilian Exclusion Order No. 34 issued by Commanding General J. L. DeWitt. His conviction was affirmed. *Korematsu* v. *United States*, 323 U.S. 214, 65 S.Ct. 193, 89 L.Ed. 194 (1944).

Mr. Korematsu now brings this petition for a writ of coram nobis to vacate his conviction on the grounds of governmental misconduct. His allegations of misconduct are best understood against the background of events leading up to his conviction.

On December 8, 1941 the United States declared war on Japan.

Executive Order No. 9066 was issued on February 19, 1942 authorizing the Secretary of War and certain military commanders "to prescribe military areas from which any persons may be excluded as protection against espionage and sabotage."

Congress enacted § 97a of Title 18 of the United States Code, enforcing the exclusions promulgated under the Executive Order. Section 97a made it a misdemeanor for anyone to enter or remain in any restricted military zone contrary to the order of a military commander.

In the meantime, General DeWitt was designated Military Commander of the Western Defense Command which consisted of several western states including California.

On March 2, 1942 General DeWitt issued Public Proclamation No. 1 pursuant to Executive Order 9066. The proclamation stated that "the entire Pacific Coast . . . is subject to espionage and acts of sabotage, thereby requiring the adoption of military measures necessary to establish safeguards against such enemy operations."

Thereafter, several other proclamations based upon the same justification were issued placing restrictions and requirements upon certain persons, including all persons of Japanese ancestry. As a result of these proclamations and Exclusion Order No. 34, providing that all persons of Japanese ancestry be excluded from an area specified as Military Area No. 1, petitioner, who lived in Area No. 1, could not leave the zone in which he resided and could not remain in the zone unless he were in an established "Assembly Center." Petitioner remained in the zone and did not go to the Center. He was charged and convicted of knowingly remaining in a proscribed area in violation of § 97a.

It was uncontroverted at the time of conviction that petitioner was loyal to the United States and had no dual allegiance to Japan. He had never left the United States. He was registered for the draft and willing to bear arms for the United States.

In his papers petitioner maintains that evidence was suppressed or destroyed in the proceedings that led to his conviction and its affirmance. He also makes substantial allegations of suppression and distortion of evidence which informed Executive Order No. 9066 and the Public Proclamations issued under it. While the latter may be compelling, it is not for this court to rectify. However, the court is not powerless to correct its own records where a fraud has been worked upon it or where manifest injustice has been done.

The question before the court is not so much whether the conviction should be vacated as what is the appropriate ground for relief. A description of the procedural history of these proceedings explains this posture.

Procedural History of These Proceedings

Petitioner filed his petition for a writ of coram nobis on January 19, 1983. The first scheduled status conference was conducted on March 14, 1983, when all parties appeared before the court. At that time the petition was deemed a motion and the government was ordered to respond by August 29, 1983. Petitioner's reply to the government's response was set for September 26, 1983, and a hearing on the petition was scheduled for October 3, 1983. Informal discovery was conducted in accordance with the agreement arrived at during the conference. Thereafter, the government moved for an extension based upon the forthcoming report of the Commission on Wartime Relocation and Internment of Civilians ("Commission"), which it anticipated would have a substantial bearing on these proceedings. The motion for a continuance was opposed. The court granted the motion, giving the government until September 27, 1983 to respond, and setting October 25, 1983 for petitioner's reply and November 4 for a hearing on the petition. Thereafter, the government was given a further extension, to October 4, for the filing of its response. On October 4, 1983, a document entitled "Government's Response and Motion Under L.R. 220–6" ("Response") was filed. The substance of the Response consists of less than four pages. In fact, it is not an opposition to the petition, but a counter-motion to vacate the conviction and dismiss the underlying indictment.[1] It is denominated a motion under Local Rule 220–6, pertaining to the hearing of related motions.

On October 31, petitioner filed his reply and Request for Judicial Notice. The government filed its Preliminary Response to the Request for Judicial Notice on November 7, 1983. A hearing on the petition and counter-motion was conducted on November 10, 1983.

Because the government maintains that the court should grant its motion and not reach the merits of the petition, the counter-motion is considered first.

The Government's Counter-Motion

[1] The government does not specifically designate in its memorandum the grounds for its motion. It relies upon *Rinaldi* v. *United States*, 434 U.S. 22, 98 S.Ct. 81, 54 L.Ed.2d 207 (1977) and *United States* v. *Hamm*, 659 F.2d 624, 631 (5th Cir. 1981) (en banc), in which motions were made pursuant to Fed.R.Crim.P. 48(a). At the hearing the government acknowledged Rule 48(a) as the premise for its motion.

Rule 48(a) has its antecedents in the common law doctrine of *nolle prosequi*. An understanding of that doctrine is necessary to a discussion of the Rule's application here. As the literal translation of *nolle prosequi*—"I am unwilling to prosecute"—makes clear, the primary purpose of the doctrine was to allow the government to cease active prosecution. At common law, and before Rule 48(a) was enacted, prosecution was within the exclusive jurisdiction of the prosecuting attorney at the early stages of the proceedings and a *nolle prosequi* could be entered at any time before the jury was empaneled. *Confiscation Cases*, 74 U.S. (7 Wall.) 454, 457, 19 L.Ed. 196 (1868).

However, as the case progressed, the prosecuting attorney lost the unilateral right to enter a *nolle prosequi*. After the jury was sworn and evidence heard, the defendant had the right to object to the entry of a *nolle prosequi* and the effect of the entry at that stage was a verdict of acquittal. *United States* v. *Shoemaker*, 27 F.Cas. 1066 (C.C.D.Ill.1840) (No. 16,279). While the prosecutor's unilateral power to enter a *nolle prosequi* apparently revived just after the verdict was returned, once a sentence had been handed down or final judgment entered, that unilateral

---

[1] Although the government referred in its papers to dismissal of the indictment, the defendant was in fact convicted upon an information.

right of the prosecutor was again extinguished. *United States* v. *Brokaw*, 60 F.Supp. 100 (S.D.Ill.1945).

With the adoption of Rule 48(a), the absolute authority of the prosecutor was tempered and leave of court was required for dismissal of an indictment, information or complaint at *any* stage of the proceedings. Although there is a substantial body of case law dealing with the scope of the court's authority to grant or deny leave to dismiss, little has been written about the times within which a Rule 48(a) dismissal may be brought.

There is nothing to suggest that the Rule was intended to extend the *nolle prosequi* privilege beyond that allowed at common law. In fact, the purpose of the Rule was to place some fetters on prosecutorial discretion. Fed.R.Crim.P. 48(a) advisory committee note 1. The plain language of the section is also instructive. The Rule allows for dismissal, with leave, of an indictment, information or complaint, whereupon "the prosecution shall . . . terminate." As the Rule provides that upon the court's approval of a *nolle prosequi*, the prosecution will terminate, it clearly contemplates action by the prosecuting agency only while control of the prosecution still lies, at least in part, with it. By contrast, the prosecutor has no authority to exercise his *nolle prosequi* prerogatives at common law or to invoke Rule 48(a) after a person has been subject to conviction, final judgment, imposition of sentence and exhaustion of all appeals and, indeed, after a lapse of many years. At that stage, there is no longer any prosecution to be terminated.

United States v. *Weber*, 721 F.2d 266 (9th Cir.1983) does not compel a different interpretation. In *Weber*, as in the cases upon which it relies, the Rule 48(a) motion was made during the pendency of the proceedings. Applying the same rationale, that dismissal is a possibility while the case is still being actively prosecuted, the Supreme Court, even after it has granted a petition for a writ of certiorari, has remanded to allow the government to dismiss charges against the petitioner. E.g., *Watts* v. *United States*, 422 U.S. 1032, 95 S.Ct. 2648, 45 L.Ed.2d 688 (1975). This is because Rule 48(a) and the right of *nolle prosequi* emanate from the Executive's power to initiate a criminal prosecution and to terminate a pending prosecution. *See United States* v. *Cowan*, 524 F.2d 504, 507 (5th Cir.1975), cert. denied sub nom. *Woodruff* v. *United States*, 425 U.S. 971, 96 S.Ct. 2168, 48 L.Ed.2d 795 (1976) (citing *United States* v. *Cox*, 342 F.2d 167 (5th Cir.1965), cert. denied sub nom. *Cox* v. *Hauberg*, 381 U.S. 935, 85 S.Ct. 1767, 14 L.Ed.2d 700 (1965)).

The court finds no authority for the proposition that a Rule 48(a) motion may be made long after the prosecution has come to rest, the judgment is final, appeals have been exhausted, judgment imposed and the sentence served.

The Petition for a Writ of Coram Nobis

[2] A writ of coram nobis is an appropriate remedy by which the court can correct errors in criminal convictions where other remedies are not available. Although Rule 60(b), Fed.R.Civ.P., abolishes various common law writs, including the writ of coram nobis in civil cases, the writ still obtains in criminal proceedings where other relief is wanting. *United States* v. *Morgan*, 346 U.S. 502, 74 S.Ct. 247, 98 L.Ed. 248 (1954). See also *James* v. *United States*, 459 U.S. 1044, 103 S.Ct. 465, 74 L.Ed.2d 615 (1982) (dissenting opinion in denial of petition for writ of certiorari explaining purpose of coram nobis); *Chresfield* v. *United States*, 381 F.Supp. 301, 302 (E.D.Pa.1974).

[3] While the habeas corpus provisions of 28 U.S.C. § 2255 supplant most of the functions of coram nobis, particularly in light of the federal courts' expanded view of custody, habeas corpus is not an adequate remedy here. Petitioner's sentence has been served. He cannot meet the "in custody" requirements of § 2255 under any interpretation of that section. See *Hensley* v. *Municipal Court*, 411 U.S. 345, 93 S.Ct. 1571, 36 L.Ed.2d 294 (1973) (discussing meaning of custody in context of 28 U.S.C. § 2254 requirements); *Jones* v. *Cunningham*, 371 U.S. 236, 83 S.Ct. 373, 9 L.Ed.2d 285 (1963) (finding the restraints of parole sufficient to constitute custody for the purposes of habeas proceedings under § 2254); *Azzone* v. *United States*, 341 F.2d 417 (8th Cir.1965), cert. denied sub. nom. *Azzone* v. *Tahash*, 390 U.S. 970, 88 S.Ct. 1090, 19 L.Ed.2d 1180 (1968) (applying the custody requirement in § 2255 proceedings). It is in these unusual circumstances that an extraordinary writ such as the writ of coram nobis is appropriate to correct fundamental errors and prevent injustice. *United States* v. *Correa-De Jesus*, 708 F.2d 1283 (7th Cir.1983).

[4, 5] The source of the court's power to grant coram nobis relief lies in the All Writs Act, 28 U.S.C. § 1651(a). The petition is appropriately heard by the district court in which the conviction was obtained. *Morgan*, 346 U.S. at 512, 74 S.Ct. at 253. This is so even though the judgment has been appealed and affirmed by the Supreme Court. Appellate leave is not required for a trial court to correct errors occurring before it. *Standard*

Oil of California v. *United States*, 429 U.S. 17, 97 S.Ct. 31, 50 L.Ed.2d 21 (1976).

Coram nobis being the appropriate vehicle for petitioner to seek relief, I turn to the question of how the court shall proceed in this unusual case.

While the government would have this court grant its motion and look no further, petitioner asks this court to look behind the conviction, view the "evidence" that has now come to light and make findings of fact. The court concludes that the first alternative, although easy, is not available; the second alternative is unnecessary.

[6] Even were the government in a position to move under Rule 48(a) of the Fed.R.Crim.P., the court would not automatically grant dismissal. A limited review by the court is necessary, even where the defendant consents. The purpose of this limited review is to protect against prosecutorial impropriety or harassment of the defendant and to assure that the public interest is not disserved. *United States* v. *Cowan*, 524 F.2d at 512–13.[2]

[7] This Circuit has resolved that petitions for a writ of coram nobis should be treated in a manner similar to § 2255 habeas corpus petitions. *United States* v. *Taylor*, 648 F.2d 565 (9th Cir.), cert. denied, 454 U.S. 866, 102 S.Ct. 329, 70 L.Ed.2d 168 (1981). Thus, the nature of the court's inquiry is substantially more expansive than under Rule 48(a). For example, § 2255 considerations apply in determining whether an evidentiary hearing is required. 648 F.2d at 573 n. 25.

[8] In *Townsend* v. *Sain*, 372 U.S. 293, 83 S.Ct. 745, 9 L.Ed.2d 770 (1963), the Supreme Court provided instructions to the district courts as to when evidentiary hearings should be held in state habeas cases under 28 U.S.C. § 2254. It is clear that care must be taken and a hearing afforded when a palpable claim is raised by the petitioner and there is an inadequate record or disputed factual issues. However, the Court acknowledged that district courts have substantial discretion and should not be put to conducting unnecessary evidentiary hearings. The parties may choose to rely upon the record or an expanded record and forego an evidentiary hearing. The same standards apply in habeas proceedings under § 2255. See *Sosa* v. *United States*, 550 F.2d 244, 250–56 (5th Cir.1977) (separate opinion of Judge Tuttle and collected citations therein). And where "on the facts admitted, it may appear that, as matter of law, the

---

[2] Indeed, it has been suggested that Rule 48(a), Fed.R.Crim.P., "contemplates public exposure of the reasons for abandonment of an indictment, information or complaint. . . . *United States* v. *Greater Blouse, Skirt & Neckwear Contractors Ass'n*, 228 F.Supp. 483, 486 (S.D.N.Y.1964).

prisoner is entitled to the writ" no hearing need be held. *Walker* v. *Johnston*, 312 U.S. 275, 284, 61 S.Ct. 574, 578, 85 L.Ed. 830 (1941).

[9, 10] On a motion under § 2255, the government must establish that there is no genuine issue of material fact; the petitioner is entitled to the benefit of favorable inferences. *Honneus* v. *United States*, 509 F.Supp. 1135, 1138 (D.Mass.1981). Where, as here, the government offers no opposition and, in effect, joins in a similar request for relief, an expansive inquiry is not necessary. In fact, the government agrees petitioner is entitled to relief and concedes: "There is, therefore, no continuing reason in this setting for the court to convene hearings or make findings about petitioner's allegations of governmental wrongdoing in the 1940's." Response at 3. However, even where the government has acknowledged that the conviction should be set aside, albeit on different grounds, the court must conduct some review to determine whether there is support for the government's position.

[11] Ordinarily, in cases in which the government agrees that a conviction should be set aside, the government's position is made clear because it confesses error, calling to the court's attention the particular errors upon which the conviction was obtained. A confession of error is generally given great deference. Where that confession of error is made by the official having full authority for prosecution on behalf of the government it is entitled to even greater deference. See *Sibron* v. *State of New York*, 392 U.S. 40, 58–59, 88 S.Ct. 1889, 1900–1901, 20 L.Ed.2d 917 (1968). Even so, the court must conduct its own review. *Young* v. *United States*, 315 U.S. 257, 62 S.Ct 510, 86 L.Ed. 832 (1942).

In this case, the government, joining in on a different procedural footing, is not prepared to confess error. Yet it has not submitted any opposition to the petition, although given ample opportunity to do so. Apparently the government would like this court to set aside the conviction without looking at the record in an effort to put this unfortunate episode in our country's history behind us.

The government has, however, while not confessing error, taken a position tantamount to a confession of error. It has eagerly moved to dismiss without acknowledging any specific reasons for dismissal other than that "there is no further usefulness to be served by conviction under a statute which has been soundly repudiated." (R.T. 13:20–22, November 10, 1983). In support of this statement, the government points out that in 1971, legislation was adopted requiring congressional action before an Executive Order such as Executive Order 9066 can ever be issued again; that in 1976, the statute under which petitioner was convicted was repealed; and that in 1976, all authority conferred by Executive Order 9066 was formally proclaimed terminated as of December 31, 1946. While these are compelling reasons for concluding that vacating the conviction is in the best interests of this petitioner, respondent and the public, the court declines the invitation of the government to treat this matter in the perfunctory and procedurally improper manner it has suggested.

On the other hand, this court agrees that it is not necessary to reopen the partially healed wounds of an earlier period in order to perform its role of conducting independent judicial review. Fortunately, there are few instances in our judicial history when courts have been called upon to undo such profound and publicly acknowledged injustice. Such extraordinary instances require extraordinary relief, and the court is not without power to redress its own errors.[3]

Because the government has not acknowledged specific errors, the court will look to the original record and the evidence now before it to determine whether there is support for the petition and whether manifest injustice would be done in letting the conviction stand.

Evidentiary Issues

The "evidence" before this court consists of certain documents and reports of which petitioner asks the court to take judicial notice. The posture of this request is curious. In response to the request, the government filed a "Preliminary Response." This was filed three days before the hearing on the petition. In its "Preliminary Response," the government did not take issue with the merits of petitioner's request for judicial notice. Its response was merely "designed to convey our general objections" and the government offered to file a full response if requested by the court. It then went on to make further arguments in favor of its own motion. Again, this was on the eve of a hearing which had been postponed and for which the government had had ample opportunity to formulate a response. At the first hearing, as noted below, the question of judicial notice had been raised and discussed.

The matters which petitioner asks the court to judicially notice are the

---

[3] As discussed above, a full evidentiary hearing is not always required. Petitioner's submissions in this case would ordinarily justify a hearing and the court could not, in light of those submissions, deny the petition without affording a hearing. See *Lujan* v. *United States*, 424 F.2d 1053 (5th Cir.1970). However, it is clear from the results reached herein, that petitioner is not prejudiced by the failure to conduct an evidentiary hearing. The government is deemed to have waived its right to a hearing.

Report of the Commission on Wartime Relocation and Internment of Civilians, entitled *Personal Justice Denied* (Washington, D.C., 1982) ("Report") and certain government documents, the authenticity of which is not in dispute.

[12] When the parties are in agreement that the court may take judicial notice of certain matters, or that records may be admitted as public records, the court need not make as searching an inquiry as when notice or admissibility is disputed. Similar considerations apply here, as the government, rather than actually opposing the request and supplying reasons for such opposition, has merely suggested it may oppose the request. In fact, at the hearing on March 14, 1983, in answer to the court's question whether it "would agree that it is appropriate for the court to take judicial notice of the Report," the attorney for the government responded, "absolutely." Despite this acquiescence, care should be taken to consider only trustworthy and reliable evidence. Thus, I look first to whether the documents proffered may be judicially noticed or otherwise admitted.

[13, 14] Judicial notice may be taken of adjudicative facts in accordance with Fed.R.Evid. 201, as well as of legislative facts. The distinction between the two is not always readily apparent. See 1 Weinstein's Evidence ¶ 200[04], at 200–19. Adjudicative facts are usually those facts that are in issue in a particular case. Judicial notice of adjudicative facts dispenses with the need to present other evidence or for the factfinder to make findings as to those particular facts. Rule 201 provides that only those adjudicative facts which are not subject to reasonable dispute because they are generally known or "capable of accurate and ready determination by resort to sources whose accuracy cannot reasonably be questioned" may be judicially noticed.

[15] Legislative facts are "established truths, facts or pronouncements that do not change from case to case but [are applied] universally, while adjudicative facts are those developed in a particular case." *United States* v. *Gould*, 536 F.2d 216, 220 (8th Cir.1976). Legislative facts are facts of which courts take particular notice when interpreting a statute or considering whether Congress has acted within its constitutional authority. For example, courts frequently take judicial notice of legislative history, including committee reports. See *Territory of Alaska* v. *American Can Co.*, 358 U.S. 224, 227, 79 S.Ct. 274, 276, 3 L.Ed.2d 257 (1959). So, too, historical facts, commercial practices and social standards are frequently noticed in the form of legislative facts. See *Leo Sheep Co.* v. *United States*, 440 U.S. 668, 99 S.Ct. 1403, 59 L.Ed.2d 677 (1979); *Jay Burns Baking Co.* v. *Bryan*, 264 U.S. 504, 517–33, 44 S.Ct. 412,

415–420, 68 L.Ed. 813 (1923) (Justice Brandeis' dissent takes an expansive view of when scientific and commercial practices may be judicially noticed); and *United States* v. *Various Articles of Obscene Merchandise, Schedule No. 1303*, 562 F.2d 185, 187 n. 4 (2d Cir.1977).

However, petitioner seeks to have this court take judicial notice of the actual findings of the Commission and matters stated in documents contained in government files. To the extent these matters are offered on the issue of governmental misconduct they are offered on the ultimate issue. Taking judicial notice of them would be inappropriate, as it would render them conclusive according to Rule 201(g).

Care must be taken that Rule 201 not be used as a substitute for more rigorous evidentiary requirements and careful factfinding. For example, if the Commission's findings were proffered as public records under Rule 803(8), Fed.R.Evid., the foundational requirements of subparagraph (8) would need to be met and the findings, if admitted, would be weighed along with other evidence. Judicial notice cannot be used to shortcut the evidentiary hearing process. Nevertheless, courts have found it appropriate to take judicial notice of current economic conditions, *Mainline Investment Corp.* v. *Gaines*, 407 F.Supp. 423, 427 (N.D.Tex.1976) and historical evidence, *Oneida Indian Nation of New York* v. *New York*, 691 F.2d 1070, 1086 (2d Cir. 1982), as adjudicative facts under Rule 201. In these instances the facts judicially noticed went to the matter in issue, such as the defense of extraordinary economic cause asserted in a breach of contract claim in *Mainline Investment*. In *Oneida Indian Nation* the Second Circuit generally approved taking judicial notice of individual records, notes, correspondence, histories and other articles of the late eighteenth century as "historical evidence," but concluded that it was error for the lower court to do so where the data was in dispute. Indeed, this Circuit has urged a cautious approach, observing that "the taking of evidence, subject to established safeguards, is the best way to resolve controversies involving disputes of adjudicative facts." *Banks* v. *Schweiker*, 654 F.2d 637, 640 (9th Cir.1981).

[16] Two factors make the particular stance of this case unusual. The government has neither interposed any specific objection nor put any facts in controversy.[4] Furthermore, this is not a matter which will ultimately be decided by a jury. Where the function of the court is to act as a factfinder or exercise its discretion, more leeway to take judicial notice is jus-

---

[4]Cf. *United States* v. *Wilson*, 690 F.2d 1267, 1273–74 (9th Cir.1982) (explaining the need to state with specificity the grounds for objections and the consequences on appeal of the failure to do so).

tified. See C. McCormick, Evidence § 332 (2d ed. 1972). Still, the court should be careful in deciding whether to take judicial notice of the records proffered.

[17] In light of these concerns, the court finds it proper to take judicial notice of the purpose of the Commission, the manner in which it was established and, subject to a finding of trustworthiness, the general nature and substance of its conclusions. Judicial notice of these facts may be used to inform the court's determination of whether denial of the motion would result in manifest injustice, of the public interest to be served by the granting of the motion, and of whether there is support for the government's acquiescence. See *Southern Louisiana Area Rate Cases* v. *Federal Power Commission*, 428 F.2d 407, 438 n. 98 (5th Cir.1970) (court may take judicial notice of concerns of the Federal Power Commission as expressed in speeches given by Commissioners even though specific facts stated may not be judicially noticed); *Overfield* v. *Pennroad Corp.*, 146 F.2d 889, 898 (3d Cir.1944) (court may take judicial notice of "Congressional proceedings and the *existence* of facts disclosed by them") (emphasis supplied).

The court concludes it is not proper or necessary to take judicial notice of the specific Commission findings and conclusions as adjudicative facts under § 201, despite the government's failure to adequately object.[5]

The Commission Report

The Commission on Wartime Relocation and Internment of Civilians was established in 1980 by an act of Congress. It was directed to review the facts and circumstances surrounding Executive Order 9066 and its impact on American citizens and permanent resident aliens; to review directives of the United States military forces requiring the relocation and, in some cases, detention in internment camps of American citizens, including those of Japanese ancestry; and to recommend appropriate remedies. Commission on Wartime Relocation and Internment of Civilians Act, Pub.L. No. 96–317, § 2, 94 Stat. 964 (1980).

[5] It should be noted that the report appears to meet the requirements of Rule 803(8) of the Federal Rules of Evidence as findings resulting from an investigation made pursuant to authority granted by law. Under the Rule, it would be deemed admissible absent a showing of lack of trustworthiness. Advisory Committee Notes to Exceptions 803(8). See also *Letelier* v. *Republic of Chile*, 567 F.Supp. 1490, 13 Fed.R.Evid.Serv. 1731 (S.D.N.Y.1983). There is nothing to suggest the report lacks trustworthiness. Admission of the report under 803(8) would allow it to be weighed along with other evidence, if any, and permit the court to make its own findings. Were the court to take judicial notice of the findings under Rule 201, by contrast, the findings would become conclusive.

The Commission was mandated to submit a written report of its findings and recommendations to Congress. It was given authority to conduct hearings, and to compel attendance of witnesses and production of documents, including documents in the possession of governmental agencies and departments.

The Commission was composed of former members of Congress, the Supreme Court and the Cabinet as well as distinguished private citizens. It held approximately twenty days of hearings in cities across the United States, taking the testimony of over 720 witnesses, including key government personnel responsible for decisions involved in the issuance of Executive Order 9066 and the military orders implementing it. The Commission reviewed substantial numbers of government documents, including documents not previously available to the public.

In light of all these factors, the Report carries substantial indicia of trustworthiness.[6] Indeed, as noted above, the government conceded at the March 1983 status conference that the Report was an appropriate subject of judicial notice. It acknowledged it was awaiting the final Report before formulating any policy with respect to this petition and related Japanese internment matters. After issuance of the Report, the government announced its decision to move to dismiss the charges. It appears it is relying on the Report in substantial measure for its own recommendations.[7]

The findings and conclusions of the Commission were unanimous. In general, the Commission concluded that at the time of the issuance of Executive Order 9066 and implementing military orders, there was substantial credible evidence from a number of federal civilian and military agencies contradicting the report of General DeWitt that military necessity justified exclusion and internment of all persons of Japanese ancestry without regard to individual identification of those who may have been potentially disloyal.

The Commission found that military necessity did not warrant the exclusion and detention of ethnic Japanese. It concluded that "broad historical causes which shaped these decisions [exclusion and detention] were race prejudice, war hysteria and a failure of political leadership." As a result, "a grave injustice was done to American citizens and resident

---

[6] See *Nebbia* v. *New York*, 291 U.S. 502, 516–18, 54 S.Ct. 505, 507–508, 78 L.Ed. 940 (1934) (joint legislative committee's report on the milk industry given substantial weight where over one year period the committee conducted thirteen public hearings, heard testimony of 254 witnesses, conducted extensive research and collected numerous exhibits).

[7] *Personal Justice Denied* (Washington, D.C., 1982) presents the findings of the Commission on Wartime Relocation and Internment of Civilians. The final report, which is not before the court, apparently contains the Commission's recommendations.

aliens of Japanese ancestry who, without individual review or any probative evidence against them, were excluded, removed and detained by
the United States during World War II." *Personal Justice Denied* at 18.

The Commission's Report provides ample support for the conclusion
that denial of the motion would result in manifest injustice and that the
public interest is served by granting the relief sought.

Government Memoranda

[18] Petitioner offers another set of documents showing that there was
critical contradictory evidence known to the government and knowingly
concealed from the courts. These records present another question
regarding the propriety of judicial notice. They consist of internal government memoranda and letters. Their authenticity is not disputed. Yet
they are not the kind of documents that are the proper subject of judicial notice, and they are offered on the ultimate issue of governmental
misconduct.

The internal memoranda and letters may, however, be considered by
the court as evidence under Rule 803(1) or 803(16). Alternatively, because they are not actually offered for the truth of the statements contained in them, but rather as evidence that the statements were made (i.e.,
verbal conduct), they may be admitted as non-hearsay within the purview
of 801(c).[8]

[19] The substance of the statements contained in the documents and
the fact the statements were made demonstrate that the government knowingly withheld information from the courts when they were considering
the critical question of military necessity in this case. A series of correspondence regarding what information should be included in the government's brief before the Supreme Court culminated in two different
versions of a footnote that was to be used to specify the factual data upon
which the government relied for its military necessity justification. The
first version read as follows:

The Final Report of General DeWitt (which is dated June 5, 1943, but which was
not made public until January 1944) is relied on in this brief for statistics and
other details concerning the actual evacuation and the events that took place
subsequent thereto. *The recital of the circumstances justifying the evacuation as*

---

[8] For all intents and purposes, there may be little difference between admitting them on a non-
hearsay basis and taking judicial notice of their existence, as opposed to taking notice of the facts
contained in them.

a matter of military necessity, however, is in several respects, particularly with reference to the use of illegal radio transmitters and to shore-to-ship signalling by persons of Japanese ancestry, *in conflict with information in the possession of the Department of Justice. In view of the contrariety of the reports on this matter we do not ask the Court to take judicial notice of the recital of those facts contained in the Report.*

Petitioner's Exhibit AA, Memorandum of John L. Burling to Assistant Attorney General Herbert Wechsler, September 11, 1944 (emphasis added).

After revision, it read:

The Final Report of General DeWitt (which is dated June 5, 1943, but which was not made public until January 1944) hereinafter cited as Final Report, is relied on in this brief for statistics and other details concerning the actual evacuation and the events that took place subsequent thereto. *The recital in the Final Report of circumstances justifying the evacuation as a matter of military necessity, however, is in several respects,* particularly with reference to the use of illegal radio transmitters and shore-to-ship signalling by persons of Japanese ancestry, *in conflict with the views of this Department. We, therefore, do not ask the Court to take judicial notice of the recital of those facts contained in the Report.*

Id. (emphasis added).

The footnote that appeared in the final version of the brief merely read as follows:

The Final Report of General Dewitt (which is dated June 5, 1943, but which was not made public until January 1944), hereinafter cited as Final Report, is relied on in this brief for statistics and other details concerning the actual evacuation and the events that took place subsequent thereto. *We have specifically recited in this brief the facts relating to the justification for the evacuation, of which we ask the Court to take judicial notice, and we rely upon the Final Report only to the extent that it relates to such facts.*

Brief for the United States, *Korematsu* v. *United States*, October Term, 1944, No. 22, at 11. The final version made no mention of the contradictory reports. The record is replete with protestations of various Justice Department officials that the government had the obligation to advise the courts of the contrary facts and opinions. Petitioner's Exhibits A–FF. In fact, several Department of Justice officials pointed out to their superiors and others the "wilful historical inaccuracies and intentional falsehoods" contained in the DeWitt Report. E.g., Exhibit B and Exhibit AA, Appendices A and B hereto.

These omissions are critical. In the original proceedings, before the district court and on appeal, the government argued that the actions taken were within the war-making powers of the Executive and Legislative branches and, even where the actions were directed at a particular class of persons, they were beyond judicial scrutiny so long as they were reasonably related to the security and defense of the nation and the prosecution of the war. Plaintiff's Brief in Opposition to Demurrer before the District Court, at 11–13; Brief for the United States in *Korematsu* v. *United States*, in the Supreme Court of the United States, at 11–18.

Indeed, this emphasis on national security was reflected in the standard of review laid down in *Hirabayashi* v. *United States*, 320 U.S. 81, 95, 63 S.Ct. 1375, 1383, 87 L.Ed. 1774 (1943): "We think that constitutional government in time of war, is not so powerless and does not compel so hard a choice if those charged with the responsibility of our national defense have reasonable ground for believing that the threat is real." The Court acknowledged that it could not second guess the decisions of the Executive and Congress but was limited to determining whether all of the relevant circumstances "within the knowledge of those charged with the responsibility for maintaining the national defense afforded a rational basis for the decisions which they made." *Id*. at 102, 63 S.Ct. at 1386.

The government relied on the rationale of *Hirabayashi* in its memoranda in *Korematsu*. That rationale was adopted in *Korematsu*. 323 U.S. at 218–24, 65 S.Ct. at 195–197.

In *Hirabayashi* and *Korematsu*, the courts at each level engaged in an extensive examination of the facts known to the Executive and Legislative Branches. The facts which the government represented it relied upon and provided to the courts were those contained in a report entitled "Final Report, Japanese Evacuation from the West Coast" (1942), prepared by General DeWitt. His evaluation and version of the facts informed the courts' opinions. Yet, omitted from the government's representations was any reference to contrary reports which were considered reliable by the Justice Department and military officials other than General DeWitt.

A close reading of the briefs filed in the District Court by the government and amicus curiae State of California shows they relied heavily on the DeWitt Report for the facts justifying their military necessity arguments.[9]

---

[9] The upper echelons of the Justice Department were well aware of the unjustified reliance being placed on the DeWitt Report by the amici curiae. "It is also to be noted that parts of the [DeWitt] report which, in April 1942 could not be shown to the Department of Justice in connection with the Hirabayashi case in the Supreme Court, were printed in the brief amici curiae of the States of California, Oregon and Washington. In fact the Western Defense Command evaded the statutory requirement that this Department represent the Government in this litigation by preparing the erroneous and intemperate brief which the States filed." Exhibit B, p. 3, Memorandum from Edward J. Ennis,

There is no question that the Executive and Congress were entitled to reasonably rely upon certain facts and to discount others. The question is not whether they were justified in relying upon some reports and not others, but whether the court had before it all the facts known by the government. Was the court misled by any omissions or distortions in concluding that the other branches' decisions had a reasonable basis in fact? Omitted from the reports presented to the courts was information possessed by the Federal Communications Commission, the Department of the Navy, and the Justice Department which directly contradicted General DeWitt's statements. Thus, the court had before it a selective record.

Whether a fuller, more accurate record would have prompted a different decision cannot be determined. Nor need it be determined. Where relevant evidence has been withheld, it is ample justification for the government's concurrence that the conviction should be set aside. It is sufficient to satisfy the court's independent inquiry and justify the relief sought by petitioner.

Other Requirements for Coram Nobis Relief

Petitioner has met the other requirements necessary to have his petition for a writ of coram nobis granted. One of the factors traditionally considered relevant is generally described as "mootness," but is more specifically stated in terms of whether a petitioner who has already fully served his sentence suffers any collateral consequences such that he should be permitted to apply for a writ of coram nobis. At one time it was presumed that the burden was upon the petitioner to show the existence of collateral consequences. More recent cases have moved toward the view that collateral consequences are to be presumed from the fact of a criminal conviction. The Supreme Court has, in fact, stated that a "criminal case is moot only if it is shown that there is no possibility that any collateral legal consequences will be imposed on the basis of the challenged conviction" *Lane* v. *Williams*, 455 U.S. 624, 632, 102 S.Ct. 1322, 1327, 71 L.Ed.2d 508 (1982) (quoting approvingly *Sibron* v. *New York*, 392 U.S. at 57, 88 S.Ct. at 1899). This articulation places the burden on the government to show that petitioner suffers no collateral consequences. Petitioner has filed a certificate setting forth the collateral consequences he believes he

---

Director of the Alien Enemy Control Unit, Department of Justice to Assistant Attorney General Herbert Wechsler, September 30, 1944.

suffers and will continue to suffer as a result of the conviction. The government, by its "Response" has failed to come forward with evidence to overcome the presumption.

The government has also failed to rebut petitioner's showing of timeliness. It appears from the record that much of the evidence upon which petitioner bases his motion was not discovered until recently. In fact, until the discovery of the documents relating to the government's brief before the Supreme Court, there was no specific evidence of governmental misconduct available.

There is thus no barrier to granting petitioner's motion for coram nobis relief.

Conclusion

[20] The Supreme Court has cautioned that coram nobis should be used "only under certain circumstances compelling such action to achieve justice" and to correct "errors of the most fundamental character." *United States* v. *Morgan*, 346 U.S. 502, 511–12, 74 S.Ct. 247, 252–253, 90 L.Ed. 248 (1954). It is available to correct errors that result in a complete miscarriage of justice and where there are exceptional circumstances. See *United States* v. *Hedman*, 655 F.2d 813, 815 (7th Cir.1981).

[21] Coram nobis also lies for a claim of prosecutorial impropriety. This Circuit noted in *United States* v. *Taylor*, 648 F.2d at 573, that the writ "strikes at the veracity *vel non* of the government's representations to the court" and is appropriate where the procedure by which guilt is ascertained is under attack. The *Taylor* court observed that due process principles, raised by coram nobis charging prosecutorial misconduct, are not "strictly limited to those situations in which the defendant has suffered arguable prejudice; . . . [but also designed] to maintain public confidence in the administration of justice." *Id.* at 571.

At oral argument the government acknowledged the exceptional circumstances involved and the injustice suffered by petitioner and other Japanese-Americans. See also Response at 2–3. Moreover, there is substantial support in the record that the government deliberately omitted relevant information and provided misleading information in papers before the court. The information was critical to the court's determination, although it cannot now be said what result would have obtained had the information been disclosed. Because the information was of the kind peculiarly within the government's knowledge, the court was dependent upon the government to provide a full and accurate account. Failure to do so presents the "compelling circumstance" contemplated by *Morgan*. The judicial process is seriously impaired when the government's law enforcement officers violate their ethical obligations to the court.[10]

This court's decision today does not reach any errors of law suggested by petitioner. At common law, the writ of coram nobis was used to correct errors of fact. *United States* v. *Morgan*, 346 U.S. 502, 507–13, 74 S.Ct. 247, 250–253, 90 L.Ed. 248 (1954). It was not used to correct legal errors and this court has no power, nor does it attempt, to correct any such errors.

Thus, the Supreme Court's decision stands as the law of this case and for whatever precedential value it may still have. Justices of that Court and legal scholars have commented that the decision is an anachronism in upholding overt racial discrimination as "compellingly justified." "Only two of this Court's modern cases have held the use of racial classifications to be constitutional." *Fullilove* v. *Klutznick*, 448 U.S. 448, 507, 100 S.Ct. 2758, 2789, 65 L.Ed.2d 902 (1980) (Powell, J., concurring and referring to *Korematsu* and *Hirabayashi* v. *United States*, 320 U.S. 81, 63 S.Ct. 1375, 87 L.Ed. 1774 (1943)). See also L. H. Tribe, *American Constitutional Law* §§ 16–6, 16–14 (1978). The government acknowledged its concurrence with the Commission's observation that "today the decision in *Korematsu* lies overruled in the court of history."

Korematsu remains on the pages of our legal and political history. As a legal precedent it is now recognized as having very limited application. As historical precedent it stands as a constant caution that in times of war or declared military necessity our institutions must be vigilant in protecting constitutional guarantees. It stands as a caution that in times of distress the shield of military necessity and national security must not be used to protect governmental actions from close scrutiny and accountability. It stands as a caution that in times of international hostility and antagonisms our institutions, legislative, executive and judicial, must be prepared to protect all citizens from the petty fears and prejudices that are so easily aroused.

Order

In accordance with the foregoing, the petition for a writ of coram nobis is granted and the counter-motion of the respondent is denied.

It Is So Ordered.

---

[10]Recognizing the ethical responsibility to make full disclosure to the courts, Director Ennis pointed out to the Assistant Attorney General that "[t]he Attorney General should not be deprived of the present, and perhaps only, chance to set the record straight." Exhibit B, p. 4, Appendix A hereto.

Appendix A, Exhibit B: Memorandum for Mr. Herbert
Wechsler from the Director of the Alien Enemy Control Unit
of the Department of Justice, Washington, re Korematsu *v.*
United States, *September 30, 1944.*

I understand that the War Department is currently discussing with the Solicitor General the possibility of changing the footnote in the Korematsu brief in which it is stated that this Department is in possession of information in conflict with the statements made by General DeWitt relating to the causes of the evacuation. Mr. Burling and I feel most strongly that three purposes are to be served by keeping the footnote in its present form. (1) This Department has an ethical obligation to the Court to refrain from citing it as a source of which the Court may properly take judicial notice if the Department knows that important statements in the source are untrue and if it knows as to other statements that there is such contrariety of information that judicial notice is improper. (2) Since the War Department has published a history of the evacuation containing important misstatements of fact, including imputations and inferences that the inaction and timidity of this Department made the drastic action of evacuation necessary, this Department has an obligation, within its own competence, to set the record straight so that the true history may ultimately become known. (3) Although the report deals extensively with the activities of this Department and with the relationship of the War Department to this Department, the report was published without its being shown to us. In addition, when we learned of its existence, we were on one occasion advised that the report would never be published and, on another occasion when we asked that release be held up so that we could consider it, we were told that the report had already been released although in fact the report was not released until two weeks thereafter. In view of the War Department's course of conduct with respect to the report, we are not required to deal with the report very respectfully.

I

As to the propriety of taking judicial notice of the contents of the report, it will be sufficient to point out that (1) the report makes an important misstatement concerning our published alien enemy procedures; (2) the report makes statements concerning radio transmissions directly contradicted by a letter from the Federal Communications Commission, and (3) the report makes assertions concerning radio transmissions and ship-to-shore signaling directly contradicted by a memorandum from the Federal Bureau of Investigation.

II

The wilful historical inaccuracies of the report are objectionable for two different reasons. (1) The chief argument in the report as to the necessity for the evacuation is that the Department of Justice was slow in enforcing alien enemy control measures and that it would not take the necessary steps to prevent signaling whether by radio or by lights. It asserts that radio transmitters were located within general areas but this Department would not permit mass searches to find them. It asserts that signaling was observed in mixed occupancy dwellings which this Department would not permit to be entered. Thus, because this Department would not allow the reasonable and less drastic measures which General DeWitt wished, he was forced to evacuate the entire population. The argument is untrue both with respect to what this Department did and with respect to the radio transmissions and signaling, none of which existed, as General DeWitt at the time well knew. (2) The report asserts that the Japanese-Americans were engaged in extensive radio signaling and in shore-to-ship signaling. The general tenor of the report is not only to the effect that there was a reason to be apprehensive, but also to the effect that overt acts of treason were being committed. Since this is not so it is highly unfair to this racial minority that these lies, put out in an official publication, go uncorrected. This is the only opportunity which this Department has to correct them.

III

As to the relations of this Department to the report, the first that we knew of its existence was in April, 1942, when we requested Judge Advocate General Cramer to supply any published material in the War Department's possession on the military situation on the West Coast at the time of the evacuation to be used in the Hirabayashi brief in the Supreme Court. Colonel Watson, General DeWitt's Judge Advocate, stated that General DeWitt's report was being rushed off the press and would be available for consideration. I was then advised, however, that the printed report was confidential and I could not see it but I was given 40 pages torn out of the report on the understanding that I return them which, unfortunately, I have done. Because these excerpts misstated the facts as I knew them and misstated the relations between the Department of Justice and the War Department, I suggested to the Solicitor General that he might wish to discuss with the Attorney General the matter of the Attorney General taking up with the Secretary of War the question of showing us this report before it was released. Colonel Watson then advised me that Mr. McCloy was treating the report as a draft and my personal recollection is that Mr. McCloy stated in Mr. Biddle's presence that it was not intended to print this report. We did not hear about this report again until over six months later when I learned accidentally from Mr. Myer of WRA that he had a copy of the report which the War Department was going to publish. I borrowed his copy and then Mr. Burling called Captain Hall, Mr. McCloy's Assistant Executive Officer, and pointed out to him that the report undertook to discuss relations between the War and Justice Departments without giving us a chance to examine it and it was my understanding that Mr. McCloy did not intend to have the report released. Captain Hall admitted that Mr. McCloy had stated that the report was not to be issued but stated that he was sorry but the report had already been released and there was nothing that could be done. We accepted his statement as true and did not check on it until two weeks had passed without any publicity and then when the report was discussed in the newspapers we checked with the public relations office of the War Department and they advised that the report had just been released and had not been released at the time Captain Hall said it had.

It is also to be noted that parts of the report which, in April 1942 could not be shown to the Department of Justice in connection with the Hirabayashi case in the Supreme Court, were printed in the brief amici curiae of the States of California, Oregon and Washington. In fact the Western Defense Command evaded the statutory requirement that this Department represent the Government in this litigation by preparing the erroneous and intemperate brief which the States filed.

It is entirely clear that the War Department entered into an arrangement with the Western Defense Command to rewrite demonstrably erroneous items in the report by reducing to implication and inference what had been expressed less expertly by the Western Defense Command and then contrived to publish this report without the knowledge of this Department by the use of falsehood and evasion.

For your information I annex copies of (a) my memorandum of April 20, 1943 to the Solicitor General, (b) my memorandum of January 21,

1944 to the Solicitor General, (c) my memorandum of February 26, 1944 to the Attorney General, and (d) a transcript of Mr. Burling's conversation of January 7, 1944 with Captain Hall which clearly brings out the evasion and falsehood used in connection with the publication of the report.

I also annex copies of memoranda from the FBI and of an exchange of correspondence between the Attorney General and the Chairman of the Federal Communications Commission which establish clearly that the facts are not as General DeWitt states them in his report and also that General DeWitt knew them to be contrary to his report.

Recommendation: In view of the Attorney General's personal participation in, and final responsibility for, this Department's part in the broad administrative problem of treatment of the Japanese minority, I urge that he be consulted personally on this problem. Much more is involved than the wording of the footnote. The failure to deal adequately now with this Report cited to the Supreme Court either by the Government or other parties, will hopelessly undermine our administrative position in relation to this Japanese problem. We have proved unable to cope with the military authorities on their own ground in these matters. If we fail to act forthrightly on our own ground in the courts, the whole historical record of this matter will be as the military choose to state it. The Attorney General should not be deprived of the present, and perhaps only, chance to set the record straight.

/s/ Edward J. Ennis
Edward J. Ennis

Appendix B, Exhibit A: Memorandum from Mr. J. L. Burling of the Alien Enemy Control Unit of the Department of Justice to Herbert Wechsler, Assistant Attorney General, War Division, re Korematsu v. United States, *September 11, 1944*

The Solicitor General has gone over the revised page proof and has made certain additional changes. I desire to invite your attention particularly to the footnote which appears on page 11 of the revised page proof. As set out in the first page proof at page 26, the footnote read:

The Final Report of General DeWitt (which is dated June 5, 1943 but which was not made public until January 1944) is relied on in this brief for statistics and other details concerning the actual evacuation and the events that took place subsequent thereto. The recital of the circumstances justifying the evacuation as a matter of military necessity, however, is in several respects, particularly with reference to the use of illegal radio transmitters and to shore-to-ship signalling by persons of Japanese ancestry, in conflict with information in the possession of the Department of Justice. In view of the contrariety of the reports on this matter we do not ask the Court to take judicial notice of the recital of those facts contained in the Report.

As Mr. Fahy has revised it, it reads:

The Final Report of General DeWitt (which is dated June 5, 1943, but which was not made public until January 1944) hereinafter cited as Final Report, is relied on in this brief for statistics and other details concerning the actual evacuation and the events that took place subsequent thereto. The recital in the Final Report of circumstances justifying the evacuation as a matter of military necessity, however, is in several respects, particularly with reference to the use of illegal radio transmitters and shore-to-ship signalling by persons of Japanese ancestry, in conflict with the views of this Department. We, therefore, do not ask the Court to take judicial notice of the recital of those facts contained in the Report.

You will recall that General DeWitt's report makes flat statements concerning radio transmitters and ship-to-shore signalling which are categorically denied by the FBI and by the Federal Communications Commission. There is no doubt that these statements were intentional falsehoods, inasmuch as the Federal Communications Commission reported in detail to General DeWitt on the absence of any illegal radio transmission.

In addition, there are other misstatements of fact which seek to blame this Department with the evacuation by suggesting that we were derelict in our duties. These are somewhat more complicated but they are nevertheless demonstrably false.

In view of the fact that General DeWitt in his official report on the evacuation has sought to justify it by making important misstatements of fact, I think it important that this Department correct the record insofar as possible and certainly we should not ask the Court to take judicial notice of those facts.

The War Department has no proper complaint as to our disavowal of the recital of the facts. When we were preparing the Hirabayashi brief we heard that the report had been made and asked for a copy of it for our use. We were told that it was secret but that the Army would temporarily lend us certain pages torn out of the report. We did examine these pages in May 1943 and then returned them to the War Department. (Some of these pages then turned up in a brief filed in the *Hirabayashi* case, without our knowledge, by the States of California, Oregon and Washington as amici curiae.) Mr. McCloy advised Mr. Ennis at this time that DeWitt's Final Report would not be made public.

We next heard of the report in January 1944. At Mr. Ennis' direction, I called Captain Hall, who was Captain Fisher's predecessor, and asked that the publication of the report be withheld until this Department might examine the full report and make comments concerning the report's discussion of the role played by this Department. Captain Hall stated that the report had already been published and it was too late to do anything about it. The report, however, was not published until two weeks later when it was released to the press. I verified this through the Army's Publications and Public Relations officers and there was no question but that Captain Hall's statement on this subject was untrue and that there would have been time to permit this Department to make representations with respect to the publication of a report placing the responsibility on it in part for the necessity of the evacuation, had the War Department seen fit to permit this Department to inspect the report prior to publication.

In view of all these circumstances, it seems to me that the present bowdlerization of the footnote is unfortunate. There is in fact a contrariety of information and we ought to say so. The statements made by General DeWitt are not only contrary to our views but they are contrary to detailed information in our possession and we ought to say so.

I press the point not only because I would like to see the footnote restored to its earlier form, if possible, but because it is now contemplated that the revised brief be submitted again to the War Department. I assume that the War Department will object to the footnote and I think we should resist any further tampering with it with all our force.

Hirabayashi v. United States

Transcript of Arguments on Coram Nobis Petition,
U.S. District Court for the Western District of Washington

June 19, 1985

After he rejected numerous government motions to dismiss Gordon Hira-bayashi's coram nobis petition, Judge Donald S. Voorhees of Seattle's U.S. district court scheduled an evidentiary hearing for June 17, 1985. Before the hearing, Victor Stone submitted a forty-page brief arguing that Hirabayashi had waited too long to file his petition, had not suffered any continuing injury from his conviction, and had no dispute with the government over the relief he sought. Judge Voorhees told Stone to argue these points after the hearing.

Rod Kawakami made the opening argument for Hirabayashi and Victor Stone responded for the government. The most important witness for Hirabayashi was Edward Ennis, who had prepared the government's Supreme Court brief in 1943 and who repeated the "suppression of evi-dence" charge he made then. Stone's chief witness was David Lowman, a retired intelligence official who claimed that decoded Japanese cables (code-named "Magic") gave evidence of a "vast espionage network" of Japanese Americans. Stone argued that the Magic cables supported the internment orders Hirabayashi had challenged.

Participants:

Judge Donald S. Voorhees
Rodney Kawakami for Gordon Hirabayashi
Victor Stone for United States

> *The Court:* Good morning. Will you call the calendar, please?
>
> *The Clerk:* C83-122V, Gordon Hirabayashi vs. The United States.
>
> *The Court:* Are the parties ready?
>
> *Mr. Kawakami:* Yes, Your Honor.
>
> *The Court:* Very well. I said this at the hearing the other day, but I hate to have you people have to stand. Even though I normally don't permit

this, those of you may sit in the jury box and fill that up. As far as the artists are concerned, I am going to ask you to sit back there. I guess there are a couple more seats here, if you would care to. Why don't you just walk around the front of the jury box here?

Mr. Kawakami, are you prepared to give your opening statement?

Mr. Kawakami: Yes, Your Honor.

May it please the Court: I wish to first thank the Court on behalf of my client, Gordon Hirabayashi, for this opportunity to present this coram nobis petition.

This case is an American case. This is not just Gordon Hirabayashi's case, and this is more than just a Japanese-American case. This is truly an American case.

Morton Grodzins in his book, *Americans Betrayed*, in discussing the evacuation and internment of Japanese-Americans during World War II states in his conclusion on page 374, "Japanese-Americans were the immediate victims of evacuation, but larger consequences are carried by the American people as a whole. Their legacy is a lasting one of precedent and constitutional sanctity for a policy of mass incarceration under military auspices. This is the most important result of the process by which the evacuation was made. That process betrayed all Americans."

This is a case where an American citizen with a deep and abiding faith in American principles stood up and was one of the few voices to proclaim that as an American, evacuation and incarceration based solely on ancestry was contrary to the most fundamental concept of what being an American is all about.

He believed so strongly in his principles that he was willing to risk incarceration to put the Government's actions to a legal test. Unfortunately, however, the legal test failed.

The Government, in an earlier motion to dismiss this coram nobis petition, acknowledged the contribution made by Mr. Hirabayashi to the cause of civil liberty and characterized him as "a standard bearer." However, the Government does not even today seem to realize that carrying the weight of the standard was then and continues to be today an incredible burden on the Petitioner. The weight he carries on his shoulders has never been lifted off, and has never, even after forty years, gotten any lighter.

The coram nobis petition is a unique case in several respects. First, the coram nobis proceedings themselves are not commonplace legal proceedings. It's a little known and seldom used type of procedure which allows the Court to overturn a criminal conviction on equitable principles. This the Court can do if fundamental errors were committed at trial which made the procedure by which the defendant was convicted unfair.

It is, therefore, the procedure or process by which the defendant was convicted at which the Court should look. Second, the case is unique because it was certainly not an ordinary conviction. This involved a test case which ultimately was used to uphold the constitutionality of the evacuation and incarceration of 120,000 persons of Japanese ancestry.

Further, the three test cases, *Hirabayashi*, *Yasui* and *Korematsu*, were the first and only court decisions which legalized and gave judicial sanction to discrimination against Americans based solely on ancestry. But these were not true test cases. This was not an "all the cards on the table and let the chips fall where they may" fair fight. The Government was so intent on defending the evacuation decision and to win at all costs that it fixed the tests.

In doing so, it involved the Court in a process which resulted in what Justice Murphy called "the most sweeping complete deprivation of constitutional rights in the history of this nation." The quote is taken from Justice Murphy's dissenting opinion in *Korematsu*.

Finally, our coram nobis petition is unique in that it affords this Court a rare opportunity to correct its own judicial record on this matter. The executive branch has had its opportunity to confront its mistakes and has, for example, in 1976, rescinded Executive Order 9066.

The legislature has also been able to deal with its role by repealing Public Law 503 under which Petitioner was convicted. The legislature has also commissioned a commission to study the internment of American citizens during World War II and has also had an opportunity to pass and enact the Japanese-American Claims Act of 1948.

Up until our petition, it has only been the judicial branch which has remained under the cloud cast upon it in 1943. It is our hope that this Court will issue a strong and direct warning to the Government and, by doing so, remind the Government that the Government's duty goes beyond prosecuting the guilty; that the Government's duty, more importantly, is to see that justice is done.

We are here today to determine whether or not, as alleged by the Petitioner, governmental misconduct precluded Mr. Hirabayashi from obtaining a fair trial. As I understand the scope of the hearing, whether or not the decision to evacuate was wise remains a subject for debate at another time in another forum.

In the eyes of history, most of the scholars who have looked at the sad episode of our past have concluded that evacuation was wrong and not justified. President Ford in his 1976 executive proclamation entitled "An American Promise," in rescinding Executive Order 9066, called the evacuation "a national mistake" and "a setback of fundamental American principles."

It will, however, be our focus to examine the method and means by which the Government obtained their conviction; not whether there was in fact military necessity. Even assuming for the sake of argument that the military decision was wise, this case would then be a classic case of ends not justifying the means. Since this is a "means" and not an "ends" hearing, it is critical that we demonstrate, as we believe we conclusively do, that there was exculpatory evidence which was suppressed, altered and later destroyed. We also believe the record will reflect that the Government made material misrepresentations to the Court.

It is our position that evidence of a potentially incriminating nature does not excuse the Government's actions and only diverts attention away from the central issues, and that is due process and governmental misconduct. As stated by the Ninth Circuit in *Taylor*, cited in our memo, "This Court has rejected the notion that because the conviction was established on incontestable proof of guilt, it may stand no matter how the proof was secured. Observance of due process has to be not with the question of guilt or innocence but the mode by which guilt or innocence was ascertained."

Now, Your Honor, what I'd like to do next, very briefly, is give a basic framework for our case and the documents that will be presented. First of all, we believe the documents refer to a delimitation agreement, and the delimitation agreement was an agreement between the intelligence gathering agencies, the FBI, G-2 and ONI, and this agreement attempted to define the lines of authority and provided for the sharing of intelligence between the agencies.

Next, I would like to very briefly compare three things for the Court. One is what the Government knew; a brief outline of what we believe the Government knew. Then I would like to go over very briefly what the Government's positions were with respect to what they knew. And, finally, I'd like to cover what the Government represented to the Court.

Your Honor, we have prepared a timeline which at this point we would like to put up, just for demonstrative purposes.

Your Honor, in terms of what the Government knew, starting with around December 17th, 1941, in documents that we have presented or we will present to the Court, there is a document which indicates first that the FBI on December 17, 1941, knew that the Army would be requesting from them a list of persons whom they considered dangerous. The FBI also at this time did not believe that they could put over any plan to clear people out of the area unless there were some very imminent prospect of attack.

On 12-20-41, is the date of the last of the Munson Reports. Mr. Munson had written several reports.

The Court: Who is Munson?

Mr. Kawakami: Mr. Munson was a well-to-do Chicago businessman who was performing an informal investigation on behalf of the President of the United States. He went around the West Coast gathering information from the various intelligence agencies and wrote a series of reports to the President, the last of which, as I indicated, was on December 20, 1941.

On January 9th, 1942, the documents will reflect that the Federal Communications Commission had a conference with General DeWitt of the Western Defense Command and advised General DeWitt at that time that there was no evidence of any illegal transmissions.

At that time he also, after discussions with DeWitt, formed the Radio Intelligence Division which was under the control of the military but run by personnel from the Federal Communications Commission.

On December 30th, 1941, the Chief of Naval Operations has read or learned of the Munson Reports and requests of his staff that they prepare for him a report regarding the question of potential espionage and sabotage by Japanese-Americans, and the person he selected to do the report was Lieutenant Commander Ringle.

Lieutenant Commander Ringle completed his task on January 26th, 1942, and submitted a report, the conclusions of which indicated that it was not necessary to evacuate Japanese and that most of the Japanese were Americanized. Those who posed a risk of sabotage or espionage could have been readily and easily identified.

On January 27th, 1942, the Attorney General advises Congressman Ford that the Justice Department did not deem it advisable to evacuate, and on February 14th, 1942, DeWitt issues his final recommendations in which even he at that time acknowledges that there was no sabotage or evidence of sabotage.

On 2-17-42, the Attorney General advises the President that the last advice from the War Department that he obtained was that there was no evidence of imminent attack and no evidence of planned espionage or sabotage.

In March, March 9th, 1942, we know that the Attorney General of the United States has read and sends to McCloy of the Department of War the Ringle Report which was written on January 26th, 1942.

In March, March 21st, 1942, Mr. McCloy in a letter acknowledges that he received the report and indicates that he in fact talked at length with Ringle and that he was very impressed with Lieutenant Commander Ringle's knowledge of the situation.

We know that on or about May 6th, 1942, the War Relocation Authority specifically requested the services of Lieutenant Commander Ringle to help them with their job in settling the evacuees. We also know that on April 15th, 1943, General DeWitt and his staff circulates a printed and bound volume of what we will call the Final Report. In that Final Report, the salient points of that are that in General DeWitt's opinion, shortness of time to separate the loyal from the disloyal was not a factor in his decision. In the second point that he makes, amongst others, was that in his view you could not separate the loyal from the disloyal.

Four days later, after Mr. McCloy reads this version of the Final Report, Mr. McCloy requests revisions to this Final Report, and he emphasizes two changes that he wished to make, and that was (1) that loyalty could be determined, and (2) in his view time was of the essence, was the argument that should be posed.

Between April 19th, 1943 and June of 1943, revisions in the Final Report were made. On June 29th, 1943, we have a document in which it was witnessed that the galley proof pages, galley pages, drafts and memos of the original Final Report were destroyed.

Then, Your Honor, we know that from documents we have received which occurred after the arguments in Hirabayashi, which was on May 10th and May 11th of 1943, we know that the FBI from the beginning of the war, at least through Mr. Hirabayashi's case and on through including Mr. Korematsu's case, reported that there was never any evidence of sabotage, espionage or fifth column activity.

We also know from documents received from the Federal Communications Commission that after their investigation there was never any evidence of illicit radio transmissions or signaling of any kind.

This is a short summary of the kinds of evidence that the Government had in its possession. The Government's position with respect to that evidence, as near as we can determine, was as follows: First, the Department of Justice felt that evacuation was not necessary. Measures taken short of evacuation were sufficient. The military, and therefore the War Department, or the military and also the War Department determined that there was a military necessity, although they articulated it nowhere except in the Final Report.

The Final Report, in its first version, again recommended that you cannot separate loyal from disloyal, regardless of how much time there was or how much time he had to do that, and they specifically state that time or shortness of time to separate the loyal from the disloyal was not a factor.

Now, the Final Report in its altered version contradicts and states the opposite; that loyalty could be determined, but changes the time factor to state merely that there were no ready means available to determine loyalty. The intelligence community, which I have already gone over, basically Munson and Ringle reports, all indicated that by and large, Japanese-Americans were "Americanized." They further stressed that potential disloyalty could and in fact was at the time they wrote the reports, these people were already rounded up, so it was very easy to identify and select and to then detain and question those individuals.

They also emphasized that the Japanese "problem" was blown way out of its true proportions. This is, again, what positions the Government took with respect to the evidence they had. What the Government then represented with these facts to the Court was that their facts regarding the Japanese population on the West Coast, which they urged the Court to take judicial notice of, included alienage—alienation toward the Kibei— these are just characteristics that I'm going over. Kibei are Americans with Japanese—

The Court: Let me just ask you to go back. Did you say the Government was urging the Courts to take judicial notice of this?

Mr. Kawakami: Yes, Your Honor. That's correct.

The Government, citing these racial characteristics, urged the Court to take judicial notice of them and, further, to take judicial notice of the fact that because of these racial characteristics, that the Japanese-Americans were therefore predisposed to disloyalty.

The other characteristics, amongst others, and I'll just list a few more that the Government urged the Court to take judicial notice of, included participation in Japanese organizations, Japanese language schools, dual nationality, and the fact that apparently most of the Japanese-Americans were concentrated or lived on or near the West Coast war industries.

The Government also represented to the Court that the identity of potentially disloyal American citizens were not readily identifiable. They also urged the Court, that immediate evacuation was necessary.

Finally, we contend that the Government presented improperly through the amicus briefs of the states of Washington, Oregon and California certain selected facts which they obtained from the first version of the final report, which they presented to the Court in *Hirabayashi*, notwithstanding the fact that the final report itself was suppressed and not before the Court in *Hirabayashi*.

Your Honor, with that brief overview, we would like to call our first witness, Mr. Edward Ennis.

The Court: Let me give Mr. Stone a chance to respond.

Mr. Kawakami: I'm sorry.

The Court: Are you through with your opening argument?

Mr. Kawakami: Yes.

The Court: Mr. Stone.

Mr. Stone: Good morning, Your Honor.

Although I had anticipated a slightly different opening statement, I feel obliged to respond to as many of the points that were made in my co-counsel's opening statement as I can, so please excuse me if I don't look that composed.

I think that the Court is aware, as we all are, that although I was—well, the other side has pointed out that in 1976, President Ford on behalf of the Executive Branch called the treatment of Japanese-Americans on a group basis a tragic mistake. That is and that was and that will always be now the final position of the Executive Branch of the Government.

The statement that was made a moment ago that only the Legislative Branch or perhaps the Executive Branch has taken back and apologized for the extreme actions they took under the pressure of a wartime emergency, and that the Judicial Branch still needs to do something is to argue not something which had anything to do with prosecutorial misconduct.

If a record was presented to the Supreme Court that was improper, indeed if there was prosecutorial misconduct, that in no way taints the Judicial Branch. That has nothing to do with the judges of the Supreme Court. If there is a taint—if there is a taint—it is a taint upon the Executive Branch, the branch which has already issued a presidential proclamation. So to say that there is some overriding obligation that has never been cleared and that a cloud still hangs over the Judicial Branch is totally absurd in our view. It has nothing to do with reality.

The reality is when the case was presented the Court, the Judicial Branch, certainly acted based as it felt upon the case before it, and certainly there is no even allegation that the Judicial Branch of the Government ever engaged in any misconduct.

Now, the second thing that I think I need to take up is the point made that this is a unique case, a Japanese-American case. That has nothing to do with this case. As Your Honor had ruled, the question before the Court, the question that they later finally got to, was whether or not there was something in the way the case was prosecuted originally which was not proper according to the rules of how a case is prosecuted. That is no different than any other of hundreds of kinds of criminal cases that are prosecuted every day and handled every day in the court system.

If there was prosecutorial misconduct, then yes, that is something which may or may not need to be addressed, and it may or may not have affected the outcome of this case or of any case. But that has absolutely nothing to do with the subject matter of the prosecution. If someone didn't present something to the Court that they should have, or if someone didn't present evidence to the other side that they should have, that can and does happen, as this Court well knows, in every kind of case, sometimes based on simple neglect of a prosecutor, sometimes based on a prosecutor's particular view of the evidence, that he in his own mind doesn't happen to think it's exculpatory, and sometimes, I will concede, it is based on a little bit of overzealousness which the Court may find was not appropriate.

But there are various reasons and innumerable neutral contexts in which a prosecutor can make a mistake in determining what he should give to the other side. So the Japanese-American aspect of this case has nothing to do with it. As Mr. Kawakami has pointed out, the Japanese community has long ago been apologized to by the Executive Branch. They went to the Legislative Branch and got the statute repealed. Those are all points that the Government pointed out in our very first motion to dismiss when we tried to make the point that we are not trying to bring up again allegations of Japanese-American espionage or whatever.

However, despite our coming in and suggesting that it had long been conceded, now close to ten years ago by President Ford, that there were lots of tragic mistakes that people may have done in connection with this episode because of the pressure in this very city, among others, of the wartime emergency. That's not the same thing as saying that there was a plan, a plot, a conspiracy if you will, among those high decision makers to deprive Japanese-Americans purely because of their race.

Frankly, we find those allegations as a whole to be not only spurious but also almost incredible. To suggest that Franklin Roosevelt gave his go ahead and his okay—a president who was the first one to try and treat all Americans and enact laws in programs treating all Americans as equals; a president who is considered by the longest run of historians to have been on the liberal spectrum of the political scene. That he and Secretary of War Stimson, a person from a different political party and different backgrounds, who also was well known to be a liberal, and Attorney General Biddle, also a lifelong public servant, and the prosecutors in this case, one of whom is going to be their first witness whose testimony will be that when he left the Government where he held several important posts, became a director and sat on the Board of Directors of the ACLU, who had filed amicus briefs in this case and indeed has sought leave to intervene again now. He sat as a director for the ACLU and still does for the last forty years, that he also is part of this conspiracy, intentionally trying to deprive people—it doesn't matter if they're Japanese-Americans—any American, to suggest that he would prosecute a case like that, that he intentionally wanted to deprive people of their rights, not that perhaps he made a mistake, is to us incredible.

To suggest that he and John Burling, two people about whom you will hear very much, two people whose views my opponent keeps saying were the Department of Justice's views, even though they get overruled by their superiors—

The Court: Let me hear what you intend to introduce as evidence.

Mr. Stone: Mr. Ennis will testify, Your Honor, and I certainly hope he will testify that his views were not the Attorney General's views, nor Mr. Burling, who was his subordinate.

The allegation has been made that the prosecutorial actions in this case were intentional efforts to deprive these people of their constitutional rights, and only that. There is no allegation that simile extended to Filipinos, Koreans, Chinese, or other people of the same racial characteristics who were resident on the West Coast. Only Japanese-Americans were singled out.

You heard Mr. Kawakami say how he's complaining that the Government was improper in its brief in the Supreme Court; that this is the crucial test of their misconduct, in citing the fact that Kibei and people who believed in the Shinto religion should have to be dealt with more harshly than others perhaps.

In the first place, I want to be sure the Court recognizes that the focus of the case in the Supreme Court, the focus of the prosecution, the focus of the opinion in this case was on whether there was a curfew violation. The Supreme Court only accepted certification of the Yasui case and this case when the cases were certified up to it. It had an option if it wished, because the petition for certification also included the Korematsu case, but it didn't take that case which was only an evacuation case. Instead, it took the Yasui case, which was only a curfew case, and it accompanied it by this case and chose only to reach curfew issues, specifically reserving anything more.

The Government's brief that was filed in the Supreme Court in this case opens its statement of facts by saying that the Government and the Court is well aware that the factors which went into the military decision were not able during that wartime period to be put on the record because we were in a war zone. We were in a time of war even then, even more than a year after the activities which were being complained about.

So the Government said very clearly, we think where a curfew is involved, you may take judicial notice of certain things which distinguish certain citizens of Japanese extraction, and about those characteristics which we don't have enough time to separate people out.

Now, just to discuss those two things for a moment. Was there anything outrageous about suggesting that individuals who had been born in this country to Japanese citizens and whose parents had sent them for long periods of time to Japan for their primary education and for their military training, and to retain their dual citizenship and came back to this country, was there at that time in the eyes of those people, the people briefing this, as they thought about it in 1942 after we had been attacked at Pearl Harbor, was there something to worry about with respect to other people? Or with respect to people who were advocates or are advocates of the Shinto religion?

I will direct the Court to Mr. Ringle's memo which Mr. Kawakami makes so much of. Mr. Ringle—

The Court: I don't really want a final argument.

Mr. Stone: Okay, Your Honor.

The Court: What I do want you to do is state what the Government intends to show.

Mr. Stone: Okay. The Government intends to show, Your Honor, that the evidence that will come into the case will show that the factors which were pointed to were perfectly legitimate factors which the intelligence community as a whole at that time was busy advising everybody was a problem. The only question which the intelligence community brought up at that time, the Government's evidence will show, was the question of can we separate people out. Do we have enough time to do it? Is the situation so emergent [*sic*] that we can do that or not?

Now, much has been made of how the Department of Justice felt differently. Well, first of all, I don't think they were talking to the Department of Justice. The evidence will show they're talking about Mr. Ennis and Mr. Burling. Mr. Ennis will tell you, I hope, that that was not his call to make at that time. It was the call of the man who was put in charge of the war zone to make, and he simply had to tell that to the Supreme Court, which is exactly what he did. And he did it in a very objective way.

He said to the Supreme Court both in this case, and if you'll look at the oral argument which will be a piece of evidence in the Korematsu case when the Solicitor General's office was involved, they said, "Court, we ask you, because the evidence which there is is classified, it's not for public consumption, we ask you to see if you can decide this on the basis of judicial notice. If you can't, you may have to remand it for a hearing. If you can, we think we win."

Now, what happened? In the first case that only involved curfew, nine of the justices, a unanimous court, agreed that they could uphold a curfew, an order that didn't kick anybody out of his home; it didn't evacuate anybody from his community; it didn't separate families; didn't make people leave their possessions or their jobs. They said unanimously that they could uphold based on judicial notice.

The Court: When you say "this case," you're talking about the first case?

Mr. Stone: Yes. That's this case, the Hirabayashi case. In this case none of the justices were troubled that an incursion onto liberties could not be justified by fears and potential threats of disruption in the Western Defense Command, espionage and perhaps sabotage, not incidents.

We will present the evidence, as you will see, that in the certification documents that came to the Supreme Court, Judge Denman of this Circuit, then the Chief Judge, specifically pointed out in the Court of Appeals, Mr. Ennis was the first one to admit to Judge Denman that we didn't have any prosecution pending of any of those 70,000 people for sabotage, espionage or fifth column activity.

What General DeWitt had been talking about was a threat, he felt, a fear that he had in 1942 at the time in question, and it was said to the Supreme Court, very openly, "We think if you look at the facts in public notice, that is enough to justify the fears that were in the mind of General DeWitt." The Court unanimously agreed.

Later on when the next case, the Korematsu case, a year later gets to the Supreme Court, the Government said the same thing. When the Supreme Court disposes of the Hirabayashi case, they are very clear, particularly, I believe, the dissents are very—excuse me—the concurring opinions—it was a unanimous opinion with no dissents—but the concurring opinions are very clear that they are not at all sure that they could take judicial notice of something more stringent, less preventative in nature, perhaps more punitive in impact, even if not in intention, that being curfew, and indeed that is precisely what happens.

When the Supreme Court gets to look at the Korematsu case, three of the justices who were perfectly happy to concur in the first decision, feel obligated to dissent, and one of them dissents very strongly from the practices that are openly put before them. Justice Murphy writes a ringing dissent with long footnotes, making all the same arguments that Mr. Kawakami has made, complaining about General DeWitt's Final Report, complaining that there is no evidence, and taking up the claim that they can't decide the case on judicial notice. It has got to go back for a hearing.

But six of the justices did not agree. They still felt there was probably enough to decide it on judicial notice, even in an evacuation context. Now, in later years some of those justices have said "I think I decided the case wrong; maybe we should have sent that part of the case back for hearing." But that is a far cry from this case. And the Government's position in the case was open and well known.

We will never know what would have happened if the Court had taken up Mr. Hirabayashi's suggestion at the time. Mr. Hirabayashi at that time, at Mr. Korematsu's suggestion in those briefs, does not say "We are entitled to those reports that we think show our innocence." He didn't say that at all, because they know they weren't entitled to classified military information during wartime, and it was still wartime. They said "We're entitled to a remand, we think, for an evidentiary hearing."

Now, at that point the Government would have been put in the position—

The Court: Let me say again, I don't really want a final argument.

Mr. Stone: The Government will show, Your Honor, the Government will show that that is the open process by which the case was decided, and everybody was well aware of the options that were open to everybody. The Supreme Court simply chose, we will show, not to send the case back and put the Government in the difficult position of deciding whether it would produce classified material or dismiss the case.

Now, we have come in now, as you know, and said we're happy to dismiss the case. That certainly indicates where we're going. Instead, the prosecu—Mr. Kawakami and Mr. Hirabayashi now are forcing us to hold that evidentiary hearing. Our evidence at this hearing is, in our view, going to be much different than the evidence might have been forty years ago for two distinct reasons.

The first is, for whatever reason, most of the evidence that we assembled has been excluded, so we will have to be in the position of making proffers to the Court. The second reason is, even if our evidence had not been excluded, forty years have passed. You will hear Mr. Ennis sit on the stand, and I will be very surprised if he can remember with the kind of clarity that certain written documents may have what kinds of information, the specifics, he actually had in his hands at that time or that General DeWitt had in his hands at that time. Documents are lost, memories fade, most of the critical witnesses are all dead.

It happens that Mr. Ennis is still around, so is Mr. Hirabayashi. General DeWitt is not here. General DeWitt's G-2, Mr. Forney, is not here. Mark Clark, who is on the chart that we've been shown by the petitioners, is dead. General G-2, GHQ, who advised Mark Clark, Robinett, who was at that time one of the most well-respected intelligence officers in the United States Army, is dead. President Roosevelt is dead. Mr. Ringle's boss, Mr. Canaga, is dead. Mr. Canaga's boss is dead. The heads of the ONI are all dead.

Can we go back and figure out what was in their minds? The Government's evidence will show that the picture that has been drawn of Mr. Ringle, who was an Assistant District Intelligence Officer, not even the District Intelligence Officer, in a single Naval District of fifteen Naval Districts, did not speak to the Chief of Naval Operations. He was respected because he was in a position where he had a lot of information, but he didn't speak to the Office of Naval Intelligence.

The Government's evidence will show that he was not in a position to do that, to the extent that we can, because he is not here to take the stand.

Now, I make this point, and I think it's quite important, the evidence which Mr. Kawakami will present, which he has already mentioned to you, shows that Mr. Ringle's papers were widely distributed.

John J. McCloy, one of the supposed conspirators to deprive these litigants of their rights by prosecutorial misconduct, openly admits that Mr. Ringle had a certain amount of expertise. He doesn't say, as you would think if he were a conspirator, "This guy doesn't know what he's talking about."

The Court: I don't want to say it again. I simply want to know what the Government intends to produce.

Mr. Stone: The Government will show that the people at that time treated the case in the best way that they could; that in the Western Defense Command the people who were involved acted in accordance with normal customary procedures, acted like responsible officials. If mistakes were made, they were due to the impression of the war, and many of the mistakes were not even apparent to them.

The Government will show that General DeWitt acted in a way that he truly believed was correct, and again, Mr. Irons may have concluded he made a mistake, but the Government will show he acted according to his beliefs.

The Government will also show that in Washington the War Department exercised independent control over what was going on, and that they acted separately, and in fact, they acted based on different information, information to which both Mr. Ennis and probably most of the other individuals in this country were not privy. The highest officials in Washington consulted and relied on information that was ultimately derived from the most important intelligence coup that existed during World War II. The United States, on the basis of some cryptological breakthroughs had secretly been reading the diplomatic telegraph traffic that the Japanese consuls were sending back and forth to their home offices. The airways were open, obviously, and people could intercept any signal, but the cryptological experts had broken various codes and continued to break the updated codes. The result was that excellent information about the moves that the Japanese government were making with respect to World War II was given to this country.

Because it was such an important intelligence breakthrough, there was a very strict control on who was allowed to know that we even had made the breakthrough and had this project in being, which, because the evidence that was obtained by transcripted secret messages was so amazing in their description of what was going on, was entitled "Magic," and so they're called "Magic" documents, because people thought that the whole idea that we had broken these codes and gotten terrific information, the Japanese continued to use it, was like magic.

It was a very small circle of people who was allowed to know that we had done that. There was an even smaller circle of people who got to actually handle the cables in their roll-up form and who got to see a cable and to read a cable. However, the intelligence community as a whole, our evidence will show, was given the meat of those cables on a regular basis. It was distributed. It was run back and forth. It was all over the intelligence community. That is what our evidence will show.

And although to the lawyers who were involved in that case, and the people who have drafted the petition in this case, they may not see the meat of that intelligence and how it affected the decision-makers in the War Department, that is what we will show you, that the meat of that intelligence was why people in Washington had an independent basis to resist rejecting the necessity for curfew.

Did they care much about—our evidence will show that they didn't care much about the final report. That was a published document during the war. The evidence will show that anything that is published was not something that the War Department was relying on during the war, because the evidence, as I have already pointed out, shows the Government came in to the Supreme Court and said, "We can't give you the evidence because it is not something we can publish."

So our evidence will show you that the Final Report of General DeWitt was not the final say-so on the evacuation of the Japanese. Indeed, our evidence will show you that the final say-so was the official report of the evacuation of the Japanese which was published in 1959 by the Government itself and written by Stetson Conn.

Now, ultimately we will show you through that evidence that the decision makers had a basis to go ahead, although Mr. Ennis may have been unaware of it, although General DeWitt may have been unaware of it, although they may have had separate views that allowed them to proceed, but that no one in this whole circle was busy conspiring to deprive only one Oriental group on the West Coast of their rights. Only one. Not the people of Korea or people of Chinese origin or people of Filipino origin.

That's what our evidence will show. We think that the evidence will also show that to the extent that we can make a case, our evidence will show you that our case has been irreparably damaged by time. I was very pleased to hear in the opening, right at the very beginning of Mr. Kawa-kami, that he spoke about Morton Grodzins' book, *Americans Betrayed*.

Our evidence will show you that Morton Grodzins went and spoke to Mr. Ennis in 1942, within six months of the events that we're now trying to unscramble; that he was given access to the Department of Justice files in 1942, partly because Mr. Ennis wasn't so happy with this whole series of events, personally he was unhappy.

Mr. Grodzins published all of this in 1949. Every critical document was published and discussed by Mr. Grodzins in 1949, including Mr. Grodzins' suggestion that maybe somebody should reopen this in the Supreme Court. The only thing that was not published by Mr. Grodzins, and maybe it was out of respect to Mr. Ennis because Mr. Ennis agreed to be interviewed by him, was Mr. Ennis's personal views rather than his institutional views about the way the cases were handled.

But Mr. Ennis, our evidence will show you, was himself counsel to the Japanese-American citizenry and went around the country lobbying for that bill that was discussed by Mr. Kawakami in opening, to give redress to Japanese-Americans. Mr. Ennis was and is among one of the most ardent admirers of Japanese-Americans in this country that there is.

The Court: Anything further about the Government's evidence?

Mr. Stone: The Government's evidence ultimately will show you, Your Honor, that to the extent that there has been any evidence out there that anybody wants to discuss, either Mr. Ennis personally or Morton Grodzins, was available to the defendant in this and the other two cases since the late 1940's, and to come back now, thirty years later, and tell us what Morton Grodzins was saying back then, at a time when the Government is unable to really reconstruct for you by the testimony of witnesses what happened, and we all have to surmise about the intent behind documents, prejudices the Government's ability to stand here and say the case was prosecuted in a proper fashion.

To the extent that the evidence may show that it prejudices the Government's ability to defend it, the actions that were taken, that's not an issue in the case. So to the extent that there is a laches problem, a problem with waiting too long, we are glad that they have opened the subject of what Morton Grodzins has done, because we certainly hope to ask Mr. Ennis if he remembers Morton Grodzins.

Consequently, in sum, Your Honor, we will try and show you that this case is not—what is before you right now, this hearing, has nothing to do with Japanese-American rights. It has nothing to do with the Commission on Wartime Relocation and Internment of Civilians which made recommendations for redress. It has nothing to do with the Japanese-American Claims Act of 1949.

Our evidence will show it has to do with whether the prosecutors in one of many cases they prosecuted, acted properly, and whether or not we can show that at this late date is something that's very difficult, thirty years after all the events have been made a part of the public record.

Thank you, Your Honor.

Hirabayashi v. United States

Petitioner's Post-Hearing Brief, U.S. District Court for the
Western District of Washington

July 31, 1985

*At the conclusion of the evidentiary hearing on the Hirabayashi petition,
Judge Voorhees asked the lawyers on both sides to submit briefs summarizing the evidence and presenting the legal arguments they wished the
judge to consider. Hirabayashi's lawyers produced a brief that relied
largely on the documents submitted with the petition. Focusing on the
"suppression of evidence" charges in the petition, this brief carefully
traced the paper trail that proved them: the preparation of General
DeWitt's initial evacuation report, the Justice Department's request for
this report, the War Department's decision to withhold the report and
alter crucial passages about the racial basis for the internment, and the
concealment of the initial report from the Supreme Court. The record of
the evidentiary hearing, Hirabayashi's lawyers concluded, "proved a
shocking and indefensible pattern of governmental misconduct" in the
original trials and appeals.*

I. Introduction

Petitioner seeks issuance of a writ of error coram nobis to vacate his
October 20, 1942 criminal convictions of two violations of Public Law
No. 503: failure to observe a curfew as required by Public Proclamation No. 3 and refusal to be evacuated as required by Civilian Exclusion
Order No. 57. The relief requested by Petitioner is based on numerous
acts of misconduct by agencies of the Government during and after Petitioner's trial.

II. Issues

A. Did the Government suppress evidence, present evidence it knew or should have known to be false, or destroy evidence in its attempt to secure Petitioner's convictions and defend those convictions on appeal?

B. If so, should the Court grant Petitioner's prayer for relief and vacate Petitioner's convictions?

III. Legal Standards

A. Relief Is Warranted Because Government Misconduct Deprived Petitioner of His Right to Due Process Under the Fifth Amendment and Violated the Sanctity of the Courts

The writ of error coram nobis is available by statute, 28 U.S.C. §1651(a), to challenge a federal criminal conviction obtained by the Government through constitutional or fundamental errors that render a proceeding irregular and invalid. *United States* v. *Morgan*, 346 U.S. 502 (1954).

Coram nobis relief is warranted where Government abuses "offend elementary standards of justice," cause "serious prejudice to the accused," or, even absent such prejudice, "undermine public confidence in the administration of justice." *United States* v. *Taylor*, 648 F.2d 565, 571 (9th Cir.), cert. denied, 454 U.S. 866 (1981). As stated in *Taylor*, the leading Ninth Circuit case,

prosecutorial misconduct may so pollute a criminal prosecution as to require a new trial, especially when the taint in the proceedings *seriously prejudices the accused.* . . . When a conviction is secured by methods that *offend elementary standards* of justice, the *defendant may invoke the Fourteenth Amendment* guarantees of a fundamentally fair trial. . . . Moreover, this principle is not strictly limited to those situations in which the defendant has suffered arguable prejudice, the principle is designed to *maintain also public confidence in the administration of justice.*

Id. at 571 (emphasis added). Guilt or innocence is not the fundamental consideration in due process arguments. The Court cites Justice Frankfurter:

This Court has rejected the notion that because a conviction is established on incontestable proof of guilt it may stand, no matter how the proof was secured. Observance of due process has to do not with questions of guilt or innocence but the mode by which guilt is ascertained. *Irvine v. California*, 347 U.S. at 148, 74 S.Ct. at 391 (Frankfurter, J. dissenting.)

Id. at 571, n.20.

Here, the Government misconduct is so egregious that the Court should find that the Government's misconduct deprived Petitioner of a fundamentally fair trial and appeal. Even absent a finding that Petitioner suffered sufficient prejudice, Petitioner's convictions were secured by methods that offend elementary standards of justice, violate the sanctity of the courts, and undermine the public confidence in the administration of justice. For these reasons alone, the Court should grant the petition for writ of error coram nobis.

Although in *Taylor*, the Ninth Circuit expressly withheld judgment "as to the extent of prosecutorial malfeasance or prejudice to appellant necessary to warrant relief," *Taylor*, 648 F.2d at 574, n.28, this Court should, however, rule that Petitioner need only show that the Government misconduct *could have affected* the Court's determination of the constitutionality of Public Law 503 and the curfew and evacuation orders. The Government misconduct, therefore, rendered the proceedings unfair.[1]

1. Suppression of evidence. In *United States* v. *Agurs*, 427 U.S. 97 (1976), the Court stated that the reversal of a conviction is warranted where the omitted evidence raises a "reasonable doubt" that did not otherwise exist. This does not mean that the accused must show that the omitted evidence, if considered, would have resulted in acquittal. This is clear from the fact that the Court states that the standard is higher than the harmless-error standard, but is *not* so high as to require "probability" of acquittal. *Id.* at 111. See also, *United States* v. *Goldberg*, 582 F.2d 384, 489 (9th Cir. 1978), cert. denied, 440 U.S. 973 (1979), (this test is stricter than the harmless-error standard, but is not so severe as to require the defendant to show that the undisclosed evidence probably would have resulted in acquittal); and *United States* v. *Imbruglia*, 617 F.2d 1 (9th Cir. 1980).

Here, the suppressed evidence is material to the question of the constitutionality of Public Law 503 because it was more than harmless-error for the Government to suppress the intelligence reports indicating that the security problems, if any, posed by the West Coast Japanese population

---

[1] The *Taylor* Court ruled that "Taylor's claim of government fraud would, if proven, meet the various tests for relief in the nature of coram nobis." *Taylor*, 648 F.2d at 571, n.22. Thus, it was not necessary for petitioner Taylor to prove that he would have been acquitted but for the government's misconduct. Instead, it was enough that the misconduct involved important evidence that rendered the proceedings unfair.

did not warrant the issuance of the military curfew and evacuation orders. Petitioner *need not* prove that Public Law 503 probably would have been held unconstitutional if the Supreme Court had considered the suppressed evidence.

2. Use of evidence that the Government knew or should have known to be false. The Court "has consistently held that a conviction obtained by the knowing use of perjured testimony is fundamentally unfair, and must be set aside if there is *any reasonable likelihood that the false testimony could have affected the judgment of the jury.*" (Emphasis added.) *Agurs*, 427 U.S. at 103. Presumably this same standard applies where the prosecution knowingly uses false evidence. Thus, the Court should grant the petition if it determines that the false evidence used by the Government could have affected the judgment of the Court.

3. Destruction of evidence. In *United States* v. *Heiden*, 508 F.2d 898, 902 (9th Cir. 1974), the Court declared that,

When there is loss or destruction of such evidence, we will reverse a defendant's conviction if he can show (1) bad faith or connivance on the part of the Government or (2) that he was prejudiced by the loss of evidence.

Id. at 902. After *Heiden*, the courts have suggested that prejudice will be *presumed* if there is intentional destruction of evidence by the prosecution. In *United States* v. *Arra*, 630 F.2d 836, 849-850 (1st Cir. 1980), the Court stated that,

It may be, though we do not now so decide that intentional wrongful misconduct on the part of the Government would warrant an assumption that the evidence destroyed would have been favorable to the defense.

IV. Analysis

A. Suppression of Evidence

Petitioner does not deny that he knowingly violated Public Law 503 and the underlying military curfew and evacuation orders. Instead, Petitioner argued and still argues that the Fifth Amendment "prohibits the discrimination made between citizens of Japanese descent and those of other ancestry." *Hirabayashi* v. *United States*, 320 U.S. 81, 89. In response to Petitioner's due process argument, the Government presented to the courts a "tailored" factual record to support its argument that military necessity justified the imposition of the military curfew and exclusion orders. The Government attorneys and their agents suppressed exculpatory evidence that would have permitted the Petitioner to rebut the Government's arguments. The suppressed evidence, examined below, seriously prejudices Petitioner, offends elementary standards of justice, and even absent prejudice, undermines public confidence in the administration of justice.

In addition, it was more than harmless error for the Government to suppress the following intelligence reports. Therefore, the evidence suppressed by the Government raises a "reasonable doubt" that did not otherwise exist.

1. The Delimitation Agreement. Discussion of the Delimitation Agreement is essential to understanding the significance of the evidence that was suppressed by the Government. In a memo dated June 26, 1939, President Roosevelt directed that,

. . . the investigation of all espionage, counter-espionage, and sabotage matters be controlled by the Federal Bureau of Investigation of the Department of Justice, or the Military Intelligence Division of the War Department and the Office of Naval Intelligence of the Navy Department.

. . . the directors of these three agencies are to function as a committee to coordinate their activities.

. . . no investigation should be conducted by any investigative agency of the Government into matters involving actually or potentially any espionage, counter-espionage or sabotage, except by the three agencies mentioned above.

(Exhibit 94, Tab 1.)

On June 5, 1940, in accordance with the Presidential Directive of June 26, 1939, the three agencies charged with the investigation of espionage and sabotage activities entered into the "Delimitation Agreement." (Exhibit 95, Tab 2.) This Agreement spelled out the basic working relationship between the agencies. The FBI was given primary responsibility for investigating all domestic and civilian matters related to espionage and sabotage in the continental United States and in certain of its territories.

For many years prior to this Agreement, ONI had been keeping a particularly close watch on the activities of Japan since Japan was an unfriendly major naval power. The ONI had already established an extensive investigatory network related to Japanese activities. Because the FBI would have had to establish a whole new network, it was agreed that ONI would continue to conduct investigations on Japanese espionage activities. (See Exhibit 133, Admission No. 24, p. 32.) This arrangement was later formally recognized by a revised Delimitation Agreement dated February 9, 1942, in which it was agreed that ONI would be responsible for "jointly with FBI, the coverage of Japanese activities in the categories enumerated in Paragraph I [espionage, counterespionage, subversion and sabotage]." (Exhibit 96, Tab 3, p. 4.)

2. The Ringle Report. After Pearl Harbor, the Navy reviewed the investigative reports which had been done on the Japanese American and Japanese resident alien population. In reviewing one such report, the Chief of Naval Operations noted in a memo of December 30, 1941 (Exhibit 46, Tab 6), that Curtis Munson reported that,

Ninety-nine per cent of the most intelligent views on the Japanese by military, official and civil contacts in honolulu and the mainland, was best crystallized by two intelligence men before the outbreak of the war. These two men are Lieutenant Commander K. D. Ringle of the 11th Naval District in Los Angeles and Mr. Shivers, in Honolulu, of the FBI.

The Chief of Naval Operations (CNO) ordered that Lt. Com. Ringle submit to him a report "on the Japanese referred to in Mr. Munson's report." Lt. Com. Ringle was thereafter relieved of all other responsibilities so that he could devote full time to Japanese issues. (Exhibit 148.)

Four other exhibits submitted herein establish the point that Lt. Com. Ringle was widely considered to be an expert on Japanese issues: (1) a letter from John Franklin Carter, Presidential consultant, advised Roosevelt that Munson's general recommendations for allaying racial antagonism be acted upon. Carter stated "[t]he best qualified officer to handle this work, in Munson's opinion, is Lieutenant Commander K. D. Ringle . . ." (Exhibit 45, Tab 7); (2) a letter from McCloy to Biddle, dated March 21, 1942 (Exhibit 34, Tab 8), in which McCloy thanks Biddle for sending him the Ringle Report. In the letter McCloy states that,

. . . while out there [West Coast], I talked at some length with Commander Ringle and other officials of the Office of Naval Intelligence, 12th Naval District. I was greatly impressed with Commander Ringle's knowledge of the Japanese problem along the Coast.

(3) the transcript of a telephone conversation of August 3, 1942 (Exhibit 80, Tab 10), between Colonel Bendetsen and Colonel Tate in which they discussed the problem of transferring Ishimaru, a Japanese American internee, from one internment camp to another. Bendetsen stated: "Ishimaru [the internee] is one of the people by the way whom Commander Ringold [*sic*] seemed to feel was all right, and he told me that he considered Ishimaru to be pretty reliable," (p. 2). Bendetsen thereby acknowledged Lt. Com. Ringle's expertise regarding the Japanese Americans; (4)

a letter dated May 6, 1942 (Exhibit 100, Tab 69), after the evacuation in the Los Angeles area had commenced, Milton Eisenhower, then director of the War Relocation Authority (WRA) put in a special request to Rear Admiral Wilkinson, Director of Naval Intelligence, specifically requesting the services of Lt. Com. Ringle to assist the WRA in developing a program for evacuation and relocation. Eisenhower stated in part,

Many of us in the War Relocation Authority have conferred from time to time with Commander K. D. Ringle because we have found that he has a deep understanding of the problem we are now facing in evacuating and relocating the Japanese . . . He has been extremely helpful.

Lt. Com. Ringle was subsequently assigned to assist the WRA and wrote a report for them which was essentially an expansion of his original views in his January 26, 1942 report to the Chief of Naval Operations. This second report to WRA was later excerpted and published anonymously in the *Harper's* magazine article of October 1942.[2]

In terms of distribution of the Ringle Report to ONI (Exhibit 32, Tab 4), the Chief of Naval Operations received this report on or about January 29, 1942 (Exhibit 47, Tab 5). The Department of Justice had the Report prior to March 9, 1942, when it was transmitted by the Attorney General to the Department of War (Exhibit 33, Tab 11).

The Ringle Report to ONI is significant for several reasons. It was written by an expert on the Japanese American population (Ringle) in his capacity as a Naval Intelligence Officer at the direct order of the Chief of Naval Operations. As previously discussed, ONI was primarily responsible for investigation of the ethnic Japanese population. The Report dated January 26, 1942, was written before the issuance of Executive Order 9066, February 19, 1942, and before DeWitt's military curfew and exclusion orders went into effect.

Salient points of the Ringle Report to ONI can be summarized as follows:

a. . . . within the last eight to ten years the entire "Japanese question" in the United States has reversed itself. The alien menace is no longer paramount, and is becoming of less importance almost daily . . . (p. 1.)

b. . . . of the Japanese-born alien residents, the large majority are at least passively loyal to the United States. (p. 2.)

[2] See Exhibit 35, Tab 36, p. 2, where Ennis states that, "A comparison of this memorandum with the article leaves no doubt that the author of the *Harper's* article is Lt. Com. K. D. Ringle." Ennis went on to state that he was unofficially advised that Lt. Com. Ringle was, "lent to the War Reloca-

c. . . . however, there are among the Japanese both alien and United States citizens . . . who would act as saboteurs or agents. This number is estimated to be less than three percent of the total, or about 3,500 in the entire United States. (p. 2.)

d. . . . of the persons mentioned in 'c' above, the most dangerous are either already in custodial detention or are members of organizations . . . The membership of these groups is already fairly well known to Naval Intelligence service or the Federal Bureau of Investigation . . . (p. 2.)

e. . . . as a basic policy tending toward the permanent solution of this problem, the American citizens of Japanese ancestry should be officially encouraged in their efforts toward loyalty and acceptance as bona fide citizens . . . (p. 2.)

f. . . . the most potentially dangerous element of all are those American citizens of Japanese ancestry who have spent the formative years of their lives, from 10 to 20, in Japan . . . [Kibei] (p. 2.)

g. . . . the writer heartily agrees with the reports submitted by Mr. Munson . . . (p. 3.)

h. . . . in short, the entire "Japanese Problem" has been magnified out of its true proportion, largely because of the physical characteristics of the people; that it is no more serious than the problems of the German, Italian and Communistic portions of the United States population, and, finally it should be handled on the basis of the *individual*, regardless of citizenship, and *not* on a racial basis. (p. 3, emphasis original.)

In his Report, Ringle supported his conclusions with the following:

1. The Japanese American Citizens League at their January 11, 1942 convention required that each member, as a prerequisite to membership, take a loyalty oath in support of the Constitution of the United States. (p. 5.)

2. Many of the Nisei leaders have voluntarily contributed valuable anti-subversive information to this and other government agencies. (p. 5.)

3. That the Japanese consular staff, leaders of the Central Japanese Association, and others who are known to have been sympathetic to the Japanese cause do not themselves trust the Nisei. (p. 5.)

4. That a very great many of the Nisei have taken legal steps through the Japanese consulate and the Government of Japan to officially divest themselves of Japanese citizenship (dual citizenship), even though by so doing they become legally dead in the eyes of the Japanese law, and are no longer eligible to inherit any property which they or their family may have held in Japan. (p. 5.)

Edward J. Ennis, Director, Alien Enemy Control Unit, Department of Justice, crystallized the significance of the Ringle Report in a memorandum to the Solicitor General, dated April 30, 1943 (Exhibit 35, Tab 36).

---

tion Authority to prepare a manual on the background of the Japanese who were being evacuated from an Intelligence or security viewpoint, for the use of the WRA personnel. After this memorandum was prepared permission was obtained to abstract it and publish it anonymously in *Harper's*."

In this memo, Ennis reviewed the *Harper's* magazine article (Exhibit 78, Tab 13) written by "an Intelligence Officer." Ennis later traced the authorship of this magazine article to Lt. Commander Ringle. He highlighted for the Solicitor General several key points extracted from the *Harper's* article, including:

1. The number of Japanese aliens and citizens who act as saboteurs and enemy agents was less than 3,500 throughout the entire United States;
2. Of the Japanese aliens, "the large majority are at least passively loyal to the United States";
3. "The Americanization of Nisei (American-born Japanese) is far advanced";
4. "With the exception of a few identified persons who were prominent in pro-Japanese organizations, the only important group of dangerous Japanese were the Kibei (American-born Japanese predominantly educated in Japan)";
5. "The identity of Kibei can be readily ascertained from the United States Government records";
6. "Had this war not come along at this time, in another ten or fifteen years there would have been no Japanese problem, for the Issei would have passed on, and the Nisei taken their place naturally in the American communities and national life."

Ennis also highlighted the article's conclusion:

To sum up: The "Japanese Problem" has been magnified out of its true proportion largely because of the physical characteristics of the Japanese people. It should be handled on the basis of *individual*, regardless of citizenship and *not* on a racial basis. (Emphasis in original.)

Having determined that the anonymous magazine article was written by Ringle, Ennis in his April 30th memo stated, "I now attach more significance to it [the magazine article] because a memorandum prepared by Lt. Com. K. D. Ringle . . . has come to my attention." (pp. 1–2.) He later stated that,

I have furthermore been most informally, but altogether reliably, advised that both the article and the WRA memorandum prepared by Lt. Com. Ringle represent the views, if not of the Navy, at least of those Naval Intelligence officers in charge of Japanese counterintelligence work. It has been suggested to me quite clearly that it is the view of these officers that the whole evacuation scheme was carried on very badly and that it would have been sufficient to evacuate the following three groups: (1) Kibei; (2) the parents of Kibei; and, (3) a known group of aliens and citizens who were active members of pro-Japanese societies such as the Japanese Navy League, Military Virtue Society, etc. Since the Naval officers believe that it was necessary to evacuate only about 10,000 people, they could have identified by name, they did not feel it was necessary to evacuate all the Japanese. (p. 2.)

Ennis understood that under the Delimitation Agreement it was agreed that Naval Intelligence should specialize on the Japanese, while Army Intelligence occupied other fields, Ennis stated that,

Had we known that the Navy thought that 90% of the evacuation was unnecessary, we could strongly have urged upon Gen. DeWitt that he could not base a military judgment to the contrary upon Intelligence reports, as he now claims to do. (p. 3.)

Ennis discussed the Government's position with respect to the *Hirabayashi* case pending before the Supreme Court as follows:

In view of the fact that the Department of Justice is now representing the Army in the Supreme Court of the United States and is arguing that a partial, selective evacuation was impracticable, we must consider most carefully what our obligation to the Court is in view of the fact that the responsible intelligence agency regarded a selective evacuation as not only sufficient but preferable . . . Thus, in one of the most crucial points of the case, the Government is forced to argue that individual, selective evacuation would have been impractical and insufficient when we have positive knowledge that the only Intelligence agency responsible for advising Gen. DeWitt gave him advice directly to the contrary. (p. 3.)

He urged the Solicitor General to reveal the Ringle Report to the Court by advising:

In view of this fact, I think we should consider very carefully whether we do not have a duty to advise the Court of the existence of the Ringle memorandum and of the fact that this represents the view of the Office of Naval Intelligence. It occurs to me that any other course of conduct might approximate the suppression of evidence. (p. 4.)

3. The Munson Reports. Prior to the war, President Roosevelt had developed his own informal intelligence system through John Franklin Carter, a journalist, who helped Roosevelt obtain information and estimates by exploiting sources outside the Government. One such source was Curtis B. Munson, a well-to-do Chicago businessman who gathered intelligence for Carter under the guise of being a Government official. Munson sent to Carter several reports based on his investigation of the Japanese population on the West Coast. These reports, in turn, were transmitted to Roosevelt. (*Personal Justice Denied*, pp. 51, 52.)

Munson's first report was dated November 7, 1941 (Tab 14). He stated, "Our Navy has done by far the most work on this problem, having given it intensive consideration for the last 10 or 15 years." (p. 2.) Munson had canvassed the entire West Coast and obtained opinions of the various services and "also of business, employees, universities, fellow white workers, students, fish packers, lettuce packers, farmers, religious groups, etc." (p. 2.) He reported the religious, family and cultural background of the Japanese on pages 2 through 8. He went on in his report to describe the family set-up in the United States and Japanese organizations and activities. On page 11 of his report he stated,

There are still Japanese in the United States who will tie dynamite around their waist and make a human bomb out of themselves. We grant this, but today they are few. Many things indicate that very many joints in the Japanese set-up show age, and many elements are not what they used to be. The weakest from a Japanese standpoint are the Nisei. They are universally estimated from 90 to 98% loyal to the United States if the Japanese element of the Kibei is excluded. The Nisei are pathetically eager to show this loyalty. They are not Japanese in culture. They are foreigners to Japan. (p. 11.)

As to potential sabotage, Munson stated that,

As interview after interview piled up, those bringing in results begin to call it the same old tune. Such it was with only minor differences. These contacts ranged all the way from two-day sessions with Intelligence services, through businessmen, to Roman Catholic priests . . . The story was all the same. There is no Japanese 'problem' on the West Coast. There will be no armed uprising of the Japanese. There will undoubtedly be some sabotage financed by Japan and executed largely by imported agents or agents already imported . . . In each Naval District there are about 250 to 300 suspects under surveillance. It is easy to get on the suspect list, merely a speech in favor of Japan at some banquet, being sufficient to land one there . . . The Japanese are hampered as saboteurs because of their easily-recognized physical appearance. It will be hard for them to get near anything to blow it up *if it is guarded*. There is far more danger from Communists and people of the Bridges type on the Coast than there is from Japanese. The Japanese here is almost exclusively a farmer, a fisherman or a small businessman. He has no entry to plants or intricate machinery. (pp. 13–14.)

As for espionage, Munson noted that, "a great part of his work (espionage) was probably completed and forwarded to Tokio [*sic*] years ago, such as soundings and photography of every inch of the Coast." (p. 14.) He noted that while Japanese would be effective as far as movement of supply troops and ships are concerned,

They occupy only rarely positions where they can get to confidential papers or plants. They are usually, when rarely so placed, a subject of perpetual watch and suspicion by their fellow workers. They would have to buy most of this type of information from white people. (p. 15.)

The next Munson report, entitled "Report on Hawaiian Islands by Curtis B. Munson," was undated but was transmitted from Carter to

Roosevelt on December 8, 1941. (See cover letter, Tab 15.) After his investigation in Hawaii, Munson concluded, as in his earlier report, that the second generation was estimated as approximately 98% loyal. He further stated:

However, the FBI state that there are about 400 suspects, and the FBI's private estimate is that only 50 or 60 of these are sinister. (In all figures given, only aliens are considered. Should it be possible to pick up citizens, this figure would have to be materially increased.) There are also a few Germans and Italians in the Islands who should be picked up . . . The Army Intelligence showed this reporter a secret map with pins of different colors to denote first generation, second generation and other nationalists who are suspect, and their distribution in the Islands. Each one of these men's address is known and they showed me that it would be a comparatively easy job to pick them up almost in a few hours, should the necessity arise . . . (pp. 2–3.)

In his report dated December 20, 1941 (Exhibit 5, Tab 16), Munson stated on page 1 that this report should be read in conjunction with his other reports: "Japanese on the West Coast" (Exhibit 139, Tab 14) and "Report on the Hawaiian Islands" (Exhibit 140, Tab 15). He noted, "We did not repeat many basic statements originally embodied in the earlier reports as these statements had already been made and held good in both cases." He emphasized that, "An attack is the proof of the pudding." (p. 3.)

In the latter report (Exhibit 5, Tab 16), Munson discussed a statement made by Secretary of Navy Knox, who had said, "I think the most effective fifth column work of the entire war was done in Hawaii, with the possible exception of Norway." (p. 1.) Munson commented that,

We suggest this paragraph creates the wrong impression and that it uses the term "fifth column." This term is loose and has been widely abused. Should not the term "complete physical espionage" have been used instead? "Physical espionage" is supplied unwittingly by the gabble of Navy wives, by the gabble of loyal second generation Japanese, by the gabble of the postmen and the milkmen and classified by definite agents of a foreign government . . . Fifth column activities, such as in Norway, impugns the loyalty of a certain population. Your observer still doubts that this was the case in Honolulu. He doubts, for instance, that outside of sabotage, organized and paid for by the Imperial Japanese government beforehand (i.e. professional work), that there was any large disloyal element of the Japanese population which went into action as a Fifth Column running around and intentionally disrupting things on their own hook. (pp. 1–2.)

Also as to Secretary Knox's statement, Munson further stated: "It is not the measured judgement of 98% of the Intelligence services or the knowing citizenry on the mainland or in Honolulu." (p. 2.)

4. The Final Report. The Final Report (Exhibit 4, Tab 17) represented General DeWitt's military justification for the military orders issued.[3] This report was suppressed by the War Department not only from the Supreme Court in *Hirabayashi*, but from the Department of Justice as well. After the Justice Department obtained copies of the Final Report, Edward Ennis, in a memo to the Attorney General, dated February 26, 1944 (Exhibit 93, Tab 18), revealed:

We learned of the existence of General DeWitt's report last Spring when we were trying to get some information for the *Hirabayashi* brief in the Supreme Court and we were refused a copy of the printed report . . . but we were given a few pages torn out of a copy merely because they wanted us to have selected facts to support the evacuation . . .

It is perfectly clear from the course of events that the War Department deliberately evaded submitting this report, discussing our mutual activities, to us before publication. (pp. 1, 2.)

5. FCC Reports. As early as January 1, 1942, the Federal Communications Commission (FCC) advised DeWitt in a letter (Exhibit 102, Tab 20) that as of that date, it had no active cases on file indicating the possession of radio transmitters by any alien enemies. In this letter to DeWitt, V. Ford Greaves, Chief Inspector, Western Area of the FCC, described the FCC monitoring operations and advised DeWitt:

These stations maintain a continuous radio intercept watch, and their normal duty is the detection and location of subversive and fifth-column radio activities, and the collection of evidence in cooperation with the FBI for court action. (p. 2.)

On January 9, 1942, George E. Sterling, of the FCC, and a few members of his staff met with General DeWitt and Western Defense Command (WDC) staff to review and discuss transmission monitoring operations (Exhibit 107, Tab 21). During this conference it was proposed that a joint FCC and military center be established to facilitate the reporting and monitoring of suspected illegal transmissions (p. 4). By agreement, the operating personnel were all to be from the FCC and the Army and Navy representatives were merely to help in identifying their stations and traffic (p. 4). On January 13, 1942, Lt. Col. Smith of the Signal Corps sent to General DeWitt a report and recommendation for the establishment of a Radio Intelligence Center (RIC) to be operated and controlled by the FCC. (Exhibit 106, Tab 22, p. 2.) The report recommended that the

---

[3] See Exhibit 98, Tab 19, where Solicitor General Fahy argued to the Supreme Court in *Korematsu*: "We say that the report proves the basis for the exclusion orders. There is not a line in it that can be taken in any other way. It is a complete justification and explanation of the reasons which led to his [DeWitt's] judgement." (pp. 9–10.)

equipment and personnel be supplied by the FCC (p. 2). On January 15, 1942, General DeWitt requested funding for the RIC. (Exhibit 104, Tab 23.) In a letter from General DeWitt to Mr. Greaves of the FCC, dated April 9, 1942 (Exhibit 103, Tab 24), DeWitt acknowledged receipt of a report covering the first month's operation of the Radio Intelligence Center and stated he appreciated being kept informed of the activities at the Center. He also stated in the letter, "I am very much pleased over the results so far achieved and am grateful to you and your splendid organization for your invaluable assistance."

The Radio Intelligence Division (RID) of the FCC summarized its work performed for other agencies in a report dated March 10, 1943 (Exhibit 88, Tab 26). This report acknowledged that the RIC was set up at the request of General DeWitt and further detailed tracking and monitoring procedures. The report also stated:

As a result of a conference, February 17, 1942, arrangements were completed for furnishing to the Office of the Chief Signal Officer, War Department, copies of all messages intercepted from clandestine radio stations under surveillance by the Radio Intelligence Division. (p. 1.)

Once the Final Report was released and available to the Department of Justice, Justice Department attorneys began an investigation into the accuracy of the factual statements made in the Final Report regarding the reasons for the issuance of the military orders by General DeWitt. In a letter dated February 26, 1944 (Exhibit 75, Tab 28), the Attorney General specifically requested that the FCC respond to allegations made in the Final Report regarding illicit radio transmissions and shore-to-ship signalling. The Attorney General was also concerned about the allegation that authorities would be unable to obtain a search warrant quickly enough for the full removal of these unlawful transmitters. Biddle asked Fly to confirm the following:

The experience of the Department of Justice which, of course, itself investigated great numbers of rumors concerning signal lights and radio transmitters, was that without exception the rumors proved to be baseless; and so far as this Department is aware, there is no evidence of the existence of any illicit signaling by lights or by radio transmitters . . .

Biddle also requested that he be informed of the extent to which General DeWitt or his subordinates were kept advised regarding FCC findings.

Finally, the Attorney General noted:

This Department did not discover any unlawful radio signalling or any unlawful shore-to-ship signalling with lights. Great numbers of all kinds of reports from the public, however, were received but these did not diminish in number following the evacuation. I would be interested in knowing whether the number of reports of unlawful radio transmissions received by the Commission varied in accordance with the pattern suggested by General DeWitt or varied in accordance with the experience of this Department. (p. 2.)

In response to the Attorney General's requests, an internal FCC memorandum was prepared identifying the tracking stations and equipment utilized, and summarized the establishment of a joint Radio Intelligence Center with the Army. (Exhibit 43, Tab 29.) The FCC reported that from December 1941 to July 1, 1942, there were 760 reports of unidentified or unlawful radio signals in areas evacuated (p. 3). Each case was investigated and there were no cases involving signals which could not be identified by the FCC (p. 4). The findings indicated that in 641 of the 760 cases the FCC found no radio signalling involved at all. The remaining 119 cases in which radio signalling was found all came from identified and lawful stations. With respect to the alleged reduction in reported cases after the evacuation, the FCC report indicated:

It will be seen that the number of complaints requiring investigation received before and after July 1st are comparable. It is quite evident that these complaints were influenced only to a small degree, if at all, by the evacuation of the Japanese. . . . (p. 4.)

In a letter from James Fly, Chairman of the FCC, to the Attorney General, dated April 3, 1944 (Exhibit 76, Tab 30), regarding DeWitt's Final Report on Japanese evacuation from the West Coast, Fly reported:

Time after time, the Army reported stations transmitting in Kana code, a code used almost exclusively by Japanese military stations, had been located at various points along the West Coast by Army direction finders . . . The Commission's investigations disclosed that all such reports were unfounded; that the transmissions involved were in each case from a station outside the United States, usually in Japan itself. (p. 1.)

In a follow-up letter of April 4, 1944 (Exhibit 40, Tab 31), Fly restated to Biddle that the reference in the Final Report to hundreds of reports of signalling by means of signal lights and unlawful radio transmissions proved after investigation, without exception, to be baseless. He further reported to Biddle that from December of 1941 to July 1, 1942 the FCC was engaged in monitoring and identifying signals reported to be from unlawful transmitters and in locating any such transmitters on the West Coast. RID was engaged in a comprehensive 24-hour surveillance of the entire radio spectrum to guard against any unlawful radio activities.

In the April 4th letter, Fly also reported:

The General and his staff were kept continuously informed of the Commission's work, both through occasional conferences and day-to-day liaison. . . . And as the result of a request of General DeWitt in January 1942, the Commission established a Radio Intelligence Center in San Francisco for coordinating radio intelligence information collected by the Army, Navy and the Commission. . . . As part of the plan for coordinating activities, Army and Navy personnel maintained a liaison attendance at this Center. (p. 3.)

Finally, in response to the inquiry from Biddle, Mr. Fly reported:

You note that the memorandum suggested that available means were inadequate to locate and seize any such radio transmitter, but state that if your understanding that equipment was available for locating such a transmitter is correct, the problem with which General DeWitt is concerned would not arise in practice. Your understanding is correct. As noted above, equipment developed by the Commission's engineers was on and after December 7, 1941 in the hands of its personnel on the West coast, which enabled them easily to locate the individual house and even the exact room containing a concealed transmitter. (p. 4.)

In fact, there is evidence as early as September 27, 1942, which suggested that General DeWitt himself acknowledged that reports of illicit transmissions were not well-founded. In a letter to Sterling, dated September 27, 1942 (Exhibit 81, Tab 25), DeWitt acknowledged:

It is true that during the months coastal patrols have operated in this area none of the reported suspicious stations have proven to be enemy, clandestine, or illegal; however, the work of the patrols has been of considerable assistance to this command in the prompt identification of signals.

6. Department of Justice. The Department of Justice had either information or reports that should have been provided to the Supreme Court. For example, the FBI's belief that the Japanese population did not constitute a threat on the West Coast was evidenced by an internal memo from J. Edgar Hoover to Tolson, Lamm, and Ladd, dated December 17, 1941 (Exhibit 38, Tab 32). In this memo, Hoover recognized that by giving them a list, "we won't be giving them anything they don't already have, as we have given them two or three lists already." (p. 1.) Hoover further stated:

I thought the Army was getting a bit hysterical, and although I believe the condition is very critical and serious, I do not believe that they can put over any plan to clean people out of that area unless there is some very imminent prospect of attack. . . . [T]here was no sense in the Army losing their heads as they did in the Bonneville Dam affair, where the power lines were sabotaged by cattle scratching their backs on the wires, or the "arrows of fire" near Seattle, which was only a farmer burning brush as he had done for years. (p. 1.)

[W]e must have proof not just allegations against these people . . . (p. 2.)

[I]f the Army wanted to take in thousands predicated upon lists furnished by us we wanted to be very careful to have specific recommendations on every person on any of our lists so that if there is any howl afterwards, we will not be left holding the bag. (p. 3.)

A letter from the Attorney General to Representative Leland Ford, dated January 27, 1942 (Exhibit 83, Tab 33), summarized the Department of Justice's early positions relative to evacuation. In that letter, Biddle stated:

As a result of these conferences, the decision of this Department that the program I have outlined above [which did not include wholesale evacuation], together with the extensive investigations which have been carried on by the Federal Bureau of Investigation, would adequately control the problem of the Japanese population of the Pacific coast.

For this reason, and also because of the legal difficulties involved in attempting to intern or evacuate the thousands of American born persons of Japanese race who are, of course, American citizens, this Department did not deem it advisable at this time to attempt to remove all persons of the Japanese race into the interior of the country. (p. 2.)

The Justice Department's position was also recorded in a memorandum to the President, dated February 17, 1942 (Exhibit 79, Tab 14), only two days before the President signed Executive Order 9066. Therein Biddle informed the President of the following: "My last advice from the War Department is that there is no evidence of imminent attack and from the FBI that there is no evidence of planned sabotage." (p. 1.) Biddle further advised the President to allay public fears regarding danger to the United States and noted:

It is extremely dangerous for the columnists, acting as "Armchair Strategists and Junior G-Men," to suggest that an attack on the West Coast and planned sabotage is imminent when the military authorities and the FBI have indicated that this is not the fact. It comes close to shouting FIRE! in the theater. . . . (pp. 1–2.)

In an April 19, 1943 memo to Solicitor General Charles Fahy (Exhibit 1, Tab 35), Ennis acknowledged that in preparation for briefing and arguments before the Supreme Court in *Hirabayashi*, *Yasui* and *Korematsu:*

[T]he War Department has today received a printed report from General DeWitt about the Japanese evacuation and is now determining whether it is to be released so that it may be used in connection with these cases. (p. 1.)

Ennis further noted that the Justice Department had an outstanding request to the War Department to furnish any public materials which might be helpful to the Department of Justice.

As noted in the section regarding FCC documents, after the Department of Justice obtained copies of DeWitt's Final Report, the DOJ attorneys requested that the FBI review the Final Report and report on the accuracy of the allegations contained in the Final Report which the FBI investigated. In a memo to the Attorney General from J. Edgar Hoover, dated February 7, 1944 (Exhibit 41, Tab 37), Hoover reported:

. . . there is no information in the possession of this Bureau as the result of investigations conducted relative to submarine activities and espionage activity on the West Coast which would indicate that the attacks made on ships or shores in the area immediately after Pearl Harbor have been associated with any espionage activity ashore or that there has been any illicit shore-to-ship signalling, either by radio or lights. (Cover letter.)

. . . no information is possessed relative to the number or percentage of ships attacked immediately after Pearl Harbor, nor is there any information to indicate that these attacks were associated with any espionage activity ashore. (p. 3.)

Hoover noted that as to General DeWitt's statement:

"there were many evidences of the successful communication of information to the enemy, information regarding positive knowledge on his part of our installations," it is generally known that the Japanese had for years prior to the outbreak of the war collected information as to locations of military and naval installations, as well as data relative to the coast lines of the United States, but it should not be assumed that any part of this information came to the Japanese through shore-to-ship signaling by lights or illicit radio operation. Every complaint in this regard has been investigated, but in no case has any information been obtained which would substantiate the allegation that there has been illicit signaling from shore-to-ship since the beginning of the war. (p. 3.)

The FBI was asked to determine the accuracy of DeWitt's assertions that interceptions of suspicious or unidentified radio signals and shore-to-ship signal lights were virtually eliminated and attacks on out-bound shipping from the West Coast ports appreciatively reduced following the evacuation. Hoover reported to Biddle in his February 7, 1944, memorandum: "There has been no material reduction in the number of complaints received pertaining to submarine activities on the West Coast as a result of persons of Japanese ancestry having been removed from the coast." (p. 3.)

In analyzing the three known attacks on the West Coast mentioned in the Final Report, Hoover indicated that after the FBI investigated each incident, it was unable to find any evidence of shore-to-ship signalling or of landing in the area. Hoover further stated there was never any evidence found which would link Japanese Americans or Japanese resident aliens to any of these activities.

In a February 23, 1944, memorandum to Edward Ennis (Exhibit 42, Tab 38), John Burling, a Justice Department attorney, indicated that he had met with the FCC. Burling wrote that after this meeting he concluded that General DeWitt's statements in the Final Report were made by him at a time when he personally knew the facts to be otherwise and, therefore, were either deliberately untruthful or at least deliberately misleading. Burling explained:

The significance of this is that one of General DeWitt's principal arguments in favor of mass alien enemy raids was that it was impossible to locate radio transmitters precisely and, therefore, impossible to obtain search warrants . . . Mr. Sterling stated categorically that a search warrant could always be obtained since his men would be in a position to swear to the precise location of the transmitter . . .

His [Sterling's] men also reported to the Army in every case in which the Army referred a complaint for them, and thus the Army had notice that every complaint was unfounded . . .

In conclusion, General DeWitt's report suggests there was a great deal of illicit radio communication and that the failure of the Department of Justice adequately to provide for prevention of it necessitated the evacuation of the Japanese. If the report can be construed as stating this directly, then, as General DeWitt well knew, the statement is a lie (a) because there were no illicit transmissions and, (b) if there had been they could have been located and dealt with by the FCC and by the use of judicial search warrants. If General DeWitt's statement is construed as being merely ambiguous, then his intent was to mislead without directly lying.

On April 13, 1944, in a memorandum to the Solicitor General (Exhibit 92, Tab 41), John Burling reviewed the Final Report and outlined the factual inaccuracies regarding the military justification for the evacuation. He further stated:

The most important statements of fact advanced by General DeWitt to justify the evacuation and detention were incorrect, and furthermore that General DeWitt had cause to know, and in all probability did know, that they were incorrect at the time he embodied them in his final report to General Marshall . . . [I]t is my view that his flat misstatements of fact as to evacuation discredit his statements as to detention . . . Contrary to the assumptions upon which we in this office have been going for some time, the original detention was not ordered as a mere temporary expedient, to be in effect for a few days while the persons were removed from California, nor was it in any sense hypothetical or speculative . . . It may also be shown that it was the intention of the Army at that time to continue with detention (with very few exceptions) at least for more than a few weeks . . . Our further assumption that the detention was ordered so as to give time to sift the loyal from the disloyal Japanese Americans is likewise unfounded . . . In view of this statement in General DeWitt's official report, it is apparent that we could only defend detention on the ground that evacuation could not be carried out without detention. This, however, is not a matter of law, but is a matter of fact, and almost the only available confirmation of the alleged fact is General DeWitt's statement . . . General DeWitt, however, says that this is so; and this Department can support detention only if it informs the Court, on the strength of its own reputation for veracity, that it is so. We, however, believe it is not so; we know that General DeWitt has made false statements in his evacuation report, and we therefore should not take the position in court. (p. 3.)

Shortly after his memo to the Solicitor General, Burling wrote to Philip Glick, Solicitor, War Relocation Authority on April 24, 1944 (Exhibit 90, Tab 42). In preparing the brief to the Supreme Court in *Korematsu*, Burling reviewed a memorandum prepared by the WRA entitled "Fifth Column Threat" and advised Glick:

It is a mistake to try to justify detention in terms of specific evidence of overt acts indicating a fifth column threat, since there probably is no such evidence . . . The legends surrounding the Japanese fishing fleet remain legends, and this Unit could give you little help in supplying authority to insert as indicated in your memorandum. I do not point these matters out in any spirit of criticism, but merely to correct the record since, as I feel sure you will agree, it is important that the Government not place its official stamp of approval on the vast mass of fifth column folklore which, insofar as concrete evidence is concerned, is almost entirely baseless.

7. G-2 Periodic Reports. The G-2 Periodic Reports were weekly summaries of intelligence as analyzed by the Military Intelligence Division (MID) of the Army. Information in these reports included assessments of: the enemy situation at end of period; enemy operations during period; miscellaneous (enemy casualties, morale, supply and equipment, terrain not under our control, weather and visibility, and enemy's probable knowledge of our situation); and, enemy capabilities.

The first G-2 report (No. 1) dated January 3, 1942 (Exhibit 57, Tab 44) states:

No hostile ground forces are believed to be nearer than the enemy occupation forces at WAKE ISLAND. (p. 1.)

No hostile operations conducted in this theatre of operations except harassing attacks by submarines . . . (p. 1.)

The enemy's probable knowledge of our situation has not been gained by observation or reconnaissance but by information learned during peace and the activities of the fifth columnists . . . (p. 2.)

Negative reports relative to *a*. [surprise attacks against HAWAII or a portion of the PACIFIC COAST, including the PANAMA CANAL and ALASKA, by carrier-borne aircraft or possibly accompanied by naval action], and *d*. [attacks on the Maritime Provinces in eastern SIBERIA to eliminate menacing Russian air power . . .] and known activity relative to *b*. [harassing attacks by submarine or surface craft . . .], and *c*. [intensification of campaigns in CENTRAL CHINA, MALAYASIA, PHILIPPINES and other objectives in the Far East] leads to the assumption that Japan will confine itself to this capability for the present, combined with a possible renewal of *b*. at some future date. (p. 2.)

The G-2 reports for the week ending January 10, 1942 (Exhibit 58, Tab 45) and January 17, 1942 (Exhibit 59, Tab 46) contained the same relevant information as in the prior report (No. 1) but added the following: "The last attack on shipping by hostile submarines was reported on 24 December." (p. 1.) G-2 report No. 4 (Exhibit 60, Tab 47) placed the nearest hostile ground forces at "2,000 miles west by south of the Hawaiian Islands." (p. 1.)

Report No. 6 for the week ending February 7, 1942 (Exhibit 61, Tab 48), had a significant change from all previous reports in the section assessing the enemy's probable knowledge of our situation. Report No. 6 stated that the enemy's probable knowledge was gained by "information learned during peace by the activities of accredited diplomatic, military and naval attaches and their agents." (p. 2.) The deletion of "fifth columnists" as a source of information was a significant admission by the Army that they had no evidence to support this assertion in the first place. This reassessment as to the source of information was repeated in the next four weekly reports.

In Reports Nos. 10–13 (Exhibits 65–68, Tabs 52–55), the enemy forces remained over "2,000 miles from Hawaii," and the Army continued to believe the Japanese would confine itself to its Far Eastern campaign, with a possible extension into Australia.

Report No. 14 for the week ending April 4, 1942 (Exhibit 69, Tab 56) was the first report of suspected sabotage. The report states, "sabotage was definitely indicated in the burning of two Southern Pacific Railroad bridges near Niland, California, 29 March." Report No. 15 (Exhibit 70, Tab 57), however, concluded that the fires reported in Report No. 14 were "apparently the work of a pyromaniac or person with a grudge against the railroad and are not the result of co-ordinated efforts at sabotage." (p. 3.)

Reports No. 14 (Exhibit 69, Tab 56), No. 15 (Exhibit 70, Tab 57), No. 16 (Exhibit 71, Tab 58), No. 17 (Exhibit 72, Tab 59), No. 18 (Exhibit 73, Tab 60), and No. 19 (Exhibit 74, Tab 61) covered the periods through the week ending May 9, 1942 (Petitioner was arrested May 16, 1942). Throughout these reports the enemy basically stayed 2,000 miles away and confined themselves to the Far Eastern campaign.

As for any active sabotage during this period, G-2 Report No. 17 (Exhibit 72, Tab 59) reported the "possibility of sabotage in connection with burning of a short trestle on the Oregon Trunk Line . . ." (p. 2), which after investigation by the FBI the following week "revealed that no sabotage was involved." (Exhibit 73, Tab 60, p. 3.) Report No. 19 (Exhibit 74, Tab 61) stated: "Investigation discloses that the fire at Western Pipe and Steel Company . . . was not of incendiary origin but caused by a short circuit . . ." (p. 4.)

B. Alteration and Suppression of Evidence

Several branches of Government collaborated to alter and destroy the original Final Report. This destruction not only constituted suppression of evidence, but also raises an independent ground of misconduct upon which this Court may vacate the Petitioner's convictions.

When the prosecution and affiliated Government agencies are responsible for the loss or destruction of evidence, the courts will find a due process violation if bad faith lies behind the Government's actions or if the defendant can show prejudice by the loss of evidence. *United States* v. *Heiden*, supra. Here, the destruction of the Final Report and the alteration of the dates of transmittal letters shows bad faith, and, in any event, prejudiced the Petitioner.

The Government's claim of military necessity rested on the assumption that there was insufficient time to determine the loyalty of Japanese Americans on an individual basis. Yet, General DeWitt's own statement that insufficiency of time was not the reason for the orders, was destroyed with the original Final Report. Petitioner was thereby prejudiced in his ability to challenge the factual justification for the military orders put forth by the Government. The bad faith exhibited by the War Department in altering and destroying the original Final Report was so egregious and calculated that the Court should presume that the evidence destroyed favored Petitioner. *United States* v. *Arra*, supra.

1. Alteration and suppression of Final Report. The evidence of alteration of the Final Report is clear from the trail of documents presented by the Petitioner. The significance of the alteration is that it allowed the Government to present after-the-fact, tailored and more defensible arguments to the Court rather than the actual indefensible justifications. The alterations occurred before oral arguments to the Supreme Court were heard (May 10 and 11). The evidence that the Report was available for use in *Hirabayashi* was also altered, and an attempt was made to cover up this fact by "adjusting" department records of receipt of the Report and recalling and destroying original versions.

Executive Order 9066 authorized the appropriate military commander in his judgment to issue military orders designating military zones. It further authorized him to exclude people from these areas and subject them to whatever restrictions he deemed necessary to protect against espionage and sabotage. Thus, the military orders relevant to these proceedings (Public Proclamation No. 3 and Civilian Exclusion Order No. 57) were issued pursuant to what DeWitt, in his sole discretion, believed necessary. Therefore, the only relevant justifications for the issuance of the orders are what DeWitt utilized in his decision to order curfew and evacuation. Even McCloy, who pushed for the changes in the Final Report, acknowledges that it is Dewitt's report and that he strongly desired to "avoid creating the impression he could prescribe what the commanding General should say or should not say in the final report." (Exhibit 6, Tab 70, p. 3.)

Two exhibits herein contain statements from DeWitt demonstrating his true attitude about the loyalty of Japanese Americans and the ability to make loyalty determinations. This is the attitude expressed in the original version of the Final Report but which was subsequently altered in the later version. First, based on notes of a January 4, 1942 conference between DeWitt and James Rowe of the Justice Department (Exhibit 30, Tab 62), DeWitt stated:

I have little confidence that the enemy aliens are law-abiding or loyal in any sense of the word . . . particularly the Japanese. I have no confidence in their loyalty whatsoever. I am speaking now of the native born Japanese . . . (p. 1.)

. . . we have lots of aliens who are perfectly loyal who are not American citizens, and some . . . but it is particularly hard to separate the sheep from the goats. (p. 5.)

Second, on January 14, 1943 (Exhibit 12, Tab 63), in a telephone conversation with General Gullion, DeWitt stated, "I don't see how they can determine the loyalty of a Jap by interrogation . . ." Later in the conversation he said, "There isn't such a thing as a loyal Japanese and it is just impossible to determine their loyalty by investigation—it just can't be done."

The evidence of alteration began with transmittal letters dated April 15, 1943 to John J. McCloy (Exhibit 3, Tab 64) and General Marshall (Exhibit 24, Tab 65), in which DeWitt sent to each two printed and bound volumes of his Final Report. He stated in each letter that he was "officially" forwarding these bound copies on that date. He later stated in each letter:

These are going forward via Air Express because I am advised that there is an urgent need of the material contained therein for use in the preparation of the Federal Government's brief in the cases now pending before the Supreme Court of the United States challenging the constitutionality of the entire program.

On April 19, 1943, McCloy called Bendetsen (DeWitt's aide) (Exhibit 5, Tab 66) and said he was worried about the content and form of the Final Report and was upset that the report as transmitted was in final form. The pertinent parts of the conversation were as follows:

B: . . . That isn't—hasn't been distributed except as an official report . . . This is merely his report to—from him on to the War Department.

M: . . . There is no such thing as a separate report—it contains a lot of stuff that I question the wisdom of and it certainly complicates it to get it into a written form such as this. I thought it was perfectly clear that you were going to let us have a galley before it was bound up.

M: . . . I'm not trying to tell you that you can't say what you want to say, but I wanted to put some considerations—we might want to put some considerations before you before you made any report to anybody. But this is all in the air of finality—the letter of transmittal is already printed and signed—completed—done—pat. That is what disturbs me . . . There are a number of things in it which I feel should not be made public—I feel that it, to a large extent, is a sort of self-serving document on this matter of relocation . . .

M: . . . Now it is a sort of document to support the contention that no Jap is ever going to get back into the Western Defense Command. Which was not at all the purpose of the original idea—it was a report on the evacuation and that was all.

B: Sir, I don't think that there was ever any thing that the report should not contain the basis on which the action was taken—and that has been attempted religiously.

M: Bendetsen, you know as well as I do that when you go through that report, that it is pointed to this issue—this question that is now up. Even negation of the suggestion that it wasn't a question of time—it was a matter of—as you put it—facing the facts—clearly—too clearly—pointed to the issue at hand to make any mistake about it.

M: The difference is this. This way it comes up in a completely definitive form—with a letter of transmittal already printed and bound into it and signed, sealed and delivered. The act of the Final Report has now been consummated as of April 15. That is what disturbs me. There is no taking it back.

M: . . . [Y]ou have got to treat this as a report of DeWitt has been made. Final recommendations—even as to how the—how long the Japanese are going to stay there—how a man can make a recommendation without knowing what developments the war is going to take, I don't see. It looks to me as if there is a prejudgment of the problem without getting the facts, but, however, that is done, that's over the dam. I think it is unfortunate that it is over the dam because if any action is taken now it involves the question of overruling which we might have avoided.

After this phone conversation, Bendetsen went to Washington as DeWitt's emissary to discuss changes in the Final Report with McCloy. In a telegram of April 26, 1943 (Exhibit 14, Tab 67), Barnett tells DeWitt:

BENDETSEN TOLD ME THAT HE COULD RECOMMEND ACCEPTANCE OF SOME PARTS OF THE SUGGESTED REVISIONS BUT THAT TWO POINTS WENT TO THE FUNDAMENTAL CONCEPT OF EVACUATION STOP THE PRINCIPAL ONE OF THESE WAS THAT LOYALTY COULD NOT BE DETERMINED AND FOR THAT REASON MASS EVACUATION WAS ORDERED STOP HE REQUESTED INSTRUCTIONS STOP I TOLD HIM IT WAS YOUR REPORT AND THAT THE WAR DEPARTMENT COULD NOT TELL YOU WHAT TO SAY STOP . . .

The next day, DeWitt sends his response back to General Barnett in a telegram (Exhibit 101, Tab 68), which stated:

MY REPORT AS SIGNED AND SUBMITTED TO CHIEF OF STAFF WILL NOT BE CHANGED IN ANY RESPECT WHATSOEVER EIGHER [*sic*] IN SUBSTANCE OR FORM AND I WILL NOT REPEAT NOT CONSENT TO ANY REPEAT ANY REVISION MADE OVER MY SIGNATURE STOP HIGHER AUTHORITY MAY OF COURSE PREPARE AND RELEASE WHATSOEVER THEY DESIRE AS VIEWS OF THAT AUTHORITY BUT STATEMENTS IN MY SIGNED REPORT OF EVACUATION ARE MINE AND SO SUBMITTED STOP SUBMISSION OF PREPARED REVISIONS FOR PRESENTATION TO ME FOR ACCEPTANCE OR REVISION WILL ACCOMPLISH NOTHING AS FINAL WORD ON SUBJECT SO FAR AS I REPEAT I AM CONCERNED HAS BEEN SAID.

On May 3, 1943 (Exhibit 16, Tab 69), Barnett reported to DeWitt:

MCCLOY ANXIOUS THAT BENDETSEN CONFER WITH YOU AT ONCE CONCERNING CHANGES IN FINAL REPORT SUGGESTED BY ASSISTANT SECRETARY WHICH THE LATTER FEELS YOU MAY MAKE ONCE THE BASIS HAS BEEN FULLY EXPLAINED PERIOD . . . SECRETARY CONVINCED THAT FINAL REPORT IMPORTANT TO GOVERNMENT CASE IN SUPREME COURT AND THAT TIME IS SHORT PERIOD HE DOES NOT ASK ANY REVISIONS BE MADE UNLESS YOU CONSIDER THEM AS NOT REPEAT NOT COMPROMISING YOUR PERSONAL VIEWS PERIOD IN SUBSTANCE THESE CHANGES RELATE TO CONFINDING SCOPE OF REPORT TO FACTUAL STATEMENT INCLUDING REASONS FOR EVACUATION SEGREGATING YOUR PROPOSALS FOR FUR-

THER DISPOSITION OF EVACUEES AND PLACING LATER AND SEPARATE DOCUMENT PERIOD . . .

In a memorandum to DeWitt from Bendetsen, also dated May 3, 1943, Bendetsen recorded his discussions with McCloy regarding suggested changes to the Final Report (Exhibit 6, Tab 70), and summarizes the substance of the week's conferences with McCloy relating to, "(a) the attitude and position of the War Department with regard to continued exclusion of the Japanese . . . and (b) the final report of the Commanding General." (p. 1.) Bendetsen reported it was McCloy's position that there no longer existed any military necessity for the continued exclusion of all Japanese from the evacuated zone. McCloy stated: "[T]he War Department, of its own motion, would not take any action to direct or require the revision or revocation of present restrictions in this regard." (p. 1.) Bendetsen reported that McCloy did say, however,

that if the question were to be presented officially to the Secretary of War by the White House or by any other official federal agency having a legitimate interest whether from the viewpoint of the War Department there is any longer any military objection to the return of those Japanese "whose loyalty had been determined," the answer would be, "no." (p. 1.)

Bendetsen responded to McCloy:

if the War Department thought no further military necessity existed and that therefore it could not justify the maintenance of present restrictions . . . then how could the War Department justify the existence of military areas coincident with each relocation center. (The undersigned reminds Mr. McCloy that there never was any military necessity for this action and that it was based only upon the request of the War Relocation Authority for War Department assistance in maintaining proper public relations with the interior states in which the relocation centers exist.) (p. 2.)

Bendetsen related McCloy's two recommended changes in the Final Report relevant to the instant Petition. First, in paragraph 2 of the letter of transmittal the statement appeared that "the necessity of exclusion of all Japanese from the Pacific Coast 'will continue for the duration of the present war.'" A second objection was,

to that portion of Chapter II which said in effect that it is absolutely impossible to determine the loyalty of Japanese no matter how much time was taken in the process. He said that he had no objection to saying that time was of the essence and that in view of the military situation and the fact *that there was no known means of making such a determination with any degree of safety* . . . (Emphasis original, p. 4.)

In a telegram dated May 5, 1943, (Exhibit 18, Tab 71) DeWitt told
Barnett:

HAVE NO DESIRE TO COMPROMISE IN ANY WAY GOVT CASE IN SUPREME COURT
AND DO NOT UNDERSTAND HOW SUBSTANCE AND FORM OF REPORT AS SUBMITTED
CAN HAVE THIS EFFECT STOP . . . DO NOT UNDERSTAND MCCLOYS PROPOSAL STOP
REPORT IS NOW FACTUAL AND I <u>SOLEMNLY</u> SEE MY VIEWS AND ACTIONS DETER-
MINED AS NECESSARY AT TIME OF EVACUATION WEAKENED OR UNDERMINED IF
REPORT CHANGES STOP I CANNOT CONSCIENTIOUSLY CHANGE OR PUT INTO SEPA-
RATE DOCUMENT PROPOSALS FOR FUTURE DISPOSITION OF EVACUEES WITHOUT BY
MY OWN ACT INVALIDATING MY ASSIGNED MISSION AND RESPONSIBILITIES THERE-
UNDER STOP.

General DeWitt then directed the version of the Final Report be revised
and ordered:

ALL COPIES HERETOFORE SENT TO THE WAR DEPARTMENT PAREN NOT INCLUDING
INCLOSURES CLOSE PAREN WILL BE CALLED IN BY YOU AND YOU WILL HAVE WAR
DEPARTMENT RECORDS OF RECEIVING REPORT DESTROYED INASMUCH AS SUCH
REVISION IS FINALLY SENT TO WAR DEPARTMENT WILL HAVE A LATER DATED
TRANSMITTAL LETTER PD. (Exhibit 19, Tab 72.)

Exhibit 7, Tab 73; Exhibit 15, Tab 74; Exhibit 20, Tab 75 are all documents evidencing recommended changes to the original version of
DeWitt's Final Report. These were more than changes in form since they
significantly altered what General DeWitt was putting forth as his rationale for the evacuation. For example, on page iii, paragraph 2, second
sentence of the original version of the Final Report (Exhibit 4, Tab 17),
the words, "and will continue for the duration of the war," were eliminated and were replaced with the words, ". . . their loyalties were unknown and time was of the essence." On page 9, second complete
paragraph, the fifth and sixth sentences of the Final Report (Exhibit 4,
Tab 17), including DeWitt's assertion that it was not that there was insufficient time to separate the loyal from disloyal, was substituted for the
following, "to complicate the situation, no ready means existed for determining the loyal and disloyal with any degree of safety . . ." In the telegram of May 9, 1943 (Exhibit 20, Tab 75), Barnett reviewed the changes
and confirmed that, ". . . changes fifteen through fifty five, inclusive,
which include number twenty seven [It was not that there was insufficient
time . . . (p. 9)] have been adopted."

Also on May 9, 1943, in a telegram from Bendetsen to Barnett (Exhibit
8, Tab 76), Bendetsen ordered Barnett to, "take action to call in all copies
previously sent to WD less inclosures and to have WD destroy all records
of receipt of report as when final revision is forwarded letter of transmittal

will be redated." Exhibits 9, 25, 21, 10, 26, 27, 22, 23, with the Tabs 77 through 84, document the attempt to recall all copies of the original version of the Final Report. As requested by DeWitt, War Department records regarding receipt of the original version of the Final Report were "adjusted accordingly." (See Exhibit 10, Tab 80.) The revised version of the Final Report was mailed to the Chief of Staff on June 18, 1943, with the transmittal letter dated June 15, 1943. (Exhibits 27, 22 and 23, Tabs 82, 83 and 84.) The galley proofs, galley pages, drafts and memorandum of the Final Report were destroyed on June 29, 1943. (Exhibit 11, Tab 87.)

C. Use of Evidence That the Government Knew or Should Have Known To Be False

The Government presented the Courts with false "evidence" suggesting that Japanese Americans engaged in acts of espionage and sabotage. This "evidence" was contradicted by information in the possession of the Government. The Court, unaware of the falsity of these allegations, relied on these "facts" to uphold the constitutionality of the curfew and exclusion orders. It is established law that a conviction of a defendant based on false evidence is "inconsistent with the rudimentary demands of justice." *Mooney* v. *Holohan*, 294 U.S. 103 at 112 (1935). Following *Mooney*, courts have consistently held that the prosecutor's knowing use of false evidence is unconstitutional. *Pyle* v. *Kansas*, 317 U.S. 213 (1942); *Hysler* v. *Florida*, 315 U.S. 411 (1942); *Giglio* v. *United States*, 405 U.S. 150 (1972). It is not only improper for the prosecution to affirmatively misrepresent facts, but it is just as improper for the prosecution to create an inference of guilt by omitting material facts. As stated in *Imbler* v. *Craven*, 298 F. Supp. 795, 806 (C.D. Cal. 1969), affd sub nom., *Imbler* v. *California*, 424 F.2d 631 (9th Cir.), cert. denied, 400 U.S. 865 (1970):

omissions and half-truths are equally damaging and prohibited, and their use is no less culpable. Creating an *inference* that a fact exists when in fact to the knowledge of the prosecution it does not, constitutes the knowing use of false testimony.

Evidence may be false either because it is perjured, or, though not in itself factually inaccurate, because it creates a false impression of facts which are known not to be true. (Citations omitted. Emphasis added.)

In Petitioner's case, the central issue before the Court was whether the Public Law 503 and the underlying military orders were constitutional.

To support its argument of military necessity, the Government used the false evidence described herein to paint a false and misleading picture of imminent threat to the security of the West Coast. Whether by affirmative misrepresentation, suggestive inference, or by failure to disclose contrary evidence, the Government knowingly and purposefully made a false impression on the courts.

As mentioned above, the Government had in its possession intelligence reports and other documents that rebutted statements it made to the Court. Based upon these reports from responsible intelligence agencies, the Government knew or should have known that it was presenting false information to the Court.

The misrepresentations made to the courts offended elementary standards of justice, seriously prejudiced the accused, violated the sanctity of the courts, and undermined the public confidence in the administration of justice. Therefore, this Court should grant Petitioner's prayer for relief.

In addition, where the prosecutor used perjured testimony to obtain a conviction, the courts have reversed the conviction if there was "any reasonable likelihood that the false testimony *could have affected the judgment of the jury.*" *Agurs*, 427 U.S. at 103 (emphasis added). The same standard of materiality should apply when, as here, the Government knowingly used false evidence to obtain Petitioner's convictions and defend those convictions on appeal.

1. Misrepresentation. During the evidentiary hearing, Edward Ennis testified that because no factual record was developed at the trial court level, the Government in its brief to the Supreme Court relied almost exclusively on the doctrine of Judicial Notice to create its "factual basis" for the military orders. (See also Exhibit 99, pp. 10–11.) The Government argued: (1) the racial, religious and cultural characteristics of Japanese Americans predisposed them to disloyalty; (2) there was not sufficient time to separate the loyal from the disloyal; and (3) the Government's military necessity claim was supported by evidence which it could not reveal to the Court because it was a "closely guarded military secret." (Government's brief, Exhibit 99, p. 12.)

In its brief (Exhibit 99), the Government first asked the Court to take judicial notice of "facts" such as: concentration of Japanese population on the West Coast (pp. 17, 33–34, 46); religion (Shintoism and Buddhism) (pp. 25–28); attendance at Japanese language schools (pp. 30–31); membership in cultural or social organizations (p. 31); dual citizenship (pp. 24–25); and Japanese Americans who were educated in Japan (Kibei) (pp. 28–29). The Government then argued that these "racial characteristics" proved that a great number of Japanese Americans were very likely to be disloyal. Respondent made this argument despite evidence indicating the "facts" were in dispute, and therefore, not appropriate for judicial notice. Petitioner's convictions were gained based upon racist characterizations which Respondent misrepresented were not subject to reasonable dispute.[4]

The Ringle Reports (to ONI on January 26, 1942 and the expanded version to WRA in June of 1942) and the Munson Reports directly contradicted the Government's arguments about loyalty, except for the part of the argument as it related to the Kibei. These comprehensive intelligence reports discussed and refuted the very same "racial characteristics" used by the Government in its argument to the Court. These were the only intelligence reports which evaluated and analyzed these characteristics as they related to the ethnic Japanese population after Pearl Harbor. Thus, had the Government been required to put forth facts to support its judicial notice argument, its own "expert witnesses" (Ringle, Munson, ONI and FBI) would not have supported the Government's case as represented to the Court.

The Government further argued that not only did racial characteristics predispose Japanese Americans to disloyalty, but an attack by Japan on the West Coast was imminent and the disloyal element was organized into a "fifth column" which would aid the attack. The Government's brief states:

. . . the military situation was so grave, the danger of an enemy attack was so far within the realm of probability, and the peril to be apprehended from treacherous assistance to the enemy on the part of an unknown number of Japanese concentrated in critical areas along the West Coast was so substantial it was a matter of high military necessity to take prompt precautionary steps. (p. 61.)

These representations were made to the Court despite the fact that the G-2 reports indicated there was no threat of imminent attack. On February 17, 1942, the Attorney General directly stated to the President: "There is no evidence of imminent attack and from the FBI that there is no evidence of planned sabotage." (Exhibit 79, Tab 34.) Thus, these representations were made in the Government's brief in spite of the fact that the only Government reports which investigated and analyzed this entire issue, the Munson, Ringle and FBI reports, stated there was no evidence of fifth column activity.

---

[4] See Discussion of judicial notice as utilized by the Government in *Hirabayashi* in Exhibit A-66, Dembitz, *Racial Discrimination and the Military Judgment: The Supreme Court's Korematsu and*

Further compounding this misrepresentation, the Government supported its fifth column position by first noting how Japanese espionage aided the Pearl Harbor attack (p. 45) and then noting:

The overwhelming majority of persons of Japanese ancestry in the United States resided on the West Coast . . . a number of them, citizen and aliens alike might be disposed to assist the enemy, particularly in the case of an attack. (p. 46.)

The Government thereby asked the Court to draw the false inference that Japanese Americans were involved in the Pearl Harbor attack. There was never any evidence to support this allegation and the Munson Reports, Ringle Reports and FBI reports in the Government's possession did not support the Government's position.

The Government also argued that time was of the essence and that there was no ready means to identify and separate the loyal from the disloyal. (Exhibit 99, pp. 34, 46, 62, 63.) However, DeWitt did not base his decision to issue the orders on either of these reasons. DeWitt's position was that loyalty could not be determined regardless of whether or not there was sufficient time.[5] Thus, by presenting a justification which was not a consideration for the issuance of the orders and by not telling the Court the true basis for the decision, the Government falsely represented the true facts to the Court on this crucial issue.

As to the Government's ability to identify and separate the loyal from the disloyal, it should be noted that those considered most dangerous were not only easily identifiable, but, in fact, before issuance of EO 9066, were all arrested and detained. The FBI and ONI had prepared lists of suspected dangerous individuals from even before Pearl Harbor.

Furthermore, Government witnesses at the evidentiary hearing testified that the investigative agencies thoroughly and competently conducted investigations on all reports of suspected subversive activities. The Respondent's own documents clearly show that these agencies had compiled lists of names, addresses, employment and membership in organizations of all individuals considered dangerous. See Exhibits A17f; A17h; A22; and A40. Thus, despite the fact the Government had lists of identified potentially dangerous people even prior to Pearl Harbor and despite the fact that each one of these individuals had been investigated, monitored and

---

Endo Decisions, 45 Columbia Law Review 174, 183–189 (1945). Nanette Dembitz was herself a former Government attorney who participated in preparation of the U.S. brief in *Hirabayashi*.

[5] See Exhibit 30, Tab 62 and Exhibit 12, Tab 63. See also the first version of the Final Report (Exhibit 4, Tab 17), which states that the evacuation will continue for the "duration of the present war." (p. iii), and: "It was not that there was insufficient time in which to make such a determination . . ." (p. 9.)

later arrested, the Government nonetheless represented that this could not be done.

Finally, by identifying, investigating and arresting suspicious individuals, the Government showed that "ready means" were available to make a loyalty determination. Also, as Mr. Ennis testified, loyalty hearings were conducted and determinations were made for enemy aliens, Japanese and Germans, but not for Japanese Americans, which thereby resulted in aliens receiving "more due process than citizens." Although the Government was utilizing a "ready means," it represented to the Court that there was no workable method (i.e., no "ready means") to make loyalty determinations.

The Government's last main argument was a suggestion to the Court that secret information in its possession proved military necessity. (Exhibit 99, p. 12.) The Government in fact had no evidence which would justify evacuation of over 120,000 people. It was suggested by the Government during the course of the instant proceedings that diplomatic intercepts provided the basis for the decision to evacuate. There is no evidence which even suggests that DeWitt utilized the diplomatic intercepts in any form or even that he utilized the information from the intercepts as a basis for his decision to order evacuation.

The intercepts offered by the Respondent in the instant case are totally irrelevant to the issues of governmental misconduct and violation of Petitioner's due process. Assuming arguendo they are relevant, the intercepts themselves at most contain a request from Tokyo to the consulate to recruit second generation Japanese for information collecting. Assuming arguendo the consulates were successful in this assigned mission, as Colonel Herzig testified there is an enormous and significant difference from a military intelligence perspective between the collection of raw information obtained from publicly available sources and intelligence or espionage operations, which refer to covertly obtaining and analyzing information.

However, there is not a single cable nor group of cables taken collectively, which can reasonably demonstrate that recruitment efforts were successful. There was never any evidence of a second generation espionage network which operated for Japan. No Japanese American was ever convicted of espionage or sabotage activities in the U.S. Furthermore, all suspected individuals and organizations were easily identifiable and thoroughly investigated by the proper authorities and the results of all investigations were negative.

The Supreme Court in its opinion in *Hirabayashi* accepted in total these misrepresentations about racial characteristics, loyalty and fifth column threat. The Court stated:

The German invasion of the Western European countries had given ample warning to the world of the menace of the "fifth column." Espionage by persons in sympathy with the Japanese Government had been found to have been particularly effective in the surprise attack on Pearl Harbor . . . At a time of threatened attack upon this country, the nature of our inhabitants' attachment to the Japanese enemy was consequently a matter of grave concern.

Hirabayashi v. *United States*, supra at 96.

In incorporating the Government's arguments, the Court discussed the social factors preventing assimilation of the ethnic Japanese; Japanese language schools; Japanese Americans born and educated in Japan; and, dual citizenship (*Id.* at 96–99) and then concluded:

. . . Whatever views we may entertain regarding the loyalty to this country of the citizens of Japanese ancestry, we cannot reject as unfounded the judgment of the military authorities and of Congress that there were disloyal members of that population, whose number and strength could not be precisely and quickly ascertained. We cannot say that the war-making branches of the Government did not have ground for believing that in a critical hour such persons could not readily be isolated and separately dealt with, and constituted a menace to the national defense and safety, which demanded that prompt and adequate measures be taken to guard against it.

Id. at 99.

. . . But as we have seen, those facts, and the inferences which could be rationally drawn from them, support the judgment of the military commander that the danger of espionage and sabotage to our military resources was imminent, and that the curfew order was appropriate to meet it.

Id. at 103–104.

2. Abuse of Amici. Not only did the Government misrepresent the facts to the courts by tailoring a set of facts by judicial notice and by suppressing obviously exculpatory evidence, but the Government used the States of California, Washington and Oregon as amici curiae to present its tailored facts to the Court.

As discussed above, War Department officials withheld DeWitt's Final Report from the Justice Department until January 1944. Nonetheless, War Department officials did release the initial version of the Final Report for presentation to the Supreme Court through the amici curiae. DeWitt personally delegated a member of his legal staff, Captain Herbert E. Wenig, to assist the Attorney General of California in preparing the amici brief on behalf of the three West Coast states. (Exhibit 91, Tab 88.)

As both Burling and Ennis realized when they finally received the Final Report and the amici brief, much of the material contained in the amici brief was taken from the Final Report. (Exhibit 111, Tab 89; Exhibit 2, Tab 90.) In his memo to Wechsler dated September 30, 1944, Ennis states:

It is also to be noted that parts of the report which, in April 1942 could not be shown to the Department of Justice in connection with the Hirabayashi case in the Supreme Court, were printed in the brief amici curiae of the States of California, Oregon and Washington. In fact the Western Defense Command evaded the statutory requirement that this Department represent the Government in this litigation by preparing the erroneous and intemperate brief which the States filed.

It is entirely clear that the War Department entered into an arrangement with the Western Defense Command to rewrite demonstrably erroneous items in the report by reducing to implication and inference what had been expressed less expertly by the Western Defense Command and then contrived to publish this report without the knowledge of this Department by use of falsehood and evasion.

(Exhibit 2, Tab 90, pp. 3–4.)

3. *Continued Misconduct*. The Government continued its pattern of misconduct beyond the decision by the Supreme Court in Petitioner's case. Petitioner asserts that Government attorneys are obligated to disclose to a defendant or the courts obviously exculpatory and newly discovered evidence which comes to the Government's attention even after the close of a case. However, not only did it fail to make such disclosures, the Government continued to make misrepresentations to the Court despite its knowledge of evidence to the contrary.

As discussed before, once DeWitt's Final Report was released and available to the Department of Justice, Justice Department attorneys investigated the accuracy of allegations asserted in the Final Report. After receiving reports from the FBI and the FCC directly refuting the allegations, Government attorneys responsible for the Supreme Court brief in the pending *Korematsu* case attempted to advise the Court of the situation. Pursuant to this, John Burling inserted the following footnote into the brief to the Supreme Court in *Korematsu*:

The Final Report of General DeWitt (which is dated June 5, 1943, but which was not made public until January 1944) is relied on in this brief for statistics and other details concerning the actual evacuation and the events that took place subsequent thereto. The recital of the circumstances justifying the evacuation as a matter of military necessity, however, is in several respects, particularly with reference to the use of illegal radio transmitters and shore-to-ship signalling by persons of Japanese ancestry, in conflict with information in possession of the Department of Justice. In view of the contrariety of the reports on this matter we do not ask the Court to take judicial notice of the recital of those facts contained in the Report.

(Exhibit 84, Tab 43.) In explaining the footnote to Herbert Wechsler, Burling stated:

You will recall that General DeWitt's report makes flat statements concerning radio transmitters and ship-to-shore signalling which are categorically denied by the FBI and by the Federal Communications Commission. There is no doubt that these statements were intentional falsehoods, inasmuch as the Federal Communications Commission reported in detail to General DeWitt on the absence of any illegal radio transmission. . . . The statements made by General DeWitt are not only contrary to our views but they are contrary to detailed information in our possession and we ought to say so.

(Exhibit 84, Tab 43.)

The War Department objected to this footnote and undertook to remove it from the Justice Department's brief. In a memo to Ennis, Burling stated:

It became necessary for you to suggest the possibility to Captain Fisher that the brief had gone for final printing and, presumably as a result of this, Mr. McCloy called the Solicitor General and particularly referred to the footnote. Presumably at Mr. McCloy's request, the Solicitor General had the printing stopped at about noon.

(Exhibit 85, Tab 92.) Ennis urged to Wechsler that the footnote remain unchanged:

This Department has an ethical obligation to the Court to refrain from citing it [the Final Report] as a source of which the Court may properly take judicial notice if the Department knows that important statements in the source are untrue and if it knows as to other statements that there is such contrariety of information that judicial notice is improper.

(Exhibit 2, Tab 90.)

The War Department implicitly recognized that the Final Report was problematic, but did not wish to present any criticism of the Final Report to the Court's attention:

Captain Fisher came to the Solicitor General's office and discussed the footnote. Captain Fisher took the position that he would not defend the accuracy of the report but that the Government would deal with sufficient honesty with the court if it would merely refrain from reciting the report without affirmatively flagging our [Burling and Ennis] criticism thereof.

(Exhibit 85, Tab 92.)

Pursuant to the War Department's efforts, the footnote was finally revised to read:

The Final Report of General DeWitt (which is dated June 5, 1943, but which was not made public until January 1944), hereinafter cited as *Final Report*, is relied on in this brief for statistics and other details concerning the actual evacuation and the events that took place subsequent thereto. We have specifically recited in this brief the facts relating to the justification for the evacuation, of which we ask the Court to take judicial notice, and we rely upon the *Final Report* only to the extent that it relates to such facts.

(Exhibit 87, Tab 91; Exhibit 86, Tab 93; Exhibit A-48a, page 11.)

This revised footnote did not fulfill the Government's obligation to disclose to Petitioner and the Court evidence contrary to the misrepresentations of the Final Report. Therefore, the Government's failure to make a proper disclosure constituted a continuation of the pattern of misconduct which denied Petitioner of his rights to due process.

However, the pattern of misconduct did not stop there. Charles Fahy, in oral argument before the Supreme Court in the *Korematsu* case, discussed the brief's footnote:

It is even suggested that because of some foot note in our brief in this case indicating that we do not ask the Court to take judicial notice of the truth of every recitation or instance in the final report of General DeWitt, that the Government has repudiated the military necessity of the evacuation. It seems to me, if the Court please, that that is a neat little piece of fancy dancing. There is nothing in the brief of the Government which is any different in this respect from the position it has always maintained since the Hirabayashi case—that not only the military judgment of the general, but the judgment of the Government of the United States, has always been in justification of the measures taken; and *no person in any responsible position has ever taken a contrary position*, and the Government does not do so now. Nothing in this brief can validly be used to the contrary.

(Emphasis added. Exhibit 98, Tab 19, p. 7.)

V. Adverse Legal Consequences

The existence of present adverse legal consequences flowing from Petitioner's criminal convictions is presumed. *Sibron* v. *New York*, 392 U.S. 40 (1968). The Government has the burden of overcoming this presumption. *Id.* The Government has failed to show that there is no possibility of collateral legal consequences.

Moreover, Petitioner has demonstrated the possibility of adverse legal consequences. These include moral stigma and injury to reputation. See Exhibits 134 and 138. These also include the possibility that the conviction will be used for impeachment purposes in some future legal proceeding or that the conviction will become a consideration in some future sentencing. Even though the adverse use of Petitioner's conviction appears remote, a coram nobis petition must be available to prevent manifest injustice. *Holloway* v. *United States*, 393 F.2d 731, 732 (9th Cir., 1968).

VI. Conclusion

As established in the instant proceedings, Petitioner, through its witnesses and exhibits, developed a record which proved a shocking and indefensible pattern of governmental misconduct. In contrast, the record as developed by the Respondent did not significantly rebut the evidence submitted by the Petitioner. No document the Government put into evidence even suggests the misconduct, as presented by the Petitioner, did not in fact occur. No document in evidence legally justifies the misconduct.

Both John McCloy and Karl Bendetsen, former Government officials, had first-hand knowledge of suppression, misrepresentation, alteration and destruction of evidence from the Government's perspective. Both, as Ennis testified, are alive and available to testify, and yet the Government elected not to call these witnesses. Instead, the Government paraded a series of witnesses whose testimonies provide absolutely no insight into the real issues at hand.

After 40 years of enduring his convictions, Mr. Hirabayashi has remained steadfast in his belief and faith in the American judicial system. He comes before the Court to vindicate that faith in the Constitution. Mr. Hirabayashi is motivated by his belief that the Constitution is more than just a scrap of paper. The record of his convictions, as they stand today, based upon a record of suppression, alteration and destruction of evidence, remains a violation of the Constitution and lies like a "loaded weapon."[6] As Justice Jackson stated in his dissent in *Korematsu* v. *United States*, 323 U.S. 214, 246 (1944):

---

[6]The errors and violations of Petitioner's due process rights are not restricted to those arising from prosecutorial misconduct. Offer of Proof Exhibit 142 establishes that the original trial court denied Petitioner his constitutional right to a jury trial when that court directed the jury to find the Defendant guilty based upon the ancestry of the Defendant.

[O]nce a judicial opinion rationalizes such an order to show that it conforms to the Constitution, or rather rationalizes the Constitution to show that the Constitution sanctions such an order, the Court for all time has validated the principle of racial discrimination in criminal procedure and of transplanting American citizens. *The principle then lies about like a loaded weapon ready for the hand of any authority that can bring forward a plausible claim of an urgent need.* Every repetition imbeds that principle more deeply in our law and thinking and expands it to new purposes.

But if we review and approve, that passing incident becomes the doctrine of the Constitution. There it has a generative power of its own, and all that it creates will be in its own image. Nothing better illustrates this danger than does the Court's opinion in this case. (Emphasis added.)

As evidenced by the person who from the audience during the evidentiary hearing announced "the reason is because *they* bombed Pearl Harbor"; by the letters received by the Petitioner (Exhibits 134 and 138); by the recent slaying of Vincent Chin, a Chinese American who was beaten to death by out-of-work auto workers who blamed the Japanese for their unemployment; and even as evidenced by the defense offered by the Government in the instant proceedings, the distinction between citizens of Japan and Japanese Americans which was not made over 40 years ago is still pervasive in our society. Americans did not bomb Pearl Harbor, yet Americans were unjustly deprived of their constitutional rights.

To be an American citizen will only be a cherished, treasured and respected status when all rights are preserved for all citizens. By correction of this Court's record, a statement would be made that rights guaranteed to all Americans, whatever their ancestry, will be safeguarded and upheld in the American system of justice. As Mr. Hirabayashi stated before this Court, "This is not just a Japanese American case; this is an *American* case."

Respectfully submitted,

Rodney L. Kawakami, Attorney for Petitioner
Arthur G. Barnett, Attorney for Petitioner
Camden M. Hall, of Foster, Pepper & Riviera, Attorneys for Petitioner
Michael Leong, Attorney for Petitioner
Daniel J. Ichinaga, Attorney for Petitioner
Craig Kobayashi, of Foster, Pepper & Riviera, Attorneys for Petitioner
Benson D. Wong, Attorney for Petitioner

Hirabayashi v. United States

Government's Post-Hearing Brief, U.S. District Court for
the Western District of Washington

September 5, 1985

*The government answered Hirabayashi's post-hearing brief by firmly
denying that any of the documents or testimony presented at the evidentiary hearing supported his claim "that there was prosecutorial misconduct which resulted in a fundamental miscarriage of justice." The brief
cast the testimony of Edward Ennis in a light favorable to the government, arguing that Ennis had testified that "none of the governmental
activities" in the trial and appeals of the Hirabayashi case "were improper or unconstitutional." On its own side, the brief cited the testimony
of David Lowman on the Magic cables to support a conclusion that
"General DeWitt's recommendation to evacuate all 'potentially dangerous' individuals" from the West Coast was based on evidence of
espionage activity by Japanese Americans. The brief concluded that
Hirabayashi had been unable to meet the burden of showing that the
evidence he presented would have resulted in the Supreme Court's reversal of his convictions.*

I. The Proceedings Below

On May 8, 1942, an indictment was filed in the United States District
Court for the Western District of Washington charging the petitioner,
Gordon Kiyoshi Hirabayashi, a resident of a designated military area,
with two misdemeanors, i.e., failing to report to the Civil Control Station
on May 12, 1942 as required by Civilian Exclusion Order No. 57 (Count
I) and failing to remain within his residence between 8:00 p.m. and
6:00 a.m. on May 4, 1942 as required by Public Proclamation No. 3
(Count II), both of which military regulations were issued pursuant to
Presidential Executive Order 9066 (Feb. 19, 1942). (Ex. 141, pp. 1–3.)
On September 15, 1942, in the district court, United States District Judge

Lloyd L. Black, rejected both petitioner's pretrial demurrer and amended demurrer to the charges (*id*. at 9; reprinted at 46 F. Supp. 657), expressly invoking the doctrine of judicial notice:

The defendant, after filing an original demurrer, later, pursuant to court permission, interposed an amended demurrer to each such count of the indictment upon the grounds that the orders and proclamations involved are unconstitutional by virtue of being in violation of the Fifth Amendment and of Article 4, Section 2, Clause 1 of the Constitution of the United States, and also are not authorized by Executive Order of the President or by any valid legislative act or law of Congress.

. . . The matter was presented to the court after oral argument supplementing very extensive briefs which in the aggregate cited about one hundred thirty court decisions and several texts. . . .

In substance and effect the defendant's position is that *regardless of how critical the war perils, of how necessary and vital the military area, and of how essential to American success in this conflict the curfew provisions and evacuation orders applicable to those of Japanese ancestry in such military area may be,* that the armed forces of this country and our government are absolutely helpless to make or enforce any such curfew provisions or exclusion orders until a Constitutional amendment has been proposed, voted by both houses of Congress, and finally adopted by three-fourths of the states. (*Id*. at 10, emphasis added.)

It was recently stated in *State of California* v. *Anglim*, 129 F.2d (CCA 9th) 455:

". . . The same act at one time may be regarded as constitutional by facts *judicially noted* or other facts then shown, and at another time, on other known or proved facts, be held unconstitutional. It was so held in an opinion by Mr. Justice Holmes in *Chastleton Corp.* v. *Sinclair*, 264 U.S. 543, 548, 549, 44 S.Ct. 405, 67 L.Ed. 841, in determining the constitutionality of the rent regulating law for the District of Columbia."

And so the decision of this case must be in the light of the unprecedented world conflict which so suddenly engulfed this nation, in the light of this being a declared Military Area, in the light of the dangers that would confront us if defendant should prevail, in the light of the advantage to this nation and actually to those of Japanese ancestry from the orders and proclamations which defendant attacks.

This Pacific Coast has been shelled at Santa Barbara, Seaside, Vancouver Island, ships have been submarined without warning in sight of shore, sinking has occurred near the entrance to the straits that lead to Puget Sound, Dutch Harbor has been bombed, and a formidable force of Japanese soldiers occupies Kiska Island. Who can guarantee that they who have already invaded the western Aleutians have not since Pearl Harbor been perfecting plans to attack by carrier planes and suicide parachutists the vital Seattle bomber factories, our docks so essential to Alaska's life, the navy yard at Bremerton just across the bay? (*Id*. at 11–12, emphasis added.)

In the very recent opinion under date of July 29, 1942 of the United States District Judge F. Ryan Duffy in the Lincoln Seiichi Kanai habeas corpus proceeding before him [*Ex parte Kanai*, 46 F. Supp. 286 (E.D. Wisc.)], in which such petitioner, an American citizen of Japanese ancestry, challenged the constitutionality of said Presidential Order 9066 and attacked the validity of the same Military Area No. 1 herein involved, the court said:

". . . This court will not constitute itself as a board of strategy, and declare what is a necessary or proper military area.

". . . The field of military operation is not confined to the scene of actual physical combat. Our cities and transportation systems, our coastline, our harbors, and even our agricultural areas are all vitally important in the all-out war effort in which our country must engage if our form of government is to survive. . . . This court can take *judicial notice* of the extensive manufacturing facilities for airplanes and other munitions of war which are located on or near our west coast." (*Id*. at 13–14, emphasis added.)

The defendant may most properly *be deemed* by the President, military forces and Congress as residing in a portion of a vital military fortress and factory arsenal. (*Ex parte Ventura*, supra, 44 F. Supp. 520 [W.D. Wash. 1942].)

In view of the war emergency the President and the Commander of this defense command, as authorized by Congress in said Public Law 503, may determine whether persons of Japanese ancestry shall observe curfew in a military area and whether they shall be removed therefrom. (*Id*. at 15, emphasis added.)

Petitioner's one day jury trial followed on October 20, 1942 at which he was convicted on both counts and sentenced to concurrent three month terms of imprisonment (*id*. at 24). In lieu of utilizing a trial transcript in his direct appeal, petitioner's counsel filed a bill of exceptions summarizing the trial testimony and proceedings, which summary was certified as accurate by the district court (*id*. 31–37). That summary shows that petitioner unsuccessfully sought jury instruc. ons that would have required the jury to find that he personally was guilty of a crime such as espionage or sabotage before the jury could convict him for failing to obey the military regulations (*id*. 20–22, 35). By motion for directed verdict, petitioner renewed his constitutional arguments, and he made a different judicial notice argument than he makes here, i.e.,

that the court erred in *taking judicial notic* of Executive Order #9066, Public Proclamations 2 and 3 and Civilian Exclusion Order #57 of the Military Commander as they were unconstitutional and void, and that Public Law #503 under which the action was prosecuted was not a valid criminal statute. (*Id*. 35–36, emphasis added.)

As petitioner concedes, he did not and "does not deny that he knowingly violated Public Law 503 and the underlying military curfew and evacuation orders" (Pet.'s Post-Hearing Br. at 4:22–23) since "the central issue before the Court was whether the Public Law 503 and the underlying military orders were constitutional." (*Id.* at 37:10–11.)

Petitioner did not take exception to the district court's written pretrial statement that petitioner's legal position did not depend upon "how critical the war perils, . . . how necessary and vital the military area, and . . . how essential to American success" were the military regulations. (Ex. 141 at 10.) Petitioner also did not take exception to the district court's "taking judicial notice" in its written pretrial opinion that there existed a West Coast "war emergency," including a realistic exposure to airplane and submarine raids on the "vital" West Coast bomber factories, docks and navy yards in that very military area which the district court "deemed . . . a vital military fortress and factory arsenal." (*Id.* at 10–15.) Both petitioner's bill of exceptions and the testimony of Edward Ennis (at the coram nobis hearing) confirm that at petitioner's trial which followed the trial court's written opinion, petitioner did not make any factual record nor seek to make any factual record disputing the existence of a bona fide West Coast "war emergency."

Moreover, during the government's case in chief, the prosecution called Captain Michael Revisto, the "officer of the U.S. Army in Charge of Japanese evacuation in Seattle under Lt. Gen. J. L. DeWitt" (*id.* at 33), who was an Assistant G-2, i.e., an intelligence officer (coram nobis hearing testimony of William Hammond; see also the original subpoena contained in the original district court file). Petitioner's 1942 bill of exceptions reflects that the petitioner neither sought nor received testimony from this intelligence officer about the particular intelligence information in that military area which was pending before General DeWitt. In addition, after the prosecution rested, petitioner did not prove nor proffer any "other facts" (Ex. 141 at 11) in his direct case to contradict the district court's judicially noticed conclusion that there was a "war emergency."

In his Statement of Points on Appeal, petitioner listed the constitutional claims and the cases upon which he relied (*id.* at 40–43). He did not note any factual arguments.

Petitioner's case was briefed and argued in the Ninth Circuit prior to the time that the Supreme Court ordered the whole case certified up to it on April 5, 1943 (Ex. 141 at 43; Ex. 126 at 4). Petitioner's opening Ninth Circuit brief raised only legal errors (Ex. 124 at 1–2, Argument *Summary* I.–IV.) i.e., "the constitutionality or validity of the President's Executive Order No. 9066 . . . and of the Public Proclamation Nos. 1, 2, and 3 and Civilian Exclusion Order No. 57 . . ." (*id.* p. 2 of "Statement of Pleadings and Facts"). Regarding the "emergency of war" asserted by the government (*id.* at 8), petitioner responded that absent martial law, which was not in effect on the West Coast, factual proof of a war emergency was irrelevant and "the President, Secretary of War and Military Commanders were and are without constitutional power or authority to enforce either the exclusion order or the law against American citizens." (*Id.* at 10.) Alternatively, petitioner argued that the "due process" clause of the Fifth Amendment requires that each Japanese American who was a citizen must be convicted of a crime such as treason before being interned (*id.* 10–12).[1]

In petitioner's Ninth Circuit reply brief, petitioner quoted at length from the October 1942 *Harper's* magazine article "The Japanese in America" (Ex. A-5 at 2-4) and stated that individual loyalty consideration of each Japanese American was required because the author of that article considered that "at least 75% of them (American born United States citizens of Japanese ancestry) are loyal to the United States." (*Id.* at 3.) Petitioner went on to urge the Ninth Circuit to "take judicial notice" (*id.* at 3) that the FBI had the situation well in hand, and that published statements of Secretary of War Stimson, Assistant Attorney General Rowe, and California Attorney General Earl Warren stated that there was no sabotage in Pearl Harbor and no sabotage or Fifth Column activity in California. (*Id.* 3–6.)

Petitioner continued (Ex. A-5 at 11):

> We commend to the court for reading in its entirety the clear, able and decisive opinion of Judge Fee in the Yasui case [*United States* v. *Yasui*, 48 F. Supp. 40 (D. Or. 1942)], *supra*. Judge Fee's digest of the law on this subject and his reasoning is so persuasive that we contend that the law as stated in his opinion is still the law of this land and is controlling and conclusive in this case.

Judge Fee's *Yasui* opinion emphasized the legal significance of the failure to declare martial law and also states that "it is obvious during the clash of arms the evidence of the military necessities cannot be adduced in a civil court." 48 F. Supp. at 52.[2]

---

[1] Petitioner acknowledged, however, that there was a potential loyalty threat presented by Japanese *aliens* in the United States, stating: "There exists a sound reason for a suspicion that alien enemies, those who owe their allegiance to hostile powers, would commit such acts of treason—it would be but the natural thing for them to do. . . ." (*Id.* at 11.)

[2] As the coram nobis petition here pointed out, at Yasui's federal district court trial Judge Fee had sustained Yasui's objection to the government's proffers of direct evidence—offered to prove the necessity for a curfew and the government's concern about divided loyalties—on the ground that such evidence was irrelevant. (Hirabayashi's coram nobis petition at p. 74 fn. 6 & 7, and p. 76 fn. 10.)

Summing up all his arguments, petitioner's 1943 Ninth Circuit Reply Brief concludes (Ex. A-5 at 18):

Conclusion

In conclusion, appellant contends that the real issues in this case have not been met and cannot be met by counsel for the Government and that this court must hold that it is the law of this land that,

(a) Until martial law is established by the Congress, the Military Commanders have no jurisdiction of civilians;

(b) That until he was granted a hearing on the question of his loyalty to this country, where he would be given his day in court and a right to establish that loyalty, appellant could not be forced to leave his home and go into internment;

(c) That the war powers of the President do not and cannot supercede the jurisdiction of the civil courts, and

(d) That Public Law No. 503 for the reasons set forth in appellant's opening brief and this brief is unconstitutional and void.

Therefore the verdict of the jury must be set aside, the judgment of the trial court overruled and the demurrer of the appellant to the indictment sustained.

Edward Ennis, then Director of the Department of Justice Alien Enemy Unit, testified (at the coram nobis hearing) that in 1943 he argued the *Hirabayashi* and *Yasui* cases in the Ninth Circuit on behalf of the government. During that 1943 oral argument Ennis readily admitted that from December 7, 1941 to May 12, 1942 "not one of these 70,000 Japanese descended citizen deportees had filed against him in any federal court of this circuit an indictment or information charging espionage, sabotage or any treasonable act." (Ex. 126 at 41.)

In the Supreme Court, petitioner contended

. . . only that Congress unconstitutionally delegated its legislative power to the military commander by authorizing him to impose the challenged regulation, and that, even if the regulation were in other respects lawfully authorized, the Fifth Amendment prohibits the discrimination made between citizens of Japanese descent and those of other ancestry. (320 U.S. 81, 89.)

His current petition argues that the Supreme Court was misled by the government in its resolution of this latter "due process" claim (Pet.'s Post-Hearing Br. at 4).

In disposing of petitioner's due process claim, the Supreme Court specifically noted—as had the district court in its pretrial written opinion—that "Appellant [Hirabayashi] does not deny that, given the danger, a curfew was an appropriate measure against sabotage." (320 U.S. at 99.)

The Court also noted:

. . . The alternative which appellant insists must be accepted is for the military authorities to impose the curfew on all citizens within the military area, or on none. In a case of threatened danger requiring prompt action, it is a choice between inflicting obviously needless hardship on the many, or sitting passive and unresisting in the presence of the threat. We think that constitutional government, in time of war, is not so powerless and does not compel so hard a choice if those charged with the responsibility of our national defense have reasonable ground for believing that the threat is real. (320 U.S. at 95.)

. . . Congress, and the military authorities acting with its authorization, have constitutional power to appraise the danger in the light of facts of public notoriety. We need not now attempt to define the ultimate boundaries of the war power. We decide only the issue as we have defined it—we decide only that the curfew order as applied, and at the time it was applied, was within the boundaries of the war power. In this case it is enough that circumstances within the knowledge of those charged with the responsibility for maintaining the national defense afforded a rational basis for the decision which they made. Whether we would have made it is irrelevant. (320 U.S. at 102.)

. . . as we have seen, those facts, and the inferences which could be rationally drawn from them, support the judgment of the military commander, that the danger of espionage and sabotage to our military resources was imminent, and that the curfew order was an appropriate measure to meet it.

. . . It is unnecessary to consider whether or to what extent such findings would support orders differing from the curfew order.

The conviction under the second count is without constitutional infirmity. Hence we have no occasion to review the conviction on the first count since, as already stated, the sentences on the two counts are to run concurrently and conviction on the second is sufficient to sustain the sentence. For this reason also it is unnecessary to consider the Government's argument that compliance with the order to report at the Civilian Control Station did not necessarily entail confinement in a relocation center. (320 U.S. at 103–105.)

Petitioner did not move the Supreme Court for rehearing of this 1943 decision or file any subsequent legal challenge until 1983 although he testified (at the coram nobis hearing) that he had long been aware of the *Korematsu* case, *Korematsu* v. *United States*, 323 U.S. 214 (1944), and historical works such as *Americans Betrayed* by Morton Grodzins (1949) (Ex. A-49), and *Prejudice* by Carey McWilliams (1944) (Ex. A-67), the latter two criticizing the Supreme Court decision in his case. Petitioner testified (at the coram nobis hearing) that he did not approach any attorneys to seriously discuss reopening his case prior to the early 1970's.

On May 24, 1984, this Court issued an order "that it must hold an evidentiary hearing in order to permit petitioner to attempt to demonstrate by competent evidence that he was in fact denied due process at his trial or upon his appeal."

II. The Standard of Review

Petitioner's Post-Hearing Brief alleges that egregious government misconduct "deprived Petitioner of a fundamentally fair trial and appeal" (Pet.'s Post-Hearing Br. 2:UN15/-16). He first argues, consistent with this Court's May 24, 1984 order, that he is entitled to have his convictions vacated if fundamental errors seriously prejudiced his trial and appeal (*id.* at 2:2).

In the alternative, citing language in *United States* v. *Taylor*, 648 F.2d 565, 574 n. 28 (9th Cir.), cert. denied, 454 U.S. 866 (1981), he urges this Court to create a new lower standard upon which to grant coram nobis relief: that even absent proof of prejudice this Court may vacate convictions if it concludes that government conduct had the potential to or "*could have affected* the Court's determination of the constitutionality of Public Law 503 and the curfew and evacuation orders." (*Id.* at 2:26– 3:1). Petitioner goes on to argue that he "*need not* prove that Public Law 503 probably would have been held unconstitutional if the Supreme Court had considered the suppressed evidence" (*id.* at 3:20–21) as long as there is "*any reasonable likelihood*" that the government's 1943 actions "could have affected the judgment of the Court." (*Id.* at 4:7; see also *id.* at 5:8–9 & 38:1–7.) Finally, petitioner urges this Court to hold that prejudice to his case should be "*presumed* if there is intentional destruction of evidence by the prosecution." (*Id.* at 4:14.)

Petitioner's alternate legal theories are contrary to applicable law.

1. Petitioner Bears the Burden of Proving That the Outcome Would Have Been Different

Petitioner's proposed lower standard—an "*any* reasonable likelihood which *could* have affected" test—is improper even in the case of a direct appeal. Even in such an appeal, "considerations of justice," "judicial integrity" and intentional "illegal conduct" are not enough, standing alone, to warrant vacating a conviction if the resultant "errors alleged are harmless" since "the conviction would have been obtained notwithstanding the asserted error." *United States* v. *Hastings*, 461 U.S. 499, 505–506 (1983). Accord, *United States* v. *Morrison*, 449 U.S. 361, 365–367 (1981).

The instant coram nobis petition, however, is not a direct appeal, but rather is a forty year old collateral attack which is resolved in a manner similar to a habeas corpus petition. *United States* v. *Taylor*, 648 F.2d

565, 571 n.21 & 573 n.25 (9th Cir.), cert. denied, 454 U.S. 866 (1981). In *United States* v. *Frady*, 456 U.S. 152, 166 (1982) the Supreme Court "reaffirm[ed] the well-settled principle that to obtain collateral relief a prisoner [or petitioner] must clear a significantly higher hurdle than would exist on direct appeal." Consequently, on collateral attack, even a "massive violation of due process" must be "causally related to the conviction," *Leiterman* v. *Rushen*, 704 F.2d 442, 444 (9th Cir. 1983).

The Supreme Court stated in *United States* v. *Morgan*, 346 U.S. 502, 511 (1954) that "Continuation of litigation after final judgment and exhaustion or waiver of any statutory right of review should be allowed through this extraordinary remedy only under circumstances compelling such action to achieve justice." Simply because "errors in certain matters of fact" may have occurred is not enough, standing alone, to warrant relief since coram nobis "jurisdiction was of limited scope [applying only] in those cases where the errors were of the most fundamental character, that is, such as rendered the proceeding itself irregular and invalid." *Id.* 346 U.S. at 509 n.15. In *United States* v. *Darnell*, 716 F.2d 479, 480 fn.5 (7th Cir. 1983), cert. denied, 104 S.Ct. 1454 (1984), which this Court has previously quoted and relied upon in its April 29, 1985 order (at p. 3), the Seventh Circuit stated:

. . . The principle that coram nobis is not a substitute for appeal limits the issues that may be raised to those "of the most fundamental character." *United States* v. *Morgan*, 346 U.S. at 511, 74 S.Ct. at 252. This limited scope ensures that coram nobis will not be utilized as a substitute for appeal. It is presumed that the challenged proceedings were correct and a heavy burden rests on the petitioner to demonstrate otherwise. In addition, a standard akin to the "actual prejudice" standard is applied: the coram nobis petitioner must demonstrate that but for the fundamental errors committed a more favorable judgment would have been rendered. *United States* v. *Dellinger*, 657 F.2d 140, 144 n.6 (7th Cir. 1981).

Although petitioner (Post-Hearing Br. 1–3) relies primarily upon *United States* v. *Taylor*, supra, that case cites the above language in *Morgan*, 648 F.2d at 570 n.14, and acknowledges that Taylor sought to prove "a great prejudice" to his case, 648 F.2d at 571. Of course, in *Taylor* the Court was only ruling that an evidentiary hearing on the coram nobis petition was warranted at that point, specifically "withholding judgment on the extent of prosecutorial malfeasance or prejudice to the appellant necessary to warrant relief," 648 F.2d at 574 n.28. That question was left to the district court which, after remand, simply denied the coram nobis petition without reaching that question, 527 F. Supp. 863.

There is, therefore, no controlling Supreme Court or Circuit case support for petitioner's argument that collateral coram nobis relief is permissible forty years after conviction, simply because of the speculative observation that an error "could have" resulted in prejudice where the petitioner fails to carry his burden of proving that the outcome of his case was prejudiced. Indeed, the caselaw is directly to the contrary. See *Frady*, *Hastings*, *Morrison*, *Morgan*, *Darnell* and *Leiterman*, supra.

2. This Case Involves No Misrepresentations Made to the Trier of Fact

Petitioner's reliance upon *United States* v. *Agurs*, 427 U.S. 97 (1976) and cases following it is inapposite. Those cases deal with factually exculpatory evidence withheld from the trier of fact. No such facts are placed in issue in petitioner's Post-Hearing Brief, nor was the legal issue now raised—whether judicial notice was appropriate—previously submitted (in 1942) by the Court to the trier of fact, i.e., the petit jury.

Petitioner here has at all times conceded that he knowingly and intentionally violated the military regulations at issue. Thus, the question of petitioner's factual innocence or guilt was never disputed and there is no allegation that it was incorrectly decided by the trier of the fact. Nor does petitioner's Post-Hearing Brief in this case identify any perjured testimony offered at trial. Instead, petitioner attacks the government's legal argument in its appellate pleadings, i.e., the government's Supreme Court discussion of judicial notice. This issue was raised before trial by the district judge and after trial by petitioner in the Ninth Circuit and the Supreme Court. The original district court and Ninth Circuit pleadings show that at least up until this case reached the Supreme Court, petitioner's position (in full agreement with Judge Fee's *Yasui* opinion) was that facts relating to the military necessity for a curfew were not relevant due to the admitted absence of a formal declaration of martial law and the government's admitted failure to give this particular citizen petitioner any individualized attention before subjecting him to the military regulations he intentionally violated. Consequently, despite the fact that the government called as a witness at trial Assistant G-2 Captain Michael Revisto, the Army officer in charge of evacuation in Seattle under General DeWitt, petitioner did not question him about the Army's basis to believe that there was a bona fide "war emergency." In sum, there was neither false nor incomplete evidence on this question submitted to the trier of fact.

Consequently, legal standards such as *Brady* that apply to fact finders misled by perjurious or incomplete testimony do not apply to this case.

The gravamen of petitioner's coram nobis complaint is no longer the constitutionality of the military regulations on their face, but rather the wholly different question whether there was a sufficient administrative record basis in 1942 to implement such regulations. Petitioner argues that the government was required in 1943 to bring to the Court's attention not only the declassified considerations which lay behind the actions adopted by the War Department and the Commander-in-Chief (the President), but also the then classified internal dissenting policy views which were not adopted, some of which urged more extreme measures (e.g., by General DeWitt) and some of which urged less extreme measures (e.g., by Lt. Com. Ringle) than the War Department adopted.

The universe of differing internal policy positions which lead up to official actions are not discoverable, *N.L.R.B.* v. *Sears, Roebuck & Co.*, 421 U.S. 132, 150–151 (1975). Moreover, here the government openly informed the Supreme Court in 1943 that it was not declassifying all the confidential military information which went into the difficult policy decisions to issue these regulations (Ex. 99, p. 12). This fact was acknowledged and accepted by both Judge Fee in his *Yasui* opinion, 48 F. Supp. at p. 52 ("during the clash of arms the evidence of the military necessities cannot be adduced in a civil court") and the Supreme Court, 320 U.S. at 99 ("these are only some of the many considerations"). Nonetheless, this petitioner argues that it was misconduct to seek, even openly, judicial notice of only those considerations which were not classified. Compare, the 1944 Supreme Court argument of Solicitor General Fahy in *Korematsu*, Ex. 98, pp. 8–9 (Supreme Court cannot take judicial notice of General DeWitt's report where it goes beyond facts of public general knowledge and if the Court believes more facts are needed it will have to remand the case to the trial court). Today, a special ex parte in camera procedure exists which provides an alternative approach. See the Classified Information Procedures Act (CIPA), Pub. L. 96-456, 94 Stat. 2025 (Oct. 15, 1980) reprinted in 18 U.S.C. App. § 1–16 at pp. 549–554 (1982); *United States* v. *Wilson*, 732 F. 2d 404, 414 (5th Cir.), cert. denied, 105 S.Ct. 609 (1984) (ex parte review by court reveals no *Brady* violation); *United States* v. *Wilson*, 750 F.2d 7, 9 (2d Cir. 1984) (same). No similar statutory nor judicial procedure existed in the 1940's. See *Korematsu* v. *United States*, 323 U.S. 214, 245 (Jackson, J., dissenting, "Neither can courts act on communications made in confidence.")

At all events, since the allegation of prosecutorial misconduct in this case has nothing to do with intentionally perjurious evidence misleading the trial court or petit jury, *Morgan*, *Frady*, and *Hastings* control. Even if those cases did not control, petitioner incorrectly describes a defendant's burden under *Agurs* and *Brady*. In *United States* v. *Bagley*, ____ U.S. ____, 105 S.Ct. 3375, 3384 & 3385 (1985), the Supreme Court stated that in all *Agurs* and *Brady* situations "evidence is material only if there is a reasonable probability that, had the evidence been disclosed to the defense, the result of the proceeding would have been different." Consequently, even if this were an *Agurs* and not a *Morgan* situation (which we deny), petitioner is incorrect that he need not show a probability that "the result of the proceeding would have been different" but that he can prevail even if he only shows that the result of the proceeding *could have* been different.

3. Even If Evidence Has Been Destroyed, Prejudice Is Not Presumed

Petitioner also argues that this Court should hold that prejudice should be "presumed if there is an intentional destruction of evidence by the prosecution" (Pet.'s Post-Hearing Br. 4:14). Such a presumption is contrary to the caselaw.

Again, even in a direct appeal which imposes a lower burden upon a defendant, a defendant still must "show (1) bad faith or connivance on the part of the government, *and* (2) that he was prejudiced by the loss or destruction of the evidence." *United States* v. *Jennell*, 749 F.2d 1302, 1308 (9th Cir. 1985) citing *United States* v. *Loud Hawk*, 628 F.2d 1139, 1146 (9th Cir. 1979) (en banc), cert. denied, 445 U.S. 917 (1980). Petitioner's reliance on contrary dicta in *United States* v. *Arra*, 630 F.2d 836, 849–850 (1st Cir. 1980) and the language in *United States* v. *Heiden*, 508 F.2d 898, 902 (9th Cir. 1974) which was modified by the en banc Ninth Circuit in *Loud Hawk*, supra, is inapposite. See also *United States* v. *Bagley*, supra, 103 S.Ct. at 3379–3381 (reversing a Ninth Circuit "automatic reversal" rule which did not require the court to appraise whether the newly discovered evidence was "likely to have changed the verdict").

Where a defendant has delayed a significant period of time before commencing a collateral attack upon his conviction and is also required to show "sound reasons" for his "failure to seek appropriate earlier relief," the rule that his prejudice must be proven and not merely assumed from the destruction of a piece of evidence is even more compelling. In describing the procedure to be followed in a coram nobis proceeding where the transcript of the original criminal proceeding was no longer available, the Supreme Court in *Morgan*, supra, 346 U.S. at 512, stated in words equally applicable here:

. . . the absence of a showing of waiver from the record does not of itself invalidate the judgment. It is presumed the proceedings were correct and the burden rests on the accused to show otherwise.

Similarly here, there is a presumption that the original proceedings were correct, not incorrect, and the burden rests on petitioner "to show otherwise." See also *INS* v. *Miranda*, 459 U.S. 14, 18 (1982). Thus, petitioner's suggestion that the Court should presume prejudice from the destruction or loss of evidence at this late date is contrary to the controlling caselaw.

III. A Chronology of Events

1. The Official Previously Classified War Department MID Reports

The evidence at the hearing showed that prior to the bombing of Pearl Harbor, the Office of Naval Intelligence (ONI) and the Military Intelligence Division (MID) of the Army secretly intercepted and decrypted Japanese diplomatic cables, a few of which were declassified during the 1946 Congressional Pearl Harbor hearings but the bulk of which were not declassified until the 1970's (coram nobis testimony of David Lowman). These cables reveal that in 1941 the Japanese government believed that it had recruited some "second generation" Japanese Americans in West Coast airplane factories and in the United States Army in order to learn about the disposition in the United States of critical war materials and manpower.[3] These secretly obtained cables formed the basis for warnings

---

[3] Discussing the "utilization of our 'Second generations' and our resident nationals" as spies, one Japanese diplomatic cable sent from Tokyo to Washington, D.C. (Ex. A-17) states that "the utmost caution must be exercised." Another cable sent to Tokyo from Los Angeles (Ex. A-22) states:

". . . We have already established contacts with absolutely reliable Japanese in the San Pedro and San Diego area, who will keep a close watch on all shipments of airplanes and other war materials, and report the amounts and destinations of such shipments. The same steps have been taken with regard to traffic across the U.S.-Mexican border.

"We shall maintain connection with our second generations who are at present in the (U.S.) Army, to keep us informed of various developments in the Army. We also have connections with our second generations working in airplane plants for intelligence purposes."

A third cable sent to Tokyo from Seattle (Ex. A-23) states "we have made arrangements to collect intelligence from second generation Japanese draftees on matters dealing with the troops, as well as troop speech and behavior [at p. 2] . . . [and] we are making use of a second generation Japanese lawyer . . ." [at p. 3].

which the Office of Naval Intelligence and the Military Intelligence Division of the War Department widely distributed in sanitized form both at the time of interception of these various messages[4] and in year-end survey reports issued during December 1941.[5]

On January 3, 1942, the War Department Military Intelligence Division issued a "Summary of Information" (Ex. A-6) which (at p. 1) specifically referenced by name Ex. A-17h, the ONI December 24, 1941 memorandum, and is noted G2/CI: G2 designates military intelligence; CI designates counterintelligence, compare Ex. A-17a. This exhibit

---

[4]The information contained in Ex. A-17 was sent by the Chief of the Intelligence Branch of the War Department MID General Staff to the Chief of the Army Counter Intelligence Branch and to the FBI (Ex. A-17a). The Director of the Office of Naval Intelligence forwarded the information to the Chief of Naval Operations and a copy was sent to the FBI (Ex. A-17b). The Military Intelligence Division of the War Department distributed the information with a rating that both the source and information were "reliable" to Army units in its nine Corps Areas, including General DeWitt's (coram nobis testimony of William Hammond), in Puerto Rico, in the Canal Zone, in the Philippine Islands, in the Territory of Hawaii, to the FBI and to ONI. (Ex. A-17c, see also A-17e). The FBI distributed the information to twenty two of its top officials (Ex. A-17d). The Special Agent in Charge of the Boston FBI field office communicated this same information to the Director of the FBI in Washington, D.C. (Ex. A-17c). Officials of the FBI later incorporated this information in a personal and confidential June 1941 FBI report (Ex. A-22; pp. 15–16) which was sent to the Secretary to the President at the White House for his information and the President's (Ex. A-22k), to the Assistant Secretary of State (Ex. A-22L) and to the Attorney General (Ex. A-22m); other FBI reports issued in September and October 1941 distributed this information to the FBI field offices (Ex. A-17f and Ex. A-17g).

The information contained in Ex. A-22 was likewise distributed in O.N.I. and the FBI (Ex. A-22a and A-22b); to the Chiefs of the Intelligence and Counter Intelligence Branches of the Office of Chief of Staff of the War Department Military Intelligence Division (Ex. A-22c and A-22d); to the B-7-J unit (Japanese Counter Intelligence Section) of O.N.I. and Naval Districts 1 to 15, the Military Intelligence Division of the War Department and the FBI (Ex. A-22e and A-22f); to the Attorney General (Ex. A-22g); to FBI field offices in Los Angeles and San Diego (Ex. A-22h); to the Army G-2 of the 9th Corps Area with a rating from the War Department Military Intelligence Division that both the source and information was "reliable"; and in the June 1941 FBI memorandum sent to the White House, State Department, and Attorney General (Ex. A-22j, pp. 25–26; and Ex. A-22k, Ex. A-22L and Ex. A-22m). The information was still being distributed by O.N.I. to the FBI, the 15 Naval Districts and M.I.D. on new sets of O.N.I. index cards entitled "ESPIONAGE (Japanese Intelligence Network in the U.S.)" as late as December 1, 1941 (Ex. A-22o).

The information contained in Ex. A-23 showed similar MID, ONI and FBI distribution (Ex. A-23a and Ex. A-23b).

[5]The initial December 1941 intelligence survey report (Ex. A-40 at pp. 2 and 10) was used as a model for other post Pearl Harbor counterintelligence surveys (Ex. A-40b). See also Ex. A-17h (dated December 24, 1941) at pp. i, iii, iv, 22, 23. This latter report states in part 1, pp. 21 22 (emphasis added):

". . . It must constantly be kept in mind in this connection that Japan strove to put into operation in the United States and its territories a highly integrated and specialized intelligence network which could 'take over' from regular established agencies in wartime.

"Under such circumstances, Japanese nationals and pro-Japanese *nisei* who are well settled in normal and yet strategic occupations are likely to be the mainstay of Japanese espionage-sabotage operations in this country."

Both Ex. A-140 (at p. 26) and Ex. A-17h (at p. 27) show wide distribution to naval districts, to the FBI, M.I.D., the Coordinator of Information (C.O.I., Colonel Donovan), the State Department and (of Ex. A-17h) to the Special Defense Unit of the Department of Justice.

shows that a file copy was retained in MID's Japanese activities file (No. 000.24), and shows distribution to FBI, MID, State Department, Special Defense Unit of the Department of Justice, and all the Army Corps Areas. It also rated both the source and information it contained as "reliable" (see the "x" on the "o" in "source" and on the "n" in "information," p. 1 of Ex. A-6). In pertinent part, it stated:

. . . Approximately 5,000 Japanese are congregating at some undetermined point in strategic Baja California. . . .

The Japanese practice of cloaking subversive operations with "legitimate business fronts" exists in Mexico as well as in the United States. . . .

. . . In the United States there is a possible infiltration of Japanese espionage agents through Cuban and Florida ports. A similar danger exists on the Pacific Coast and Mexican border.

In streamlining their Intelligence Machine the Japanese have been guided by two major considerations—that of a system of "total intelligence" such as the Germans have developed; and establishment of a completely integrated intelligence organization which in time of war and the breaking off of official relations would be able to take over intelligence operations on a major scale.

Although never fully developed, this new espionage organization was characterized by a high degree of decentralization. The general pattern included individuals, small groups, and commercial organizations functioning separately yet directly controlled by Imperial Japanese Government through Embassy and Consulate.

The new program provided for the utilization of citizens of foreign extraction, aliens, Communists, Negroes, Labor union members, anti-Semites, and individuals having access to Government Departments, experimental laboratories, factories, transportation facilities and governmental organizations of various kinds. Nisei and Japanese aliens were not overlooked.

In event of open hostilities, Mexico was to be the Japanese intelligence nerve center in the Western Hemisphere, and in anticipation of war, U.S.–Latin American intelligence routes were established, involving extensive cooperation among Japanese, German and Italian intelligence organizations.

In this connection there should be kept in mind the proximity of San Diego to Tiajuana [*sic*] and of El Centro to Mexicali. [Illegible] along with Yuma, Nogales, El Paso, Laredo, and Brownsville are well known Japanese "post offices" and espionage centers.

. . . A widespread decentralized system of Japanese "clubs," labor organizations, and legitimate business groups has been converted into an important unit of the central Japanese Intelligence Network. There can be no doubt that most of the leaders have been and still continue to function as key operatives for the Japanese Government along the West Coast.

Finally, on January 21, 1942, Lieutenant Colonel P. M. Robinett, G-2 of the U.S. Army General Headquarters, issued a confidential Information Bulletin (No. 6) entitled "Japanese Espionage" (Ex. A-50) which was for high level dissemination "Not . . . lower than division." (*Id.* p. 3). At that time, Robinett was among the select group of government officials authorized to have personal access to the decrypted Japanese cables (coram nobis testimony, Hannah Zeidlik). Brigadier General Mark W. Clark was then Deputy Chief of the U.S. Army General Headquarters which was stationed at the Army War College, Washington, D.C. (coram nobis testimony of Hannah Zeidlik, and Ex.'s A-6 and A-50). This information bulletin entitled "Japanese Espionage" mentions Japanese organizations in Hawaii, New York City, Los Angeles, Washington D.C., San Francisco, Seattle, and Ogden, Utah. It concludes:

6. *Conclusions. a.* It may be expected that Japanese diplomatic and consular communications will be replaced now by using the diplomatic and consular organization of an allegedly neutral power identified with the Axis. They may also use officials of other neutral countries whom they have subverted.

b. Their espionage net containing Japanese aliens, first and second generation Japanese and other nationals is now thoroughly organized and working underground.

c. In addition to their communications net through neutral diplomats, they may be expected to have their own underground communications net.

On February 13, 1942, Brigadier General Mark Clark furnished the above information bulletin "published by [his] headquarters on the subject of Japanese Espionage" to Assistant Secretary of War John J. McCloy "confirming" their telephone conversation of the previous day in order to assist the Assistant Secretary of War "in settling this question" as it related to the West Coast. McCloy needed this information because his immediate superior, Secretary of War Stimson, was the recipient of General DeWitt's recommendation to evacuate all "potentially dangerous" individuals or classes of persons, which was then being prepared (Ex. 4, pp. 25, 33–38; Ex. 29, pp. 33–38). General Clark goes on to assure Assistant Secretary of War McCloy "that the G-2 of the Western Defense Command has all this information . . ." (Ex. A-81). After General DeWitt's recommendation was received by the War Department on February 16, the War Department conferred with the Justice Department and then submitted a draft order to President Roosevelt which on February 19 became Executive Order 9066 (Ex. 4, p. 25; Ex. 29, p. 25).

Petitioner argues that the above described intelligence data and reports—which data his own witness testified derived from the most important source of wartime intelligence data (coram nobis cross-examination of testimony of John Herzig)—were not important. Instead, petitioner rests his case upon reports written by Curtis B. Munson and Lt. Com. K. D. Ringle and the alleged destruction for improper reasons of the first draft of General DeWitt's evacuation report.

2. The Munson Reports

In November 1941 and January 1942, the FBI wrote internal analyses of the reports prepared by Curtis B. Munson, a forty-nine year old business-man. The January 16, 1942 FBI analysis (Ex. A-157) was prepared for Mr. Tamm, then the first assistant to J. Edgar Hoover (coram nobis testimony of Ed Ennis, Tr. 377:22) and the November analysis was prepared for FBI Director Hoover (Ex. A-155, p. 1; Ex. A-157, p. 4). These analyses pointed out that Munson was the brother-in-law of former Congressman Richard M. Russell (Ex. A-157, p. 1), that Munson admitted having "no knowledge of . . . investigative work" (*id.* at p. 2) and stated "he would like to enroll" in the FBI training program (*id.* at p. 9). Twenty-six years earlier he had been employed as a "cub reporter for three months" (*id.* at p. 1), and two days after Pearl Harbor he told the Special Agent in Charge of the FBI Los Angeles field office that he had better access to President Roosevelt than the Director of the FBI "and that he [Munson] could get in touch with the President directly from Los Angeles in fifteen minutes, and he wished that [the Los Angeles field office of the FBI] be aware of this fact." (Ex. A-156.)

In November 1941 Munson visited the West Coast FBI field offices "as well as the Military and Naval agencies." (Ex. 157, p. 3.) At that time "the nature of Mr. Munson's mission was not generally made known or under-stood by [the FBI], ONI and G-2 and Mr. Munson carried no credentials." (*Id.* at p. 9, see p. 3.) "Munson made no attempt to pry into the Bureau's confidential matters and limited himself to requests for general informa-tion." (*Id.* at p. 3.) Munson did, however, obtain confidential access to lists of Japanese suspects in the Naval Districts on the West Coast (Ex. A-155, pp. 2–3 and Ex. A-157, p. 4), lists of Japanese associations (Ex. 139, p. 8), and secret Naval documents (*id.* at p. 11). Since Munson's primary source of confidential information appears to have been the Navy, it is not surprising that he told an Army Intelligence officer "that the ONI on the California coast had a better understanding of the Japanese situation than that possessed by the FBI and MID. . . ." (Ex. A-157, p. 8.)

The FBI noted that Munson's November report (Ex. 139) "contains no specific factual information of importance to the Bureau" and that Munson's statement "that the Japanese rarely occupy positions in defense plants" was merely the repetition of what the Portland, Oregon FBI agent told Munson (Ex. A-157, p. 4). The FBI's analysis stated that Munson "minimized the danger of sabotage" from all Japanese persons in the United States and limited the "espionage threat" to their ability "to obtain information as to movement of supplies by ship and railroad." (*Id.* at p. 4.) The Bureau commented (Ex. A-155, p. 2) that Munson's psychological and sociological

. . . suppositions as to the manner in which the Japanese will react in the event of war between the United States and Japan are purely theoretical and conjectural and for that reason would not appear to be as significant in a practical way as his observations concerning the need for physical protection of important facilities.

See also *id.* at 3 (Munson's reasoning is "purely theoretical"); Ex. A-157, p. 4 (Munson's "conclusions were . . . purely theoretical and conjectural.") Both the FBI and President Roosevelt stated that there was "nothing much new" in Munson's reports (Ex. A-68, p. 1; Ex. A-15).

The FBI report noted that one of Munson's recommendations—that 600 Japanese suspects "should be placed under continuous surveillance" by FBI agents—was internally inconsistent with Munson's view that there "are only 100 or 120 really dangerous suspects" (Ex. A-155, pp. 2–3). The FBI also believed that the recommendation was impractical since such surveillance would have required 2,400 agents.

In his December 20 report (Ex. _____, Tab 16) Munson recommended that all Japanese nationals and their property in the continental United States, not simply on the West Coast, should "be immediately placed under absolute Federal control" supervised perhaps by "loyal Nisei" who were "rigidly approved by and under the thumb" of a military or naval intelligence agency (Tab 16, pp. 9–10, also reprinted in Ex. A-157, p. 6). Two days after Pearl Harbor, Munson advised the FBI Special Agent in Charge of the Los Angeles Field office, Richard Hood, to ignore the Attorney General because the Attorney General was "not in favor of picking up citizens for custodial detention." (Ex. A-156.) FBI Agent Hood noted that absent instructions from the Bureau, he had no intention of following Mr. Munson's advice which was "that it would be all right if this office went ahead and picked up any citizens where there was any doubt about it, and let them get out the best way they can." *Id.*, also reprinted in Ex. A-157, pp. 8–9. In one report, Munson states that the number of suspects "would have to be materially increased" if Japanese American citizens were added. (Ex. 140, p. 4.) The FBI also noted that Munson's findings were all formulated prior to Pearl Harbor (Ex. A-157, p. 6), and that Munson's desire to break radio silence after the outbreak of war "without apparently appreciating the inadvisability of such a course" caused "some concern," *id* at p. 9. The FBI analysis concluded (Ex. 157, p. 9) by noting that FBI Agent Shivers (whom Munson regarded as highly as Munson regarded Ringle, Ex. 5, pp. 3–4) reported that "Munson did considerable talking and probably gave people more information than he got out of them." Former FBI Special Agent in Charge Richard Hood testified (at the coram nobis hearing) that in his professional opinion Munson's reports could not have been relied upon without additional evidentiary support.

At all events, Munson's reports, albeit colorful and unprofessional, reflect his perception of the difficulties encountered on the West Coast. For example, Munson states:

Take the Shinto religion, Buddhist religion, Christian religion, ancestor worship, family worship, all tied back to sun worship of which the Emperor of Japan is the living titular head on earth; add to this, the Oriental mind, western business culture, innate politeness and fear; add also the fact that each individual Japanese is playing all by himself in a field the size of the Yale Bowl with his own conscience as umpire, carrying the ball with as much competitive spirit as an American, the while the stands—whom he wishes to please—are filled to overflowing with his departed ancestors each of whom is vitally interested and sitting in judgment on his personal gyrations; add again a number of other things of varying importance,—such as the fact that the Japs are the greatest joiners in the world and have associations for everything to join from "Fixing Flowers Properly in a Bowl" to "War Relief for Japanese Soldiers in China". You then have a picture so complex to western minds that it cannot be solved by facts and pencil. When it is all added up no westerner will say on the coast here how any individual Japanese will act under given circumstances, how reliable he is, nor what the mass of them will do. (Ex. A-69, pp. 1–2.)

. . . You have to feel this problem–not figure it out with your pencil. We only cite the sand that our reader may never forget the complexities of even a shovel full of sand. (Ex. 139, Report p. 1.)

As noted above, Munson had access to some confidential naval intelligence reports and therefore concluded "that the ONI on the California coast had a better understanding of the Japanese situation than that possessed by the FBI and MID. . . ." (Ex. A-157, p. 8.) In two different reports, Munson relied upon a secret Navy Department report entitled "Japanese Organizations and Activities in the 11th Naval District" (Ex.

139, Report p. 11; Ex. 140, Report p. 11) and Munson stated in his final report that Assistant District Intelligence Officer Lt. Com. K. D. Ringle of the 11th Naval District was one of two intelligence officers who appeared to him to be a "crystallization" of "99% of the most intelligent views on the Japanese. . . ." (Ex. 5, Report p. 2.)

Starting with his December 20, 1941 report and continuing through the end of January 1942, Munson had his political friends urge the President to have General DeWitt (in the War Department "Corps Area Headquarters at San Francisco") put Lt. Com. Ringle in charge of Munson's West Coast Japanese plan (Ex. 45). This did not occur. However, Ringle's views did get circulated to the Attorney General (Ex. 33) who passed them along to the Assistant Secretary of War McCloy (Ex. 34), and Ringle was consulted on relocation by the Director of the War Relocation Authority (WRA) (Ex. 100), which in May 1942 (see Ex. 78, p. 490) printed and circulated a "compilation" of Ringle's personal memoranda (including Ringle's January 26 memo) prefaced by the disclaimer that the memorandum did "not necessarily reflect the policies of the War Relocation Authority or the Navy Department." (Ex. 77, p. 3.) In any event, the language in Munson's December 20, 1941 report did directly result in a December 30, 1941 request from the Chief of Naval Operations (received January 5, 1942) for "a report from Lieutenant Commander Ringle concerning his views on the Japanese referred to in Mr. Munson's report." (Ex. 46.) Thereafter, Ringle wrote a report dated January 26, 1942 (Ex. 32) which was mailed to Washington on January 29, 1942 (Ex. 47).

3. The Ringle Reports

The January 26 Ringle report was sent by the Office of the Chief of Naval Operations to the FBI, the M.I.D., and to the Department of Justice's Special Defense and Alien Enemy Control Units, the latter then headed by Edward Ennis (Ex. A-77, coram nobis testimony of Edward Ennis, Tr. 191:22–24). The cover letter from the Navy Department made it clear that the Ringle report was prepared at ONI's request due to the Munson Report's endorsement of Lt. Com. Ringle and that the Ringle report "does not represent the final and official opinion of the Office of Naval Intelligence on this subject." (Ex. A-77.) Ringle went on to write an expanded version of his report for the WRA in May 1942 (Ex. 77) and received permission to publish a shortened version of it in the October 1942 issue (Ex. 78, p. 490) of *Harper's* magazine (Ex. 35, pp. 1–2).

Ringle, who like Munson had no personal access to or awareness of the decrypted Japanese diplomatic cables, was of the opinion that many Japanese born alien residents would do no more than "surreptitious observation work for Japanese interests if given a convenient opportunity" (Ex. 32, p. 2; Ex. 77, p. 6); that about 3,500 Japanese aliens and citizens would actively "act as saboteurs or agents" (*id.*); and that the most dangerous are members of Japanese military associations in the United States who as of May 1942 (see Ex. 78, p. 490) still had "not yet been apprehended" (Ex. 77, p. 7). Ringle also believed that "the most potentially dangerous element of all" were the Kibei of whom Ringle estimated there were 8–9,000 (Ex. 77, p. 30) and who, in spite of their citizenship and "the Bill of Rights" (Ex. 32, p. 3; Ex. 77, p. 7) should be guarded in detention camps, stripped of their citizenship, and deported to Japan "at the first opportunity" (Ex. 77, p. 30), along with their parents or guardians (*id.*, pp. 32 and 35). Procedurally, Ringle recommended that these people should be "considered guilty unless proven innocent." (*Id.*)

Regarding Japanese resident aliens, Ringle also believed it would be "perfectly legal" and "may be more expeditious in the long run" to declare them all suspect and have them prove their innocence, as with the Kibei (*id.* at 35–36). According to Ringle's estimates, that would require only about 25% of the total evacuee population to be held in custody (Ex. 32, p. 4; Ex. 77, p. 37; Ex. 78, p. 490). Ringle recommended that American citizens of Japanese ancestry be given a role "in the national war effort . . . even though subject to greater investigative checks as to background and loyalty, etc., than Caucasian Americans." (Ex. 77, p. 7.) However, Ringle discouraged the use of Japanese Americans as teachers for any Japanese descended detainees (Ex. 77, p. 51) and recommended that Shintoism be banned as "it is not a true religion but a form of patriotism toward Japan." (Ex. 77, p. 53.) Ringle also said that in the pre-war period Japanese Americans were not discriminated against on the basis of race, but rather because they "belonged to a minority group in the American population of whose loyalty and integrity the people at large were not sure." (Ex. 77, p. 20; Ex. 78, p. 496.)

Ringle also wrote an intelligence report dated February 7, 1942 which, unlike the earlier report, was officially approved by Ringle's superior, District Intelligence Officer of the 11th Naval District, Bruce L. Canaga (see also, coram nobis testimony of Richard Hood), and circulated to the Director of Naval Intelligence, the Assistant Chief of Staff G-2 of the War Department Military Intelligence Division (in whose Japanese activities file, No. 000.24, it still appears), the Aliens Division of the War Department Office of Provost Marshall, to the FBI (Ex. A-7), and by the FBI to their Los Angeles field office (Ex. A-70).

This report, entitled "Japanese Menace on Terminal Island, San Pedro, California," noted that more than 80% of the population were Japanese American citizens (Ex. A-7, Report p. 1). Ringle's report warns that there is a 75% chance of physical observation and espionage since "known alien sympathizers, even though of American citizenship" were present (Ex. A-7, Report pp. 3–4). Ringle also warned about a 20% chance of sabotage which he stated he would have increased but for "the rather rigid and effective guards and protections which have been placed into effect within the last six months." (Ex. A-7, Report p. 4.) He also estimated a 5% chance of "fifth column activity" (*id.*).

From the above, we submit that petitioner has failed to show that there is any hard intelligence data in the Munson or Ringle reports—of a nature similar to the intercepted Japanese diplomatic cables about which they were totally unaware—which could have been considered exculpatory.

4. General DeWitt's Curfew Orders and Evacuation Report

In July 1942 after most of the Japanese Americans were detained, Civil Affairs Officer Col. Karl R. Bendetsen recommended to General DeWitt that the curfew order, which this petitioner violated, be modified or revoked (Ex. A-111). General DeWitt, however, felt the curfew was important and continued it after obtaining the views of his Assistant Chief of Staff G-2 (Intelligence), Col. John Weckerling, who agreed with General DeWitt about its importance vis à vis German and Italian aliens, despite the objections of both Bendetsen and, later, of Assistant Secretary of War John J. McCloy (Ex. A-111). Even by that date, G-2 Weckerling advised General DeWitt that Weckerling still continued to be concerned about "sabotage or attempted sabotage on a mass scale . . ." (*id.*). At that time, no West Coast FBI officers nor West Coast Army G-2 officers objected to the curfew and evacuation orders or argued that they were unnecessary (coram nobis testimony of William Hammond, Richard Hood, Robert Mayer and Richard Hamm).

On January 18, 1943, General DeWitt had a telephone conversation with Assistant Secretary of War McCloy in which they disagreed about allowing evacuees into the U.S. Army. General DeWitt, who "didn't concur" in this plan (Ex. A-84, p. 2), had been overruled by the War Department and was upset that he had been instructed to prepare for about

30,000 investigations (Ex. A-84, p. 1). General DeWitt told Assistant Secretary of War McCloy that "we wouldn't have evacuated these people at all if we could determine their loyalty." (*Id.*). McCloy responded (*id.*):

McCloy: I don't know whether we are at one on that—

DeWitt: I know we are not one on it—

McCloy: We evacuated them from the West Coast because we thought the front was immediate. We couldn't sort them out immediately.

About three months later on April 19, 1943, McCloy received DeWitt's report on the evacuation. McCloy immediately complained that "it is sort of a document to support the contention that no Jap is ever going to get back into the Western Defense Command" (Ex. 5, p. 2), and "that the Western Defense Command is taking a view which is a little at variance with that of the War Department view" (Ex. 5, p. 3) on "the question as to whether the Japanese should be relocated now or not until after the duration [of the war]" (Ex. 5, p. 2). McCloy pointed out that the War Department might well overrule issuing that part of the report. (*Id.* at p. 4.)

Colonel Bendetsen responded that the report was similar to a galley proof and not meant to constitute "a thing of finality" (*id.* at p. 1 and see pp. 2, 4, 5), and that the War Department's and DeWitt's differences were not insoluble (*id.* at pp. 2 and 5). Bendetsen also stated that General DeWitt had been misquoted in the newspapers (*id.* at p. 3). As petitioner's original 1943 Supreme Court briefs brought to everyone's attention, on April 14, 1943, the *Washington Post* quoted General DeWitt as stating, *inter alia*, "A Jap's a Jap" and "There is no way to determine their loyalty" in his testimony before a Congressional Subcommittee on the question of the resettlement of Japanese Americans on the West Coast. (Ex. 130, p. 25; Ex. 127, p. 114.)

Subsequently, Bendetsen (through Barnett, Ex. 14) and McCloy (through Adler, Ex. 16 and through Bendetsen, Ex. 6, p. 3) told DeWitt he need not accept changes to his evacuation report. DeWitt at first stood firm against even the idea of any changes (Ex. 101), but by May 5 sought a meeting on the subject with Bendetsen (Ex. 18; Ex. A-45). Finally, by May 9, DeWitt decided to make his *own* changes (Ex. 8 and 19). In fact, he adopted most of the War Department's suggestions (Ex. 15, pp. 1–4) but added many more (Ex. 15, pp. 4–9; Ex. 20). The first set of changes went to the printer on May 27, 1943 (Ex. 21) and a revised second printing of DeWitt's evacuation report was mailed to Chief of Staff General George C. Marshall in Washington, D.C. on June 18, 1943 (Ex. 27) and received on June 21, 1943 (Ex. A-42). General Marshall did not forward DeWitt's report to the Secretary of War until July 19, 1943 (Ex. 29, p. iii). Thereafter, several dozen additional changes were requested on September 11 and 14, 1943 before publication of what was called the "Final official, or 3rd Printing" by Sunset Press for the G.P.O. (Ex. A-108, Ex. 26, and coram nobis testimony of Hannah Zeidlik).

Bendetsen sought to live up to his representations to Assistant Secretary McCloy on April 19, 1943 that the first version of the report should be treated no differently than a draft (Ex. 5). Consequently, after DeWitt decided to change the first printing, Bendetsen recalled the original cover letters (Ex. 19 and 10) and the ten copies of that version which had been printed (Ex. 26, 9, 25). No attempt was made to hide this recall. In fact, the new cover letters sent with the second printing openly referred to the first printing previously recalled and revised (Ex. 27, 23) and dozens of documents memorializing the recall and amendment of the first printing were preserved (see, e.g., Ex. 28, 27, 23, 26, 9, 25, 19, 10, 5, 21, 20, 8, 18, 101, 6, 16, 14). Under the prevailing procedures during World War II (Army Regulation 380-5 § 22, Ex. A-63 at p. 11, and War Department Circular 201, Ex. A-73), both the first and second printing drafts and plates were destroyed and a certificate of destruction prepared (Ex. 11 and Ex. A-43). However, two copies of the first printing and two copies of the second printing were each carefully preserved and inventoried (Ex. A-108). One of these early ten copies of the first printing was offered by petitioner at the hearing (Ex. 4). Contrary therefore to petitioner's claim that allegedly exculpatory documents were intentionally destroyed, all the documents still exist. None have been intentionally destroyed.

5. The Supreme Court Litigation

On the same day that the War Department first received General DeWitt's original version of his evacuation report, April 19, 1943, Edward Ennis at the Justice Department was informed that the War Department was "determining whether it [the report] was to be released" for use in this case (Ex. 36, p. 1). At that same time, Ennis declined to use a statement by the Director of War Relocation Authority which also was "prepared post and propter litem motem" (*id.* at p. 2)—after the fact and for use in the controversy which had arisen. Ennis also raised the question with the Solicitor General whether the government could cite confidential investigative reports to the Supreme Court (*id.*).

As it turned out, the War Department did not decide to declassify and publicly distribute DeWitt's Report until January 1944, nearly six months after the *Hirabayashi* case was briefed, argued and decided (Ex. A-48a, p. 11, fn.2). This delay appears to have resulted from the War Department's concern that General DeWitt was seeking to utilize his evacuation report to gain support for his separate but continuing disagreement with the War Department concerning whether Japanese American servicemen should be permitted to return to the West Coast prior to the end of the war (Ex. A-84, pp. 1–2; Ex. 5, pp. 2–4; Ex. 6, pp. 1–3). The report was, however, made public by the War Department well in advance of the Supreme Court litigation in the *Korematsu* case, but was not relied upon by the government (A-48a, p. 11, fn.2). During the six month hiatus between the drafting and publishing of Dewitt's evacuation report during which time DeWitt disagreed with the War Department over the return of Japanese American servicemen to the West Coast, General DeWitt was replaced by General Emmons, who favored such a return (Ex. A-84, p. 3).

On April 30, 1943, just prior to filing the government's Supreme Court *Hirabayashi* brief, Ennis advised the Solicitor General that he obtained a copy of the Ringle report from attorneys for the War Relocation Authority who also advised Ennis "that the Ringle memorandum represent[ed] the view of the Office of Naval Intelligence" at the time of the evacuation, Ex. 35, p. 4. Ennis also stated that he was told that under the delimitation agreement, ONI was "the intelligence agency having the most responsibility for investigating the Japanese from the security viewpoint . . ." (*id.* at p. 3). Ennis prepared a draft letter for the Solicitor General to send to the Secretary of the Navy in order to ascertain if these facts were true. If they were, then Ennis stated that he believed the government should "advise the Court" of these facts. (*Id.*)

Although the petitioner now echoes Ennis' 1943 concerns, petitioner has not produced any additional correspondence or testimony to bear out Ennis' concerns. Indeed, just to the contrary, Ennis testified (at the coram nobis hearing) that his understanding, ultimately, was that Ringle's views were only accepted by individual Naval intelligence officers, but not officially by ONI (Tr. 438:11–13). Ennis also testified that none of the government activities which ultimately occurred or government papers filed in this case or in the *Yasui* or *Korematsu* cases were improper or unconstitutional. Although Ennis left the government and worked with the Japanese American Citizens League (J.A.C.L.) in 1946 and became a member of the board of directors of the A.C.L.U. that same year, it never struck him that there remained to be corrected some intentional government misconduct in this case that he should communicate either to the

J.A.C.L. or the A.C.L.U. (Tr. 336:19–24). Indeed, he testified that the whole incident was so unexceptional that Ennis testified "the whole matter had entirely left [his] memory" until it was brought to his attention in 1981 or 1982 (Tr. 335:24–Tr. 336:9).

Other evidence confirms Ennis' testimony. The cover letter of both Ringle's January 26, 1943 report (Ex. A-77, p. 1) and the preface to the longer WRA version (Ex. 77, p. 3) and the published version (Ex. 78, p. 490) all disclaim that they represent anything other than Ringle's personal views. Although Ennis states in 1943 (Ex. 35, pp. 2–3) that knowledge of ONI's Ringle report would have made a difference to him fourteen months earlier, Ennis no doubt forgot in 1943 that he was in fact privy to the original distribution of the Ringle report fourteen months earlier, before Executive Order 9066 was signed (Ex. A-77, p. 1), but the report apparently made little or no impression upon him or his office at that time.

Ennis was also misinformed about ONI being the intelligence agency with the most direct responsibility. From the later half of 1940 until February 9, 1942, ONI and the FBI shared the responsibility for investigating Japanese espionage, counterespionage, sabotage and subversive activities since

... the Navy Department [did] not want the full responsibility for the checking of the Japanese because of a lack of personnel, etc. Admiral Anderson furnished ... the background of Commander McCollom and pointed out that the Commander had resided in Japan, knows the Japanese language and has excellent Japanese contacts. Admiral Anderson agreed to make Commander McCollom and the Far Eastern Division of the Navy Department available for consultation and advice to the FBI at any time it was necessary or desirable.

(Ex. A-86, pp. 1–2.)

These facts contradicted Ennis' 1943 "informal" information. Even so, the government's opening *Hirabayashi* brief did bring Lt. Com. Ringle's anonymous October 1942 *Harper's* magazine article to the Supreme Court's attention (Ex. 99, p. 29, fn.46). Of course as noted above, in January 1943, five months earlier, petitioner's Ninth Circuit Reply Brief (Ex. A-5, p. 1 and Brief, pp. 2–4) and petitioner's Ninth Circuit brief answering amicus California (Ex. 125, p. 1 and Brief, pp. 1–2) made major arguments citing the intelligence views of the *Harper's* article. The *Harper's* article was also brought to the Supreme Court's attention by petitioner (Ex. 126, p. 21) and two of his amici (Ex. 127, pp. 92, 93; Ex. 128, p. 15).

Moreover, neither in this case, nor in the *Yasui* and *Korematsu* cases did the government defend the wisdom of General DeWitt's decision nor argue that Japanese Americans were in fact disloyal. Rather, the government's position was that the government as a whole, not just General DeWitt, was faced with a difficult decision during wartime in a declared war zone, and under those conditions its actions were rational and therefore minimally acceptable. See Ex. 98, pp. 10, 14–15; Tr. 422:2–5.)

The government's Supreme Court *Hirabayashi* brief (Ex. 99) stated:

The situation which gave rise to the curfew and evacuation measures was wholly unprecedented in the history of this country. The validity of those measures must be tested, not in the light of the military situation as it exists today, nor even in the light of the military situation as it existed at that time viewed as a matter of hindsight. (p. 60.)

The exact and detailed military situation affecting the Pacific Coast after the attack on Pearl Harbor, which was within the personal and official knowledge of the President, the Secretary of War and General DeWitt when it was determined that the entire Japanese population should be evacuated, was a closely guarded military secret. It was not a matter of public knowledge then or now, and probably cannot be a matter of public knowledge at least until the military authorities decide that there is no possible military risk. However, the facts about the military situation which were then publicly known or have since been disclosed may be stated in support of the action taken. (p. 12.)

Our Pacific Fleet had been rendered all but powerless for the time being, and the Japanese forces were making bold and impressive strides. Indeed, our very coast had been shelled. Faced with the responsibility of repelling a possible Japanese invasion which might have threatened the very integrity of our nation, it was the duty of the commanding general to take into account the plain fact that over 100,000 Japanese were grouped along the coast. It was essential to recognize that although the majority of these people might be regarded as loyal to the United States, a disloyal minority, if only a few hundreds or thousands, strategically placed, might spell the difference between the success or failure of any attempted invasion. (p. 61.)

. . . Even assuming that administrative hearings might have been held for each Japanese, such hearings would have been virtually worthless unless each were preceded by an investigation carefully conducted by a trained investigator. Many months, or perhaps years, would be required for such investigations and hearings.* Meanwhile the threat of a Japanese attack would persist. (p. 62.)

*Based on investigations by the Federal Bureau of Investigation over a course of years, about 10,000 hearings have been granted to alien enemies throughout the United States since December 7, 1941.

. . . The rationale of the action here in controversy is not the loyalty or disloyalty of individuals but the danger from the residence of the class as such within a vital military area. If there was a rational basis for this judgment, then the only question that remains is whether a given individual was or was not a person of Japanese ancestry. (p. 64.)

After the oral Supreme Court argument, the government filed an additional pleading on May 14, 1943, to clarify its position in this case:

. . . Our position is not that hearings are an inappropriate method of reaching a decision on the question of loyalty. The Government does not contend that, assuming adequate opportunity for investigation, hearings may not ever be appropriately utilized on the question of the loyalty of the persons here involved. It is submitted, however, that in the circumstances set forth in our brief, this method was not available to solve the problem which confronted the country. The situation did not lend itself, in the unique and pressing circumstances, to solution by individual loyalty hearings. In any event, the method of individual hearings was reasonably thought to be unavailable by those who were obliged to decide upon the measures to be taken. If the Government's brief (pp. 62–64) is thought to be inconsistent with the views set forth herein, it is requested that this memorandum be considered as superseding the brief to this extent. (Ex. 131, pp. 1–2.)

At the coram nobis hearing, Ed Ennis supported this assessment of the situation. He testified that holding just the 5,000 Japanese alien hearings took between one and two years (Tr. 242:1–7; Tr. 275:14–17).

Approximately one year later when the *Korematsu* case was being briefed and argued in the Supreme Court, the government made essentially the same arguments (Ex. A-48a, pp. 22–24). Even though a modified version of DeWitt's report was published by that time, the War Department reluctantly acquiesced in the Department of Justice's decision not to rely generally upon DeWitt's report, see Ex. A-48a, p. 11, fn.2. The War Department did not choose to reveal to the Court or even the Department of Justice attorneys (Ex. A-85), the still classified fact that intercepted Japanese diplomatic cables, only the substance of which were widely distributed in early 1942, lay behind the fears of the leaders of the professional intelligence community. Ennis testified that throughout the war he was kept ignorant of that entire intelligence operation, which remained highly classified until the 1946 Pearl Harbor hearings. See Ex. A-71 and testimony of David Lowman. However, neither Ennis nor Burling had clearance for nor received any confidential military information (Tr. 315:1–6 & 11–17; Tr. 324:9–11; Tr. 325:6–19). For this reason, Ennis and Burling's perceptions of the War Department's motives were not based on a full appreciation of all the relevant facts.[6]

_____

[6] Ennis testified that he also had no confidence in and disagreed strongly with the military judgment calls made by Admiral Nimitz and General Richardson in Hawaii (Tr. 343:25–345:22), by General Drum in the Eastern Defense Command (Tr. 420:1–9), and by General Gullion (Tr. 397:2–3). Ennis and Burling's protests were also prompted by their view that General DeWitt's evacuation report sought "to blame this Department with the evacuation by suggesting that *we* were derelict in *our* duties." Ex. 84, p. 2 (Burling, emphasis added); accord, Ex. 44, p. 2 (Ennis).

IV. Petitioner Has Not Carried His Burden of Proof

1. The Outcome of Petitioner's Case Was Unaffected by the Facts He Has Adduced

Petitioner claimed that he and the Supreme Court were knowingly and prejudicially misled both in his case and in the *Korematsu* Supreme Court proceeding.

At the coram nobis hearing, Ennis testified that prior to 1943 he had supervised hundreds of cases and was sensitive to the need to disclose exculpatory information at trial (Tr. 263:12–23). He went on to state that since the Supreme Court was not the trial court, no question of disclosing exculpatory evidence was presented in this case, or is ever presented at that stage of a case (Tr. 406–407; Tr. 338:2–5). Rather, the problem presented was "what we should call to the attention of the Court . . . as subject to judicial notice." (Tr. 222:7–9.) Ennis testified that the government's position in the *Hirabayashi* case—that there was not sufficient time to hold individual hearings—was "a correct" and "appropriate" government representation (Tr. 279:10–18) which he himself might have constructed (Tr. 246:14–15) and with which the Solicitor General agreed (Tr. 280:16), even assuming that General DeWitt personally took the more extreme and injudicious position that hearings were useless. Ennis testified that his objections to the evacuation were not based on the availability of hearings. Rather, Ennis objected to evacuation because he was not aware of facts which suggested that there was "a serious enough danger in the Japanese community to have any exclusion program at all. . . ." (Tr. 279:13–15.)[7]

Ennis stated that in his personal meetings with General DeWitt in December 1941 and January 1942, DeWitt exhibited a "general fear of sabotage and espionage" (Tr. 288:14), but exhibited no personal animus toward people of Japanese ancestry (Tr. 343:4–8). Ennis testified that J. Edgar Hoover "was neutral" and "didn't seek to make any recommendation or urge any course of action" with respect to Executive Order 9066 (Tr 382:1–13), even though "there were differences of opinion between

---

[7] Ennis admitted, however, that he and Burling did not have any special clearances for decrypted cable information (Tr. 315:5–6; Tr. 324:11), did not regularly receive ONI reports (Tr. 315:15–16) or General DeWitt's military reports (Tr. 313:13), and did not attend meetings of Joint Chiefs of Staff, meetings with Chief of Staff George C. Marshall nor meetings with the military "G-2"s (Tr. 324:6–16).

the civilian Department [of Justice] and the military Department [of War] as to what was required in Continental United States." (Tr. 314:23–25.)

With regard to the briefs in these cases, Ennis stated that he did not believe that the government was entitled to introduce classified military intelligence reports, rather than public information, in support of a judicial notice argument (Tr. 318:19–20). Consequently, the government did not discuss any such reports and candidly told the Supreme Court that no such material was being made available (Tr. 318:21–23; Ex. 99, p. 12).

Even at the time of the writing of the government's *Korematsu* briefs more than one year later and after the publication of General DeWitt's evacuation report, Ennis' proposed footnote did not seek to offer conflicting classified military information to the Supreme Court (Tr. 338:16–17). Rather, Ennis simply sought to notify the Supreme Court not to rely generally upon General DeWitt's written recitation of the publicly known facts since parts of DeWitt's published report were disputed by other classified information (Tr. 326:10; Tr. 338:16–21; Tr. 208:14–22; Tr. 253:2–4, 10–11, 17–20), with which Ennis never confronted DeWitt (Tr. 321:23–Tr. 322:1). Ennis went on to testify that the footnote that *was* used (Ex. A-48, p. 11, fn.2), which Ennis also proposed (Tr. 254:15–16), was "the narrowest way to deal with the problem . . . and avoided any censurable misconduct" even if the A.C.L.U. brief had not been filed in the *Korematsu* case (Tr. 377:2–4). That footnote, carefully narrowing the government's reliance on General DeWitt's report only to the extent that its facts were actually repeated in the government's brief (Tr. 208:17–22), was approved by Ennis, Burling, Assistant Attorney General Herbert Wechsler of the War Division of the Justice Department, and Solicitor General Charles Fahy, none of whom disassociated themselves from the brief (Tr. 327:12–Tr. 328:19), although Ennis had previously warned Fahy that he might do so (Tr. 254:8; Tr. 325:20–24). Ennis testified that the *Korematsu* footnote as it finally appeared "wasn't misleading if it was carefully read . . ." (Tr. 326:2–3) and met the required minimum standard of disclosure (Tr. 328:13–19).

In addition, Ennis testified that the A.C.L.U.'s brief included a "statement of the same problem" raised in his memoranda (Tr. 372:22), identified the same concerns Ennis expressed in his memoranda (Tr. 374:13–15), and its discussion was "longer" and "clearer" than even the proposed footnote which was not used. (Tr. 375:2–11.) Thus, Ennis testified, the A.C.L.U. brief "leads correctly to the inference that this problem was called to the Court's attention *more clearly* than in our footnote . . ." (Tr. 376:17–19, emphasis added). Thus, Ennis' prospective fears memorialized in his and Burling's pre-argument memoranda were never realized.

Furthermore, Ennis stated (Tr. 418:6–15) that Korematsu's October 1944 A.C.L.U. amicus brief was signed by Carey McWilliams, see also Ex. A-46, p. 27. McWilliams published a book called *"Prejudice"* in October 1944 (Ex. A-67, p. viii) identifying at p. 114 Lt. Col. K. D. Ringle as the intelligence officer who prepared the *Harper's* magazine article cited by all the parties (Ex. A-66, p. 191, fn.55). Ennis testified that Justices Murphy's and Jackson's dissents in the *Korematsu* case (323 U.S. 233–242) showed that the Supreme Court was not misled by the government's position in these cases (Tr. 374:16–18). Ennis testified that the dissents of both Justices Murphy and Jackson showed that the Court was indeed alerted "that the Army's justification was disputed" (Tr. 326:8–10). Ennis stated that the Justices "said the [DeWitt] report is full of erroneous statements, and the erroneous statements they referred to were the information I tried to get into the footnote." (Tr. 256:25–Tr. 257:3.) Moreover, in that part of Justice Murphy's dissent attacking DeWitt's final report, Justice Murphy cited McWilliams' book *Prejudice* four times (323 U.S. at p. 237, fn.6, at p. 238, fn.7 and fn.9, and at p. 239, fn.12).

The Supreme Court simply chose to reject the suggestion to remand the case for a detailed factual exposition of all the confidential military reports, which suggestion was candidly noted at oral argument by the Solicitor General (Ex. 98, p. 9), advocated by dissenting Justice Murphy (Tr. 331:9–10), and later urged by Korematsu in his unsuccessful rehearing petition (at p. 9–11) to the Supreme Court, 324 U.S. 885 (1945). In addition, Nanette Dembitz, one of the government's attorneys in the *Hirabayashi* case (Ex. 99, p. 82), made this same point in a 1945 law review article (Ex. A-66, p. 227) which criticized the Supreme Court for making the policy choice not to remand the *Korematsu* case for a detailed evidentiary hearing. Accord, Rostow, "The Japanese American Cases— A Disaster," 54 Yale L.J. 489, 520 (1945) (pointing out the significance of footnote two in the government's brief). All of the above shows that neither the parties, the Supreme Court, nor the legal community were misled by government officials into believing that the decisions in these cases should be based upon an uncritical acceptance of all the details of General DeWitt's evacuation report.

Petitioner also complains about illicit radio signalling fears expressed in General DeWitt's evacuation report and about the use of data from

General DeWitt's evacuation report in the *Hirabayashi* Supreme Court brief of amici California, Oregon and Washington.

Initially, we point out that as noted above, General DeWitt's report and views were not declassified in 1943 and therefore played no part in the outcome of the *Hirabayashi* case. Even if General DeWitt's personal views had mattered, it is clear that even if misinformed, General DeWitt sincerely *believed*: (1) that the FBI's post Pearl Harbor arrests of Japanese aliens were not sufficiently thorough[8]; (2) that mobile radio transmitting units were illegally operating on the West Coast[9] assisting enemy submarines which were attacking our coastal shipping[10]; that the resources

[8] When asked to comment in April 1944 upon the fears expressed by General DeWitt in his evacuation report, Dillon S. Meyer, then Director of the WRA wrote to the Secretary of War in a confidential memorandum that General DeWitt's "confidence in the thoroughness of the clean-up operations immediately following the outbreak of war was something less than complete." Ex. 112, p. 4. All versions of DeWitt's report begin by complaining that in the post-Pearl Harbor period "little was done to implement the presidential proclamation. No steps were taken to provide for the collection of contraband and no prohibited zones were proclaimed." Ex. 4, p. 3; see also Ex. 29, p. 3. As noted in this pleading at pp. 20–21, General DeWitt's Corps Area was "reliably" advised by M.I.D. on January 3, 1942 (by Ex. A-6): (1) that "[a]pproximately 5,000 Japanese are congregating at some undetermined point in strategic Baja California"; (2) that the border towns on both sides of the United States–Mexican border "are well known Japanese 'post offices' and espionage centers"; and (3) that most of the leaders of Japanese "clubs," labor organizations and legitimate business groups were still functioning at that time as key operatives of the Japanese Intelligence Network along the West Coast. See also Ex. A-50, of which Ex. A-81 reports the Western Defense Command was aware. Ennis also testified to DeWitt's general fear of espionage and sabotage (Tr. 288:14; Tr. 285:25–Tr. 286:1–7). General DeWitt's fears were certainly not put to rest by FBI raids as late as February 7, 1942 resulting in the confiscation from enemy aliens of twenty one sticks and one half box of dynamite, one hundred sixty six dynamite blasting caps, three pounds of black powder, one hundred sixty three feet of fuse, eight millimeter film containing photographs of battleships and fortifications, four cameras, several firearms and ammunition, two shortwave radio sets, seven radios capable of receiving shortwave, three telegrapher's keys, one radio oscillator, a microphone, and four boxes of assorted radio equipment. Ex. A-1. Former FBI Special Agent in Charge Richard Hood testified that suspicious persons of Japanese descent continued to be rounded up for months after Pearl Harbor. Ennis testified that approximately 4,000 Japanese aliens not picked up shortly after Pearl Harbor were ultimately apprehended. (Tr. 273:10–274:20.)

[9] As of January 9, 1942 ". . . Gen'l DeWitt seemed concerned and, in fact, seemed to believe that the woods were full of Japs with transmitters . . ." (Ex. 107, p. 1). DeWitt's operational personnel "report to their commanding officers that they have fixes on Jap agents operating transmitters on the West Coast. These officers, knowing no different, pass it on to the general and he takes their word for it." (Ex. 107, p. 2). All versions of DeWitt's report describe DeWitt's concern "during the closing weeks of December" which "was in part based upon the interception of unauthorized radio communications which had been identified as emanating from certain areas along the coast." Ex. 4, pp. 3–4; and Ex. 29, pp. 3–4.

[10] All versions of General DeWitt's report state: "Of further concern . . . was the fact that for a period of *several weeks following December 7th*, substantially every ship leaving a West Coast port was attacked by an enemy submarine. This seemed conclusively to point to the existence of hostile shore-to-ship (submarine) communications." Ex. 4, p. 4; Ex. 29, p. 4. An FCC report also notes that shortly before January 9, 1942 "a Jap sub off the coast . . . was destroyed by bombing from the air." Ex. 107, p. 2. G-2 Periodic Reports reflected the presence of enemy submarines on the West Coast during late December and January. Ex. 57, pp. 1–2 and Ex. A-51 (map); Ex. 58, p. 1 and Ex. A-52 (map); Ex. 59, pp. 1–2 and Ex. A-53 (map); Ex. A-54 (map); Ex. 61, p. 1 and Ex. A-55 (map). The 1944 FBI retrospective comment upon these submarine attacks did not dispute that they took place

then available were not sufficient to resolve that problem [11]; and that there was a realistic possibility of both enemy air and naval (especially submarine) raids upon the Western Defense Command. [12] As the Supreme Court noted, retrospective analyses with the perfect hindsight it affords does not undercut the authority of a military commander who acted in good faith on the basis of the information then at hand. *Mitchell* v. *Harmony*, 54 U.S. (13 How.) 115, 134–135 (1851) (". . . the state of facts, as they appeared to the officer at the time he acted, must govern the decision . . . and the discovery afterwards that it was false or erroneous, will not [control or] make him a trespasser."); *Sterling* v. *Constantin*, 287 U.S. 378, 399–400 (1932). In any event, even if petitioner's case had been remanded, the now declassified cables and the intelligence reports which relied upon the cables show that there was some military intelligence basis for General DeWitt's and the War Department's fears.

Finally, even though amici California, Oregon and Washington may have consulted or even used parts of an early version of General DeWitt's evacuation report, the amici did not represent or even suggest that the Supreme Court should give special consideration to those portions of their brief because such portions originated with General DeWitt's com-

---

but simply "pointed out that undoubtedly the Japanese Navy had made preparations for submarines to proceed to the West Coast immediately after Pearl Harbor and, quite naturally . . . these attacks would follow." Ex. 41, Memo p. 3.

[11] On December 31, 1941, San Francisco FCC supervisor Greaves (see Ex. 102) told Lt. Col. L. R. Forney, General DeWitt's G-2 in charge of counterespionage (see Ex. 107, p. 1) that he operated "only a monitoring service and has only a very few men" and that there "probably are a large number of . . . records in Washington pertaining to [suspected illegal radio sets on the West Coast] but they are not immediately available to him." Nonetheless, he guessed that there were not "more than ten to twenty-five cases of reasonably probable illegal operation of radio sending sets on the entire Pacific Coast." The impression Lt. Col. Forney gained was that the FCC was "not in a position to take an extensive part in solving the problem being considered by the Commanding General." (Ex. A-83). At a subsequent meeting with the FCC on January 9, 1942, General DeWitt's officers "stressed the necessity of finding the transmitter quickly. . . ." Ex. 107, p. 3. The FCC representative, George Sterling, who was the Chief of the FCC's National Defense Operations (see Ex. 102, p. 2), told General DeWitt "that . . . while time is of the essence . . . not to be surprised if it took several hours and possibly days if [the transmitter] were moving about." Ex. 107, p. 3. This led General DeWitt to immediately concur in the plans for a well equipped and staffed Joint Radio Intelligence Center (Ex. 107, p. 4), and General DeWitt went so far as to agree to finance its $30,000 start up cost and $200,000 annual operating cost (Ex. 107, p. 4; Ex. 106, Ex. 104). The Center did not actually begin operating, however, until March 1942 (Ex. 43, p. 3) and did not change General DeWitt's sincere belief that in the event of an emergency, "a number of illegal stations will come into being." Ex. 81. As late as January 24, 1942, General DeWitt continued to believe that illegal transmitters were aiding the enemy, and DeWitt freely said so to the Secretary of War, who informed the Attorney General that he had independently confirmed General DeWitt's apprehensions. Ex. A-2.

[12] See the G-2 Periodic Reports, Part 4, e.g., Ex. 57, p. 2; Ex. 58, p. 2; Ex. 59, p. 2; Ex. 60, p. 2; Ex. 61, pp. 2–3; Ex. 62, p. 2; Ex. 63, p. 3; Ex. 64, p. 4. Petitioner's observation that the nearest hostile ground forces were more than 2,000 miles away (Pet. Post-Hearing Br. 27:18, 28:5) is beside the point.

mand. At the coram nobis hearing, petitioner's witness, Ennis, could not recall whether these amici on behalf of the government got the same pages of the early version of DeWitt's report that were made available to Ennis and Burling at the Department of Justice at that time (Tr. 282: 15–24), as suggested in Ex. 84, p. 2, or whether the amici got other portions as well, as suggested in Ex. 2, p. 3. Ennis was offended not so much by the amici, as at the Army officials who made DeWitt's draft available to the amici without Ennis' knowledge or permission (Tr. 283:4–12). Ennis conceded, however, that if his permission had been asked he probably would not have objected to making the material available to the amici (Tr. 284:15–285:1). At all events, Ennis testified that no part of the amici brief that was filed was particularly offensive (Tr. 284:3–6), and none of these actions materially altered the way this case was argued and decided (Tr. 283:13–15). There was, therefore, no evidence that this conduct had any effect on the outcome of this case.

In sum, petitioner has not carried his heavy burden of demonstrating that any errors of a fundamental magnitude occurred, and that "but for [them] a more favorable judgment would have been rendered." *United States* v. *Darnell*, supra, 716 F.2d at 481, n.5. This is true not only as to petitioner's curfew conviction—which is all, we submit, that was at issue in the Supreme Court in 1943—but, as we have demonstrated above, even as to petitioner's evacuation conviction.[13]

At bottom, petitioner suggests that it was improper for the government simply to brief a judicial notice argument, and erroneous for the Supreme Court to have utilized judicial notice to deal with confidential military information (which included the highly secret decrypting of intercepted Japanese cables), rather than remanding the case for a public trial of these matters during an ongoing war. This is the same procedural issue which concerned Justice Jackson in the *Korematsu* case (dissenting, 323 U.S. at 245) where he complained that military decisions are not susceptible of "intelligent judicial appraisal" because they "do not pretend to rest on evidence, but are made on information that often would not be admissible[,] assumptions that could not be proved," and confidential national defense information that "could not be disclosed to courts. . . ." That issue, however, was thoroughly discussed and decided in 1943 and the

---

[13] At the coram nobis hearing, petitioner's own counsel candidly told the court: "We can't sit here today and say that if this information had been made available to the Court it would have changed the Court's opinion. I don't think anyone can say that." (Tr. 114:16–19.) Accord, *Korematsu* v. *United States*, 584 F. Supp. 1406, 1419 (N.D. Ca. 1984) ("Whether a fuller, more accurate record would have prompted a different decision cannot be determined.")

doctrine of *res judicata* bars the petitioner from reopening his case simply to relitigate this issue because it might be more favorably treated now than in 1943. The Supreme Court in *Federated Department Stores, Inc.* v. *Moitie*, 452 U.S. 394, 398, 401–402 (1981), stated in words equally applicable here:

> . . . the *res judicata* consequences of a final . . . judgment on the merits [are not] altered by the fact that the judgment may have been wrong or rested on a legal principle subsequently overruled in another case. *Angel* v. *Bullington*, 330 U.S. 183, 182 (1947); *Chicot County Drainage District* v. *Baxter State Bank*, 308 U.S. 371 (1940); *Wilson's Executor* v. *Dean*, 121 U.S. 525, 534 (1887).

This court has long recognized that "[p]ublic policy dictates that there be an end of litigation; that those who have contested an issue shall be bound by the result of the contest, and that matters once tried shall be considered forever settled as between the parties." *Baldwin* v. *Traveling Men's Assn.*, 283 U.S. 522, 525 (1931).

2. Laches Bars Relief

Petitioner has failed to carry his burden of showing "sound reasons" for his failure to seek appropriate earlier relief.

A recent Ninth Circuit opinion, *Maghe* v. *United States*, 710 F.2d 503 (9th Cir.), cert. denied, 463 U.S. 1212 (1983), restated the rule announced by the Supreme Court in *United States* v. *Morgan*, 346 U.S. 502, 512 (1954):

> To be entitled to a writ of *coram nobis*, Maghe must show that, there are "sound reasons" for his failure to seek relief earlier. *United States* v. *Morgan*, 346 U.S. 502, 512, 74 S.Ct. 247, 253, 98 L.Ed. 248 (1954). The district court properly denied Maghe's petition without a hearing because he failed to allege an adequate factual basis justifying his 25-year delay in seeking relief. See *United States* v. *Taylor*, 648 F.2d 565, 573 (9th Cir.), cert. denied, 545 U.S. 866, 102 S.Ct. 329, 70 L.Ed.2d 168 (1981).

The court then went on to explain that a prior lack of interest or a newly acquired interest in seeking relief is not a "sound reason" that will justify a long delay in seeking legal relief. *Accord United States* v. *Correa-DeJesus*, 708 F.2d 1283, 1286 (7th Cir.), cert. denied, 464 U.S. 1010 (1983).

The factual circumstances which this petitioner raises have all been matters of public record for nearly forty years. This petitioner's 1943 Supreme Court brief explicitly complained to the Supreme Court about General DeWitt's statements that "There is no way to determine [Japanese

American] loyalty." Ex. 130, p. 25. Korematsu's 1944 pleadings (Ex. A-46, pp. 21–23) argued to the Supreme Court about the government's footnote in its *Korematsu* brief and about: (1) General DeWitt's reported illegal radio signals; (2) the *Harper's* article conclusions; and (3) the lack of ONI or FBI reports in the record. The 1944 McWilliams book (Ex. A-67, p. 114) [and the 1945 Dembitz law review article (Ex. A-66, p. 191, fn.55)] identified Lt. Com. K. D. Ringle of the ONI as author of the *Harper's* magazine article. Morton Grodzins published *Americans Betrayed* in 1949 (Ex. A-49) and recounted in great detail the controversy among the Department of Justice, the FBI, the FCC, Ringle's supporters, and the War Department.[14] Since petitioner conceded in his testimony at the coram nobis hearing that he was not unfamiliar with these source materials but nonetheless made no real effort to seek to challenge his conviction until the 1970's, he has contributed by his own inaction to the four decades of delay which have made it impossible for a court to re-examine and redecide what originally occurred. In addition, as the testimony of Ennis and the government witnesses showed, detailed recollections about these very specific forty year old events are no longer available. Even where old records of these events were made (see Ex. A-78, p. 132, fn.17 and Ex. A-11, p. 121, fn.20, quoting and recounting in 1960 the importance in 1942 of Ex. A-50), the notes of those now enfeebled military historians, e.g., Stetson Conn (coram nobis testimony of Hannah Zeidlik), though available at least as late as 1969 (see Ex. A-74, p. vii), have also been lost (coram nobis testimony of Hannah Zeidlik).

All the while, the archival material—from which petitioner's attorney was able to obtain and construct the bulk of the petition in four months

---

[14]Chapter nine, particularly pp. 280–297, of Grodzins' 1949 book, (which this Court agreed to judicially notice for laches purposes, Tr. 535:20–21) detailed most of the same publicly available declassified intelligence information and exhibits discussed by the petitioner. The book commented upon the policy position of Lt. Com. Ringle of the Office of Naval Intelligence (*Americans Betrayed*, pp. 145–146 & n.46, 188–189), the FBI (*id.*, pp. 188, n.23, 257–258 & n.49), and the FCC (*id.*, pp. 291–293) contradicting the Final Report's references such as to off-shore and radio signalling. Grodzins' book also highlights the position of General DeWitt and the conflict between McCloy at the War Department and Ennis at the Department of Justice. As a result, Grodzins suggested going back to the judicial system in 1949 because, citing Justice Jackson, "the Court's validation of evacuation remains like a loaded weapon. . . ." (*Id.*, pp. 357–358.) This is the identical justification petitioner urges today (Post-Hearing Br. 49:16). The research for Grodzins' book included access in the 1940's to the Department of Justice files (*id.*, 182, n.6, 208, n.6) and personal interviews with Ed Ennis (*id.*, 231, n.1, 232, n.3, 255, n.57), James Rowe, Jr., then assistant to the Attorney General (*id.*, 240, n.21, 266, n.78), John J. McCloy, then Assistant Secretary of War (*id.*, 259, n.65, p. 264, n.74), and Francis Biddle, then Attorney General (*id.*, 270, n.85). See also the earlier 1946 WRA publication (Ex. A-47, pp. 154–159, 167), which reprinted the text of the 1944 FBI and FCC letters disparaging General DeWitt's evacuation report.

(between August 28, 1981, Tr. Ex. A-76, and December 9, 1981, Ex. A-8)—and the different versions of DeWitt's evacuation report were publicly available at the National Archives (Ex. A-124, Ex. A-109, Ex. A-108, and coram nobis testimony of Hannah Zeidlik). Petitioner testified that prior to the filing of the petition, he never even made an FOIA request to review the original documents and memoranda from his case.

The district court decision in *Hohri* v. *United States*, 586 F. Supp. 769 (D.D.C. 1984, app. pending No. 84-5460) (Japanese American internment related civil damage suit) is instructive in this respect. Almost the identical factual allegations of misconduct made here were made there (see 586 F. Supp. 772–781). That court stated that the same books and public records offered by the government in the instant case showed on their face that even under the plaintiff's version of the facts, "the underlying documents concealed from the Supreme Court in 1944 became public and were available to diligent plaintiffs from the late 1940's onward." *Id*. at 790. The court continued:

The publication in the late 1940's of the previously concealed Ringle, Fly, and Hoover documents, not the publication in the 1980's of the Ennis and Burling memoranda, provided the basis on which plaintiffs could have filed a complaint challenging the military necessity finding . . . (*Id*.)

It may be that timely claims on their behalf would have prevailed. But it is now close to forty years after the camps were closed, and almost that long after the facts essential to those claims were published. Much time has passed, memories have dimmed, and many of the actors have died.* (*Id*. at 795.)

---

*For example, General DeWitt, a critical witness, died in 1962.

The conclusion is inescapable. Petitioner has offered no sufficient justification for his forty year delay in seeking relief.

3. Petitioner Labors Under No Legal Disabilities and Presents No Cognizable Injury Which This Court Could Redress

If there are no present adverse legal consequences flowing from a conviction, there is no justiciable case or controversy.

Collateral attacks upon old criminal convictions, where the sentence has already been served, are moot "if it is shown that there is no possibility that any collateral legal consequences will be imposed on the basis of the challenged conviction." *Sibron* v. *New York*, 392 U.S. 40, 57 (1968); *United States* v. *Morgan*, supra, 346 U.S. at 512–513; *Ybarra* v. *United States*, 461 F.2d 1195 (9th Cir. 1972); *Chavez* v. *United States*, 447 F.2d

1373 (9th Cir. 1971). This doctrine was recently discussed in *Lane* v. *Williams*, 455 U.S. 624, 632 (1982). There, the Supreme Court noted that the typical legal consequences which warranted an exercise of collateral relief involved civil penalties such as loss of the right to vote, the right to serve as an official of a labor union for a specified period of time, or to engage in certain businesses. None of those allegations are made here.

This petitioner offered no testimony at the coram nobis hearing that his convictions ever resulted in the loss of a job or impeachment in any legal proceeding. His only claim is that he suffers from moral stigma and that there is the "remote" possibility (Pet.'s Post-Hearing Br. 48) that his now forty year old test case misdemeanor convictions could be used in some legal forum to impeach his credibility or affect some future sentence.

There is no allegation that the misdemeanor convictions at issue deprive petitioner of any of his civil rights (to vote, etc.). As in *Lane* v. *Williams*, supra, since no felony violations are involved

. . . No civil disabilities such as those present in *Carafas* [v. *La Valle*, 391 U.S. 234] result . . . At most, certain nonstatutory consequences may occur; employment prospects, or the sentence imposed in a future criminal proceeding, could be affected. . . . The discretionary decisions that are made by an employer or a sentencing judge, however, are not governed by the mere presence or absence of a recorded violation . . . Any disabilities that flow from what respondents did . . . are not removed or even affected by a District Court order . . . In these circumstances, no live controversy remains.

In *St. Pierre* v. *United States*, 319 U.S. 41, 43 (1943), the Supreme Court stated that it is an insufficient allegation, *as a matter of law*, to allege as a present adverse legal consequence "that the judgment may impair [the petitioner's] credibility . . . in any future legal proceeding." In *Sibron*, the Court did not overrule that holding, but rather revalidated it and took considerable pains to distinguish it on the unique facts present in *Sibron*. In this regard, the *Sibron* opinion states, 392 U.S. at 56, fn.17:

We note that there is a clear distinction between a *general* impairment of credibility, to which the Court referred in *St. Pierre*, see 319 U.S., at 43, and New York's *specific statutory* authorization for use of the conviction to impeach the "character" of a defendant in a criminal proceeding. The latter is a clear legal disability deliberately and specifically imposed by the legislature. (Emphasis added.)

In the instant case, this "clear distinction" between a general and specific impairment of credibility is totally absent. There is no specific statutory disability imposed by the federal legislature attaching to this misdemeanor conviction. Indeed, just the opposite is true here. The federal legislature has repealed the statute involved in the instant case, 18 U.S.C. § 1383, and enacted 18 U.S.C. § 4001(a) to prohibit the repetition of any similar executive orders.

If petitioner were correct that the "remote" possibility of impeachment from a forty year old already-repealed *malum prohibitum* misdemeanor in some undetermined state or foreign legal forum is a sufficient disability to maintain a case or controversy, then the above-quoted language from *Sibron* was totally unnecessary and *St. Pierre* has been overruled, not distinguished. Every outstanding conviction, no matter how slight its effect, could hypothetically lead to impeachment in some forum and would therefore be sufficient, per se, to maintain collateral review. That result would render *St. Pierre* a nullity and would have obviated the *Sibron* decision's careful language distinguishing, not overruling, *St. Pierre*. See, e.g., 392 U.S. at 56, fn.17 supra and also at pp.51, 53 and fn.13, and 57.

The second adverse legal consequence that petitioner has identified, "that the conviction will become a consideration in some future sentencing," is also legally insufficient. That too is universally true of all convictions in every conceivable hypothetical situation. Therefore, this ruling is also in direct conflict with the continued viability of *St. Pierre*. Once again, in *Sibron* a *specific* legislative provision in the New York Criminal Code mandated that any subsequent repetition of that misdemeanant conduct (possession of burglary tools) by Sibron would thereafter be treated as a felony. 392 U.S. at 56 and at 48, fn.5. That kind of *specific* legislative penalty enhancement is not present in this case. In contrast, the legal sufficiency of the mere speculative possibility that "the sentence imposed in a future criminal proceeding, could be affected" not only by the underlying conduct (which a federal judge is *always* free to consider, see 18 U.S.C. § 3577), but additionally by the formal judgment of conviction, was recently reconsidered in *Lane* v. *Williams*, 455 U.S. 624, 632 (1982) and rejected, over Justice Marshall's dissent on that very point, 455 U.S. at 637. See also *United States* v. *Ray*, 683 F.2d 1116, 1120–1122 (7th Cir.) cert. denied, 459 U.S. 1091 (1982) (even conduct underlying a prior acquittal may be considered at a subsequent sentencing); *United States* v. *Grayson*, 438 U.S. 41, 50 (1978).

Furthermore, the record in this case shows that this conviction is not within the *Sibron* rule because it is not like "most criminal convictions" which we readily concede ordinarily entail adverse consequences. Most criminal convictions, however, either involve a felony with its concomitant loss of civil rights, or involve moral turpitude, or are *malum in se*, or involve statutory crimes which have not long ago been legislatively repealed and discredited. The do not commonly involve situations where the defendant marches into the police station demanding to be arrested for a regulatory violation in order to test its constitutionality in the Supreme Court.

Since the government has challenged and rebutted the presumption of adverse legal consequences which would attach in the ordinary felony case, and since petitioner's unmeritorious suggestion of remote legal consequences provides a legally insufficient basis for Article III jurisdiction, there is no case or controversy and the petition must be dismissed.

Conclusion

For all the above described legal and factual reasons, petitioner has not demonstrated that there was prosecutorial misconduct which resulted in a fundamental miscarriage of justice. Because petitioner has been unable to carry the heavy burden he must bear to overturn these forty year old misdemeanor convictions, the petition should be denied.

Respectfully submitted,

Gene S. Anderson, United States Attorney

Susan E. Barnes, Assistant U.S. Attorney, Western District of
    Washington

Victor D. Stone, Richard L. Edwards, Attorneys, General Litigation and
    Legal Advice Section, U.S. Department of Justice

Hirabayashi v. United States

Petitioner's Reply Brief, U.S. District Court for the
Western District of Washington

October 4, 1985

In the reply brief filed in response to the government's post-trial brief, Hirabayashi's lawyers argued that government lawyers had misquoted the trial testimony of Edward Ennis to suggest that Ennis had no objections to the Justice Department arguments before the Supreme Court in 1943. The reply brief also argued that government lawyers had withheld exculpatory evidence from the Supreme Court. Finally, Hirabayashi's lawyers attacked the government's efforts to introduce the so-called Magic cables into the case, arguing first that the cables were "irrelevant" to the misconduct charges in the coram nobis petition and, second, that the cables failed to show any evidence of espionage on the part of Japanese Americans.

I. Introduction

Petitioner is respectfully requesting the following relief from this Court:

1. Vacation of his two misdemeanor convictions under Public Law 503;

2. Dismissal of the indictments filed against him under Public Law 503;

3. Granting of his Petition for a Writ of Error Coram Nobis herein;

4. Findings of Fact as bases for the above-requested relief that Petitioner was denied his due process rights by the Government by the suppression of material evidence.

II. The Government Misconduct

A. The Government Misled the Court on the Issue of Military Necessity

Petitioner's defense against the indictments was that the statute and orders were unconstitutional. The Supreme Court's ruling on this challenge of constitutionality turned upon the military necessity of General DeWitt's action. Upon this crucial issue, the Government misled the Supreme Court to believe that General DeWitt issued the military orders pursuant to a duly made factual basis of military necessity.

In reviewing the constitutionality of the challenged orders, the Court stated the issue as follows:

. . . our inquiry must be whether *in light of all the facts and circumstances* there was any substantial basis for the conclusion, in which Congress and the military commander united, that the curfew as applied was a protective measure necessary to meet the threat of sabotage and espionage which would substantially affect the war effort and which might reasonably be expected to aid a threatened enemy invasion.

(Emphasis added.) *Hirabayashi* v. *United States*, 320 U.S. 81 at 95 (1943). However, the Court was given only a limited set of facts by the Government through resort to judicial notice and the amici curiae. From this carefully tailored set of facts, the Government argued the military orders were issued as a matter of military necessity grounded upon a factual basis, despite possession by the Government of persuasive military and intelligence reports directly contrary to this position.

The Government in its brief to the Court asserted:

[the military orders were] founded upon the fact that the group [of Japanese residents] as a whole contained an unknown number of persons who could not readily be singled out and who were a threat to the security of the nation; and in order to impose effective restraints upon them it was necessary not only to deal with the entire group, but to deal with it at once.

(Ex. 99, p. 35.)

If those Japanese who might aid the enemy were either known or readily identifiable, the task of segregating them would probably have been comparatively simple. However, the identities of the potentially disloyal were not readily discoverable.

(Ex. 99, pp. 61–62.) The Government argued that the insufficiency of time determined the need to impose the military orders on the entire Japanese West Coast population. This is reflected in Mr. Ennis' testimony below:

Q. (By Mr. Hall) In the context of the Government's presentation of its case to the Supreme Court, either in written form or oral form, Mr. Ennis, how important to the Government's case was the concept that there was not sufficient time within which to make a distinction between the sheep and the goats?

A. Well, really, our formula or our argument that there was not time was the whole center of our argument, and as I understand it, that was the center of the Supreme Court's decision by the Chief Justice, who said that if the military commander believed that there were possible espionage agents or saboteurs in the group and there was not sufficient time to take—to determine their existence, that then he could remove the whole group. It was the whole argument.

(Tr. 243:19–244:7.)[1] The Government re-emphasized that position to the Supreme Court subsequent to oral argument before the Court. (Ex. 131.)

Subsequently, the Court accepted the argument of the Government and stated:

We cannot say that the war-making branches of the Government did not have ground for believing that in a critical hour such persons could not readily be isolated and separately dealt with, and constituted a menace to the national defense and safety, which demanded that prompt and adequate measures be taken to guard against it.

320 U.S. at 99. The Court went on to conclude:

[the military orders] themselves followed a standard authorized by the Executive Order—the necessity of protecting military resources in the designated areas against espionage and sabotage. And by the Act [Public Law 503], Congress gave its approval to that standard. We have no need to consider now the validity of action if taken by the military commander without conforming to this standard approved by Congress, or the validity of orders made without the support of findings showing that they do so conform. *Here the findings of danger from espionage and sabotage, and of the necessity of the curfew order to protect against them, have been duly made.* . . .

The military commander's appraisal of facts in the light of the *authorized standard,* and the inferences which he drew from those facts, involved the exercise of his *informed* judgment.

(Emphasis added.) 320 U.S. at 103. The Court clearly relied upon the Government's misrepresentation that General DeWitt, in his informed

---

[1] Respondent in its Closing Argument at page 40 misquotes Mr. Ennis' testimony representing that Mr. Ennis believed the position of the Government represented to the Supreme Court was appropriate. Mr. Ennis' actual testimony was "[T]he statement in the brief was correct, if you accept the

judgment of the facts, issued his orders as a matter of military necessity because there existed an unidentifiable group of Japanese residents who posed a threat of espionage or sabotage and the potentially disloyal could not be readily identified.

This misrepresentation was contrary to persuasive military and intelligence reports possessed by the Government at that time. Those reports established that:

1. There was no factual basis for concluding that the Japanese population posed a threat of espionage or sabotage (Ex. 41, Tab 37; Ex. 43, Tab 29; Ex. 76, Tab 30);

2. The information in General DeWitt's possession was that the military orders were not necessary (Ex. 40, Tab 31; Ex. 42, Tab 38; Ex. 38, Tab 32);

3. General DeWitt's actual assertion of military necessity was based upon his misinformed judgment that the loyal and potentially disloyal Japanese could not be identified regardless of how much time the identification required (Ex. 42, Tab 38); and

4. The potentially disloyal were readily identified such as not to require the imposition of the military orders on the entire Japanese population on the West Coast (Ex. 4, Tab 17; Ex. 32, Tab 4; Ex. 77, Tab 12).

1. The proceedings below. The Government now attempts to argue that it was under no obligation to come forward with the exculpatory evidence because Petitioner did not make a factual record disputing the existence of a war emergency. (Gov't. Closing Argument, "G.C.A." hereafter, p. 5.)[2] This argument is transparently groundless. First, Petitioner does not challenge the existence of a war emergency. His challenge then and now is that the military orders were unconstitutional and that they were not necessary to meet the "war emergency." Secondly, Petitioner's inability to perfect a factual record does not excuse the affirmative misrepresentations by the Government to the Court.

Finally, the Government's position renders the Government's obligation meaningless. It is illogical to require a defendant to demand production of evidence of which defendant has no knowledge. If the Government had disclosed the exculpatory evidence to Petitioner, he could have developed

---

proposition that there was a severe—a serious enough danger in the Japanese community to have any exclusion program at all, which I did not . . ." (Tr. 279:12–15.)

[2]Respondent misconstrues the record on this point. Nothing in the record reflects whether or not Petitioner attempted to solicit facts on the issue of military necessity.

the factual record which the Government now criticizes Petitioner for failing to do.

Here the Government knew Petitioner's defense to the indictments was that the military orders were unconstitutional. Here the Government knew the Court's review of the constitutionality of the orders turned upon the military necessity for the orders. Here the Government argued a factual basis of military necessity directly contrary to the persuasive evidence in its possession. Therefore, the Government was under an obligation to disclose the exculpatory evidence to the Court and to Petitioner.

2. *Continued misrepresentation.* Even after high Government officials debated amongst themselves about the duty to advise the Court of the contrary evidence (*See*, Ex. 2, Tab 90; Ex. 35, Tab 36), the Department of Justice deliberately chose to continue its misrepresentations to the Court. Although Mr. Ennis believed a footnote placed in the U.S. Brief to the Court in *Korematsu* met the minimum standards for disclaiming any reliance on General DeWitt's factual assertions in support of military necessity (Tr. 252:17–254:16; Tr. 325:20–362:3), Solicitor General Fahy, in oral argument before the Supreme Court, disclaimed the significance of the footnote such as to render it totally meaningless. (Ex. 98, Tab 19.) More to the point, the footnote disclaimer did not sufficiently disclose to Petitioner and to the Court the body of persuasive exculpatory evidence which directly contradicted the Government's statements to the Court.

B. The Exculpatory Military and Intelligence Reports

The first version of General DeWitt's Final Report (Ex. 4, Tab 7) was material to the issues before the courts in the prosecution of Petitioner because it established what General DeWitt's actual military considerations were in issuing his military orders. His true position was the insistence that the loyal and potentially disloyal Japanese could not be distinguished regardless of any consideration of time. This true expression of General DeWitt's position was withheld by the War Department from the Department of Justice attorneys, from Petitioner and from the courts in violation of the Government's obligation to disclose exculpatory evidence. *U.S.* v. *Butler*, 567 F.2d 885 (9th Cir., 1978); *U.S.* v. *Bryant*, 439 F.2d 642 (D.C. Cir. 1971). The Government misconduct was compounded by the subsequent alteration of the Final Report.[3]

---

[3] Among the crucial changes to the Final Report were the following changes made on page 9 of the Final Report:

The Ringle Report (Ex. 32, Tab 4) and FBI reports (e.g., Ex. 38, Tab 32) establish that the potentially disloyal were readily identifiable, contrary to what the Government represented to the Supreme Court. The Ringle, FBI and FCC reports also establish that there was no factual basis in support of General DeWitt's military orders and that there was no evidence of sabotage and espionage by Japanese Americans. Thus Mr. Ennis testified:

[T]he Department of Justice was responsible under the law for order and dealing with espionage and sabotage through our Federal Bureau of Investigation, and the Bureau did not feel that there was any evidence sufficient to support the proposed eventual evacuation of all persons of Japanese ancestry from the West Coast, and there were numerous conferences between the Attorney General and the Secretary of War and Mr. Stimson on that level, and the Assistant Secretary of War and Mr. Biddle's first assistant, and myself on the second level.

(Tr. 201:23–202:7.)

[The] Bureau had no evidence which would indicate that the Japanese-American population were a danger or that anything more was required than the couple of thousand Japanese aliens that we had picked up very quickly and detained because of possible loyalty to Japan . . .

(Tr. 203:15–20.)[4] Mr. Ennis further testified that the Department of Justice knew of these military and intelligence reports during the course of Petitioner's appeals through the Supreme Court but did not disclose them to the Court or to Petitioner. (Tr. 208:1–8; Tr. 209:5–15; Tr. 210:1–10)[5]

C. "Magic"

The Government argues that the intercepted and decrypted Japanese diplomatic cables formed the basis for General DeWitt's military orders. The "Magic" cables are both factually incorrect and irrelevant to this

---

"It was impossible to establish the identity of the loyal and the disloyal with any degree of safety. It was not that there was insufficient time in which to make such a determination . . ." Ex. 4, Tab 17, page 9 (first Final Report).

"To complicate the situation no ready means existed for determining the loyal and the disloyal with any degree of safety." Ex. 29, Tab 85, page 9 (rewritten Final Report).

Exhibit 14, Tab 67; Exhibit 101, Tab 68; and Exhibit 18, Tab 71 establish that the changes were substantively significant alterations of General DeWitt's expressions of his bases for his military orders and that he resisted the alterations strenuously.

[4] All of the Government's former G-2 and FBI trial witnesses testified that they knew of no evidence that Japanese Americans had committed acts of espionage or sabotage.

[5] Respondent at G.C.A., page 15 argues that it was not required to make disclosures because in 1943 there existed no procedure allowing for in camera review of classified documents. This argument is untenable. See, *United States* v. *Andolschek*, 142 F.2d 503 (2nd Cir., 1944).

coram nobis petition. The Government's argument seems to be that the substance of these MAGIC cables indicates that second generation Japanese Americans were being recruited into an espionage network and critical military information was being relayed by them to Japan. The Government then maintains this information was widely circulated in FBI, ONI and MID memos and reports. Therefore, according to what seems to be the Government's argument, this information formed the basis for General DeWitt's military orders. The evidence introduced at trial conclusively refutes this argument.

First, the cables do not establish that a Japanese American espionage network was ever successfully implemented. The cables speak of Japan's desire to create a network through the use of all resources, including communists, labor unions and blacks, as well as Japanese Americans. (Ex. A-17)

Second, according to the evidence at trial, the military information which was relayed to Japan was publicly available information which did not require any clandestine network. For example, Exhibit 144, which is the first half of a cable transmission submitted by Respondent (Ex. A-24), reveals that the military information was released by the president of the Boeing Company to a Senate Committee or was from public statements made by General DeWitt. Exhibits 145 and 146 establish that military plane production data, including contract award figures, payroll size and numbers of employees, were available to and published by the newspapers.

Third, there is no evidence that the "Magic" cables or their substance formed a basis for any of General DeWitt's military orders. The Government's argument ignores General DeWitt's actual statement of his military considerations as written in his first Final Report. Moreover, to the extent that the substance of "Magic" was widely distributed to the ONI and FBI, those agencies nonetheless concluded after further investigation that there was no factual basis or need for the military orders. As Colonel John Herzig testified, any responsible intelligence agency would use the raw information contained in "Magic" and conduct further investigations before arriving at any conclusion. Exhibits 149 and 150 illustrate the course of investigation by the ONI and FBI.

A reading of the "Magic" cables submitted as exhibits by the Government reveals that they are simply irrelevant to this coram nobis petition. Assuming arguendo that "Magic" may have some probative value on the issue of military necessity, "Magic" still has no bearing on the suppression of exculpatory evidence by the Government.

III. Standard of Review

The leading Ninth Circuit case regarding coram nobis is *United States* v. *Taylor*, 648 F.2d 565 (9th Cir.), cert. denied, 454 U.S. 866 (1981). Coram nobis relief is warranted where Government abuses "offend elementary standards of justice," cause "serious prejudice to the accused," or, even absent such prejudice, "undermine public confidence in the administration of justice." *Taylor*, 648 F.2d at 571. The Court noted that new trials had been ordered when the prosecution knowingly uses perjured testimony or withholds materially favorable evidence from the defense. 648 F.2d at 571. Here the Government used false evidence, suppressed evidence and misrepresented evidence to obtain a favorable determination with respect to the constitutionality of Public Law 503 and the underlying curfew and evacuation orders. The Court should, therefore, apply the standards of materiality discussed in Petitioner's Hearing Memorandum and Post-Hearing Brief and in *Mooney* v. *Holohan*, 294 U.S. 103 (1935), *Brady* v. *Maryland*, 373 U.S. 83 (1963), and *United States* v. *Agurs*, 427 U.S. 97 (1976).[6]

In this case, the Government misconduct so violated the most fundamental standards of justice that the Court should grant the requested relief based upon any reasonable standard of materiality.[7] Contrary to the Government's misconstruction of the law, Petitioner does not bear the burden of proving that but for the Government's suppression of evidence and use of false evidence the outcome of Petitioner's trial would have been different. Under the Government's proposed new standard of review, a new trial will never be necessary because the Court would have already decided that the outcome would be different. Furthermore, common sense and logic dictate it would be impossible to know whether the outcome would be different unless the case, absent the false evidence and including the new evidence, was timely presented to the original trier of fact and original appellate courts.

[6]The Government cites *United States* v. *Badley*, _____ U.S. _____, 105 S.Ct. 3375, 53 LW 5048 (1985), for the proposition that, "in all *Agurs* and *Brady* situations 'evidence is material only if there is a reasonable probability that had the evidence been disclosed to the defense, the result of the proceeding would have been different.'" This language, however, is cited from Part III of Justice Blackmun's opinion which was joined by only one other justice. Therefore, this portion of the opinion is not controlling.

[7]In *United States* v. *Hastings*, 461 U.S. 499, (1983), the Court acknowledges there are certain errors that may involve "rights so basic to a fair trial that their infraction can never be treated as harmless error." *Hastings*, 461 U.S. at 508, n. 6, citing *Chapman* v. *California*, 386 U.S. 18, 23 (1967). Yet the Government cites *Hastings* for the proposition that "'considerations of justice,' 'judicial integrity,' and intentional 'illegal conduct' are not enough, standing alone, to warrant vacat-

IV. Laches

The Court should exercise its equitable powers to bar the Government's laches defense on the following grounds:

A. *The Government Is Estopped by Unclean Hands*

"He who comes into equity must come with clean hands." *Precision Instrument Mfg. Co.* v. *Automotive Maintenance Mach. Co.*, 324 U.S. 806, 814 (1945). This is especially true where, as here, the case involves issues of substantial public importance:

Where a suit in equity concerns the public as well as private interests . . . , this doctrine assumes even wider and more significant proportions. For if an equity court properly uses the maxim to withhold its assistance in such a case, it not only prevents a wrongdoer from enjoying the fruits of his transgression but averts an injury to the public.

Id. at 815.

The pervasive pattern of misconduct by the Government's suppression, alteration, and attempted destruction of evidence, together with a knowing presentation of false evidence in order to obtain Petitioner's convictions should preclude the Government from now invoking equity to prevent redress of that injustice.

B. *The Government Has Failed To Show Prejudice*

The Government has also failed to establish that it has been prejudiced by Petitioner's alleged delay. Despite its repeated assertion that witnesses have died and memories of living witnesses have faded, the Government has not made any showing whatsoever as to what testimony these witnesses would have been able to give to negate the plain import of the evidence offered by Petitioner in this case. This failure is especially significant since the Petition is principally based on the Government's own documents. Indeed, the Government's failure to call McCloy, Bendetsen or Wechsler as witnesses in this case—although these central actors are

---

ing a conviction if the resultant 'errors alleged are harmless' since 'the conviction would have been obtained notwithstanding the asserted error.'" G.C.A., at 11. Furthermore, the Government's misconduct cannot be characterized as harmless error. *Hastings* involved statements made by the prosecutor about the defendants' suppression of evidence and the knowing use of false evidence to establish the constitutionality of Public Law 503 and the underlying curfew and evacuation orders.

not only alive but have testified before various forums in recent years—only emphasizes the lack of merit in the Government's claim of prejudice.

C. Petitioner Exercised Due Diligence

In *Morgan*, the Supreme Court did not speak in terms of laches but required the petitioner only to show "sound reasons" for his inability to seek earlier relief. *Morgan* v. *United States*, 346 U.S. 502 (1954). Furthermore, Petitioner can only be found lacking diligence if his delay in filing is both unreasonable and inexcusable and if the Government is prejudiced by the lapse of time and changed conditions occasioned by such delay. As stated before, the Government has failed to establish a prejudice due to Petitioner's delay, and the Petitioner has demonstrated that the long delay was both reasonable and justifiable.

Petitioner is not a professional archival researcher. From the testimony of Hannah Zeidlik and Aiko Herzig-Yoshinaga, it is apparent that the relevant documents which gave rise to this petition for writ of error coram nobis are located in various geographic locations across the country and the retrieval of those documents would require technical skills and knowledge of repositories of archival materials. Petitioner did not have the financial resources or technical skills necessary to discover and retrieve these documents.

Victor Stone, attorney for the Government, has had the financial and personnel resources available to him as a Government attorney in this litigation. He represented to this Court that even he, after working on this case over one year, determined that screening the relevant materials for this case presented such difficulty that he would have to hire a historical researcher. (Tr. 117:13–16, May 18, 1984) Moreover, as an attorney responding to specific allegations, Victor Stone was in a position to focus his archival research towards obtaining specific information. Mr. Hirabayashi, working on his own, with no special training or knowledge, could not reasonably be expected in the exercise of due diligence to venture into the archives on a generalized mission to discover governmental misconduct in the handling of his original case.

Moreover, the Government would impose an onerous burden on Mr. Hirabayashi to overcome a laches defense. To expect an ordinary person to meet such a standard would create an undue burden such that coram nobis petitioners would rarely, if ever, survive a laches defense.

Finally, Mr. Hirabayashi is not an attorney and has had no legal training. Even if he had flown to Washington, D.C., and to other repositories year after year as documents became available or declassified, it is unreasonable to expect that he would be in a position to determine what causes of action he might have after examining the bulk of the documents introduced as evidence in his trial on the coram nobis petition.

D. The Defense of Laches Is Inappropriate Because the Misconduct Constitutes a Fraud on the Court

Even assuming that Petitioner may not have been diligent, which is not conceded here, the defense of laches nonetheless remains inappropriate. As the Supreme Court declared in *Hazel-Atlas*, wherein it rejected the contention that relief from a ten-year old judgment obtained on the basis of fabricated evidence was barred by laches:

But even if Hazel did not exercise the highest degree of diligence Hartford's fraud cannot be condoned for that reason alone. This matter does not concern only private parties. . . . It is a wrong against the institutions set up to protect and safeguard the public, institutions in which fraud cannot complacently be tolerated consistently with the good order of society.

Hazel-Atlas Glass Co. v. *Hartford-Empire Co.*, 322 U.S. 238, 246 (1944); see also, *Toscano* v. *C.I.R.*, 441 F.2d 930, 933–935 (9th Cir. 1971) (recognizing that lack of diligence is not a bar to relief for fraud on the court).

This case presents an injustice which is "sufficiently gross to demand a departure from rigid adherence" to procedural rules which might be applicable in other circumstances and to require redress irrespective of the diligence of the parties. *Hazel-Atlas*, 322 U.S. at 244. The injustices clearly established by Petitioner's evidence require no less from this Court. The Government's spurious claim that Petitioner is guilty of laches must be rejected.

V. Conclusion

Forty-three years ago, a twenty-four-year-old college student had such a deep and abiding faith in the United States Constitution and the American principles embodied in this great document that he was willing to stand virtually alone against the entire United States government. He believed that the incarceration of over 120,000 people based solely on race was contrary to the very foundation of these constitutional principles. Today this same college student, now a professor emeritus, continues his quest to set the record straight and insure that the Constitution stands in practice for what it says in principle.

For his courageous stand, the Government in the instant proceedings recognizes the Petitioner as a "standard bearer." Yet, since the Supreme Court ruled in his case that the military orders were constitutional, and since the Court later in *Korematsu* used this ruling as a legal basis justifying the constitutionality of the evacuation of 120,000 people of Japanese ancestry, carrying this particular standard has indeed been a heavy burden shouldered by Petitioner.

Forty-three years ago, the Government prosecuted its case against this "standard bearer" not because it believed that Petitioner himself was a threat to the security of the United States, but rather because a military program affecting 120,000 people of Japanese ancestry was at stake. In its earnestness to assure that the military orders would be ruled constitutional, the Government developed a win-at-all-costs campaign which resulted in violating Petitioner's constitutional rights to due process.

In this instant coram nobis proceeding, the Government asserts no misconduct ever occurred. The evidence clearly establishes that the Government had in its possession throughout the original Court proceedings vast amounts of information, including military and intelligence reports, which directly refuted Government claims of military necessity. In the face of the indisputable evidence of suppression and misrepresentation, the Government now argues that the suppressed evidence was not exculpatory. This position is untenable given the misrepresentations which the Government made to the Supreme Court in support of the claims of military necessity.

Given the Government's unwillingness to acknowledge its own misconduct, it is imperative that the Court speak clearly through its ruling and declare to the Government that suppression of exculpatory evidence will not be condoned. The misrepresentations and suppression of evidence by the Government violated the integrity of the judicial process, not only depriving Petitioner of his due process rights but also resulting in a fraud upon the Courts.

Mr. Hirabayashi brings this coram nobis Petition motivated by the same steadfast belief in the Constitution that he maintained in challenging the military orders of 1942. Mr. Hirabayashi seeks vindication on three levels: (1) For himself as an individual defendant; (2) For the Japanese American community whose constitutional rights were violated wholesale by the evacuation program; and, (3) For all American citizens whose rights are protected by the Constitution. By granting the vacation of convictions based on findings that Mr. Hirabayashi was denied his due process rights by virtue of Governmental misconduct, this Court will assure Mr. Hirabayashi, the Japanese American community, and all Americans that their rights under the Constitution of the United States will be safeguarded.

Hirabayashi v. United States

Opinion of the Court on the Petition, U.S. District Court for the Western District of Washington*

February 10, 1986

Judge Voorhees submitted his written opinion in the Hirabayashi case on February 10, 1986. Although the evidentiary hearing had resulted in a 1400-page transcript and the submission of hundreds of documents in evidence, the judge based his opinion on a single document: the initial evacuation report of General DeWitt. This crucial report claimed that evacuation and internment had been ordered because it was "impossible" to distinguish loyal from disloyal Japanese Americans. General DeWitt admitted that lack of time to conduct individual loyalty hearings had not affected the internment decision, a position that contradicted the Justice Department's brief to the Supreme Court. That the War Department withheld this report from the Justice Department, Judge Voorhees concluded, "was an error of the most fundamental character" and required the vacation of Hirabayashi's exclusion order conviction. However, because he viewed the curfew imposed on Japanese Americans as a "relatively mild" burden, the judge decided Hirabayashi's conviction on that charge was not affected by the government's misconduct.

Petitioner has filed a petition for a writ of error coram nobis, seeking the vacation of his conviction in October 1942, for failing to report on May 11 or 12, 1942, to a designated Civil Control Station in Seattle, as required by Civilian Exclusion Order No. 57, and his conviction for failing, on or about May 4, 1942, to abide by Public Proclamation No. 3, requiring him to remain within his place of residence between 8:00 p.m. and 6:00 a.m.

Petitioner seeks to have these two misdemeanor convictions set aside on the ground that the government knowingly suppressed evidence favorable to him or presented evidence which it knew, or should have known,

*627 F. Supp. 1445 (W.D. Wash. 1986)

was false in order to secure those convictions or to defend them on appeal.

Testimony at petitioner's trial or at the evidentiary hearing on his petition indicated that at the time of the acts for which petitioner was convicted, he was a twenty-four year old senior at the University of Washington. He was at that time a native-born, American citizen, having been born in Seattle, Washington, on April 23, 1918. His parents had been born in Japan but had emigrated to the United States. His father had arrived in the United States in 1907, his mother in 1914. Both of his parents were nineteen when they came to the United States. They were married in this country. Neither had ever returned to Japan. Petitioner himself had never been to Japan and had never corresponded with any Japanese in Japan. Petitioner was educated in the public schools of King County and Seattle. He had been active in the Boy Scouts and had become a Life Scout and an Assistant Scoutmaster. He was also active in the YMCA at the University of Washington. He had been vice president of that organization and had attended YMCA conferences in other states as a representative of the University YMCA. He had never before been arrested on any charge. He testified at trial that his parents had taught him and his brothers and sisters that they were American citizens and how to conduct themselves as such; that he had not reported to the Civil Control Station nor remained in his residence during the curfew hours because of his honest belief that the evacuation and curfew orders were unconstitutional and violated his rights as an American citizen and that for him to obey them voluntarily would have been a waiver of his rights; that in the Boy Scouts and the YMCA and at the University of Washington he had learned what was expected of him as an American citizen and what his rights were as an American citizen; and that he had at all times tried earnestly to conduct himself as a good American citizen.

At trial the Secretary-Manager of the University YMCA testified that the petitioner had at all times conducted himself as a law-abiding American citizen, that he was a leader in the YMCA and other student organizations and affairs; that he was well-respected by his fellow students; and that he bore a very fine reputation among the people of the community.

At trial there was evidence that petitioner had violated the curfew restriction on the single night of May 9, 1942.

After the issuance of Civilian Exclusion Order No. 57, which required petitioner to report on May 11 or May 12, 1942, to a designated Civilian Control Station in Seattle, he went with his attorney to the Seattle office of the FBI and turned himself in. Although this is not clear in the record, petitioner must have stated to the FBI that he was refusing to report to a control station. During his interview by an agent of the FBI petitioner volunteered the information that for the past few nights in May he had not abided by the curfew restrictions imposed by Public Proclamation No. 3. The FBI agent advised petitioner that no charges at all would be brought if he registered with the Civilian Control Station, but this, petitioner refused, as a matter of conscience, to do.

None of this testimony was challenged by the government either at petitioner's trial or during the hearing upon petitioner's application for a writ of error coram nobis. The government presented no evidence that petitioner was anything other than a law-abiding, native-born American citizen.

Petitioner was indicted in a two count indictment returned by a grand jury on May 28, 1942. Count I of the indictment charged that defendant had failed to report to a designated Civil Control Station on May 11 or May 12, 1942, as required by Civilian Exclusion Order No. 57, which was issued by the Military Commander of the Western Defense Command on May 10, 1942. Count II charged that on or about May 4, 1942, between 8:00 p.m. and 6:00 a.m. defendant was not within his place of residence, as required by Public Proclamation No. 3, which was issued by the Military Commander of the Western Defense Command on March 24, 1942.

Petitioner was tried on October 20, 1942, and was found by the jury to be guilty on each count. On the following day petitioner was sentenced to serve three months on each count, the two sentences to be served concurrently.

Petitioner's appeal was argued before the Supreme Court on May 10 and 11, 1943. The sentence of confinement imposed upon petitioner was affirmed by the Supreme Court on June 21, 1943. *Hirabayashi* v. *United States*, 320 U.S. 81, 87 L. Ed. 1774 (1943).

In affirming the sentence imposed upon petitioner, the Supreme Court considered only the charge in the second count, the one that charged petitioner with violating the curfew restrictions of Public Proclamation No. 3.

In an opinion authored by Chief Justice Stone, the Supreme Court stated:

The conviction under the second count is without constitutional infirmity. Hence we have no occasion to review the conviction on the first count since . . . the sentences on the two counts are to run concurrently and conviction on the second is sufficient to sustain the evidence. 320 U.S. 81 at 105, 87 L. Ed. 1774 at 1788.

In consequence, the conviction of petitioner on the first count (the failure by him to report to a Civil Control Station) has never been reviewed upon appeal. (His conviction on both counts had been appealed by him to the United States Circuit Court for the Ninth Circuit, but that court certified the entire record to the Supreme Court and did not itself act upon the appeal.)

In determining whether petitioner's convictions should be vacated, the Court has carefully considered the record of petitioner's trial, the arguments made by the government in the brief submitted by it to the Supreme Court, the reasoning of the Supreme Court in its affirmance of the sentence imposed upon petitioner, the testimony of those who were called as witnesses at the hearing upon petitioner's petition, the voluminous exhibits which were admitted into evidence at the hearing, and the arguments made by counsel for petitioner and for the government in their post-hearing briefs.

The Court will first consider the conviction of petitioner for his failure to report to a designated Civil Control Station on May 11 or May 12, 1942.

The background of Civilian Exclusion Order No. 57 is, in brief, as follows: after the attack on Pearl Harbor on December 7, 1941, President Franklin D. Roosevelt issued Executive Order 9066, on February 19, 1942. That order authorized the Secretary of War or his designees to prescribe military areas from which any or all persons might be excluded. On February 20, 1942, Secretary of War Henry Stimson delegated his authority under Executive Order 9066 to Lieutenant General John L. DeWitt, the Commanding General of the Western Defense Command.

On March 2, 1942, General DeWitt issued Public Proclamation No. 1. That proclamation divided the states of Washington, Oregon, California and Arizona into two military areas. The western portions of Washington, Oregon and California and the southern portion of Arizona were designated as Military Area No. 1. The balance of each of those states was designated as Military Area No. 2. On March 21, 1942, the President signed Public Law No. 503, which had been enacted by Congress. That law made it a misdemeanor knowingly to disregard restrictions made applicable by a military commander to persons in a prescribed military area.

On March 24, 1942, General DeWitt issued Civilian Exclusion Order No. 1. That order affected about fifty Japanese families, residing on

Bainbridge Island, Washington, and provided for their evacuation from that island one week later. Thereafter, further exclusion orders were issued from time to time for the various zones in Military Area No. 1.

The order which affected petitioner was Civilian Exclusion Order No. 57, issued by General DeWitt on May 10, 1942. That order provided that from and after May 16, 1942, all persons of Japanese ancestry were excluded from a designated geographical area (this area included petitioner's place of residence) and required a responsible member of each family and each person living alone to report on May 11 or May 12, 1942, to a designated Civil Control Station in Seattle. The instructions which were posted with the exclusion order made it plain that reporting was for the purpose of receiving further instructions and that the excluded individuals were thereafter to be sent to an Assembly Center.

Because petitioner refused to report to the Civil Control Station, he was indicted for the crime of failing to comply with Exclusion Order No. 57, and was tried, convicted and sentenced for that offense.

Petitioner's appeal was heard by the Supreme Court on May 10 and 11, 1943. Shortly before that hearing, General DeWitt transmitted to the Secretary of War and to General George C. Marshall, the Chief of Staff, printed copies of a document entitled "Final Report: Japanese Evacuation from the West Coast 1942." It included a printed letter of transmittal to the Chief of Staff, dated April 15, 1943. That letter stated in part:

The evacuation was impelled by military necessity. The security of the Pacific Coast continues to require the exclusion of Japanese from the area now prohibited to them and will continue for the duration of the present war.

Chapter II of the report entitled "Need for Military Control and for Evacuation" contained the following statements:

Because of the ties of race, the intense feeling of filial piety and the strong bonds of common tradition, culture and customs, this population [the Japanese population] presented a tightly-knit racial group. It included in excess of 115,000 persons deployed along the Pacific Coast. . . . While it was believed that some were loyal, it was known that many were not. It was impossible to establish the identity of the loyal and the disloyal with any degree of safety. It was not that there was insufficient time in which to make such a determination; it was simply a matter of facing the realities that a positive determination could not be made, that an exact separation of the "sheep from the goats" was unfeasible.

He [the Commanding General of the Western Defense Command] had no alternative but to conclude that the Japanese constituted a potentially dangerous element from the viewpoint of military security—that military necessity required their immediate evacuation to the interior.

On April 19, 1943, Edward J. Ennis sent a memorandum (Ex. 35) to Solicitor General Charles Fahy relative to the briefs to be filed with the Supreme Court on behalf of the United States in *United States* v. *Hirabayashi*, *United States* v. *Yasui* and *United States* v. *Korematsu*. Ennis was at the time the director of the Alien Enemy Control Unit of the Department of Justice and was in charge of the preparation of the briefs for the Supreme Court in those three cases. In pertinent part that memorandum read as follows:

In my opinion minor differences of presentation of the Court's own authorities on the legal question of the war power, due process and martial law will have little influence on their decision in view of their own familiarity with this material and their scrutiny of the applicable law. The effective area for assisting the Court is in the presentation of the factual material. In this connection the War Department has today received a printed report from General DeWitt about the Japanese evacuation and is now determining whether it is to be released so that it may be used in connection with these cases. The War Department has been requested to furnish any published materials which may be helpful. I will continue further and so far as possible to document the facts which are not in the record but which may be judicially noticed on the constitutional question.

Coincidentally, on that same date Assistant Secretary of War John J. McCloy had a telephone conversation with Colonel Karl R. Bendetsen relative to General DeWitt's Final Report, which had just been received by the War Department in Washington, D.C. Colonel Bendetsen was at the time in charge of the Wartime Civil Control Administration of the Western Defense Command. The typed transcript (Ex. 66) of that conversation reveals that Mr. McCloy was more than a little exercised because the Final Report had been printed in final form and distributed without any prior consultation by the Western Defense Command with the War Department about its contents. Mr. McCloy was particularly disturbed that General DeWitt had stated in his report that the security of the West Coast would continue to require the exclusion of the Japanese for the duration of the war.

Thereafter, on April 26, 1943, Brigadier General James W. Barnett sent a message (Ex. 67) to General DeWitt which in pertinent part was as follows:

Bendetsen informs me he conferred on final report in Washington today. He was given oral directive to revise the report with the assistance of Capt. Hall. He made the point that he was in no position to do this since it was your report. Bendetsen told me that he could recommend the acceptance of some parts of the suggested revision but that two points went to the fundamental concept of evacuation. The principal one of these was that loyalty could not be determined and for that reason mass evacuation was ordered. He requested instructions. I told him it was your report and that the War Department could not tell you what to say. He had made that point and said that the instructions he received were to make a draft of the proposed revision for presentation to you for acceptance or revision. If you have additional instructions I will transmit them to Bendetsen by telephone.

On April 27, 1943, General DeWitt responded to the message from Brigadier General Barnett with the following message (Ex. 68):

My report as signed and submitted to Chief of Staff will not be changed in any respect whatsoever either in substance or form and I will not repeat not consent to any repeat any revision made over my signature. Higher authority may of course prepare and release whatsoever they so desire as views of that authority but statements in my signed report of evacuation are mine and so submitted. Submission of prepared revisions for presentation to me for acceptance or revision will accomplish nothing as final word on subject so far as I repeat I am concerned has been said.

On May 3, 1943, Colonel Bendetsen sent the following message (Ex. 70) to General DeWitt relative to conferences between himself and Assistant Secretary of War McCloy:

Mr. McCloy stated that he strongly desired to avoid creating the impression that he had any wish to prescribe what the Commanding General should say or not say in the final report. He did say, however, that he thought it could be improved upon. Following this vein, he expressed an earnest desire to have transmitted to the CG the nature of his specific suggestions with an explanation of why he felt the making of revisions conforming to these suggestions would result in improvement.

In brief, Mr. McCloy's suggestions cover three points:

  a. In paragraph 2 of the letter of transmittal the statement appeared that the necessity for exclusion of all Japanese from the Pacific coast "will continue for the duration of the present war." He said he could see no objection to a statement to the effect that exclusion will be essential so long as any military necessity exists therefor, but he said no one could foresee what the situation would be a year or two hence, and therefore he felt it stultified the report to make such a statement. He drew a parallel to the fact that in the last war a formal state of war continued in existence until 1921, although hostilities had ceased on November 11, 1918.

  b. The second objection was to that portion of Chapter II which said in effect that it is absolutely impossible to determine the loyalty of Japanese no matter how much time was taken in the process. He said that he had no objection to saying that time was of the essence and that in view of the military situation and the fact *that there was no known means of making such a determination with any degree of safety* the evacuation was necessary. (Emphasis in the original.)

c. His other comments related to certain changes in style and tone, which were orally described as designed to eliminate redundancy. These were indicated by him with blue pencil. In a number of cases he made comments on changes in tone which he believed were calculated to eliminate unnecessary pointedness with regard to certain sins of omission on the part of the Department of Justice. He said he felt this could be accomplished without in any way departing from an accurate factual account.

On May 5, 1943, General DeWitt sent the following message (Ex. 71) to Brigadier General Barnett:

Have no desire to compromise in any way govt case in Supreme Court and do not understand how substance and form of report as submitted can have this effect. Both you and Bendetsen know my crews [views] and my attitude. Do not understand McCloy's proposal. Report is now factual and I *solemnly* see my views and actions determined as necessary at time of evacuation weakened or undermined if report changes. I cannot conscientiously change or put into separate document proposals for future disposition of evacuees without by my own act invalidating my assigned mission and responsibilities thereunder. If time permits send Bendetsen by air to Anchorage reporting to me from there so he will know where to meet me and I can be fully informed and settle the matter. (Emphasis in the original.)

On May 9, 1943, Colonel Bendetsen sent the following message (Ex. 72) to Brigadier General Barnett:

General DeWitt directs that final report of evacuation be revised as indicated by Colonel Bendetsen to Major Moffitt in Major Moffitt's copy of report together with style changes given to Major Moffitt orally. . . . You are prohibited from submitting to Assistant Secretary of War any drafts of amended report. Further the revised report will not be given to anyone until DeWitt finally approves. All copies heretofore sent to the War Department (not including inclosures) will be called in by you and you will have War Department records of receiving report destroyed inasmuch as such revision as is finally sent to War Department will have a later dated transmittal letter. . . .

Exhibits 73 and 74 relate to the changes in the Final Report suggested by the War Department. Fifty-five changes were listed. The proposed changes most relevant to this proceeding were these:

Page iii, paragraph 2, second sentence: Eliminate the words "and will continue for the duration of the present war." Page iii, paragraph 2, end of the second sentence: Insert "The surprise attack at Pearl Harbor by the enemy crippled a major portion of the Pacific Fleet and exposed the West Coast to an attack which could not have been substantially impeded by defensive fleet operations. More than 120,000 persons of Japanese ancestry resided in colonies adjacent to many highly sensitive installations. Their loyalties were unknown, and time was of the essence."

Page 9. Strike the following: "It was impossible to establish the identity of the loyal and the disloyal with any degree of safety. It was not that there was insufficient time in which to make such a determination; it was simply a matter of facing the realities that a positive determination could not be made, that an exact separation of the 'sheep from the goats' was unfeasible."

And replace with the following: "To complicate the situation, no ready means existed for determining the loyal and the disloyal with any degree of safety. It was necessary to face the realities—a positive determination could not have been made."

On June 5, 1943, General DeWitt issued a revised version (Ex. 85) of his final report on the Japanese evacuation. In that version of the report the underlined portions of the following statements were either deleted from or added to the original version of the Final Report:

Page iii, paragraph 2: "The security of the Pacific Coast continues to require the exclusion of Japanese from the area now prohibited to them *and will continue for the duration of the present war*." (Deleted from the original version.)

Page iii, paragraph 2: "*More than 120,000 persons of Japanese ancestry resided in colonies adjacent to many highly sensitive installations. Their loyalties were unknown, and time was of the essence.*" (Added to the original version.)

Page 9: "*It was impossible to establish the identity of the loyal and the disloyal with any degree of safety. It was not that there was insufficient time in which to make such a determination; it was simply a matter of facing the realities that a positive determination could not be made, that an exact separation of the 'sheep from the goats' was unfeasible.*" (Deleted from the original version and replaced by the following sentence.)

Page 9: "*To complicate the situation, no ready means existed for determining the loyal and the disloyal with any degree of safety. It was necessary to face the realities—a positive determination could not have been made.*" (Added to the original version.)

On June 21, 1943, the Supreme Court handed down its decision, affirming the conviction of petitioner on the count charging curfew violation.

That General DeWitt did in fact believe that it was impossible to separate the loyal Japanese from the disloyal ones, is borne out by the transcripts of two telephone conversations which took place a few months before the publication of the initial version of the Final Report.

The first was a conversation between General DeWitt and Major General A. W. Gullion, the Provost Marshal General, on January 14, 1943. The subject matter of the conversation was the possibility that the Western Defense Command might be called upon to make thirty thousand or more loyalty investigations of individuals in the relocation centers. In the transcript (Ex. 63) of that telephone conversation the following appears:

DeWitt: I don't see how they can determine the loyalty of a Jap by interrogation . . . or investigation.

Gullion: They've got a questionnaire that the Navy—some psychologist over there in the Navy sold to them.

DeWitt: There isn't such a thing as a loyal Japanese and it is just impossible to determine their loyalty by investigation—it just can't be done. . .

The other was a conversation just four days later between General DeWitt and Assistant Secretary of War McCloy. General DeWitt was disturbed that he had been instructed to prepare for about 30,000 loyalty investigations. In the transcript (Ex. A-84) of that conversation the following appears:

DeWitt: Because I feel that I wouldn't be loyal to you or honest to you if I didn't say that it is a sign of weakness and an admission of an original mistake. Otherwise—we wouldn't have evacuated these people at all if we could determine their loyalty.

McCloy: I don't know whether we are at one on that—

DeWitt: I know we are not one on it—

McCloy: We evacuated them from the West Coast because we thought the front was immediate. We couldn't sort them out immediately.

It is further borne out by his statement in the original version of the Final Report that the security of the Pacific Coast required the exclusion of the Japanese from that area for the duration of the war. This can only be interpreted to mean that in his opinion the loyalty of a person of Japanese extraction could not be determined no matter how long the war might last.

In its brief to the Supreme Court in petitioner's appeal the government did not take the position that it was impossible to separate the loyal Japanese residents from those who were not. Rather, it was a lack of time that prevented that separation.

On page 35 of its brief the government stated:

The classification was not based upon invidious race discrimination. Rather, it was founded upon the fact that the group as a whole contained an unknown number of persons who could not *readily* be singled out and who were a threat to the security of the nation and in order to impose effective restraints upon them it was necessary not only to deal with the entire group, but to deal with it *at once*. (Emphasis added.)

On page 61 it stated:

The grave emergency called for *prompt* and decisive action.

On page 62 it stated:

What was needed was a method of removing *at once* the unknown number of Japanese persons who might assist a Japanese invasion, and not a program for sifting out such persons in the indefinite future. (Emphasis added.)

On page 63 it stated:

The operative fact on which the classification was made was the danger arising from the existence of a group of over 100,000 persons of Japanese descent on the West Coast and the virtually impossible task of *promptly* segregating the potentially disloyal from the loyal. (Emphasis added.)

The opinion of the Supreme Court in *Hirabayashi* v. *United States*, reflected the Court's acceptance of the government argument that the lack of time to separate the loyal from the disloyal justified action directed toward all individuals of Japanese ancestry. In its opinion the Court stated:

Whatever views we may entertain regarding the loyalty to this country of the citizens of Japanese ancestry, we cannot reject as unfounded the judgment of the military authorities and of Congress that there were disloyal members of that population, whose number and strength could not be precisely and *quickly* ascertained. We cannot say that the war-making branches of the Government did not have ground for believing that in a critical hour such persons could not *readily* be isolated and separately dealt with, and constituted a menace to the national defense and safety, which demanded that *prompt* and adequate measures be taken to guard against it. (Emphasis added.) 320 U.S. 81 at 99.

The position taken by the government with respect to the efficacy of loyalty hearings was set forth in a post-argument memorandum filed by Solicitor General Fahy with the Supreme Court on May 14, 1943. That memorandum stated in relevant part:

Our position is not that hearings are an inappropriate method of reaching a decision on the question of loyalty. The Government does not contend that, assuming adequate opportunity for investigation, hearings may not ever be appropriately utilized on the question of the loyalty of persons here involved. It is submitted, however, that in the circumstances set forth in our brief, this method was not available to solve the problem which confronted the country. The situation did not lend itself, in the unique and pressing circumstances, to solution by individual loyalty hearings. In any event, the method of individual hearings was reasonably thought to be unavailable by those who were obliged to decide upon the measures to be taken.

A great deal of additional documentary evidence was submitted by both petitioner and the government, but the evidence, outlined above, goes to the very heart of the issue before the Supreme Court, that is, the military necessity for the exclusion order. It demonstrates that General DeWitt ordered the exclusion of everyone of Japanese ancestry from the West Coast because of his belief that it was impossible to separate loyal Japanese from those who might be disloyal no matter how much time was devoted to that task.

General DeWitt's reason for ordering the exclusion was made known to the War Department in the original version of his Final Report. From the changes in that report which were insisted upon by the War Department there can be no doubt that the War Department was aware of, but did not agree with, General DeWitt's belief that it was the impossibility of separating the loyal from the disloyal Japanese that made their exclusion from the West Coast a military necessity.

A copy of the original version of the Final Report was never made available to the Justice Department. In consequence, all through the course of petitioner's appeal, that department was unaware of General DeWitt's stated reason for the exclusion of the Japanese from the West Coast. The Justice Department assumed and argued to the Supreme Court that the military necessity arose out of a lack of time to make a separation rather than out of an impossibility of making that separation.

Although the Justice Department did not knowingly conceal from petitioner's counsel and from the Supreme Court the reason stated by General DeWitt for the exclusion of the Japanese, the government must be charged with that concealment because it was information known to the War Department, an arm of the government.

It is petitioner's position that the concealment by the government of the reasons stated by General DeWitt for the exclusion of the Japanese from the West Coast was a suppression of evidence which requires the vacation of petitioner's convictions.

Whether this action by the government warrants the vacation of petitioner's convictions requires the Court to consider whether a conviction may be set aside under a writ of error coram nobis and, if so, the requirements that must be met by one seeking the remedy of that writ.

A writ of error coram nobis is a seldom-used remedy, but if a petitioner for a writ of error coram nobis is found to be meritorious, a conviction may be set aside even though the petitioner has fully served his sentence on that conviction. *United States* v. *Morgan*, 346 U.S. 502 (1954); *Holloway* v. *United States*, 393 F.2d 731, 732 (9th Cir. 1968). Petitioner is not foreclosed, therefore, from availing himself of this remedy even though he long ago served the sentence which was imposed upon him.

In order for a writ of error coram nobis to be available to petitioner with respect to his conviction on the failure to report count, he must meet a number of requirements:

1. His petition must be brought in the court in which he was convicted. *United States* v. *Morgan*, 346 U.S. 502, 507 n.9 (1954).

2. A more usual remedy must not be available to him. *James* v. *United States*, 459 U.S. 1044 (1982) (Brennan, J., dissenting from denial of petition for writ of certiorari).

3. He must demonstrate that he suffers present adverse consequences from his conviction sufficient to satisfy the case or controversy requirement of Article III. *United States* v. *Dellinger*, 657 F.2d 140, 144 n.6 (7th Cir. 1981).

4. He must show that there are valid reasons for his not having attacked his conviction earlier. *Maghe* v. *United States*, 710 F.2d 503 (9th Cir. 1983).

5. He must demonstrate that the error of which he complains was of the most fundamental character. *United States* v. *Morgan*, 346 U.S. 502, 512 (1954); *United States* v. *Taylor*, 648 F.2d 565, 570 (9th Cir. 1981).

6. Finally, he must demonstrate that it is probable that a different result would have occurred had the error not been made. *United States* v. *Dellinger*, 657 F.2d 140, 144 n.9 (7th Cir. 1981).

In the present action the first requirement is clearly met. Petitioner brought his petition in the Western District of Washington, the district in which he was convicted.

The second requirement is also met. Petitioner's right to appeal from his conviction was exercised and exhausted long ago. His right to petition for habeas corpus relief is unavailable because he is no longer in custody. The writ of error coram nobis is at this time the only remedy available to him.

The requirement that petitioner must demonstrate that he presently suffers adverse consequences from his conviction is less clear. Understandably, misdemeanor convictions do not carry with them the adverse consequences that flow from felony convictions. Although it is highly unlikely that his 1942 conviction on the failure to report count would ever be used to impeach his credibility in any future civil or criminal trial, nonetheless it could be so used in jurisdictions, and there are some, which permit that use of misdemeanor convictions. It is true, too, that if petitioner were ever convicted for any other crime, a sentencing judge would be advised of that 1942 conviction and could properly take the conviction into consideration in fashioning an appropriate sentence. As was said in *Holloway* v. *United States*, 393 F.2d at 732: "Coram nobis must be kept available as a post-conviction remedy to prevent 'manifest injustice' even where the removal of a prior conviction will have little present effect on the petitioner."

The Court is of the opinion that petitioner has adequately demonstrated that he presently suffers adverse consequences from his conviction in 1942 of the crime charged in the first count of the indictment.

With respect to the requirement that petitioner must present valid reasons for his not having attacked his conviction earlier, the government argues that all of the factual material presented on behalf of petitioner has been a matter of public record for nearly forty years and that petitioner is hence bound by the doctrine of laches from seeking to overturn his convictions. The government particularly relies upon the book *Americans Betrayed* by Morton Grodzins, which was published in 1949.

The Court has read with care all of the excerpts from the Grodzins book which the government presented as an exhibit and which it asked the Court to consider. At no place in those excerpts is there any reference to the statements made by General DeWitt in the initial version of his Final Report. In none of the other publications submitted by the government is there any such reference.

Although it is true that at least one copy of the initial version of the Final Report survived, petitioner cannot be faulted for not finding and relying upon that version long before he brought this action in early 1983.

Ms. Aiko Herzig-Yoshinaga, a professional researcher, testified that it would have been exceedingly difficult for a lay person to locate that copy of the initial version of the Final Report. Although she had been employed as an archival researcher on the staff of the Commission on Wartime Relocation and Internment of Civilians between June 1981 and June 1983, she testified that it was not until the end of 1982 that she became aware of the existence of the initial version and then only because she had fortuitously observed that copy on the desk of an archivist in the Modern Military Section of the National Archives and, upon examining it, recognized its wording to be different from that of the published version.

There is no evidence in the record that petitioner actually knew, or had reason to know, of the existence of the initial version of the Final Report prior to the time that Ms. Herzig-Yoshinaga happened upon it in the National Archives. Petitioner did not unduly delay the commencement of this action after he learned of the existence of the initial version of the Final Report.

The Court finds, in consequence, that petitioner has presented valid reasons for not having sooner brought his petition for writ of error coram nobis.

The requirements that the error of which the petitioner complains be of the most fundamental character and that, absent the error, it is probable that a different result would have occurred will be considered together.

The error of which petitioner complains is that, during the pendency of his appeal before the Supreme Court, neither he nor his counsel was informed by the government of the reason given by General DeWitt in the original version of his Final Report for the exclusion of all persons of Japanese ancestry from the West Coast. That statement was in essence that the military necessity, requiring the exclusion, was the impossibility of separating the loyal persons from the disloyal ones no matter how much time was devoted to that task.

It was General DeWitt who made the decision that military necessity required the exclusion of all persons of Japanese ancestry from the West Coast. The central issue before the Supreme Court in the appeal of petitioner from his conviction on the first count was whether exclusion was in fact required by military necessity. Nothing would have been more important to petitioner's counsel than to know just why it was that General DeWitt made the decision that he did. The attorneys for the Justice Department assumed, and argued to the Supreme Court, that it was the need for prompt action that made the exclusion a military necessity. The statements by General DeWitt in his Final Report belied that assumption. His statement was that it was not time that made the exclusion necessary but rather the impossibility of determining whether any particular individual was or was not loyal.

The disclosure of that information to petitioner's counsel and to the Supreme Court would have made it most difficult for the government to argue, as it did, that the lack of time made exclusion a military necessity. At the hearing on petitioner's petition Edward Ennis, who was in charge of the preparation of the brief for the government, testified that the whole thrust of the government's argument before the Supreme Court was that there was not sufficient time to make a differentiation between the loyal Japanese and those who might be disloyal. When asked what he would have done had he learned in March or April 1943 of General DeWitt's statement, he answered that it would have presented "a very serious problem" and that it would have been "very dangerous" to take that position before the Supreme Court.

Had the statement of General DeWitt been disclosed to petitioner's counsel, they would have been in a position to argue that, contrary to General DeWitt's belief, there were in fact means of separating those who were loyal from those who were not; that the legal system had developed through the years means whereby factual questions of the most complex nature could be answered with a high degree of reliability. Counsel for petitioner could have pointed out that with very little effort the determination could have been made that tens of thousands of native-born Japanese Americans—infants in arms, children of high school age or younger, housewives, the infirm and elderly—were loyal and posed no possible threat to this country. More time might have been required to consider the loyalty of those who had spent their adult lives in truck gardening or farming or fishing, but a great number of those, too, could have been rather quickly found to be loyal and of no possible threat.

Had counsel for petitioner known and been able to present to the Supreme Court the reason stated by General DeWitt for the evacuation of all Japanese, it is this Court's opinion that the Supreme Court would have felt impelled to consider and to rule upon petitioner's appeal from his conviction on the failure to report count rather than confirming petitioner's sentence by simply affirming his conviction upon the curfew count. If the asserted ground was known by the Supreme Court to be the impossibility of separating the loyal from the disloyal, the Supreme Court would have found itself in an area of inquiry where its collective wisdom and its collective experience were far greater than that of General DeWitt. The justices of the Supreme Court were intimately familiar with the process of factual determinations. If the military necessity for exclusion was the impossibility of separating the loyal from the disloyal, the Supreme Court would not have had to defer to military judgment because this particular problem, separating the loyal from the disloyal, was one calling for judicial, rather than military, judgment.

The Court finds that the failure of the government to disclose to the petitioner, to petitioner's counsel, and to the Supreme Court the reason stated by General DeWitt for his deciding that military necessity required the exclusion of all those of Japanese ancestry from the West Coast was an error of the most fundamental character and that petitioner was in fact very seriously prejudiced by that non-disclosure in his appeal from his conviction of failing to report. In consequence, petitioner's conviction on the failure to report count must be vacated.

With respect to petitioner's conviction on the curfew count, the Court has made the same analysis with respect to the requirements for the granting of a writ of error coram nobis. With respect to that conviction, the Court finds that it is unable to set aside the conviction of petitioner of violating the curfew order on a single day in May of 1942. After considering the arguments made in the government's brief before the Supreme Court with respect to the curfew violation and the lengthy opinion of the Supreme Court affirming that conviction, the Court is not persuaded that the non-disclosure of the statement made by General DeWitt with respect to the military necessity for exclusion was an error of the most fundamental character with respect to the curfew count or that the non-disclosure was actually prejudicial to petitioner with respect to that count.

Even though the curfew order was burdensome with respect to native-born Japanese since it lumped them in with alien Germans, alien Italians, and alien Japanese, the burden was nevertheless relatively mild when contrasted with the harshness of the exclusion order. Under the curfew order, petitioner and all others subject to that order, were permitted to live in their own homes, to continue to work at their places of employment, and, between six in the morning and eight in the evening, to move freely about so long as they remained within a distance of five miles from their places of residence. In addition, the curfew order was a temporary restriction. It was promulgated on March 24, 1942, and was, as a practical matter, relatively short lived. As soon as the exclusion orders became effective, the curfew order was supplanted by them.

By the time the petitioner's appeal had been heard by the Supreme Court, the curfew order had long since been replaced by the exclusion and relocation orders. The Court is persuaded that petitioner's conviction on the curfew count would without question have been affirmed by the Supreme Court even though the Supreme Court had been made aware of the reason given by General DeWitt for his ordering the exclusion of those of Japanese ancestry from the West Coast. His reason for the exclusion did not significantly undermine the earlier issuance of the curfew order. The Court must hence deny the petition of petitioner that his conviction on the curfew count be vacated.

Accordingly, the petition of petitioner that his conviction on Count I of the indictment be vacated is granted. His petition that his conviction on Count II of the indictment be vacated is denied.

The Clerk of this Court is instructed to send uncertified copies of this Memorandum Decision to all counsel of record.

Dated this 10th day of February, 1986.

Donald S. Voorhees, United States District Judge

Hirabayashi v. United States

Memorandum Opinion of the Court on Reconsideration
Motions, U.S. District Court for the Western District of
Washington

April 28, 1986

---

*After Judge Voorhees issued his written opinion on Hirabayashi's coram
nobis petition in February 1986, both sides asked him to reconsider his
rulings. The government filed a motion suggesting that General DeWitt's
racial views had not affected the internment decision and were irrelevant
to any of Hirabayashi's charges of misconduct. Hirabayashi's motion
claimed that the government's misconduct, which had led Judge Voorhees
to vacate the exclusion order conviction, applied equally to the curfew
order violation. Judge Voorhees denied both motions and reaffirmed his
initial decisions on these issues. His opinion on these motions bristles
with indignation at the tactics the government used in the 1940s and
displays his admiration for Hirabayashi. The government ignored its duty
of "absolute fairness" to Hirabayashi in his trial and appeals, the judge
wrote. At the same time, though, Judge Voorhees's opinion did not deal
with the merits of Hirabayashi's motion for reconsideration. Both rulings
set the stage for further appeals in the Hirabayashi case.*

Both petitioner and the government feel aggrieved by the rulings made
by the Court in its memorandum decision of February 10, 1986, and both
have filed motions for the Court to reconsider those rulings.

The government contends that the Court should reconsider the decision
it has rendered in this matter for the following reasons:

1. General DeWitt's beliefs were not concealed from anyone, including
the Supreme Court, in 1943.
2. General DeWitt was not the sole decision maker.
3. General DeWitt was not ordered to change his report.
4. Petitioner is barred by his delay in seeking relief since General

DeWitt's view that there was no way to determine the loyalty of Japanese-Americans was not newly discovered.

With respect to its contention that General DeWitt's beliefs were not concealed in 1943 from anyone, including the Supreme Court, the government places its reliance upon a news story, which was apparently published in the *San Francisco News* on April 13, 1943, and which was reproduced as an appendix to petitioner's reply brief in the Supreme Court. In that news story General DeWitt was quoted as saying: "I don't want any Jap back on the Coast, . . . There is no way to determine their loyalty, . . . I don't care what they do with the Japs as long as they don't send them back here. A Jap is a Jap."

The government points out that the amicus curiae brief filed by the Japanese-American Citizens League with the Supreme Court also made reference to that news story.

The basis for this Court's vacation of petitioner's conviction was the concealment by the government from petitioner's counsel and from the Supreme Court of the considered statement of General DeWitt in the first version of his Final Report that the military necessity for the evacuation was, not that there was insufficient time to separate the loyal from the disloyal Americans of Japanese ancestry, but that it was impossible to make that separation no matter how much time was devoted to that task.

The news story upon which the government relies to argue that everyone was aware of General DeWitt's beliefs did not in fact report that General DeWitt made the statements that he did in his Final Report. His reported statements were unquestionably intemperate, but the news story did not report him as saying, as he did in his Final Report, that the military necessity for his exclusion orders was the impossibility of separating the loyal Japanese-Americans from the disloyal ones no matter how much time was devoted to that task.

If it were commonly known, as the government contends, that General DeWitt believed that the evacuation was required by the impossibility of separating loyal Japanese-Americans from disloyal ones, one would have expected the Justice Department to so state in its brief to the Supreme Court and to argue forthrightly that the exclusion was justified because it was simply impossible to make that separation no matter how much time was devoted to that task.

At no place, however, in its brief before the Supreme Court did the government suggest to the Supreme Court that the military necessity for the exclusion of Japanese-Americans was the impossibility of separating the loyal from the disloyal. The Justice Department did not make that argument. Its argument before the Supreme Court was that there was not time to make that separation.

Edward J. Ennis, who was in charge of the preparation of the briefs of the government before the Supreme Court in the *Hirabayashi*, *Yasui* and *Korematsu* appeals, testified in person before this Court. The Court was tremendously impressed by his integrity, the candor with which he testified, and by his memory of events which transpired over forty years ago. Mr. Ennis testified that he was unaware of the initial version of General DeWitt's Final Report until June 18, 1985, when it was shown to him by counsel for petitioner, just the day before he appeared as a witness in this Court. The Court is convinced that had he been aware of the statements initially made by General DeWitt in his Final Report, Mr. Ennis would have felt compelled to make full disclosure of those statements to the Supreme Court.

Mr. Ennis testified that while the *Hirabayashi* appeal was pending, he did learn that the War Department had received a printed report from General DeWitt about the Japanese evacuation. He stated that when he asked for a copy of that report, he was told by an officer in the War Department that it was only an internal report that was not to be released. Later, he was told by that same officer that the report might be released later. He was given at that time only thirty pages which had been extracted from the report. One can be sure that those pages did not include the statements of General DeWitt which the War Department had found objectionable.

The testimony of Mr. Ennis is borne out by his memorandum (Ex. 39) of February 26, 1944, to Attorney General Francis Biddle in which he stated:

We learned of the existence of General DeWitt's report last Spring when we were trying to get some information for the *Hirabayashi* brief in the Supreme Court and we were refused a copy of the printed report at that time on the ground that it was confidential between General DeWitt and the War Department but we were given a few pages torn out of a copy merely because they wanted us to have selected facts to support the evacuation.

In light of this testimony of Mr. Ennis and the exhibit supporting that testimony it is simply not true that at the time of the *Hirabayashi* argument everyone knew of General DeWitt's stated belief that the military necessity for the exclusion of Japanese-Americans was the impossibility of separating loyal Japanese-Americans from disloyal ones no matter how much time was devoted to that task.

The only tangible support for the government's contention that everyone knew of General DeWitt's belief was a single news story. That news story did not state what General DeWitt stated in his Final Report. Moreover, there is a vast difference in the utility to petitioner's counsel before the Supreme Court of a newspaper account by a nameless reporter on the one hand as contrasted with a formal, printed and signed statement by General DeWitt on the other.

The government's argument that the statements by General DeWitt in his Final Report were of no significance because they simply stated what everyone knew is belied by the actions taken by the War Department. It is manifest that the War Department was not of the opinion that the beliefs expressed by General DeWitt in his Final Report were known to everyone. There can be no question but that the War Department felt that the Final Report contained statements by General DeWitt which undermined the position of the government in the Japanese-American actions then pending before the Supreme Court. Somehow or another this thought had to have been conveyed to General DeWitt, for in his message of May 5, 1943, (Ex. 71) to Brigadier General Barnett he stated that he "had no desire to compromise in any way the government's case in the Supreme Court."

The Court must reject the government's argument that General DeWitt's beliefs were not concealed from anyone. The government states in its brief that "[I]n historical perspective, the 'impossibility' argument of General DeWitt was unfortunate and misguided" but were not concealed. The Court finds that they were unfortunate, misguided *and* concealed.

In this Court's opinion, the government was under a duty to be scrupulously fair in its dealings with petitioner, for he was no ordinary criminal, his crime no ordinary crime.

Petitioner's crime was that he refused to permit himself to be imprisoned without offense and without trial. The order requiring petitioner to report to a designated Civilian Control Station was but the first step towards his ultimate imprisonment, and petitioner was aware of that when he refused to report. That his imprisonment might be referred to as an internment made it no less an imprisonment, a complete deprivation of his freedom of movement.

The exclusion order, ordering in effect the imprisonment of petitioner, was justified only if there was in fact a military necessity for his imprisonment. Under those circumstances the government owed to petitioner a duty of absolute fairness in advising him why it was that his imprisonment was required by military necessity.

At a time when he was on the New York Court of Appeals, Justice Cardozo used these words to define the duty owed by one standing in a fiduciary relationship to another: "Not honesty alone, but the punctilio of an honor the most sensitive, is then the standard of behavior." *Meinhard* v. *Salmon*, 249 N.Y. 458, 164 N.E. 545, 62 ALR 1 (1928). In this Court's opinion the standard of behavior of the government toward petitioner was no less high.

The government also argues that the 1943 amicus brief filed by the States of California, Oregon and Washington in *Hirabayashi* "reiterated General DeWitt's impossibility thesis."

Rather than supporting the government's argument that this Court was in error in setting aside the conviction of petitioner, that amicus brief reinforces this Court's belief that the government unfairly withheld knowledge of the DeWitt report from petitioner's counsel.

The final version of General DeWitt's Final Report was not made public until January 1944. The amicus brief of the States of California, Oregon and Washington was filed on May 11, 1943. This date was before the Final Report had been revised. A comparison of the wording of the initial version of the Final Report with excerpts from the amicus brief of the States of California, Oregon and Washington reveals that the initial version had to have been disclosed to the writers of the amicus brief even though it was denied to the Justice Department and to petitioner's counsel. A couple of excerpts from the two demonstrate that disclosure.

The initial version of the Final Report stated at page 10:

Research has established that there were over 124 separate Japanese organizations along the Pacific Coast engaged, in varying degrees, in common pro-Japanese purposes. This number does not include local branches of parent organizations, of which there were more than 310.

Research and coordination of information had made possible the identification of more than 100 parent fascistic or militaristic organizations in Japan which have had some relation, either direct or indirect, with Japanese organizations or individuals in the United States. Many of the former were parent organizations of subsidiary or branch organizations in the United States and in that capacity directed organizational and functional activities. There was definite information that the great majority of activities followed a line of control from the Japanese government, through key individuals and associations to the Japanese residents in the United States.

The amicus brief essentially repeats those words at page 14:

Over 124 separate Japanese organizations along the Pacific Coast were engaged, in varying degrees, in common pro-Japanese purposes, with local branches of these parent organizations numbering more than 310. There were 100 fascistic or militaristic organizations in Japan having some relation, either direct or indirect, with Japanese organizations or individuals in the United States. Many had branch organizations in the United States and directed the activities of these branches. A line of control existed from the Japanese Government.

The initial version of the Final Report stated at page 11:

The Hokubei Butoku Kai or Military Virtue Society of North America was organized in 1931 with headquarters in Alvarado, Alameda County, California, and a branch office in Tokyo. One of the purposes of the organization was to instill the Japanese military code of Bushido among the Japanese throughout North America.

The amicus brief repeats that statement at page 15:

The Hokubei Butoku Kai or Military Virtue Society of North America had headquarters in the town of Alvarado, California, and a branch office in Tokyo. Its purpose was to instill the Japanese code of Bushido among the Japanese throughout North America.

These and other instances compel the conclusion that the initial version of the Final Report was disclosed by the Western Defense Command to the Attorneys-General of California, Oregon and Washington at the time their amicus brief was being prepared.

The Department of Justice came to that same conclusion. In a memorandum (Ex. 89) to Edward J. Ennis on April 25, 1944, prior to the *Korematsu* argument before the Supreme Court, John L. Burling of the Justice Department complained of the role of the Western Defense Command. That memorandum read in relevant part as follows:

It is entirely clear . . . that the brief of the attorneys general of California, Oregon and Washington, in the *Hirabayashi* case, contained much material taken from General DeWitt's final report, which at that time was classified as confidential and which we were not given (with the exception of a few pages cut out with a knife).

The denial of the Final Report to petitioner's counsel and to the Justice Department at the same time it was being disclosed to counsel for amici in the same action is a further reason for the granting of petitioner's writ of error coram nobis.

The argument by the government that General DeWitt was not the sole decision maker is hardly worthy of consideration. It is true, of course, that Executive Order 9066 was issued by President Franklin D. Roosevelt and that it authorized Secretary of War Henry L. Stimson to prescribe military areas from which any or all persons might be excluded. The Secretary of War, however, delegated his authority under Executive Order 9066 to General DeWitt, the Commanding General of the Western Defense Command. After that delegation it is beyond question that it was General DeWitt who made the decision to designate the geographical boundaries of Military Area No. 1. It is equally beyond question that it was he who issued the series of exclusion orders which compelled the evacuation of the Japanese-Americans from Military Area No. 1.

The argument by the government that General DeWitt was not ordered to change his report may be treated no less summarily. This Court's memorandum decision stated that "changes in (General DeWitt's) report . . . were insisted upon by the War Department. . . ." The government argues that changes in General DeWitt's report were not "insisted upon" by the War Department but were rather "suggested" by the War Department.

In the Court's opinion it matters not whether the War Department "insisted" that certain changes be made or only "suggested" that they be made. A fair reading of the exhibits in this case reveals that General DeWitt must have felt himself under considerable pressure to change the wording of his report. On April 27, 1943, (Exhibit 68) he is stating: "My report as signed and submitted to Chief of Staff will not be changed in any respect whatsoever either in substance or form and I will not repeat not consent to any repeat any revision made over my signature." But by May 9, 1943, he is acquiescing in the changes which the War Department thought should be made. Between those two dates one can fairly infer an element of insistence by the War Department.

Finally, the government again makes the argument that petitioner is barred by laches. As pointed out above, the critical suppression of evidence in this case was the suppression of the initial version of General DeWitt's Final Report. That version gave his unvarnished, unedited, unrevised, considered reason for concluding that there was a military necessity for excluding Japanese-Americans from the Pacific Coast. That reason was not disclosed to petitioner's counsel nor to the Supreme Court in 1943. It did not become known to petitioner until a relatively short period of time before he filed his petition for a writ of error coram nobis. Petitioner is not barred by laches.

Petitioner has moved the Court to reconsider its refusal to vacate petitioner's conviction of the curfew violation. The Court has carefully considered the arguments made by petitioner in support of his motion.

Nevertheless, for the reasons set forth in its Memorandum Decision the Court finds it is unable to grant the petition for writ of error coram nobis with respect to petitioner's conviction on the curfew count.

Petitioner should not, however, consider that conviction to be a stigma. His refusal to obey the curfew order and, even more so, his refusal to obey the order to report for his imprisonment were in the tradition of those who have forged the freedoms which we now enjoy.

Despite petitioner's belief in his own loyalty and despite his conviction that he could not be imprisoned without offense and without trial, it took rare courage for one of his relatively young age to stand up to all the powers of government and all the forces of public opinion bearing down upon him.

His courage was comparable to the courage of those who stood up to the Crown during the reign of the Stuarts. Three of those were John Eliot, William Strode, and Benjamin Valentine. At a time when Charles I was asserting his absolute power to imprison anyone at his pleasure, those three were imprisoned by 1629. They could have secured their release at any time by conceding the power of the king to imprison them, but they, like petitioner, refused to yield. Eliot died in prison. The other two persisted in their refusal to submit and remained in prison until 1640. They accepted years of imprisonment rather than conceding that the king had the power to imprison them at all. Their steadfastness, however, helped establish the principle that the king was under and not above the law.

Like Eliot, Strode, and Valentine, petitioner accepted imprisonment rather than concede the government's power to imprison one who had committed no offense. His steadfastness, like theirs, has earned him a place in the pantheon of those who have sacrificed themselves in order to further the common good.

It is now considered by almost everyone that the internment of Japanese-Americans during World War II was simply a tragic mistake for which American society as a whole must accept responsibility. If, in the future, this country should find itself in a comparable national emergency, the sacrifices made by Gordon Hirabayashi, Fred Korematsu, and Minoru Yasui may, it is hoped, stay the hand of a government again tempted to imprison a defenseless minority without trial and for no offense.

Accordingly, the motions of petitioner and of the government for reconsideration are denied.

The Clerk of this Court is instructed to send uncertified copies of this order to all counsel of record.

Dated this 28 day of April, 1986.

Donald S. Voorhees, United States District Judge

Hirabayashi v. United States

Opinion of the Court of Appeals, U.S. Court of Appeals
for the Ninth Circuit*

September 24, 1987

*After Judge Voorhees vacated Gordon Hirabayashi's exclusion order
conviction but upheld his curfew order conviction, both sides asked the
Ninth Circuit Court of Appeals to review the decisions. The appellate
panel heard oral arguments on March 2, 1987, and issued its unanimous
opinion the following September. Judge Mary Schroeder wrote for the
panel in upholding the vacation of the exclusion order conviction and
reversing Judge Voorhees on the curfew charge. After the entire Ninth
Circuit bench rejected the government's request for a rehearing, and
after expiration, in February 1988, of the deadline for Supreme Court
review, the internment cases and the coram nobis effort ended in total
victory.*

OPINION

Schroeder, Circuit Judge.

I. Introduction

Gordon Hirabayashi is an American citizen who was born in Seattle,
Washington, in 1918, and is currently professor emeritus of sociology at
the University of Alberta. He is of Japanese ancestry. In 1942 he was
living in Seattle and was therefore subject to wartime orders requiring all
persons of Japanese ancestry, whether citizens or not, to remain within
their residences between 8:00 p.m. and 6:00 a.m. He was also subject to
subsequent orders to report to a Civilian Control Station for processing

*828 F.2d 591 (9th Cir. 1987)

requisite to exclusion from the military area. Hirabayashi refused to honor the curfew or to report to the control station because he believed that the military orders were based upon racial prejudice and violated the protection the Constitution affords to all citizens. The Supreme Court reviewed his conviction for violating the curfew order and unanimously affirmed. In an opinion by Chief Justice Stone, the Court accepted the government's position that the curfew was justified by military assessments of emergency conditions existing at the time. *Hirabayashi* v. *United States*, 320 U.S. 81, 63 S. Ct. 1375 (1943). Because Hirabayashi had received a concurrent sentence for violating the exclusion order, the Court affirmed that conviction as well. *Id.* at 105, 63 S. Ct. at 1387. The following year, a majority of what was by then a sharply divided Court applied the same military emergency rationale to uphold explicitly the exclusion of all citizens of Japanese ancestry from the West Coast. *Korematsu* v. *United States*, 323 U.S. 214, 65 S. Ct. 193 (1944).

The *Hirabayashi* and *Korematsu* decisions have never occupied an honored place in our history. In the ensuing four and a half decades, journalists and researchers have stocked library shelves with studies of the cases and surrounding events. These materials document historical judgments that the convictions were unjust. They demonstrate that there could have been no reasonable military assessment of an emergency at the time,[1] that the orders were based upon racial stereotypes,[2] and that the orders caused needless suffering and shame for thousands of American citizens.[3] The legal judgments of the courts reflecting that Hirabayashi and Korematsu have been properly convicted of violating the laws of the United States, however, remained on their records. Petitioner filed this lawsuit in 1983 to obtain a writ of error coram nobis to vacate his convictions and thus to make the judgments of the courts conform to the judgments of history.

The event which triggered the lawsuit occurred in 1982, when an archi-

---

[1] See, e.g., P. Irons, *Justice at War* (1983); R. Daniels, *The Decision to Relocate the Japanese Americans* (1975); M. Grodzins, *Americans Betrayed* (1949); Yamamoto, *Korematsu Revisited— Correcting the Injustice of Extraordinary Government Excess and Lax Judicial Review: Time for a Better Accommodation of National Security Concerns and Civil Liberties*, 26 Santa Clara L. Rev. 1 (1986).

[2] See, e.g., A. Fisher, *Exile of a Race* (1970); C. McWilliams, *Prejudice* (1944); Rostow, *The Japanese American Cases—A Disaster*, 54 Yale L.J. 489 (1954); Dembitz, *Racial Discrimination and the Military Judgment: The Supreme Court's Korematsu and Endo Decisions*, 45 Colum. L. Rev. 175 (1945).

[3] See, e.g., R. Daniels, S. Taylor & H. Kitano, *Japanese Americans: From Relocation To Redress* (1986); M. Weglyn, *Years of Infamy* (1976); D. Myer, *Uprooted Americans* (1971).

val researcher discovered the sole remaining copy of the original report prepared by the general who issued the curfew and exclusion orders. This report was intended to explain the basis for those orders. War Department officials revised the report in several material respects and tried to destroy all of the original copies before issuing the final report. The Justice Department did not know of the existence of the original report at the time its attorneys were preparing briefs in the *Hirabayashi* and *Korematsu* cases.

In his coram nobis petition Hirabayashi contended that the original report, the circumstances surrounding its alteration, and recently discovered related documents provided the proof, unavailable at the time of his conviction, that the curfew and exclusion orders were in fact based upon racial prejudice rather than military exigency. Hirabayashi further alleged that the government concealed these matters from his counsel and the Supreme Court, and that had the Supreme Court known the true basis for the orders, the ultimate decision in the case would probably have been different.

The district court held a full evidentiary proceeding on Hirabayashi's claims. It reviewed hundreds of documents and heard the testimony of several witnesses. They included Edward Ennis, who had been the Director of the Alien Enemy Control Unit at the Department of Justice and a principal author of the government's briefs in both the *Hirabayashi* and *Korematsu* cases; William Hammond, who had been the Assistant Chief of Staff for the entire Western Defense Command; Aiko Herzig-Yoshinaga, a researcher for the Commission on Wartime Relocation and Internment of Civilians from 1981 to 1983 and the person who discovered the original version of the final report.

In a careful opinion containing detailed findings of fact, the district court confirmed Hirabayashi's contentions in virtually every factual respect. See *Hirabayashi* v. *United States*, 627 F. Supp. 1445 (W.D. Wash. 1986). It rejected as factually and legally unsupported the government's arguments that Hirabayashi had not been prejudiced by the concealment of the newly discovered material, that Hirabayashi could and should have made the same claims years earlier, and that there was no remaining case or controversy because Hirabayashi suffered no continuing adverse consequences from the original convictions.

The district court held that Hirabayashi's conviction for violating the exclusion order resulted in a violation of due process and ordered it vacated. 627 F. Supp. at 1457. Another district court has reached the same result in the *Korematsu* case, *Korematsu* v. *United States*, 584 F. Supp.

1406 (N.D. Cal. 1984), and there has been no appeal.[4] The district court in this case, however, concluded as a matter of law that the curfew conviction should not be vacated. It ruled that because the curfew order less significantly infringed Hirabayashi's freedom, the Supreme Court would have distinguished it from the exclusion order and would have affirmed the conviction even if it had known the racial basis of the order. *Hirabayashi*, 627 F. Supp. at 1457.

Both Hirabayashi and the government appeal. In reviewing the district court's decision, we must uphold the findings of fact unless they are clearly erroneous, and review the legal issues de novo. *United States* v. *McConney*, 728 F.2d 1195, 1200 n.5 & 1201 (9th Cir.) (en banc), cert. denied, 469 U.S. 824, 105 S. Ct. 101 (1984). We agree with the district court's factual and legal analysis leading to its vacation of the exclusion conviction. We disagree with the court's conclusion that the curfew conviction rests upon a legal foundation different from the exclusion conviction. We therefore hold that both convictions should be vacated.

II. Factual Background

This proceeding is a collateral attack upon convictions for violating military orders promulgated in 1942. The facts underlying this litigation thus form a very small part of the great mosaic of American participation in World War II. In order to resolve the contentions of both parties on appeal, we must first understand the nature and origin of the crimes of which the petitioner was convicted; the posture of the case as it was presented to the United States Supreme Court; the material which the government suppressed from the Court; and the relevance of that material to the Supreme Court's analysis.

---

[4]Hirabayashi's case was one of three wartime Japanese internment cases in which the Supreme Court upheld the government's orders. Fred Korematsu violated a California exclusion order in May 1942, approximately the same time as Hirabayashi. Because of an intervening jurisdictional problem which was certified to the Supreme Court, we did not address the merits of his appeal until December 1943. *Korematsu* v. *United States*, 140 F.2d 289 (9th Cir. 1943). Thus, his conviction was not affirmed by the Court until a year and a half after the *Hirabayashi* decision. The Court also affirmed Minoru Yasui's conviction for violating an Oregon curfew order. The Court handed down its decisions in *Hirabayashi* and *Yasui* on the same day. *Yasui* v. *United States*, 320 U.S. 115, 63 S. Ct. 1392 (1943). In February 1983 Yasui filed a petition for coram nobis relief, which was dismissed by the district court upon the government's motion to dismiss the indictment and vacate the conviction. We held that Yasui's appeal was untimely and remanded the case to allow Yasui to make a showing of excusable neglect. *Yasui* v. *United States*, 772 F.2d 1496, 1499–1500 (9th Cir. 1985). Although we specifically retained jurisdiction over the appeal, it was subsequently dismissed as moot due to Yasui's death.

A. The Military Exclusion Orders and Hirabayashi's Conviction

On December 7, 1941, President Roosevelt issued Presidential Procla-mation No. 2525, reprinted in H.R. Rep. No. 2124, 77th Cong., 2d Sess. (1942); R. Daniels, supra note 1, at 61, delegating broad authority to the Attorney General and the Secretary of War to promulgate and enforce regulations aimed at curtailing the liberties of enemy aliens following the declaration of war against Japan, Italy, and Germany. A subject of imme-diate governmental internal debate was whether or not our Constitution permitted similar action with respect to citizens, and specifically, whether or not the evacuation of citizens of Japanese ancestry from the West Coast was appropriate. The Justice Department consistently took the view that civilian authorities could not authorize the exclusion of citizens and that the matter should be left to military judgment.[5]

Consistent with that view, President Roosevelt signed Executive Order No. 9066 on February 19, 1942. It authorized the Secretary of War or his designees to prescribe military areas from which any or all persons, citizens as well as aliens, might be excluded. Exec. Order No. 9066, 3 C.F.R. 1092 (1938–1943 Comp.). The next day, Secretary of War Stimson delegated his authority under the Executive Order to Lt. Gen. John L. DeWitt, the Commanding General of the Western Defense Com-mand. On March 2, 1942, General DeWitt issued Public Proclamation No. 1, designating "Military Areas" within the western states. 7 Fed. Reg. 2320 (1942). On March 21, President Roosevelt signed legislation making it a misdemeanor to disregard restrictions imposed by a military commander. Pub. L. No. 77-503, 56 Stat. 173 (1942).

Based upon the authority of the Executive Order and the criminal stat-ute, General DeWitt began issuing orders requiring certain persons to obey curfew restrictions and report at designated times and places for evacuation from military areas. Two of these orders provided the basis for Hirabayashi's convictions.

In Public Proclamation No. 3, dated March 24, 1942, General DeWitt proclaimed "as a matter of military necessity" that all German and Italian aliens and all persons of Japanese ancestry, whether aliens or American citizens, within established military zones would be required beginning March 28, 1942, to remain within their place of residence between 8 p.m.

---

[5]See, e.g., Letter of February 12, 1942, from Attorney General Biddle to Secretary of War Stimson reprinted in R. Daniels, supra note 1, at 107–08; Letter of January 4, 1942, from Assistant to the Attorney General Rowe to General DeWitt, quoted in M. Grodzins, supra note 1, at 238.

and 6 a.m. 7 Fed Reg. 2543. That same day, General DeWitt began issuing a series of Civilian Exclusion Orders, each relating to a specified area within the territory of his command. Order No. 57, pertaining to Seattle, issued May 10, 1942, required the petitioner to report either May 11 or May 12 to a designated civilian control station as a prerequisite to exclusion from the military area on May 16. 7 Fed. Reg. 3725. Hirabayashi went instead to the FBI where he volunteered that he had not abided by the curfew restrictions and that he, as a matter of conscience, would not register with the civilian control station. Hirabayashi's actual loyalty to this country has apparently never been questioned before, during or since World War II.[6]

A grand jury indicted petitioner on May 28, 1942. Count I charged that he had failed to report pursuant to Civilian Exclusion Order 57. Count II charged the curfew violation. He was tried by a jury in October 1942, found guilty, and sentenced to three months on each count to be served concurrently.[7] On appeal, this court certified issues to the Supreme Court, and the Supreme Court on April 5, 1943, certified the entire record to it. *Hirabayashi*, 320 U.S. at 84–85, 63 S. Ct. at 1378.

B. The Supreme Court Proceedings

Briefing to the Supreme Court took place in the spring of 1943. In his brief, Hirabayashi argued that there was no emergency justifying a racially based classification and that the orders had been issued upon invidious racial prejudice. For example, Hirabayashi's brief stated:

Whatever may have been the panicky notion about a Japanese invasion of the West Coast right after Pearl Harbor, it was quite evident by the time the orders here in question were promulgated that the Japanese were not easily going to be able to do this. They had not invaded Australia; had not even attacked Hawaii a second time. [footnote omitted] The picture of Japanese paratroops hiding among the Japanese residents of the West Coast to assist at an invasion is pure fantasy. The truth of the matter is that there was no military necessity, nor even reasonable ground for belief that such necessity required either general curfew restrictions or wholesale evacuation orders.

[6] Hirabayashi was born in the United States. His parents were born in Japan, but came to the United States in the early 1900s at the age of 19. They were married in this country and never returned to Japan. Hirabayashi had never been to Japan and had never even corresponded with anyone there. See *Hirabayashi*, 627 F. Supp. at 1447 (detailing petitioner's personal background, education, community activities, etc.).

[7] Hirabayashi's three month sentence was served after the Supreme Court affirmed his convictions. He had already been incarcerated for nine months; five pending trial and four more pending appeal before bail terms were agreed upon.

Brief for Appellant at 19, *Hirabayashi* v. *United States*, 320 U.S. 81, 63 S. Ct. 1375 (1943) (No. 870).

The Justice Department justified the exclusion and curfew orders upon what it said was a reasonable judgment of military necessity. It argued that because of cultural characteristics of the Japanese Americans, including religion and education, it was likely that some, though not all, American citizens of Japanese ancestry were disloyal. Brief for United States at 18–32. It then argued that because of the military exigencies, the government did not wait to segregate the loyal from the disloyal. The government's brief stated:

The classification was not based upon invidious race discrimination. Rather, it was founded upon the fact that the group as a whole contained an unknown number of persons who could not readily be singled out and who were a threat to the security of the nation; and in order to impose effective restraints upon them it was necessary not only to deal with the entire group, but to deal with it at once.

Id. at 35. Later in its brief, the government stated that "[w]hat was needed was a method of removing at once the unknown number of Japanese persons who might assist a Japanese invasion, and not a program for sifting out such persons in the indefinite future." *Id.* at 62.

The government claimed that the "operative fact" on which the classification was made was the danger arising from the existence of over 100,000 persons of Japanese descent on the West Coast. *Id.* at 63. It acknowledged, however, that the "record in this case does not contain any comprehensive account of the facts which gave rise to the exclusion and curfew measures here involved." *Id.* at 10–11. The government therefore made extensive use of judicial notice in order to convey its position that those responsible for the orders reasonably regarded an emergency situation to exist. It argued that "historical facts" and "facts appear[ing] in official documents . . . are peculiarly within the realm of judicial notice." *Id.* at 11.

The government's argument that the urgency of the situation made individual hearings to determine loyalty impossible was the subject of special concern. Solicitor General Charles Fahy filed a post-argument memorandum stressing that the hearings could not have been utilized because the "situation did not lend itself, in the *unique and pressing* circumstances, to solution by individual loyalty hearings." (Emphasis added.)[8]

---

[8] The memorandum from Solicitor General Fahy to the Supreme Court on May 14, 1943, states more fully:

"Our position is not that hearings are an inappropriate method of reaching a decision on the question of loyalty. The Government does not contend that, assuming adequate opportunity for inves-

The Supreme Court decided the case on June 21, 1943. The government's view prevailed; Chief Justice Stone deferred to the military assessment of necessity. The Court saw the racial classification as justifiable only as a matter of military expediency, and indicated that it had to accept the judgment of the military authorities that the exigencies of time required the entire Japanese population to be treated as a group. The Court concluded:

Whatever views we may entertain regarding the loyalty to this country of the citizens of Japanese ancestry, we cannot reject as unfounded the judgment of the military authorities and of Congress that there were disloyal members of that population, whose number and strength could not be precisely and quickly ascertained. We cannot say that the war-making branches of the Government did not have ground for believing that in a critical hour such persons could not readily be isolated and separately dealt with. . . . .

320 U.S. at 99, 63 S. Ct. at 1385.

The problem for the Court was stated with greater anguish in Justice Douglas' concurring opinion where he pointed out that "guilt is personal under our constitutional system. Detention for reasonable cause is one thing. Detention on account of ancestry is another." 320 U.S. at 107–08, 63 S. Ct. at 1389 (Douglas, J., concurring). He nevertheless rejected Hirabayashi's argument, concluding that expediency so required.

Much of the argument assumes that as a matter of policy it might have been wiser for the military to have dealt with these people on an individual basis and through the process of investigation and hearings separated those who were loyal from those who are not. But the wisdom or expediency of the decision which was made is not for us to review. . . . [W]here the peril is great and the time is short, temporary treatment on a group basis may be the only practicable expedient whatever the ultimate percentage of those who are detained for cause.

Id. at 106–07, 63 S. Ct. at 1388 (Douglas, J., concurring).

C. The Coram Nobis Proceedings: General DeWitt's Report and Other Matters Developed in the Record Below

Hirabayashi filed this coram nobis proceeding early in 1983, alleging that new material had come to light in this decade which showed that the

tigation, hearings may not ever be appropriately utilized on the question of the loyalty of persons here involved. It is submitted, however, that in the circumstances set forth in our brief, this method was not available to solve the problem which confronted the country. The situation did not lend itself, in the unique and pressing circumstances, to solution by individual loyalty hearings. In any event, the method of individual hearings was reasonably thought to be unavailable by those who were obliged to decide upon the measures to be taken." See *Hirabayashi*, 627 F. Supp. at 1453–54 (quoting memo).

Department of War had suppressed evidence from both Hirabayashi and the Justice Department during the crucial period when the case was being presented to the Supreme Court, and that this material required the court to grant the unusual writ of coram nobis to vacate the convictions. The government, recognizing that the circumstances surrounding Hirabayashi's convictions may have been unjust,[9] nevertheless asked the district court to refrain from considering the facts, and to dismiss the petition for coram nobis. It asked the court instead to utilize the provisions of Fed. R. Crim. P. 48, permitting termination of a prosecution by dismissal of the indictment, to vacate the conviction. The district court denied the government's motion to dismiss and held a full evidentiary hearing on Hirabayashi's claims.

The principal factual matter developed at the trial concerned the suppressed report of General DeWitt. This report set forth the basis for his promulgation of the orders of which Hirabayashi stood convicted. At the time General DeWitt issued his series of orders regarding curfew and exclusion in 1942, neither he nor the War Department provided any factual explanation of the reasons for the orders. After they were issued, General DeWitt prepared such a report. The official version of the report, *Final Report: Japanese Evacuation from the West Coast 1942*, was dated June 5, 1943, but was not made public until January 1944. Recent historical research, however, has uncovered in the National Archives a previously unknown copy of an original version of that report. That copy reflects that General DeWitt transmitted his original report to the War Department in Washington on April 15, 1943. See *Hirabayashi*, 627 F. Supp. at 1449, 1455–56 (describing circumstances surrounding discovery and transmittal).

The original version differed materially from the official version. Most significantly, the original report did not purport to rest on any military exigency, but instead declared that because of traits peculiar to citizens of Japanese ancestry it would be impossible to separate the loyal from the disloyal, and that all would have to be evacuated for the duration of the war. Other documents in the record below show that officials in the War Department were alarmed when they received the original report. The

---

[9]In its "response and motion," the government said it would be inappropriate to defend the convictions, noting that both the legislative and executive branches have "long since concluded that the curfew and mass evacuation were part of an unfortunate episode in our nation's history." The government cited President Ford's 1976 proclamation formally rescinding Executive Order 9066, and the 1980 congressional creation of the Commission on Wartime Relocation and Internment of Civilians, along with the repeal in 1976 of Pub. L. No. 77-503 (then codified at 18 U.S.C. § 1383) which Hirabayashi was convicted of violating in 1942.

district court observed that Assistant Secretary of War John J. McCloy was "more than a little exercised because the Final Report had been printed in final form and distributed without any prior consultation by the Western Defense Command with the War Department about its contents." 627 F. Supp. at 1450.

McCloy and Colonel Karl Bendetsen, who was in charge of the Wartime Civil Control Administration of the Western Defense Command, had a number of communications with General DeWitt in order to persuade him to change the report. *Id*. at 1450–53. At first intransigent, DeWitt stated "[I] [h]ave no desire to compromise in any way govt case in Supreme Court." 627 F. Supp. at 1451 (quoting Letter of May 5, 1943, from General DeWitt to Brigadier General Barnett). He eventually capitulated. The result was that the report was changed in several substantive respects after the War Department suggested some fifty-five alterations. The changes most relevant to this case were summarized by the district court as follows:

Page iii, paragraph 2, second sentence: Eliminate the words "and will continue for the duration of the present war." Page iii, paragraph 2, end of the second sentence: Insert "The surprise attack at Pearl Harbor by the enemy crippled a major portion of the Pacific Fleet and exposed the West Coast to an attack which could not have been substantially impeded by defensive fleet operations. More than 120,000 persons of Japanese ancestry resided in colonies adjacent to many highly sensitive installations. Their loyalties were unknown, and time was of the essence."

Page 9. Strike the following: "It was impossible to establish the identity of the loyal and the disloyal with any degree of safety. It was not that there was insufficient time in which to make such a determination; it was simply a matter of facing the realities that a positive determination could not be made, that an exact separation of the 'sheep from the goats' was unfeasible."

And replace with the following: "To complicate the situation, no ready means existed for determining the loyal and the disloyal with any degree of safety. It was necessary to face the realities—a positive determination could not have been made."

627 F. Supp. at 1451–52.

The revised, official version of the report was dated June 5, 1943. The War Department tried to destroy all copies of the original report when the revised version was prepared. This record contains a memo by Theodore Smith of the Civil Affairs Division of the Western Defense Command, dated June 29, 1943, certifying that he witnessed the burning of "the galley proofs, galley pages, drafts and memorandums of the original report of the Japanese Evacuation."

Edward Ennis, the Director of the Alien Enemy Control Unit of the Justice Department and a principal author of the government's 1942 brief, testified extensively in these proceedings. He testified as to his efforts in 1943 and 1944 in briefing both the *Korematsu* and *Hirabayashi* cases, and other efforts on the part of the Justice Department to obtain the full materials from the War Department supporting General DeWitt's decisions. While preparing the government's brief in *Hirabayashi*, Ennis learned that a report had been written but when he asked for a copy, the War Department gave him only a few selected pages. The district court observed, in denying the Government's Petition for Rehearing in this case, that it found Ennis entirely credible and that it believed that had Ennis had the original report showing the true rationale of DeWitt, he would have informed the Supreme Court of its contents.

On the basis of the evidence before it, the district court entered an extensive opinion setting forth the reasons for its decision to vacate the exclusion conviction. Judge Voorhees based that decision upon the factual record developed before him. He found first, that while the Supreme Court based its decision in *Hirabayashi* upon deference to military judgment of the need for expediency, General DeWitt, the person responsible for the racially based confinement of American citizens, had made no such judgment. The district court further found that the United States government doctored the documentary record to reflect that DeWitt had made a judgment of military exigency. Finally, the court found that had the suppressed material been submitted to the Supreme Court, its decision probably would have been materially affected. The government appeals the grant of relief.

The district court refused, however, to grant coram nobis relief with respect to the curfew conviction. It based that decision upon its conclusion that the Supreme Court would have drawn a legal distinction between the curfew and exclusion orders. It is from that denial of relief that Hirabayashi appeals. We consider first the contentions of the government.

III. The Government's Contentions in Its Appeal

The government's contentions in its appeal from the district court's decision to vacate the exclusion conviction can be classified in four general categories. They are, first, that certain factual determinations of the district court are clearly erroneous; second, that the claims are barred by laches; third, that the case is moot because Hirabayashi does not continue to suffer from any adverse consequences from the convictions; and, finally, that the district court abused its discretion in reaching the merits of the petition by not granting the government's motion to vacate the convictions pursuant to Fed. R. Crim. P. 48.

A. Factual Challenges

[1] We turn to the government's challenge to certain of the district court's findings. The government first takes issue with the district court's finding that it was General DeWitt who made the decision that exclusion of all persons of Japanese ancestry from the West Coast was required by military necessity. 627 F. Supp. at 1456. Support for the finding that the decision was General DeWitt's is abundant in this record. Secretary of War Stimson delegated his authority to General DeWitt pursuant to the power delegated to Stimson by the President. See Public Proclamation No. 1, 7 Fed. Reg. 2320 (1942). There has been no showing that General DeWitt even consulted with War Department officials in Washington before issuing the orders Hirabayashi refused to obey. It is now clear that DeWitt did not consult with Washington before preparing his final report. *Hirabayashi*, 627 F. Supp. at 1450. As one commentator wrote soon after the orders were issued: "The Japanese question had political and economic angles, but the President's Executive Order of February 19 treated it as fundamentally a military problem and placed responsibility squarely upon the Commanding General." Fairman, *The Law of Martial Rule and the National Emergency*, 55 Harv. L. Rev. 1253, 1299 (1942).

The government points to uncontroverted evidence in the record that there were those in the War Department who did not agree with the reasons given by General DeWitt for the order and would have justified the order on other grounds. This evidence, however, merely underscores the critical nature of General DeWitt's decision and his report. It was because General DeWitt had exercised the authority, and because his judgment was essential, that the War Department suppressed the original version of his report in the first place. Indeed, Solicitor General Fahy in his oral argument in 1944 in *Korematsu* conceded that it was the views of the Commanding General which counted, and that if his orders had been based upon racist precepts, they would have been invalid. The following colloquy took place in which Justice Frankfurter and the Solicitor General discussed the revised version of DeWitt's report without knowledge of the existence of the original version.

Mr. Justice Frankfurter: Suppose the commanding general, when he issued Order No. 34, had said, in effect, "It is my judgment that, as a matter of security, there is no danger from the Japanese operations; but under cover of war, I had authority to take advantage of my hostility and clear the Japanese from this area." Suppose he had said that, with that kind of crude candor. It would not have been within his authority, would it?

Mr. Fahy: It would not have been.

Mr. Justice Frankfurter: As I understand the suggestion, it is that, as a matter of law, the report of General DeWitt two years later proved that that was exactly what the situation was. As I understand, that is the legal significance of the argument.

Mr. Fahy: That is correct, Your Honor; and the report simply does nothing of the kind.

[2] To support its position the government cites language in the Supreme Court's opinion in *Hirabayashi*, referring to the judgment of Congress and military authorities, in order to suggest that somehow the Supreme Court made a factual finding contrary to the district court's finding. *Hirabayashi*, 320 U.S. at 99, 63 S. Ct. at 1385. Neither the Supreme Court's opinion nor the record before it in 1943 supports such an argument. The district court's decision correctly reflects the historical record that the orders were the direct result of General DeWitt's exercise of the authority delegated to him. The district court's finding that it was General DeWitt who decided that the curfew and exclusion orders were required is not clearly erroneous.

[3] The government next challenges as factually erroneous the district court's finding that the Supreme Court in 1943 would probably have reached a different result in the exclusion case if it had known the true basis for the General's decision. The government disagrees with the following portions of the district court's opinion:

Had the statement of General DeWitt been disclosed to petitioner's counsel, they would have been in a position to argue that, contrary to General DeWitt's belief, there were in fact means of separating those who were loyal from those who were not; that the legal system had developed through the years means whereby factual questions of the most complex nature could be answered with a high degree of reliability. Counsel for petitioner could have pointed out that with very little effort the determination could have been made that tens of thousands of native-born Japanese Americans—infants in arms, children of high school age or younger, housewives, the infirm and elderly—were loyal and posed no possible threat to this country.

Had counsel for petitioner known and been able to present to the Supreme Court the [initial] reason stated by General DeWitt for the evacuation of all Japanese,

[and] . . . [i]f the military necessity for exclusion was the impossibility of separating the loyal from the disloyal, the Supreme Court would not have had to defer to military judgment because this particular problem, separating the loyal from the disloyal, was one calling for judicial, rather than military, judgment.

627 F. Supp. at 1456–57.

The government characterizes its challenge as one to a factual finding, which we must uphold unless clearly erroneous. To the extent, however, that the government is asking us to assess the district court's judgment as to the legal materiality of the suppressed evidence, it is also raising a question of law, and we review with greater latitude. See *McConney*, 728 F.2d at 1204 (adopting functional analysis for mixed questions of law and fact).

In making this challenge, the government agrees with petitioner and the district court that the Supreme Court in *Hirabayashi* deferred to a military judgment that circumstances required the prompt evacuation of all Japanese Americans, and that there was not enough time to attempt to separate the loyal from the disloyal. The government also agrees with petitioner and the district court that General DeWitt acted on the basis of his own racist views and not on the basis of any military judgment that time was of the essence. What the government contends in this appeal is that on the basis of the record before it, the Supreme Court should have known both that General DeWitt was a racist, and that he made no military judgment of emergency. The government asks us to hold, therefore, that the Supreme Court probably would have reached the same erroneous result even if the government had not suppressed the evidence and had accurately represented to the Court the basis of General DeWitt's decision.

There are several problems with this position. First, as the district court observed when it denied rehearing, the material in the record before the Supreme Court showing General DeWitt's racism was limited primarily to a newspaper clipping. More importantly, it was principally Hirabayashi and those amici who supported him, not the government, who presented the evidence of racial bias to the Court and who argued that the decisions must have been based upon racism rather than military necessity. By contrast, the information now in the public record constitutes objective and irrefutable proof of the racial bias that was the cornerstone of the internment orders.

The basis for General DeWitt's decision was a very crucial issue which divided the government and Hirabayashi. For illustration, Hirabayashi's

brief referred to testimony by DeWitt indicating that "prejudice dominated his thinking," and quoted him as stating: "It makes no difference
whether the Japanese is theoretically a citizen . . . A Jap is a Jap." *San
Francisco News*, April 13, 1943, at 1, cited in Reply Brief for Appellant
at 1 n.2. Extracts from the newspaper article were reproduced in the appendix to that brief. The amicus brief of the American Civil Liberties
Union, in support of Hirabayashi's position, also suggested that the order
was based upon the racist view that it was impossible to segregate the
loyal from the disloyal:

There were those, of course, who claimed that it would have been impossible to
tell the loyal from the disloyal; who said that all persons of Japanese ancestry
look alike. It is a challenge to the intelligence of this nation that such childish
opinions actually carried the day.

Brief for American Civil Liberties Union at 13. Similar arguments were
made by the Japanese American Citizens League in their amicus brief in
support of Hirabayashi.

The government, on the other hand, through the device of judicial notice asked the Supreme Court to recognize that the judgment made was
one of exigency; the "principal danger to be apprehended was a Japanese
invasion." Brief for United States at 65. It argued that the "situation did
not lend itself, in the unique and pressing circumstances, to solution by
individual loyalty hearings." Post-Argument Memorandum of Solicitor
General Fahy. In deciding the case against Hirabayashi, the Supreme
Court obviously accepted the government's view of the facts as the government presented them in 1943, and rejected Hirabayashi's.

In asking us to hold that the Supreme Court would have reached the
same result even if the Solicitor General had advised Hirabayashi and the
Court of the true basis for General DeWitt's orders, the government ignores the fact that in 1943 it was clearly in a better position to know that
basis than was the defense. It also ignores the traditionally special relationship between the Supreme Court and the Solicitor General which permits the Solicitor General to make broad use of judicial notice and
commands special credence from the Court.[10] The record here shows that

---

[10]Traditionally, the Supreme Court has shown great respect for the views of the Solicitor
General—"an advocate whom the Court can trust." See Jenkins, *The Solicitor General's Winning
Ways*, 69 A.B.A. J. 734 (1983); Note, *Government Litigation in the Supreme Court: The Roles of the
Solicitor General*, 78 Yale L.J. 1442 (1969). Thus, he owes a special obligation to the Court as well
as his client. See O'Connor, *The Amicus Curiae Role of the U.S. Solicitor General in Supreme Court
Litigation*, 66 Judicature 256 (1983); Note, *The Solicitor General and Intragovernmental Conflict*,
76 Mich. L. Rev. 324 (1977). See also Speech by Rex Lee, Solicitor General of the United States
1981–85, Ohio State University College of Law (March 19, 1986) *Lawyering for the Government:*

Ennis, in preparing the government's brief, felt that responsibility keenly.[11]

The importance which the Supreme Court attached to the statements of the government regarding the factual situation at the time was brought out during the course of the proceedings in *Korematsu*, decided a year after *Hirabayashi*. By the time *Korematsu* was briefed and argued, the revised version of DeWitt's report had been made public. Justice Department attorneys with access to contemporaneous intelligence reports had had misgivings about the accuracy of even that version. This apprehension was reflected in a footnote to the government's brief in *Korematsu* limiting reliance on the report.[12] The footnote came up during oral argument, the transcript of which is in this record. Solicitor General Fahy denied that the footnote was a repudiation of the military necessity of the evacuation and reaffirmed the government's position in *Hirabayashi*.[13]

Politics, Polemics & Principle, reprinted in 47 Ohio St. L.J. 595 (1986) (discussing multiple roles of Solicitor General).

[11] As the Justice Department prepared its brief, Ennis came into possession of the intelligence work of Lt. Commander Kenneth D. Ringle, an expert on Japanese intelligence in the Office of Naval Intelligence. Ringle had reached conclusions directly contradicting the two key premises in the government's argument. Ringle found (1) that the cultural characteristics of the Japanese Americans had *not* resulted in a high risk of disloyalty by members of that group, and (2) that individualized determinations *could* be made expeditiously. See K. Ringle, *Report on the Japanese Question 3*(Jan. 26, 1942). Ennis therefore concluded:

"I think we should consider very carefully whether we do not have a duty to advise the Court of the existence of the Ringle memorandum and of the fact that this represents the view of the Office of Naval Intelligence. It occurs to me that any other course of conduct might approximate the suppression of evidence."

Memorandum from Ennis to Solicitor General Re: Japanese Brief, April 30, 1943. Notwithstanding Ennis' plea, the Justice Department's brief in *Hirabayashi* made no mention of Ringle's analysis.

[12] The footnote actually inserted in the government's brief was as follows:

"The Final Report of General DeWitt (which is dated June 5, 1943, but which was not made public until January 1944), hereinafter cited as *Final Report*, is relied on in this brief for statistics and other details concerning the actual evacuation and the events that took place subsequent thereto. We have specifically recited in this brief the facts relating to the justification for the evacuation, of which we ask the Court to take judicial notice, and we rely upon the *Final Report* only to the extent that it relates to such facts."

Korematsu, Brief for the United States at 11 n.2. Based upon the revised report, and without knowledge of the existence of the original version, lawyers within the Justice Department had pushed for a stronger footnote which would have at least partially discredited the report. The proposal for this footnote was contained in a memorandum from John L. Burling to Assistant Attorney General Herbert Wechsler dated September 11, 1944, reprinted in Appendix B, *Korematsu*, 584 F. Supp. at 1423. The full text of the footnote he proposed was:

"The Final Report of General DeWitt (which is dated June 5, 1943, but which was not made public until January 1944) is relied on in this brief for statistics and other details concerning the actual evacuation and the events that took place subsequent thereto. The recital of the circumstances justifying the evacuation as a matter of military necessity, however, is in several respects, particularly with reference to the use of illegal radio transmitters and to shore-to-ship signalling by persons of Japanese ancestry, in conflict with information in possession of the Department of Justice. *In view of the contrariety of the reports on this matter we do not ask the Court to take judicial notice of the recitals of those facts contained in the Report.*" (Emphasis added.)

[13] After being asked to make copies of the DeWitt report available to the Court, Solicitor General

The Court's divided opinions in *Korematsu* demonstrate beyond question the importance which the Justices in *Korematsu* and *Hirabayashi* placed upon the position of the government that there was a perceived military necessity, despite contrary arguments of the defendants in those cases. The majority in *Korematsu* reaffirmed the Court's deference in *Hirabayashi* to military judgments. Justice Murphy's dissent highlighted the difference between his position and the majority's. He expressly faulted the majority's acceptance of the government's justification that "time was of the essence." We now know this very phrase was inserted by the War Department into DeWitt's final report and was not a concept upon which DeWitt himself based his decision. Justice Murphy said:

> No adequate reason is given for the failure to treat these Japanese Americans on an individual basis by holding investigations and hearings to separate the loyal from the disloyal, as was done in the case of persons of German and Italian ancestry. [citation omitted] *It is asserted merely that the loyalties of this group "were unknown and time was of the essence."*

Korematsu, 323 U.S. at 241, 65 S. Ct. at 205 (Murphy, J., dissenting) (emphasis added). Justice Jackson's dissent zeroed in on the majority's acceptance of General DeWitt's revised report. He stated:

> So the Court, having no real evidence before it, has no choice but to accept General DeWitt's own unsworn, self-serving statement, untested by any cross-examination, that what he did was reasonable. And thus it will always be when courts try to look into the reasonableness of a military order.

Id. at 245, 65 S. Ct. at 207 (Jackson, J., dissenting).

The majority decision in *Korematsu* was a reaffirmation that it would defer to a military judgment of necessity in upholding first the curfew and then the exclusion orders.

Like curfew, exclusion of those of Japanese origin was deemed necessary because of the presence of an unascertained number of disloyal members of the group, most of whom we have no doubt were loyal to this country. It was because we could not reject the finding of the military authorities that it was impossible to

---

Fahy agreed and said: "It is even suggested that because of some foot note in our brief in this case indicating that we do not ask the Court to take judicial notice of the truth of every recitation or instance in the final report of General DeWitt, that the Government has repudiated the military necessity of the evacuation. It seems to me, if the Court please, that that is a neat little piece of fancy dancing. There is nothing in the brief of the Government which is any different in this respect from the position it has always maintained since the Hirabayashi case—that not only the military judgment of the general, but the judgment of the Government of the United States, has always been in justification of the measures taken; and no person in any responsible position has ever taken a contrary position, and the Government does not do so now. Nothing in its brief can validly be used to the contrary."

bring about an immediate segregation of the disloyal from the loyal that we sustained the validity of the curfew order as applying to the whole group. In the instant case, temporary exclusion of the entire group was rested by the military on the same ground.

Id. at 218–19, 65 S. Ct. at 195. The claimed emergency preventing the separation of loyal from disloyal Japanese Americans was critical to the Supreme Court's decisions upholding the internment of Hirabayashi and Korematsu. This was clearly evidenced when the Court subsequently held that detention of a concededly loyal Japanese American citizen was unlawful. See *Ex Parte Endo*, 323 U.S. 283, 65 S. Ct. 208 (1944).

[4] We cannot hold that the district court erred in deciding that the reasoning of the Supreme Court would probably have been profoundly and materially affected if the Justice Department had advised it of the suppression of evidence which established the truthfulness of the allegations made by Hirabayashi and Korematsu concerning the real reason for the exclusion order.

B. Coram Nobis Requirements: The Issues of Laches and Mootness

[5] Hirabayashi has filed a petition for a writ of error coram nobis asking the court to vacate his 1942 misdemeanor convictions. In *United States* v. *Morgan*, 346 U.S. 502, 74 S. Ct. 247 (1954), the Supreme Court held that coram nobis relief is available to challenge the validity of a conviction, even though the sentence has been fully served, *id.* at 503–04, 74 S. Ct. at 248–49, "under circumstances compelling such action to achieve justice." *Id.* at 511, 74 S. Ct. at 252. As we recently explained in *Yasui* v. *United States*, 772 F.2d 1496, 1498 (9th Cir. 1985), the coram nobis writ "fills a void in the availability of post-conviction remedies in federal criminal cases." A convicted defendant who is in federal custody and claims that his sentence "was imposed in violation of the Constitution or laws of the United States . . . or is otherwise subject to collateral attack" may move to have his sentence vacated under 28 U.S.C. § 2255. Such habeas corpus relief is not available, however, to a defendant who has served his sentence and has been released from custody. In such a situation, "no statutory avenue to relief [exists] from the lingering collateral consequences of an unconstitutional or unlawful conviction based on errors of fact." *Yasui*, 772 F.2d at 1498. See *Morgan*, 346 U.S. at 512–13, 74 S. Ct. at 253 (noting potential collateral consequences; "[s]ubsequent convictions may carry heavier penalties, civil rights may be affected"). Nor is a motion for a new trial based

on newly discovered evidence available to petitioners who have long since served their sentences because such a motion must be filed within two years of the date of the final judgment in the original proceeding. See Fed. R. Crim. P. 33; *United States* v. *Dellinger*, 657 F.2d 140, 144 (7th Cir. 1981).

[6] Thus, the coram nobis writ allows a court to vacate its judgments "for errors of fact . . . in those cases where the errors [are] of the most fundamental character, that is, such as rendered the proceeding itself invalid." *United States* v. *Mayer*, 235 U.S. 55, 69, 35 S. Ct. 16, 19–20 (1914). Although Federal Rule of Civil Procedure 60(b) expressly abolishes the writ of coram nobis in civil cases, the extraordinary writ still provides a remedy in criminal proceedings where no other relief is available and sound reasons exist for failure to seek appropriate earlier relief. *Morgan*, 346 U.S. at 505 n.4, 74 S. Ct. at 249 n.4. See also *James* v. *United States*, 459 U.S. 1044, 103 S. Ct. 465 (1982) (opinion of Justice Brennan supporting denial of petition for writ of certiorari explaining purpose of coram nobis). The Court in *Morgan* held that district courts have the power to issue the writ under the All Writs Act, 28 U.S.C. § 1651(a). See 346 U.S. at 506–09, 74 S. Ct. at 250.

[7] Based on the authority discussed above, the district court determined that a petitioner must show the following to qualify for coram nobis relief: (1) a more usual remedy is not available; (2) valid reasons exist for not attacking the conviction earlier; (3) adverse consequences exist from the conviction sufficient to satisfy the case or controversy requirement of Article III; and (4) the error is of the most fundamental character.[14] The government challenges the court's conclusions under (2) and (3).

The government argues that the district court should have dismissed the petitioner's claim on the ground of laches. It argues that the material upon which the petitioner relies had been a matter of public record for decades, or, alternatively, that petitioner by due diligence should have found the material earlier. For the reasons we have discussed in the preceding sec-

[14]627 F. Supp. at 1454–55. Relying on a footnote in *Dellinger*, 657 F.2d at 144 n.9, the court required a showing that "it is probable that a different result would have occurred had the error not been made." We note here that neither the Supreme Court nor this circuit has imposed such a requirement. In *Dellinger*, the Seventh Circuit cited *Bateman* v. *United States*, 277 F.2d 65, 68 (8th Cir. 1960), which in turn relied on the dissent in *Morgan*, 346 U.S. at 516, 74 S. Ct. at 255. The majority in *Morgan* never required a showing of prejudice. We need not decide whether there is as high a test as the *Dellinger* footnote suggests because petitioner has satisfied the higher standard.

The district court also stated, citing *Morgan*, 346 U.S. at 507 n.9, 74 S. Ct. at 250 n.9, that the petition must be brought in the convicting court. Hirabayashi satisfied this condition by bringing his petition in the Western District of Washington, the district in which he was convicted.

tion of this opinion, the district court's decision to grant the writ was clearly based upon material which was not known until very recently. The key document upon which the district court relied was the suppressed report of General DeWitt. The district court squarely confronted the government's laches contention by stating as follows:

> [T]he government argues that all of the factual material presented on behalf of petitioner has been a matter of public record for nearly forty years and that petitioner is hence bound by the doctrine of laches from seeking to overturn his convictions. . . . At no place in [the 1949 Grodzins book] is there any reference to the statements made by General DeWitt in the initial version of his Final Report. In none of the other publications submitted by the government is there any such reference.

627 F. Supp. at 1455. These findings are clearly supported.

The suppressed DeWitt Report is not the only evidence which has surfaced as a result of research during this decade. There are memos, which have only recently come to light, by Justice Department lawyers Ennis and Burling relating to the War Department's suppression of the revised report, and their doubts about the accuracy of the report. See supra notes 11–12. The discovery of these materials recently caused the District of Columbia Circuit to hold that the government's fraudulent concealment tolled the statute of limitations in cases brought by Japanese Americans for civil damages arising out of their internment. *Hohri* v. *United States*, 782 F.2d 227, 246 (D.C. Cir. 1986), vacated on jurisdictional grounds, 107 S. Ct. 2246 (1987). It appears from both the district court opinion, 586 F. Supp. 769 (D.D.C. 1984), and the court of appeals opinion in *Hohri*, decided before publication of the district court's opinion in this case, that the original DeWitt Report was not a part of the *Hohri* record. Thus, ours is an even stronger case against the government. In addition, because this is a collateral attack upon a criminal conviction, there is no statute of limitations. The petitioner does not have to prove fraud.

As to the diligence of Hirabayashi in finding the material, we must agree with the district judge who heard direct evidence on this issue and found that "petitioner cannot be faulted for not finding and relying upon [the only surviving copy of the initial version of the report] long before he brought this action in early 1983." 627 F. Supp. at 1455. Professional historians had failed to discover it as well, and the difficulty for a lay person to locate the initial version was documented in the record by testimony concerning its discovery. *Id*. at 1453–56.

Regarding the mootness issue, the district court, although noting that misdemeanor convictions do not present the same adverse consequences as do felony convictions, was satisfied that the case or controversy requirement was fulfilled. The court found that (1) Hirabayashi's credibility might be impeached in a jurisdiction that allows the use of misdemeanor convictions for that purpose, and (2) that a judge could take the convictions into account when sentencing Hirabayashi if he were ever convicted of another crime. 627 F. Supp. at 1455.

The government contends that "ordinary misdemeanors have no 'collateral consequences' and therefore are not subject to post-conviction attack absent some special legal disability." For the following reasons, we find no support for such a per se rule and conclude that the case is not moot.

Modern application of mootness principles to criminal cases must draw upon the Supreme Court's opinion in *Sibron* v. *New York*, 392 U.S. 40, 88 S. Ct. 1889 (1968), where the Court determined that it had jurisdiction to hear Sibron's appeal even though he had completely served his six-month sentence for unlawful possession of heroin. The Court held that "a criminal case is moot only if it is shown that there is no possibility that any collateral legal consequences will be imposed on the basis of the challenged conviction." *Id.* at 57, 88 S. Ct. at 1900. In *Sibron* the Court discussed its previous holding in *Pollard* v. *United States*, 352 U.S. 354, 77 S. Ct. 481 (1957), where

the Court abandoned all inquiry into the actual existence of specific collateral consequences and in effect presumed that they existed. . . . Stat[ing] that "convictions may entail collateral legal disadvantages in the future," *id.*, at 358, [77 S. Ct. at 484], the Court concluded that "[t]he possibility of consequences collateral to the imposition of sentence is sufficiently substantial to justify our dealing with the merits." *Ibid.* The Court thus acknowledged the obvious fact of life that most criminal convictions do in fact entail adverse collateral legal consequences. [footnote omitted] The mere "possibility" that this will be the case is enough to preserve a criminal case from ending "ignominiously in the limbo of mootness." *Parker* v. *Ellis*, 362 U.S. 574, 577, [80 S. Ct. 909, 911] (1960) (dissenting opinion).

Sibron, 392 U.S. at 55, 88 S. Ct. at 1898–99.

The Court acknowledged that it was applying the *Pollard* presumption and then went on to state:

This case certainly meets that test for survival. Without pausing to canvass the possibilities in detail, we note that New York expressly provides by statute that Sibron's conviction may be used to impeach his character . . . [and must be considered in subsequent sentencing]. There are doubtless other collateral consequences.

Sibron, 392 U.S. at 55–56, 88 S. Ct. at 1899. The government argues that this language and an accompanying footnote require a petitioner to show specific legislative disability. *Id.* at 56 n.17, 88 S. Ct. at 1899 n.17.[15] The *Sibron* opinion creates no such requirement. This is reflected in our own coram nobis decisions which consistently apply the *Sibron* "*no* possibility of *any* collateral legal consequences" test. See, e.g., *Chavez* v. *United States*, 447 F.2d 1373, 1374 (9th Cir. 1971) (per curiam); *Byrnes* v. *United States*, 408 F.2d 599, 601 (9th Cir.), cert. denied, 395 U.S. 986, 89 S. Ct. 2142 (1969). We have repeatedly reaffirmed the presumption that collateral consequences flow from any criminal conviction. See, e.g., *Byrnes*, 408 F.2d at 601. As we stated in *Holloway*, coram nobis relief is available to prevent manifest injustice "even where removal of a prior conviction will have little present effect on the petitioner." *Holloway* v. *United States*, 393 F.2d 731, 732 (9th Cir. 1968).

No court to our knowledge has ever held that misdemeanor convictions cannot carry collateral legal consequences. Any judgment of misconduct has consequences for which one may be legally or professionally accountable. See *Miller* v. *Washington State Bar Ass'n*, 679 F.2d 1313, 1318 (9th Cir. 1982) (letter of admonition in attorney's permanent record for which he is professionally accountable constitutes sufficient adverse consequence for Article III).

Moreover, the government's argument here that "ordinary" misdemeanors should not carry the presumption of adverse consequences is misplaced. Hirabayashi's conviction was for no ordinary misdemeanor. His conviction was one which has been the subject of controversy for more than four decades. A United States citizen who is convicted of a crime on account of race is lastingly aggrieved.

---

[15]The *Sibron* footnote provides: "We note that there is a clear distinction between a general impairment of credibility, to which the Court referred in *St. Pierre*, see 319 U.S., at 43, [63 S. Ct. at 911], and New York's specific statutory authorization for use of the conviction to impeach the "character" of a defendant in a criminal proceeding. The latter is a clear legal disability deliberately and specifically imposed by the legislature."

The government also cites *Lane* v. *Williams*, 455 U.S. 624, 102 S. Ct. 1322 (1982), for the proposition that there must be statutory consequences from a conviction to permit coram nobis relief. The case is distinguishable on several grounds. *Lane* did not involve a coram nobis petition. It did not even involve a challenge to a criminal conviction. It was an effort through habeas corpus to attack mandatory parole requirements which the court held could not be pursued beyond the expiration of the parole term. Contrary to the government's view, the Court in *Lane* reaffirmed the *Sibron* standard, quoting the no possibility of any collateral legal consequences test and explicitly stating that *Sibron* was not applicable to that case. *Id.* at 632, 102 S. Ct. at 1327.

C. The Government's Motion to Vacate and Dismiss

[8] The government contends that the trial court erred by denying its motion to vacate Hirabayashi's convictions and dismiss the underlying indictments pursuant to Fed. R. Crim. P. 48(a).

Rule 48(a) provides:

The Attorney General or the United States attorney may by leave of the court file a dismissal of an indictment, information or complaint and the prosecution shall thereupon terminate. Such a dismissal may not be filed during the trial without the consent of the defendant.

The rule vests the courts with the discretion to accept or deny the prosecution's motion. See, e.g., *United States* v. *Weber*, 721 F.2d 266, 268 (9th Cir. 1983) (per curiam); *United States* v. *Cowan*, 524 F.2d 504, 510–11 (5th Cir. 1975), cert. denied sub nom. *Woodruft* v. *United States*, 425 U.S. 971, 96 S. Ct. 2168 (1976). We therefore review the district court's decision for an abuse of discretion. *Rinaldi* v. *United States*, 434 U.S. 22, 32, 98 S. Ct. 81, 86 (1977) (per curiam).

[9] In denying the government's motion, the district court correctly stated that Rule 48(a) provides for dismissal only by leave of the court. The court then determined that "where petitioner seeks to have his petition considered on its merits, the Court is of the opinion that it is not in the public interest, over the objection of petitioner, to grant the government's motion." The government argues that the trial court erroneously relied on the second sentence of Rule 48(a) in requiring Hirabayashi's consent to dismissal because the rule only addresses the accused's consent during trial. It asserts that no consent is necessary once the trial is over.

[10] The district court, however, did not base its denial on a belief that Hirabayashi's consent was necessary. Rather, it exercised its discretion under the first sentence of Rule 48(a) which requires the prosecutor to have the leave of court to file a dismissal. The district court correctly acted within its discretion in refusing to grant the government's motion. There is no precedent for applying Rule 48 to vacate a conviction after the trial and appellate proceedings have ended. The cases cited by the government involve a prosecutor's motion made before or during the pendency of a direct appeal. See *Rinaldi*, 434 U.S. at 24–25, 98 S. Ct. at 82–83 (motion made when case was on direct appeal); *Weber*, 721 F.2d at 267 (motion made when case was on direct appeal); *United States* v. *Hamm*, 659 F.2d 624, 625 (5th Cir. 1981) (en banc) (motion made before sentencing); *Cowan*, 524 F.2d at 513 (motion made before trial).

In a case similar to this one, *Korematsu* v. *United States*, 584 F. Supp. 1406 (N.D. Cal. 1984), a district court judge recently held that the government could not move under Rule 48(a) to vacate a conviction following the lapse of 40-odd years. There, Judge Patel pointed out that Rule 48(a) had its roots in the common law doctrine of *nolle prosequi*. "As the literal translation of *nolle prosequi*—'I am unwilling to prosecute'— makes clear, the primary purpose of the doctrine was to allow the government to cease active prosecution." *Id.* at 1410–11 (discussing in detail the development of Rule 48). The court concluded that

the prosecutor has no authority to exercise his *nolle prosequi* prerogatives at common law or to invoke Rule 48(a) after a person has been subject to conviction, final judgment, imposition of sentence and exhaustion of all appeals and, indeed, after a lapse of many years. At that stage, there is no longer any prosecution to be terminated.

Id. at 1411.

We need not decide whether Rule 48 precludes a district court from ever granting a post-appeal dismissal. Based on the record in this case we cannot find that the district court abused its discretion in denying the government's motion and considering the merits of Hirabayashi's request that an injustice be corrected.

IV. Hirabayashi's Appeal of the District Court's Refusal to Vacate the Curfew Conviction

[11] The district court vacated Hirabayashi's conviction for violation of the exclusion order but left standing the conviction for violation of the curfew order. This was a result which neither side sought and which neither strenuously defends in this court.

[12] The district court based its distinction on the premise that the curfew was a lesser restriction on freedom than the exclusion. It does not follow, however, that the Supreme Court would have made such a distinction had it been aware of the suppressed evidence. The Supreme Court in 1943 reviewed only the curfew order and clearly saw it as a serious deprivation of liberty. The Court therefore held that it would be justified only on the basis of a reasonable military judgment of military necessity. 320 U.S. at 99, 63 S. Ct. at 1385.

The government suggests that the Justices in the *Hirabayashi* decision might have made a distinction between the two orders because the dissenting Justices later in *Korematsu* distinguished the level of infringement of freedom in *Korematsu* from that in *Hirabayashi*. *Korematsu*, 323 U.S. at 246–47, 65 S. Ct. at 207–08 (Jackson, J., dissenting). The relevant issue, however, is not whether a minority of the Justices might have made a distinction, but whether a majority would have. The majority of the Court in *Korematsu* followed exactly the same rationale that was followed in *Hirabayashi* and made no such distinction. The majority of the Court in *Korematsu* said "[n]othing short of apprehension by the proper military authorities of the gravest imminent danger to the public safety can constitutionally justify either [the exclusion or the curfew]." 323 U.S. at 218, 65 S. Ct. at 195.

We have seen that Hirabayashi's two convictions were based upon simultaneous indictments, were tried together, briefed together, and decided together. In its brief to the Supreme Court, the Justice Department argued a single theory of military necessity to support both the exclusion and curfew orders. At the evidentiary hearing before the district court in this case, Ennis explained why:

Q. . . . Did the Department's arguments on those two points [curfew and exclusion] differ somewhat?

A. No, not substantially.

Q. Well,—

A. Because although one was a lesser restriction, it was equally based on what was in our view the difficulty of classifying American citizens—including American citizens. That's for general curfew of the whole area.

The district court erred in distinguishing between the validity of the curfew and exclusion convictions.

Conclusion

The judgment of the district court as to the exclusion conviction is affirmed. The judgment as to the curfew conviction is reversed and the matter is remanded with instructions to grant Hirabayashi's petition to vacate both convictions.

Selected Bibliography

The literature on the wartime internment of Japanese Americans is considerable and is growing in volume as new historical and personal accounts are published. The works listed below cover both the internment experience and the legal issues it has raised. Included are books, law review articles, transcripts of congressional hearings, and lower-court opinions.

Books

Commission on Wartime Relocation and Internment of Civilians, *Personal Justice Denied* (Washington: Government Printing Office, 1982).

This 467-page report, excerpted in this book, was prepared at the request of the U.S. Congress and represents the outcome of a massive historical inquiry into the causes and consequences of the internment program. This exhaustive and illuminating report is based on the testimony of 750 witnesses and an examination of thousands of government documents, many released for the first time.

Daniels, Roger, *Concentration Camps, North America: Japanese in the United States and Canada During World War II* (Malabar, Fla.: Krieger, 1981).

Roger Daniels is the leading historian of Asians in America and of the history of the hostility toward them. This revised and updated version of *Concentration Camps USA* (Holt, 1970) analyzes the civilian and military officials in both the United States and Canada who ordered the wartime internment of ethnic Japanese. Daniels is particularly interesting in recounting the Canadian internment program, which was much harsher and longer in duration than the program in the United States.

Irons, Peter, *Justice at War: The Story of the Japanese American Internment Cases* (New York: Oxford University Press, 1983).

This historical account of the wartime internment cases traces them from their inception to the U.S. Supreme Court's decisions, with a focus on the forty-odd lawyers who participated on both sides and on the judges and justices who decided the cases. It includes much of the material on which the coram nobis petitions were based. The initial chapters examine the internal governmental debate that preceded the signing of Executive Order 9066 by President Franklin D. Roosevelt.

411

Tateishi, John, *And Justice For All: An Oral History of the Japanese American Detention Camps* (New York: Random House, 1984).

Edited by the former redress director of the Japanese American Citizens League, this book gives us the stories—told in their own words—of people of all ages and backgrounds who spent the wartime years in one of the ten internment camps. The lengthy interview with Minoru Yasui, whose curfew challenge went to the Supreme Court, is of special interest. Many of these accounts are gripping and horrifying in their revelation of the wounds of internment and the lingering pain of that experience.

ten Broek, Jacobus, Edward N. Barnhart, and Floyd W. Matson, *Prejudice, War and the Constitution* (Berkeley: University of California Press, 1954).

This early study is still the best analysis of how the internment came about and the legal issues it raised. Its first section, "Genesis," examines the background of anti-Oriental prejudice on the West Coast; the second, "Exodus," is an insightful account of the debates and decisions that led to mass internment; the third, "Leviticus," is a masterful and devastating legal analysis by ten Broek of the U.S. Supreme Court decisions.

Weglyn, Mishi, *Years of Infamy: The Untold Story of America's Concentration Camps* (New York: William Morrow, 1976).

Written for the general public, this account of the internment by a former camp inmate bristles with indignation at the government officials who administered the camps. Although organized in a way that makes it hard to follow, the book includes much important material and is particularly noteworthy in exposing the harshness of official treatment of the internees.

Articles

Dembitz, Nanette, "Racial Discrimination and the Military Judgment: The Supreme Court's Korematsu and Endo Decisions," 45 *Columbia Law Review* 175 (June 1945).

This early critique of U.S. Supreme Court decisions in the Korematsu and Endo cases was written by a former attorney of the Department of Justice who helped prepare the government's briefs. She demolishes the factual premises of the "racial disloyalty" claims that the Court adopted and that she helped to fashion.

Irons, Peter, "Fancy Dancing in the Marble Palace," 3 *Constitutional Commentary* 35 (Winter 1986).

This article includes the full transcript of Solicitor General Charles Fahy's oral argument to the U.S. Supreme Court in the Korematsu case, not discovered in government archives until 1985. The accompanying commentary argues that Fahy deliberately misled the Court on crucial issues in the case.

Iyeki, Marc Hideo, "The Japanese American Coram Nobis Cases: Exposing the Myth of Disloyalty," 13 *New York University Review of Law and Social Change* 199 (Winter 1984–85).

Based on the documentary record in the coram nobis petitions, this article attacks the assumptions of "racial disloyalty" that underlay the U.S. Supreme Court decisions in the internment cases.

Rostow, Eugene V., "The Japanese American Cases—A Disaster," 54 *Yale Law Journal* 489 (June 1945).

One of the first, and still the most influential, of the critiques of the Supreme Court decisions. Then a member of the Yale Law School faculty, Rostow subjected the opinions to a scathing analysis that exposed their abdication of judicial responsibility and the racist underpinnings of the decisions.

Takahata, Sandra, "The Case of Korematsu v. United States: Could It Be Justified Today?" 6 *University of Hawaii Law Review* 109 (Spring 1984).

This article subjects the U.S. Supreme Court's opinion to the standards of judicial review of military power and racial discrimination that have evolved since World War II and concludes that the decision could not meet those tests.

Congressional Hearings

U.S. House of Representatives, Committee on the Judiciary, Subcommittee on Administrative Law and Governmental Relations, Hearings of June 20, 21, 27, and September 12, 1984, Serial No. 90, *Japanese-American and Aleutian Wartime Relocation* (Washington: Government Printing Office, 1985).

The 1984 hearing on bills to provide monetary redress to internment camp survivors includes testimony from members of the Commission on Wartime Relocation and Internment of Civilians and from several wartime officials, most notably John J. McCloy, Karl Bendetsen, and Edward J. Ennis. Of particular relevance to the internment cases and coram nobis petitions is the conflicting testimony of David Lowman and John Herzig on the Magic cables.

U.S. Senate, Committee on the Judiciary, Subcommittee on Administrative Practice and Procedure, Hearings of July 27, 1983, Serial No. J-98-57, *Japanese American Evacuation Redress* (Washington: Government Printing Office, 1984).

Along with testimony of redress supporters and opponents, this volume includes an extensive, previously unpublished, paper by Henry David Sokolski, entitled "The Japanese Cases: Bad History, Good Law?" and submitted for the hearing transcript. It defends the U.S. Supreme Court's internment decisions as "within the Constitution." Sokolski wrote this paper in June 1983, and did not refer to the coram nobis petitions or any of the documentary record they revealed.

Judicial Opinions

Ex Parte Endo, 323 United States Reports 283 (1944).

The U.S. Supreme Court decided in this habeas corpus suit, brought by Mitsuye Endo for release from any "assembly center," that Congress had not authorized the long-term detention of loyal American citizens. However, the Court avoided decision on the constitutional challenges to internment in the suit.

Toyosaburo Korematsu v. *United States*, 140 Federal Reporter, 2d Series, 289 (9th Cir. 1943).

This opinion of the U.S. Court of Appeals for the Ninth Circuit, which sent the Korematsu case to the U.S. Supreme Court without decision, includes a lengthy dissent by Judge William Denman attacking the military orders of General John L. DeWitt.

United States v. *Hirabayashi*, 46 Federal Supplement 657 (W.D.Wash. 1942).

U.S. District Judge Lloyd Black, in denying Hirabayashi's constitutional challenges to the curfew and exclusion orders, in his opinion wrote at length about the presumed disloyalty of Japanese Americans and predicted that they would support any invading Japanese troops.

United States v. *Yasui*, 45 Federal Supplement 40 (D.Ore. 1942).

U.S. District Judge James Alger Fee wrote a lengthy opinion on Yasui's constitutional challenge to the curfew order, concluding that (1) the order was unconstitutional as applied to American citizens but that (2) Yasui had forfeited his citizenship. The U.S. Supreme Court, in upholding Yasui's conviction, reversed this opinion on both issues.

Index

415

About the Editor

Peter Irons is an attorney, political scientist, constitutional scholar, and legal historian. He is professor of political science at the University of California, San Diego. In 1988 he was the Raoul Wallenberg Distinguished Visiting Professor of Human Rights at Rutgers University.

Irons was educated at Antioch College (B.A. 1966), Boston University (Ph.D. 1973), and Harvard Law School (J.D. 1978). He is the author of numerous articles and three other books, *The New Deal Lawyers*, winner of the James Willard Hurst Prize from the Law and Society Association for the best book on American legal history; *Justice at War: The Story of the Japanese American Internment Cases*, winner of a Silver Gavel Certificate of Merit from the American Bar Association; and *The Courage of Their Convictions: Sixteen Americans Who Fought Their Way to the Supreme Court*. His home is in San Diego, California.

About the Book

Justice Delayed was typeset in Times Roman by G & S Typesetters of Austin, Texas, and designed and produced by Kachergis Book Design of Pittsboro, North Carolina.

Times Roman is a contemporary typeface designed by Stanley Morison for use in the *Times* (London). The basic design objective of Times Roman, maximum legibility with minimum waste of space, has resulted in crisp, clear, readable letters in any point size.

Wesleyan University Press, 1989